ISLAM AND THE ARAB REVOLUTIONS

USAAMA AL-AZAMI

Islam and the Arab Revolutions

The Ulama Between Democracy and Autocracy

HURST & COMPANY, LONDON

First published in the United Kingdom in 2021 by
C. Hurst & Co. (Publishers) Ltd.,
83 Torbay Road, London, NW6 7DT

Printed in India

A Cataloguing-in-Publication data record for this book is available from the British Library.

ISBN: 9781787383944

www.hurstpublishers.com

إِلَىٰ شُـهَدَاءِ الثَّوْرَات

بِسْمِ ٱللَّهِ ٱلرَّحْمَٰنِ ٱلرَّحِيمِ

مَآ أَصَابَ مِن مُّصِيبَةٍ فِى ٱلْأَرْضِ وَلَا فِىٓ أَنفُسِكُمْ إِلَّا فِى كِتَٰبٍ مِّن قَبْلِ أَن نَّبْرَأَهَآ ۚ إِنَّ ذَٰلِكَ عَلَى ٱللَّهِ يَسِيرٌ ۝ لِّكَيْلَا تَأْسَوْا۟ عَلَىٰ مَا فَاتَكُمْ وَلَا تَفْرَحُوا۟ بِمَآ ءَاتَىٰكُمْ ۗ وَٱللَّهُ لَا يُحِبُّ كُلَّ مُخْتَالٍ فَخُورٍ ۝

(سُوْرَةُ الْحَدِيْد: ٢٢-٢٣)

CONTENTS

PREFACE

This book began as a digression from my doctoral research at Princeton as I was increasingly drawn to events in Egypt in the wake of the 2013 military coup. While I was supposed to be working on a dissertation on Islamist intellectual developments in the Arab world in recent decades, current events slowly began to occupy more and more of my attention. Perhaps inevitably, I decided to include a chapter on scholarly responses to the Egyptian coup of 2013, if only to justify the amount of intellectual energy I was redirecting from my actual dissertation to events in the Middle East. Nearly eight years later, my first book would be drawn not from my dissertation, but the draft chapter that did not end up in it. In fact, it was still so much of a draft by the time I decided it would not end up in my thesis that I do not believe my adviser, Professor Bernard Haykel, ever actually saw it. I am extremely grateful to him nonetheless for helping shepherd my dissertation through to completion so that I could focus my energies on the present research more seriously.

I have incurred too many debts to be able to properly do justice to the many friends, colleagues, and teachers who offered valuable feedback, reflections, and counsel as I researched and wrote the present work. The only one of my mentors at Princeton who read the (much too early) draft chapter that served as the seed for the present work was Professor Michael Cook as part of his NES 503 dissertation workshop. I am deeply indebted to him and two colleagues, Michael Dann and Jelena Radovanović, for their suggestions with regard to the chapter at this early stage. Professor Muhammad Qasim Zaman, the third member of my examining committee at Princeton, influenced this work through his own extensive writings on the ulama. The external reader of my doctoral dissertation, Professor Jonathan A.C. Brown was the first to read the entire text as I submitted it to my publishers. He has consistently offered valuable insights throughout the writing process. My colleagues at Oxford, both in my department and the Middle East Centre at St Antony's College, have offered me an exceptionally vibrant intellectual context in which to bring this book to fruition. My academic mentor, Eugene Rogan, always offered a smile, dependable counsel, and endless encouragement and enthusiasm for my work, including reading parts of it despite his innumerable responsibilities as director of the Middle East Centre. I could not have hoped for a more supportive mentor. Similarly, my colleagues at the Middle East Centre, Walter Armbrust, Laurent Mignon, Avi Shlaim, and Michael Willis, have all made me feel right at home in the Centre's scholarly community since I joined in 2019. Librarians and administrative staff at Princeton, Markfield, and Oxford offered support without which my research would simply not have been possible.

Given the lengthy gestation of this work, I cannot conceivably thank all those who contributed to it in one way or another. The work also touches on the controversial and the politically sensitive in a part of the world in which one's views on such issues can have serious implications. I should thus highlight that my mention of individuals with whom I have had exchanges that have to some degree influenced my research for this book, or who may have facilitated my presentation of its themes in academic or more public settings, does not indicate that they agreed with my interpretation of the events recounted within it. In fact, they sometimes vehemently disagreed with me, but they still shaped the way in which I thought about the topic, and hence I register my gratitude to them here. Where I believe the risks to be too great, I have mentioned only first names or omitted them altogether.

I thus would like to express my gratitude to: Rushain Abbasi, Umar Faruq Abd-Allah, Rodrigo Adem, Haris Ahmad, Khurshid Ahmad, Taris Ahmad, Imad Ahmed, Afifi al-Akiti, Abdullah bin Hamid Ali, Mansur Ali, Muhamed Amasha, Fahimul Anam, Omar Anchassi, Ovamir Anjum, Abdullah Al-Arian, Sami Al-Arian, ‘Abdullāh al-‘Awda, Ahmed Saad Al-Azhari, Nesrine Badawi, Muhammad ‘Alī Balā‘ū, Sharif Banna, Masooda Bano, Muhammad Abdul Bari, Rahma Bavelaar, Mohamed bin Bayyah, Hatem Bazian, Rezart Beka, Youssef Belal, Adam Bensaid, Yahya Birt, Baraka Blue, Jihad Brown, Nathan Brown, Mohammed El-Sayed Bushra, Ali Galib Cebeci, Ahmet Tarık Çaşkurlu, Rashid Dar, Sara Elbanna, Shadee Elmasry, Khadijah Elshayyal, Mary Elston, Heba Raouf Ezzat, Mohammad Fadel, Dalia Fahmy, Sahar Al-Faifi, Abdullah al-Faliq, Daanish Faruqi, Maribel Fierro, Simon Fuchs, Ahmed Gatnash, Talha Ghannam, Tarek Ghanem, Amin Gharad, Sophie

Gilliat-Ray, Robert Gleave, Anas El Gomati, Omar El Gomati, Sadek Hamid, Rawan Hamoud, Sohail Hanif, Ramon Harvey and Arnold Yasin Mol, Bilal Hassam, Asif Hussain, Basit Iqbal, Sherman Jackson, Amer Jamil, Talal Kanaan, Hafsa Kanjwal, Said Salih Kaymakcı, Ataul Khabir, Khālid, Hossam El-Din Khalil, Mohammed Mokhtar Al-Khalil, Wadah Khanfar, Muʿtazz al-Khatīb, Azim Kidwai, David Kirkpatrick, Andreas Krieg, Hassan Lachheb, Stéphane Lacroix, Fulla Lahmar, Hisham Mahmoud, Aftab Malik, Maʿn, Toby Matthiesen, Christopher Melchert, Nikhita Mendis, Hizer Ali Mir, Shihan Mirza, Ruzwan Mohammed, Abdal Hakim Murad, Farooq Murad, Najah Nadi, Mohammad Akram Nadwi, Basheer Nafi, Aria Nakissa, Uwais Namazi, Iqbal Nasim, Imran Naved, Nawwāf, Nazmus Sakib Nirjhor, Dina Odessy, Thomas Parker, Davide Pettinato, Francesco Piraino, Arjan Post, Yasir Qadhi, Walaa Quisay, Asim Qureshi, Ebad(ur) Rahman, Yahya Rhodus, Sajjad Rizvi, Aaron Rock-Singer, Sohaib Saeed, Toha Salim, Saud Al-Sarhan, Mark Sedgwick, Emad Shahin, Zaqir Shaikh, Zaid Shakir, Ahmed El Shamsy, Farah El-Sherif, Wasim Shiliwala, Ataullah Siddiqui (may God show him mercy), Besnik Sinani, Ermin Sinanović, Mohamed Soltan, Sohaib Sultan, Recep Şentürk, Carl Sharif El-Tobgui, Areeb Ullah, Miqdaad Versi, David H. Warren, Suhaib Webb, Muhammad al-Yaqoubi, Yāsir, Rizwan Yoosuf, Salman Younas, Bassam Zawadi, Steven Zhou, and Adnan Zulfiqar. I hope that anyone I have missed will forgive the oversight! The reviewers and editors at Hurst also offered valuable feedback that has considerably improved this work. Naturally, any errors in this work are my responsibility alone.

On a more personal level, my eldest brother, Nabeel Al-Azami (may God show him mercy), passed away as I was approaching the completion of my first draft. His wisdom and insights in his own field of expertise, ethical leadership, a field he personally embodied, have in their own way been important in shaping my reflections about my work. His passing from illness around his forties mirrored our mother's passing from illness in her forties nearly two decades ago. That they offered so much to this world before passing on to the next is both a testament to their generosity and a reminder of what it means to live a life of service to others. My mother, my father, my grandparents, my uncles, my aunts, my siblings, and my cousins all helped me to reach this important milestone in my life of publishing my first book. *Jazāhum Allāh khayr al-jazāʾ fī al-dunyā wa-l-ākhira.* I cannot repay what they have given me, least of all my parents. In the more day-to-day process of completing the manuscript, my mother-in-law's tireless support with the children whenever she was visiting has been truly indispensable in bringing this project to fruition. I am more grateful to her than words can express. Last but not least, I wish to express my gratitude to my wife, Manal, the mother of our beautiful children. Your enduring love, companionship, and patience with my endless academic preoccupations has made everything possible. For when all is said and done, you are the home wherein my soul finds solace.

NOTE ON THE TEXT

I have generally observed the Arabic transliteration conventions followed by the *Encyclopedia of Islam* in its third edition. Occasionally, when a scholar, group, or event is especially well-known by a particular spelling in the English language that is at odds with these conventions, such as Ali Gomaa, al-Qaeda, or the Rabaa massacre, I have broken with these conventions and opted for the more widely used spelling. I also italicize any words that are not found on the website of the *Oxford Dictionary of English*, Lexico.com. Exceptions are most names and derivatives from names, such as Azharī which is used to designate a graduate of the Egyptian al-Azhar mosque and university complex. These are transliterated but not italicized. I have endeavored to use gender inclusive language in my own writing, but when presenting the writing of authors in Arabic in which such practices are rare and there are no neuter pronouns, I have generally not done so. All years of birth or death are provided after the names of individuals according to the Hijrī calendar, followed by the Common Era (e.g. 1432/2011). Finally, I have tried to ensure that all website URLs have been backed up on the Internet Archive (www.archive.org) so that they may be accessed by searching for them in the Archive's Wayback Machine even if the original link no longer works. This does not work for shortened YouTube URLs, and hence I have preserved in parentheses unshortened YouTube URLs when I first cite them.

INTRODUCTION

This is a book about religious interventions in the early phases of the ongoing Arab revolutions.[1] Perhaps exceptionally in the monographs written so far about this period of Middle Eastern history and politics, this study focuses on the activities of Islamic religious scholars, known as the 'ulama.'[2] Modern scholars argue that the ulama form a distinctive social class who often function as guardians and gatekeepers of the Islamic scholarly tradition. This sociological dimension of the ulama class is not especially explored in the present study. Rather, this book is mainly a history of the political and intellectual engagements of senior ulama in the context of the Arab revolutions. The ulama continue, in some sense, to represent the intellectual classes of Muslim societies, though the intellectual field is one in which they have an increasingly smaller market share with the inexorable rise of intellectuals of other kinds in the modern Islamic public sphere. They have also shown themselves to be effective political actors at times, as I try to demonstrate in the course of this work in which we shall find official ulama serving as political elites within the nation state. But they may also often be seen as channeling popular sentiment and advocating for democracy, albeit through an arguably elite voice, sometimes quite literally, since they overwhelmingly communicate in non-vernacular Arabic.

In the present work, I seek to trace the engagements of some key Middle Eastern ulama with the Arab revolutionary context from the outset of the Arab revolutions in early 2011 until shortly after the Egyptian coup in the summer of 2013. At the beginning of this period, it is possible to divide these scholars into at least two groups: pro-revolutionary democrats and counter-revolutionary authoritarians. A third group hold a more ambiguous position, appearing to show what might be characterized as 'wary enthusiasm' for the revolutions that soon gives way to opposition to them, allowing this group to be eventually assimilated to the counter-revolutionary group. The first group of scholars was in some sense led by the Qatar-based Egyptian Azharī, Yusuf al-Qaradawi (b. 1345/1926), who was until 2018 the president of the International Union of Muslim Scholars (IUMS).[3] As well as being an alim, Qaradawi is noted for his close affiliation with the Muslim Brotherhood (MB), Egypt and the world's oldest Islamist organization.[4] The MB was founded in 1928 by an Islamically learned school teacher, Ḥasan al-Bannā (d. 1368/1949), as a social movement dedicated to bringing about the gradual imbuing of Egyptian public life with Islamic values in the wake of the abolition of the Caliphate in 1924.[5]

By the early twenty-first century, Yusuf al-Qaradawi was the most noted Islamic scholar affiliated with the movement, but he also saw himself as transcending the movement and being concerned with the needs of the Muslim umma as a whole.[6] This pan-Islamic vision informs his prolific oeuvre and activities, especially in recent decades. He is one of the most prolific Islamic scholars of his generation, having written about almost every conceivable question of concern for Muslims over the course of an exceptionally long career. He has thus appropriately been the object of a good deal of scholarly study, with the most comprehensive overview of his output so far coming in the form of an edited volume suitably entitled *Global Mufti: The Phenomenon of Yusuf al-Qaradawi*.[7] Published in 2009, it predates his vocal pro-revolutionary advocacy from 2011 onwards. As I argue in the pages that follow, Yusuf al-Qaradawi was probably the most influential transnational scholarly advocate for the revolutions in their early weeks. He embraced the revolutions with a passion and a righteous religious zeal as soon as they succeeded in Tunisia, and then advocated for their spread well beyond that country, with an especial focus on Egypt. Qaradawi's stance towards the revolutions would be mirrored by several other scholars, but given the swiftness and significance of his particular interventions, the present work focuses on his pro-revolutionary engagements with some of the other scholars' interventions being explored only later, when they oppose the military coup in 2013.

However, Qaradawi's pro-revolutionary positions in 2011 were opposed by a number of other scholars. In the Egyptian context, two senior establishment figures who had been appointed years earlier by the thirty-year autocrat Hosni Mubarak (d. 1441/2020) came out in defense of their leader shortly before his ouster in February 2011. They were the Shaykh al-Azhar Aḥmad al-Ṭayyib (b. 1365/1946) and the Grand Mufti Ali Gomaa (b.

1371/1952).[8] The shaykh al-Azhar ranked as the Egyptian state's most senior religious official, and the grand mufti was the second most senior official. Their relatively strong opposition to the protestors was to be expected, although in the case of Gomaa, whose influence went far beyond Egypt, his pro-authoritarian stances would cause considerable controversy beyond the country. An example of Gomaa's transnational influence can be seen early in the 2011 intervention of one of his students, the young UAE-based Yemeni scholar, Ali al-Jifri (b. 1391/1971).[9] Despite being a foreigner, he was quite active in the Egyptian scene as a media personality, and he called into a satellite show in the final days of the 2011 Egyptian uprising to voice his support for the regime.

The third group of scholars mentioned above adopted a more ambiguous position in early 2011. The first of these was an American convert to Islam, and one of the West's most influential Islamic voices, namely Hamza Yusuf (b. 1377/1958).[10] He declared his enthusiastic support for the revolutions in Egypt in February 2011, while also arguing that democracy was not a priority for the country. By the second half of 2011, however, he was being interviewed on the Saudi-owned UAE-based Al Arabiya network, arguing that monarchy was less susceptible to corruption than democracy. His teacher, Abdallah bin Bayyah (b. 1353f./1935), also appeared lukewarm towards the revolutions, although in 2011 he was serving as a vice president to the enthusiastically pro-revolutionary Yusuf al-Qaradawi at the Qatar-based IUMS.[11] Their long-standing relationship would come under increasing strain with the fallout from the Arab revolutions, with the decisive break coming three weeks after the Rabaa massacre of 2013.

The year 2013 marked the period when the fortunes of the pro-revolutionary scholars would take a turn for the worse. In the course of the previous year, a member of the MB, Mohamed Morsi (d. 1440/2019), had secured the presidency in Egypt against a military establishment stalwart by a thin margin, but the counter-revolutionary Egyptian ulama we have already met had shown themselves willing and at times successfully able to thwart the new president's will. They were hardly the only opponents of the president, whose frequent missteps and miscalculations made it much easier for counter-revolutionary forces to foment a revolt against him, culminating in his removal in a popular military coup on 3 July 2013 that was supported surreptitiously by the UAE, Saudi Arabia, and even Israel.

Within weeks, this would lead to the most significant event of the revolutionary period for the ulama with whom we are concerned, namely the

Rabaa massacre of 14 August 2013 in which the coup regime's security forces fired live ammunition at thousands of unarmed protestors in full view of the international media, leaving at least a thousand peaceful pro-democracy activists dead in the streets of Egypt. The contribution of one scholar in particular to this massacre and the repercussions of his support for it form what is perhaps the centerpiece of my narrative in the present work. By the summer of 2013, Ali Gomaa was the former grand mufti of Egypt. In this book, I present the most detailed analysis in the English language of Gomaa's vociferous encouragement of the security forces to carry out the post-coup massacres, most notably the one at Rabaa Square in August that year.

The revelations of this support sent shockwaves through the ulama classes in Egypt, the Middle East, and even the Western world. As I try to illustrate towards the end of the present work, Gomaa's actions have cast a long shadow across the ulama of the particular Neo-traditionalist denomination he represents, especially in light of other ulama of the denomination (most notably Bin Bayyah and Hamza Yusuf) taking up the counter-revolutionary baton in the wider Middle East since 2014. Not all ulama opted for this path, however. Notable Neo-traditionalist and Islamist ulama loudly denounced Gomaa's actions as immoral and illegitimate. Of particular note was the fact that it was not only 'peripheral ulama' who condemned the post-coup bloodletting.[12] Rather, such denunciations came from within the ranks of senior Azharī colleagues of Gomaa, most notably Ḥasan al-Shāfiʿī (b. 1348-9/1930) and Muḥammad ʿImāra (d. 1441/2020), both senior scholars at the heart of the Azhar establishment. The former may be described as a Neo-traditionalist who was also a student of Ḥasan al-Bannā and the latter an Islamist with no formal affiliation with the MB.[13] Alongside them were many other ulama, only a few of whom are considered in the pages that follow. While these scholars could not stave off the post-coup massacres that befell Egypt, they could be seen as preserving their own reputations for independence, and thereby the reputations of some of the ulama, in rejecting the bloodbaths that punctuated that summer.

Denominations of Sunnism

Throughout these pages, I will be using certain terms to describe the 'denominational' orientation of the ulama I study. These need to be defined at the outset. The first of these is 'Islamist,' a term I define somewhat loosely for the purpose of this study as referring to those ulama whose vision of

Islamic politics has close affinities with the MB and its offshoots.[14] Roxanne Euben and Qasim Zaman describe the MB as 'the oldest and one of the most influential [...] Islamist organizations in the Sunni Muslim world.'[15] For the purpose of this particular work, however, I do not define Islamists as Muslims who are concerned with political questions through the lens of their faith, nor do I use the phrase 'political Islam' in these pages. As Peter Mandaville has pointed out, drawing on insights from the work of Talal Asad, the expression 'political Islam' presupposes problematic post-Enlightenment conceptual distinctions between the realms of religion and politics that cannot automatically be taken for granted outside relatively recent Western intellectual history.[16] Such assumptions that permeate modern Western culture cannot but view modern Islamist actors as profoundly at odds with the norms of modernity. A common Western usage of the term also blurs the lines between mainstream democratic Islamists and violent Jihadists, usually of a Salafi orientation, such as al-Qaeda and Islamic State of Iraq and Syria (ISIS).[17] It does not seem to matter that these Jihadists excommunicate and consequently legitimate the murder of MB members on account of their acceptance of democracy.[18] My use of the term Islamist tries to self-reflexively avoid these problematic assumptions. But despite the frequently pejorative usage of the term in the English language, I hesitate to discard a term that has come to be used by Islamists themselves in Arabic as *Islāmiyyūn*, though not always willingly.[19] Obviously for willing users of this self-designation, it is a positively connoted term. As I reflect in the Epilogue, they have a long way to go before they can persuade others to see matters as such.

Another term I use, to designate a second denomination of Sunnism studied here, is Neo-traditionalism. This word is used by far fewer adherents to this trend, who often simply present themselves as adherents to Sunni Islam. This is because they arguably represent the dominant form of Sunni Islam over the last five hundred or so years, although they have undergone massive transformations in the modern context.[20] This has led to them becoming simply one of several Sunni denominations in the modern period, which is why I eschew describing them simply as Sunnis, thereby suggesting that the other denominations within the broader Sunni umbrella are not really Sunni. Neo-traditionalism may be described as a modern denomination of Sunnism that promotes adherence to the four Sunni schools of law, a preference for two of the three Sunni schools of theology, namely the ones that cultivate philosophical theology (*kalām*), and the practice of Sufism.[21] As I discuss in the Epilogue, in practice the various modern denominations I speak of in the Middle Eastern context are far more imbricated than their less ideologically tolerant proponents might be willing to acknowledge.

A third Sunni denomination I refer to far less, and whose absence signals another lacuna in the present work, is Salafism.[22] These are a group of Muslims who arguably valorize the earliest period of Islam more than competing denominations. As noted by Bernard Haykel, this denomination, at its heart, represents a distinct theological outlook, although they have arguably evolved a more multifaceted identity over the course of the past century as Henri Lauzière illustrates.[23] Salafis and Salafi ulama were and continue to be important religious actors in the Arab revolutions.[24] I hope to explore their activities and mixed reputations more systematically in future.[25] Their general absence from the present work may be justified on the grounds of my focus on the direct engagement of the ulama and the state in the contestations over the highest office in Egypt, namely the presidency. The Islamic scholarly engagement of both Neo-traditionalist and Islamist ulama on issues pertaining to the Egyptian presidency, the grounds for the legitimacy of its occupant, and the grounds for removal are, to my knowledge, more directly addressed by these ulama than the Salafis in the period with which this monograph is concerned. After this period, with the meteoric rise of the Madkhalī trend, particularly in Libya, Yemen, and Saudi Arabia, Salafism has achieved a salience at the heart of the region's (counter-)revolutionary upheavals that they arguably did not enjoy between 2011 and 2013, though as noted already, they were by no means a marginal phenomenon in the earlier period.

Theoretical questions and positionality

A number of theoretical concerns underpin the present inquiry. These can be expressed through the following questions: how did scholars utilize the Qur'an and hadith to support or condemn revolutions in 2011 and the Egyptian coup of 2013? How did the selection of scriptural texts differ between the scholars who supported these events as opposed to those who condemned the Egyptian revolution and the coup? What other options were present besides outright support and outright condemnation, and how did the appeal to scriptural authority differ in such a case? Besides Qur'anic verses and hadiths, what sources of religious authority were invoked in making arguments for a given position? For example, do scholars cite the juristic tradition, consensus, and/or sources of authority other than God and the Prophet, such as appeals to the nation state, democracy, freedom, justice, and/or stability? What explains the variety of positions adopted by the ulama vis-à-vis the Arab revolutions? Are the varied positions dependent on divergent choices of scriptural texts? If so, what explains these divergent choices? To what extent did a given scholar's political commitments (association with a particular state or movement) and political orientation (pro-democracy versus authoritarianism) influence their religious position? Is 'political quietism' a useful framework for understanding counter-revolutionary scholarship? These questions lie at the heart of the present inquiry, and I will revisit them in the conclusion of the present work.

I perhaps occupy an unusual space among authors of studies in English on the ulama. Alongside my studies in the Western academy, I have also trained as an alim, primarily and most extensively in the UK, but also in studies with the ulama in France, Syria, Jordan, Egypt, Saudi Arabia, and the United States. Indeed, I have met with and in some cases learnt fairly extensively from the writings and lectures of a number of the scholars I study in this monograph. As a teenager in the late 1990s, I began listening to cassette tapes of lectures by Hamza Yusuf while still in high school in the coastal metropolis of Jeddah, Saudi Arabia, where my father worked at the time. I would continue listening to his lectures for many years. About a decade later in early 2009, while visiting the Hejaz with an elderly Indian scholar of hadith, I twice visited the home of Yusuf's most important teacher, Abdallah bin Bayyah, where I was generously hosted by his youngest son, Mohamed. Already by this point, while finishing high school and attending university in the UK in the 2000s, I had attended a number of events at which Shaykhs Bin Bayyah, Hamza Yusuf, and Ali al-Jifri had lectured. In the summer of 2002, I had also attended a lecture at SOAS, University of London, by Yusuf al-Qaradawi as part of an Arabic and Islamic studies summer course at which Bin Bayyah was also meant to lecture but was unable to in the end. So, as well as being the subject of my study, these are scholars I consider to be teachers of mine or perhaps teachers of some of my teachers. This makes my study akin to one in which I might be studying university professors of mine who have entered public life, a phenomenon that seems much rarer in the Western academy. But it gives a sense of the balancing act between personal relationships and critical distance entailed in such a study.

The scholars mentioned in the previous paragraph are only those who both feature in the present monograph and whom I have personally met, however briefly. By contrast, my Islamic scholarly formation as an alim was most systematically pursued under the tutelage of the Oxford-based scholar Mohammad Akram Nadwi (b. 1382/1963) whom I first met at the aforementioned summer course I attended in 2002. Unbeknownst to me, I would have the opportunity to study with him at greater length from early 2005 onwards when he set up, first informally, and then officially, the al-Salam Institute—a weekend seminary teaching a version of the curriculum of his Indian alma mater, Dār al-ʿUlūm Nadwat al-ʿUlamāʾ. The Nadwa, as it is sometimes referred to and whose name is often adopted by its graduates, has been an institution characterized by a kind of 'ecumenism' throughout its history, especially under its influential rector in the twentieth century, Abū al-Ḥasan ʿAli Nadwī (d. 1420/1999). The older Nadwi maintained relations with scholars across the denominational spectrum of Sunni ulama whom I have referred to above as Neo-traditionalists, Salafis, and Islamists. Indeed, the younger Nadwi noted how he in fact had fellow students at the Nadwa who were Shia—something that is difficult to imagine in most South Asian or Arab seminaries today. This relative denominational openness was a part of my own training with Shaykh Akram, as we would refer to him.

I continued studying with Shaykh Akram until I left the UK in early 2010 to pursue a PhD in North America. With my return to the UK, I have taught at the al-Salam Institute whenever I have had the opportunity. Naturally, I have studied with many other ulama over the course of my education, receiving a few *ijāza*s (licenses to narrate) along the way. Aside from my intellectual formation as an alim, I believe a scholar's family background can have a significant bearing on their work and can help a reader contextualize it. While born and raised largely in the UK, my parents are of Bangladeshi origin. My extended family in Bangladesh includes ulama of a variety of orientations including local variants of Neo-traditionalists, Islamists, and Salafis. Of course, I also have extended family members who might be characterized as secularists who are likely to be actively hostile towards the ulama, but they are far fewer. My ability to understand secularist viewpoints is doubtless assisted by my working in the secular academy for most of my academic career. I mention the foregoing not because it is particularly unusual among British ulama of South Asian origin—it is not—but because I hope it will help the reader recognize that I am able to understand the ulama I study in the present work without exclusively identifying with any one of these denominations.

The above is to illustrate, albeit briefly, aspects of my training that place me in the sociological category of those whom I study in this text, although I naturally lack the scholarly seniority of these figures much as a university lecturer and a professor share a similar sociological space but are, at the same time, different from each other in important ways. However, my positionality confers certain advantages and perhaps some disadvantages upon my study. Firstly, I hope that my background provides me with what might be called an insider's insights, namely an ability to understand the subtleties of a discourse that is self-consciously grounded in a 1400-year-old tradition of scholarship. I also hope that my training allows me to recognize some of what is at stake for the scholars in making the arguments they make. In particular, I hope that my studies with, and in some cases my personal relationships with, scholars of both Neo-traditionalist and Islamist orientations allows me to read their ideas empathetically.

A potential cost that some may see in relation to my situatedness is my own personal investment in these debates. Scholars, as human beings, have inevitable biases and preferences that will influence our ideas. In scholarship, given the attempt at approximating a kind of objectivity, this will often be subtle. Claims to perfect objectivity have appropriately come to be viewed with suspicion in much modern scholarship. I should point out that while I have been trained as an alim, I also have been trained in the Western academy in roughly the same broad field of Islamic studies. This dual training has helped me recognize the contrasting presuppositions not only between the two approaches of the Western and the Islamic but also the diversity of approaches within each tradition of scholarship. Any attempt to adjudicate the truth claims of these variegated traditions will need extensive studies of their own and will naturally not be attempted here.

In the course of the present intellectual history of the ulama, while I try to maintain a dispassionate perspective, I do not adopt a strictly insider or outsider perspective. I do not believe I can honestly choose between the two given my own intellectual formation. The most I can do is to highlight to the reader my inevitable situatedness, as I have done above, in the hope that it may at times help them understand aspects of my scholarship while avoiding the temptation to reduce my ideas to my background.

Situating the work in the literature

A significant body of scholarship has emerged on the Arab revolutions that has helped deepen our understanding of these events. This literature covers a wide range of fields including political science, anthropology, international relations, and media studies, among others, and has adopted a variety of approaches from considering the actions of military and political elites to the activism of protestors and security personnel on the streets. A number of scholars have provided excellent and occasionally prescient historical overviews of the revolutions.[26] These include quantitative studies of popular mobilization within a range of Arab countries,[27] the role of international actors supportive and opposed to revolutions in a given country, the role of state institutions and the military,[28] the significance of socio-economic factors that contributed to the uprisings, and studies of how social media was and continues to be utilized in the post-Arab Spring context by both protestors and states seeking to suppress them.[29] Scholars have written rich ethnographies from the revolutionary period that explore everything from revolutionary chants and graffiti to counter-revolutionary media and the ethics of revolutionary bloodshed.[30]

Some studies have explored the role of ideology or in some instances, the supposed lack thereof in the revolutions.[31] There have also been a number of studies regarding the religious dynamics exemplified in the behavior of a variety of Islamic actors, both individual and institutional, representing diverse Islamic orientations that participated in the revolutions.[32] Some scholars have paid special attention to sectarianism, sectarianization, and the emergence of groups like ISIS in the wake of the counter-revolutions.[33] Others have studied Islamic institutions and their affiliated scholars who sometimes have been important to the revolutions without the studies necessarily taking the revolutions as their central concern.[34] It is the more Islamic dimension of the studies of the revolutions to which I hope to contribute. Specifically, my work falls at the intersection of the revolutions and the studies of the ulama. Their discursive engagement with the revolutions in the public sphere and their interventions in the political field, grounded as they are in religious discourse, has been a blind spot, at times a glaring one, in much of the literature on these revolutions. As I discuss below, however, notwithstanding the relative marginality of ulama studies in the Arab revolutions, there have been a number of excellent articles on their discourses.

Ulama studies

In the burgeoning wider field of ulama studies, the present book is, to my knowledge, the first full-length monograph on the topic of ulama activism in the Egyptian revolution.[35] Recent scholarship on the ulama has provided a valuable corrective to the assumptions of an earlier generation of scholars who viewed the ulama as too wedded to a hidebound tradition and thus destined to disappear into irrelevance with the inexorable rise of modernity. A growing literature has illustrated how the ulama have adapted themselves to modernity in a variety of ways, sometimes as an unexpected consequence of efforts by modernizing states to exert greater control over the ulama and their institutions. This line of research was pioneered by Malika Zeghal's work on the 'peripheral ulama' in Egypt.[36] Muhammad Qasim Zaman has illustrated the transregional dimension of the modern ulama's activities with special attention directed at the Indian subcontinent, which has helped take our frames of reference for understanding their activities beyond the Arab world.[37]

A more recent transregional study is that of Henri Lauzière, whose biography of Taqī al-Dīn al-Hilālī (d. 1407/1987) begins in Morocco and ends in Saudi Arabia with significant interregna in Germany and India.[38] The ulama of Saudi Arabia have also been explored in the works of Stèphane Lacroix, whose work *Awakening Islam* has been a major contribution to studies of Saudi Arabia's Islamic activists including its ulama.[39] While Lacroix focusses on religio-political activism, Nabil Mouline has provided us with a vista into what is perhaps the clearest modern example of a Sunni clerical establishment integrated into the decision-making process of a modern state, namely the Wahhabi establishment ulama of Saudi Arabia.[40] Also on Saudi Arabia, but after the Arab Spring, Madawi Al-Rasheed's *Muted Modernists* demonstrates the creativity to be found within the Saudi Islamic scene among both the (non-establishment) ulama and 'lay' academics who have subtly attempted to question the religious basis of the absolutism that characterizes the polity.[41]

Meir Hatina's monograph on the ulama of Egypt in the late nineteenth and early twentieth centuries brings discussions closer to the geographic focus of the present monograph. He illustrates how, over recent centuries, the ulama of the Azhar have often continued to serve as an oppositional force against rulers in defense of the interests of the populace, a role they frequently played in premodern Islamic societies.[42] Thomas Pierret's recent study of the ulama in Syria illustrates the challenges faced by this social group with the rise of the modern state as well as the emergence of Islamists who they both collaborated with and opposed over time due to distinctive 'sectoral' interests.[43] There are also a number of dissertations that look promising as potential monographs. Three merit mention here as they pertain directly to the arena of ulama studies, namely the works of Youssef Belal, Walaa Quisay and Mary Elston.[44] All three adopt an ethnographic approach that seeks to understand the ways in which mainly Neo-traditionalist ulama engage tradition as a means of negotiating modernity in general and current events in particular, including the events of the Arab revolutions. There have also been a number of articles and chapters written specifically on the ulama's engagements with the Arab revolutions whether in support of or in opposition to them.[45] Several of these essays try to understand the rationale behind the support of some ulama, most notably Ali Gomaa, for the 2013 Egyptian coup and/or the violent massacres perpetrated by the Egyptian security forces in the summer of that year. I engage the scholarship on this debate most systematically in Chapter 9.

My own study augments the foregoing ulama studies in the post-Arab revolutionary context with a focus on Egyptian events. I also focus on a relatively small number of scholars. This is not because the innumerable other ulama not mentioned in my work are not important or did not engage in the revolutionary upheavals since 2011—they are and they did. Aria Nakissa and Adnan Zulfiqar have shown how ulama across the Middle East in 2011 engaged in producing fatwas and in some cases participated in protests against ruling regimes.[46] Rather, the purpose of the present work is to provide a highly textured in-depth analysis of the ideas of some of the most important and influential ulama voices in the Arab revolutions. The depth of engagement with Qaradawi, Gomaa, and a handful of other scholars has an inevitable cost in limiting the breadth of my study. Yet, given the widely recognized influence of these scholars, often well beyond the Arab world, I believe such an in-depth study is warranted and has its rewards.

The lack of deep engagement with a broader range of ulama is also offset by the fact that the figures I study here may be taken as representing many other scholars' views on these topics, particularly those scholars affiliated with the Islamist and Neo-traditionalist orientations. Many such scholars would likely not garner the kind of attention that a Bin Bayyah or Qaradawi could hope for. Their absence from the present study is a function of the social dynamics of public engagement—because most scholars are inevitably not prominent public figures, their engagements are likely to appear muted. This does not indicate that Qaradawi or Gomaa's respective opposition towards or support for the coup of 2013 were necessarily isolated opinions among scholars. As Nathan Brown notes, such disagreements were discernible among Egyptian imams he interacted with between 2013 and 2014, but explicit articulation of it was usually avoided, presumably given its political sensitivity and, with respect to those who were actually supportive of the MB, considerable risks to their well-being. This notwithstanding, Brown notes that in conversations with the imams, he could see that 'there was something like a fairly even split' between supporters and opponents of the recently deposed MB president.[47] Such figures would not necessarily have advertised their views in public for the reasons already noted. That is to say, the silence of large numbers of ulama regarding the Egyptian revolution of 2011 and the coup two years later does not indicate that they were uninterested in such matters. Ebrahim Moosa has highlighted, for example, that apparently thousands of Azhar scholars signed a petition in opposition to the Egyptian coup of 2013.[48]

On the somewhat unrelated matter of my Egyptian focus, I justify this on the following grounds. Egypt is the most populous Arab country in the region, and it often acts as a bellwether for the region as a whole. For the purpose of the present work, the institution of the Azhar exerts a centripetal force on ulama throughout the region, who will often, regardless of nationality, pursue their higher studies at this thousand-year-old institution of Islamic learning. These scholars will regularly return to their homelands to become significant religious authorities. This is why I feel that a certain amount of attention must inevitably be directed at Egypt when exploring the ulama's response to the revolutions. Doubtless future studies will further broaden our perspective to include ulama from other regions.

An outline of the chapters

This book is divided into nine chapters that generally observe chronological order. They are preceded by this Introduction and followed by a Conclusion, an Epilogue, and Appendices. To begin with the last of these first, three annotated translations are appended to the present work to give interested readers the opportunity to read some of Bin Bayyah's and Gomaa's writings and lectures cited in the course of the work. The first is a short piece by Bin Bayyah in praise of Qaradawi written in the 1990s. The second and third are the much longer transcripts of Gomaa's private lectures to the army from 2013, before and after the Rabaa massacre, respectively.

As for the core of the present work, Chapters 1 and 2 focus on Qaradawi's engagements and justifications for the revolutionary uprisings against the region's autocrats, with a focus first on Tunisia and then Egypt. As we shall see, he draws heavily on the Qur'an and hadith literature to argue for the legitimacy of peacefully but vocally opposing the tyranny of the region's despots. Chapter 3 looks at the response of pro-autocracy ulama to the Egyptian revolution. Specifically, it considers the public statements of Shaykh al-Azhar al-Ṭayyib, Grand Mufti Gomaa, and the latter's influential student Jifri, all of whom argue for the legitimacy of Mubarak's rule while casting aspersions on those encouraging the revolutions.

Chapter 4 considers the ambiguity that characterizes the initial response to the revolutions of Hamza Yusuf and his elderly teacher, the noted jurist Abdallah bin Bayyah. As mentioned earlier, both scholars have a mixed record on supporting the revolutions, and this is explored in detail in this chapter, with the discussion taking us to early 2013 when Bin Bayyah's ideas had sufficiently matured that they could readily be adapted for authoritarian purposes. The chronology of the next four chapters needs a brief explanation. As I am primarily considering events that occur in quick succession in the summer of 2013 from the divergent viewpoints of two opposing groups of scholars, I need to go back and forth between these scholars over the course of these chapters. Hence, some of the later chapters circle back to earlier events from the summer of 2013. For example, the Rabaa massacre is described in detail at the end of Chapter 5 where it is explained in relation to Gomaa's private pre-Rabaa guidance given to the security forces. We do not, however, see the pro-revolutionary ulama's reaction to the Rabaa massacre until Chapter 8 because the intervening chapters are necessary to provide relevant context. The easiest way to keep track of the temporal coverage of these chapters is to refer to the dates provided in their titles.

Chapter 5 considers the counter-revolutionary activities of the ulama, most notably that of Ali Gomaa, which can be witnessed as early as June 2012 and again in the following year in Gomaa's rationalization of the use of violence against Egypt's anti-coup protestors in private recordings to the security forces. The chapter culminates with a narration of the events of the Rabaa massacre from the summer of 2013. Chapter 6 starts back at the lead up to the Egyptian coup, exploring the discourses of the pro-revolutionary ulama at that point and in the weeks immediately following the coup that witnessed several smaller massacres that preceded the Rabaa massacre. Chapter 7 presents Gomaa and Jifri engaging in a post-Rabaa offensive, with the former privately celebrating and publicly justifying the violence. During this period, Jifri publicly lambastes Gomaa's critics as hypocrites who spread malicious rumors about the latter. We will see that Gomaa continues to justify his support for the massacre for years afterwards.

Chapter 8 considers the responses of the pro-revolutionary ulama to the Rabaa massacre and Gomaa's support for it. This includes their reactions to the leaked video of his post-Rabaa celebratory lecture to the armed forces.

The final substantive chapter, Chapter 9, critiques a reading of these events, widespread in the secondary literature, that accounts for the Egyptian coup and its accompanying massacres as best explained by premodern Sunni political theology. It concludes with a brief discussion of the post-Rabaa institutional consolidation of counter-revolutionary scholarly authority led by Abdallah bin Bayyah under the auspices of the UAE. The Conclusion brings together several threads of analysis that run through the work in an attempt to summarize and explain the divergent Islamic scholarly responses to the Arab revolutions. In the Epilogue, I offer a more personal reflection on the implications of the Arab revolutions and their aftermath on both Neo-traditionalist and Islamist ulama. All, I argue, have much to learn from these events.

1

YUSUF AL-QARADAWI

EARLY SUPPORTER OF THE ARAB REVOLUTIONS (JANUARY 2011)

In the early days of the Arab revolutions, Yusuf al-Qaradawi was probably the most prominent global religious voice advocating for the youth-led protests throughout the Arab world. Throughout his career, Qaradawi had expressed his opposition to despotic rulers, from a play he composed from his first stint in prison with the MB in his early twenties in which he celebrated an early Islamic scholar confronting a tyrant, to his excoriation of dictatorship in his encyclopedic *Fiqh al-Jihād*, published shortly before the Arab revolutions.[1] Speaking out against oppressive autocrats had been a consistent theme in his writings throughout his unusually long career and his response to the Arab revolutions was thus true to form.

The present chapter considers what were likely Qaradawi's first public statements in support of the spark that initiated the uprisings of that spring, namely Tunisia's successful revolution in January 2011. These statements were made on his then weekly Al Jazeera show, *al-Sharīʿa wa-l-Ḥayāh*, which became one of his main platforms for promoting the revolutions in this early period. In what follows, certain important features of Qaradawi's discourse will be highlighted including his insistence on the need for political freedom. He also addressed the delicate issue of the self-immolation by a Tunisian man that eventually gave rise to these uprisings. However, most of the show was dedicated to the question of tyranny (*ẓulm*) and how to confront it.

At the heart of Qaradawi's message was the important Islamic principle of commanding right and forbidding wrong (*al-amr bi-l-maʿrūf wa-l-nahy ʿan al-munkar*), an important Islamic norm grounded in both the Qur'an and Prophetic hadiths that will come up repeatedly in the chapters that follow as providing the Islamic basis for confronting tyranny. I also briefly consider the implications of Qatar's support for democracy in the region through Al Jazeera. The chapter concludes with a brief consideration of the form that Qaradawi's arguments in favor of the revolutions take at this early stage. It will be seen that they are grounded explicitly in Islamic scriptural texts that pertain to confronting tyranny while also showing a concern for social stability. This is a theme that continues into the next chapter, which addresses Qaradawi's continued engagements with the Arab revolutions as they reached Egypt later that month.

The Tunisian revolution

What was likely his first extensive public expression of support for the revolutions came on the heels of the success of the Tunisian revolution in which popular protests forced the resignation of the long-time Tunisian dictator, Zine El Abidine Ben Ali (d. 1441/2019), on 14 January 2011. Two days later, Qaradawi appeared on his then weekly primetime Al Jazeera Arabic show with that week's episode entitled '*Jihād al-Ẓulm wa-Wasā'iluh*' ('*Jihad against Tyranny and Its Means*'). The entire episode was dedicated to celebrating and religiously legitimating the Tunisian revolution, as well as encouraging peaceful protests of this kind in general.[2]

Qaradawi's weekly show on Al Jazeera, which ran for about fifteen years on the channel until late 2013, would open with a brief introduction by a presenter citing verses from the Qur'an and hadiths that were pertinent to the topic of that week before launching into an interview of Qaradawi, who was the main guest of the show over the years of its airing. The lion's share of the airtime would typically involve Qaradawi responding to a set of prepared questions in light of Islamic teachings. Most shows also allowed for audience participation via phone calls or other internet-based communication.[3] As noted by Marc Lynch in 2009, Qaradawi was an excellent barometer of Arab public opinion, and the weekly show reflected the concerns of the so-called Arab street.[4] Most significantly for our purposes, however, Qaradawi seems to have expressed enthusiasm remarkably early for the Arab revolutions.

In his episode on the triumph of the Tunisian revolution in January 2011, Qaradawi was clearly moved by the success of the protestors at ousting a dictator who had ruled since 1987. He opened the episode by expressing his support for the Tunisian people who had 'shown an example to the Arab and Islamic peoples, and oppressed people in general, that they should not despair nor fear tyrants (*ṭawāghīt*).'[5] The Arabic word he used, namely the plural form of *ṭāghiya*, is not the typical Arabic word for tyrant, but rather a more emphatic form of the word with Qur'anic resonances that is more commonly used to refer to idols and false gods.[6] Qaradawi went on to describe the Tunisians as engaged in jihad, a Qur'anic term denoting a righteous struggle against oppression.[7] In invoking this concept, Qaradawi was implying both that the cause of the revolutionaries was just and that God was on their side. He also invoked Tunisia's Islamic heritage, citing the Companion of the Prophet Muhammad, 'Uqba b. Nāfi' (d. 63/683) who led the conquest of North Africa in the seventh century, establishing the city of culture and scholarship, Kairouan, which, as Qaradawi highlighted, hosts the mosque-university complex of Zaytuna.

Qaradawi then shifted to giving more practical advice and making certain demands of a political nature. He warned the revolutionaries to be wary of those who would undermine their efforts at reform after the success of the revolutions, and he called on Tunisia's interim administration to immediately release all prisoners of conscience who, he asserted, had been incarcerated without trial or any evidence against them. 'There are things that should not be delayed: granting [...] freedom to all.' On the theme of freedom, he forcefully asserted:

> I have frequently said on this programme, and elsewhere, that in my view freedom is to be given preference over the implementation of the Sharia. We must give [people] freedoms! How can the tyrant fall and freedoms remain [restricted] after them. I am astounded at this. Tyrants fall, but their followers continue to rule! I call for freedom for all, and for the right for political participation for all. There is no isolation or exception [to who can participate]—leftists, rightists, secularists, Islamists, communists, all must unite. Except those whose hands have been stained with the blood of innocents. These people must receive punishment. Tribunals must be opened as soon as possible—*civilian* tribunals, not military ones. These should be regular courts with judges recognized as upstanding and just who will judge all of those for whom there is evidence that they tyrannized this people, and perpetrated crimes against this people.[8]

These remarks nicely illustrate the Islamist conception of political freedom that dominated their discourse at this historical moment. Qaradawi's apparent prioritizing of 'freedom' over the traditional Islamist concern for 'implementing the Sharia' arguably reflects the gradualism that has characterized Islamists of the MB variety for much of their recent history. According to such a view, without freedom the implementation of the Sharia through coercion against an unwilling public would be a meaningless exercise in religious terms. Such organizations and the Islamist denomination they represent are concerned with creating long-term Islamic social change. By willingly adopting an Islamic world view, they argue, a society would not need to be coerced into adopting the Sharia as its legal framework, but rather it would choose to do so voluntarily. Indeed, Qaradawi had as early as the 1980s argued that the *ḥudūd*, which are often associated with the notion of implementing the Sharia, were a relatively minor part of the Islamist project, and that the Sharia itself, while recognizing their validity, strongly discouraged their implementation.[9]

Qaradawi's remarks regarding the Tunisian revolution highlighted that the main menace, in his view, was authoritarianism. His appeals were deliberately broad-based: 'leftists, rightists, secularists, Islamists, communists' had to all unite against a common enemy that was more pernicious than any of these normally mutually hostile groups were to each other, namely tyranny. Indeed, his fear of tyranny seemed alive to the fact that there is often a temptation in despotic contexts to respond to the overthrowing of a tyrant with military rather than civilian tribunals which do not observe recognized rules of judicial procedure. These tools of coercion also had to be opposed, in his view. After the above statement, Qaradawi circled back to the earlier praise he directed at the Tunisian people who should be thanked, he stated, by the entire Arab and Islamic world because 'they have awakened those who were asleep, brought the heedless to their senses, and become a role model for oppressed free peoples everywhere.'[10]

On Bouazizi's self-immolation

It was not long before Qaradawi was asked about the spark that ignited the Arab revolutions, namely the self-immolation of the Tunisian street vendor Mohamed Bouazizi, which resulted in his death. Citing a viewer's question, the presenter asked whether the manner in which Bouazizi confronted the state was to be viewed as an exceptional means of jihad or as religiously condemned suicide. Qaradawi's answer considered the 'bigger picture' rather than a strictly legalistic reading of the situation. He argued that anyone who considered the matter holistically would find that Bouazizi had an Islamic legal excuse (*'udhr*). Qaradawi's interpretation of the situation is worth citing in full:

> These [tyrants] have caused this young man and his likes to live in a state of psychological crisis. I consider him to not have been free when he took this decision [to self-immolate]. He was boiling inside! Because he had earned a degree, but he could not find work. He found that he was in need of sustenance, but he could not find sustenance. As our master (*sayyidunā*) Abū Dharr (d. 32/653) said: 'I am amazed at one who does not find sustenance in his house, that he does not emerge against the people wielding a sword!' I consider him to have been in a state in which he was absolutely not in control of his will. And I said in a statement yesterday, we ask God for his sake, we humbly beseech God that He shows him clemency and forgiveness. He is Worthy of pardoning [him], Worthy of forgiving [him]. I call on the Tunisian people and I call on Muslims in general that they intercede with God to pardon this young man because he was the cause of this goodness, in awakening this umma, in kindling this revolution. So we ask God, the Exalted, to excuse him.[11]

Qaradawi's argument here is an interesting one.[12] He was clearly at pains to highlight that under normal conditions, self-immolation would constitute suicide, but he did not necessarily consider that to apply to the case of Bouazizi due to extenuating circumstances. Yet, he clearly considered the act a sin, asking God to forgive its perpetrator, and this plea with God was accompanied by his request that others also beseech God to forgive Bouazizi. In Qaradawi's view, Bouazizi's ostensibly sinful act had resulted in an opening that, at the time that he made the statement, was desperately needed in Tunisia and the wider region. Additionally, he asked others not to copy such an approach to protest since, he argued, there were so many other ways to achieve one's goal of protesting oppression. He stressed that 'Muslims should adhere to the teachings of their religion' by not committing suicidal acts, but again, he noted that these sinful responses were all a consequence of tyranny. Ultimately, he averred, it was the egregiously tyrannical regimes that were responsible for driving people to such extremes.[13] In Chapter 4, we will see that Hamza Yusuf also considered this issue at the time, but used it to criticize what he perceived as the hypocrisy of some Muslims who advocated 'suicide bombing' while condemning Bouazizi taking his own life.

Interestingly, the statement Qaradawi attributed to the Companion Abū Dharr gave rise to some criticism within days on the online Arabic discussion forum of hadith researchers, Multaqā Ahl al-Ḥadīth. On it, Qaradawi was criticized by one researcher for using a statement attributed to Abū Dharr that, in fact, had no historical basis. The discussion on the forum concluded, however, that the wider point made by Qaradawi in invoking the likely apocryphal statement was sound. One participant pointed out that the Andalusian polymath, Ibn Ḥazm (d. 456/1064), argues in a similar fashion to the apocryphal statement when he states that a person at risk of death from hunger, thirst, or exposure may fight (*yuqātil*) people who have a surplus (*faḍl*) of resources in order to save his own life. If he is killed by someone who refuses to assist them when they are in a position to, then the killer is liable for the blood money (*diya*), whereas if the one withholding the surplus resources is killed, they are deserving of God's wrath.[14]

On tyranny and acquiescing to it

After addressing these questions pertaining to Tunisia, Qaradawi turned to the question of tyranny. The presenter guided the discussion by alluding to the Prophetic statement: 'The best jihad is speaking the truth (*kalimat ḥaqq*) in the presence of a tyrannical ruler (*sulṭān jā'ir*),' a hadith considered authentic (*ṣaḥīḥ*) or sound (*ḥasan*) by Sunni hadith experts.[15] Qaradawi responded by arguing that Islam aims at establishing justice on earth, with the Qur'an considering spreading justice to be the aim of all divinely revealed traditions. He quoted the Qur'an (Q. 57:25): 'We sent Our messengers with clear signs, the Scripture and the Balance, so that people could uphold justice (*qisṭ*).' By contrast, he argued, tyranny is diametrically opposed to all revealed traditions. To justify his stance, he cited a *ḥadīth qudsī*, which is narrated by Muslim (i.e. a hadith in which the Prophet quotes God) in which God says: 'O my servants, I have prohibited myself from oppression (*ẓulm*), and I have rendered it prohibited among you, so do not oppress one another.'[16] As a consequence, Qaradawi added, God dislikes perpetrators of oppression. He additionally cited a few other partial verses to make this point and made reference to the common conclusion of ten verses in the Qur'an that 'God does not guide oppressive people (*al-qawm al-ẓālimīn*).'[17] He further declared the oppressors to be people of the Hellfire, citing several verses in quick succession (Q. 19:72; 27:52; 18:59; 11:102; 6:45) in a display of rhetorical skill, a powerful memory, and the ability to recall pertinent verses despite his advanced age—Qaradawi was eighty-four years old in this interview.[18] An informed viewer would likely have been impressed by what was clearly his deep and deliberative familiarity with the Qur'an.

The entire Qur'an, he asserted, was full of verses that prohibit oppression or supporting oppressors. Citing the Qur'an (Q. 11:113): 'And do not incline toward those who oppress (*alladhīna ẓalamū*), lest you be touched by the Fire,' Qaradawi noted that even inclining with one's heart (*al-mayl al-qalbī*) towards those engaged in oppression is prohibited.[19] Naturally, this would entail not actively supporting oppressors, he added. Oppression (*ẓulm*) has this status, he noted, because ignoring it results in complete social breakdown. Next, he cited another hadith on tyranny: 'The master of the martyrs is Hamza, then a man who stands up to a tyrannical ruler and commands him [to do what is right] and forbids him [from doing what is wrong], and so he kills him.'[20] Commenting on this hadith, Qaradawi noted that one might set out on military jihad and survive, but when one stands up to a tyrant and speaks the truth to them directly, one faced up to a greater risk. Furthermore, he cited another hadith where the Prophet is reported to have said, 'If you see my umma fearing to say to a tyrant "O tyrant," they have been bidden farewell.'[21]

Qaradawi asserted that the spread of such a 'culture of surrendering to tyrants' (*thaqāfat istislām li-l-ẓalama*) was a manifestation of deviant Sufism (*al-taṣawwuf al-munḥarif*). By contrast, he asserted that true Sufism (*al-taṣawwuf al-ḥaqīqī*) prepared believers to be people of strength (*quwwa*) and sacrifice for the sake of God. He offered historical examples of Sufis who confronted tyranny in the context of imperialism and foreign occupation. These include the example of Sufi scholars such as 'Abd al-Qādir al-Jazā'irī (d. 1300/1883) who fought against the French in Algeria; the Sanūsī Order under the leadership of 'Umar Mukhtār (d. 1350/1931) who fought the Italians in Libya; and Muḥammad Aḥmad al-Mahdī (d. 1302/1885) in the Sudan who fought the British and, Qaradawi noted, 'established a state that rules according to the Sharia' in the country. Yet, he lamented, there is a type of Sufism in which there is a certain fatalism vis-à-vis political authority that contradicts the spirit of Islam. He asserted that such Sufis respond to tyranny with statements like: '[God] places [His] servants (*'ibād*) in whatever role He wills,' (*aqām al-'ibād fi-mā arād*) suggesting that rulers have been placed in power by God, and subjects have been placed under them by Him, and so this ought to be accepted as God's will. He also cited the statement: 'Leave the creation to the Creator, and the kingdom to the Owner' (*utruk al-khalq li-*

l-Khāliq wa-l-mulk li-l-Mālik), a saying that seems to suggest not interfering with either average people or political rulers, as God is responsible for them.[22]

In this regard, Qaradawi noted how some Sufis would refer to certain verses in the Qur'an to justify certain forms of acquiescence to tyranny. He quoted 5:105 as such a verse: 'O you who believe, take care of your own selves. The one who has gone astray cannot harm you, if you are on the right path.' But Qaradawi then highlighted the conditional clause at the end of the verse. How can one be on the right path, he asked, if they set aside the obligation of commanding the right and forbidding the wrong. This is why, he noted, the first Caliph, Abū Bakr (d. 13/634), warned people against misinterpreting this verse by saying: 'I heard the Prophet, peace and blessings of God be upon him, say: "Indeed if the people see an oppressor and do not restrain him, God is at the point of subjecting them all to His punishment" (*inna al-nās idhā ra'aw al-ẓālim fa-lam ya'khudhū 'alā yadayhi awshaka an ya'ummahum Allāh bi-'iqāb min 'indih*).'[23] To this Qaradawi added the verse (Q. 8:25): 'And beware of a tribulation (fitna) that does not fall only upon the oppressors from among you,' suggesting that tyranny can also be a tribulation from God sent because people are not confronting the evil of tyrants.[24]

Excursus: On commanding right and forbidding wrong

In his magisterial study of the Islamic duty to command right and forbid wrong, Michael Cook shows that the politically subversive potential of this doctrine was felt from early Islamic times.[25] This should not be surprising for an idea, often referred to as *ḥisba*, that is ubiquitous in Qur'anic verses and Prophetic reports and whose imperatives were recognized as applying to Muslims in general. The Qur'anic support for this duty is encapsulated in the following verse: 'Let there be a community among you calling to good, and commanding right and forbidding wrong; and those are the successful ones' (Q. 3:104).[26] A number of Prophetic hadiths also emphasize the duty in some form, and we have just seen Qaradawi invoke one of them that, conveniently for Arab revolutionary activists, refers explicitly to tyranny as something that must be confronted in the name of the duty.[27] But other hadiths in this connection are even better known. Perhaps the best known, by virtue of its inclusion in the popular collection of *Forty Hadiths* compiled by the medieval Damascene scholar al-Nawawī (d. 676/1277), is what Cook refers to as the 'three modes tradition.'[28] In al-Nawawī's version of it the Prophet says, 'Whoever among you sees a wrong (*munkar*), let him put it right with his hand; if he cannot, then with his tongue; and if he cannot, then with his heart, and this [latter option] is the weakest level of faith.'[29]

This hadith has been the subject of extensive commentary in the premodern Islamic legal tradition as Cook copiously documents throughout his work. The basic message is fairly clear, however. Muslims in general have a duty to command right and forbid wrong. At the very least they must harbor in their hearts a feeling that a given action ought to be commanded or prohibited, but this is clearly the lowest level that is acceptable in the hadith. Physically changing a wrong appears to be encouraged, although jurists did place restrictions on such attempts at change in light of countervailing considerations such as the protection of privacy, where a wrong is not perpetrated in public; or the risks to social stability, which was the main reason for the classical Sunni discouragement of armed rebellion against tyrants in cases where social strife (fitna) would likely result.[30] The notion of speaking out against a wrong was frequently taken to apply to the case of tyrants, and here a scholar like Qaradawi finds himself a strong Prophetic basis, but again we find commentaries that lessen the force of this imperative in cases where one fears for one's safety.[31] Where these are not concerns, the duty is often, though not universally, upheld by premodern jurists.[32] Indeed, the way in which the duty was understood varied considerably among premodern ulama as Cook extensively documents. In the present discussion, however, the most relevant aspect of the doctrine is the extent to which it may be said to encourage protest against the tyranny of one's rulers. In this regard, Cook's summary of the classical Islamic scholarly tradition is useful: 'with regard to forbidding wrong in the face of the delinquency of the ruler, there is a clear mainstream position: rebuke is endorsed while rebellion is rejected.'[33] As he notes, premodern Islamic scholarship is replete with sympathetic portrayals of scholars who confront rulers and severely rebuke them for their tyranny.[34] By contrast, rebellion, that is to say armed insurrection, is generally seen with considerable disquiet, particularly in more mature Sunni discussions. As I will discuss in greater detail in Chapter 9, however, the antipathy towards rebellion does not quite amount to a total rejection.

As we shall see, these premodern discussions play an important role in the Arab revolutions of 2011 onwards. Despite the significantly changed context characterized by the modern nation state and a postcolonial legal order that is subordinate not to the discourses of the ulama in the form of the Sharia but to the secular logic of the modern state, religious discourse grounded in the Qur'an and Sunna still resonates with many modern Muslims. Thus, scholars like Qaradawi, while they invoke scripture from seventh-century Arabia, seek to operationalize their implications to realize political change in the present. In this regard, they are working within a modern tradition that draws heavily on the medieval scholarly heritage but adapts them to a modern context that is dramatically different to that of their premodern forbears. One of the consequences of the rise of the modern state has been for many scholars to argue that forbidding wrong with the hand, i.e. physically, should be the prerogative of the state. Cook notes with some surprise that such a view is intimated by no less an 'activist' than Ḥasan al-Bannā, the founder of the MB.[35] This may explain Qaradawi's own emphasis in early 2011 on *peaceful* protest, given that he was a devoted follower of Bannā's.[36] Indeed, as Uriya Shavit has argued, while the MB's scholars more generally recognized the central importance of the notion of commanding right and forbidding wrong, they also unanimously agreed that armed insurrection against an unjust regime was only to be undertaken as a last resort, and even then, only if success was certain and the benefits accruing from the action were less than the harm caused.[37] As Shavit notes, this reflects the dominant position of the Sunni tradition.[38] Such an attitude has more or less guaranteed that the Egyptian organization's mainstream has never engaged in a violent confrontation with the state, but it also explains Qaradawi's aversion to armed insurrection in Tunisia and Egypt in early 2011.[39] It is important to note, however, that notwithstanding the focus of the present work on the conflicts of Tunisia and Egypt which did not devolve into fully fledged civil war, Qaradawi did go on to support armed opposition to the Libyan and Syrian regimes in the context of those countries' civil wars. As Shavit notes, the MB's commitment to non-violent opposition to governments meant that they did not advocate '*launching* an armed struggle,' but this did not preclude engaging in battle where a civil war had been started by others.[40]

However, civil war aside, this generally non-violent approach to commanding right and forbidding wrong has vis-à-vis the state long been a feature of Qaradawi's thought and may help us better understand his initial response to the Arab revolutions. What may be one of his earliest discussions of the question of commanding right and forbidding wrong in relation to the state can be found in a fatwa from the 1980s.[41] In it, he argues that performing the duty of *ḥisba* vis-à-vis the state is contingent upon having the power to do so, and more generally, when one does not fear that even worse consequences may arise from attempting to change the state's behavior. He portrays having power as constituting one of three things: either controlling the army; possessing a majority in parliament in a genuine democracy; or through popular revolution. He also highlights how current regimes depend upon military might to perpetuate themselves on an unwilling public by force of arms, but it is noteworthy that he still lists armies as potential tools for commanding right and forbidding wrong with regard to wayward states if they can do so without causing fitna. The second option appears to characterize the strategy of the Egyptian MB from the 1980s onwards. For the present discussion, however, it is noteworthy that decades before the Arab revolutions, perhaps inspired by the Iranian revolution, Qaradawi argued that popular revolution is a potential means for undertaking *ḥisba* to correct a tyrannical state. In the absence of these three, he argues in his fatwa, people must be patient and restrict the duty of *ḥisba* to the second level mentioned in the hadith, namely changing with the tongue by speaking, writing, and more general advocacy so as to give rise to 'powerful public opinion that seeks to change wrongs (*taghyīr al-munkar*).'[42]

In this relatively early fatwa, Qaradawi is careful to highlight what Shavit refers to as *fiqh al-muwāzanāt* or 'the jurisprudence of balances,' an idea Qaradawi writes about elsewhere and which is concerned with balancing competing considerations in undertaking an action. Hence, one must consider the possible outcome of one's actions in performing the *ḥisba* duty. To the extent that one believes that the consequences will be worse than the wrong one is opposing, one is not permitted to attempt to change it. Qaradawi notes that if such actions are likely to precipitate loss of innocent life, the plunder of property, and exacerbate the tyranny of tyrants, then one is not permitted to undertake them. In this connection, he cites the legal principle of perpetrating the lesser of two evils.[43] These conditions will become relevant when we consider the outcome of the 2013 Egyptian coup in later chapters when Qaradawi would continue to encourage peaceful means for resisting the coup in the lead up to the Rabaa massacre. Although drastically changed circumstances arguably rendered his original fatwa inapplicable in that context, in 2011 Qaradawi was enthused by the protests which he clearly saw as falling within the third category of the means of changing corrupt governments that he had theorized decades earlier.

How to confront oppression

Returning to his 2011 interview, in response to the presenter's question of the means by which one may confront oppression, Qaradawi embarked on a discussion of the variety of means available to the believer. He spoke of resisting oppression with one's tongue (*lisān*), with the pen, through boycotts, by commanding the right and forbidding the wrong, calling to God (*da'wa ilā Allāh*), giving sincere advice regarding the religion (*naṣīḥa fī al-dīn*), and enjoining to the truth and enjoining to patience, a reference to the Qur'an (Q. 103:3). He then elaborated further. One could confront oppression by giving a sermon on Friday or through a lecture on another day, he said. One could write a book or an article, broadcast a message on the radio or television. 'There are innumerable means!'[44]

However, he did caution that the approach one took needed to be balanced, in keeping with his discourse on moderation (*wasaṭiyya*).[45] One thus finds those he labels 'retreaters' (*insiḥābiyyūn*), which he applied to the claimants to Sufism he cited earlier; in contrast with these people, one finds those who call to violence (*du'āt al-'unf*), i.e. those who call to armed rebellion against the state. This latter option was one that Qaradawi rejected in this interview 'unless many conditions and limitations are applied, because if we permit this, the lands will be overtaken by chaos (*fitan*) and people's lives will be threatened.' Predictably, given Qaradawi's discourse on moderation, he was to adopt a middle position between these two extremes. In this connection, he offered the example of the Prophet encouraging the poet Ḥassān b. Thābit to satirize his enemies' poetry as a means of defending Islam.[46] Qaradawi used the Prophet's reported deployment of poetry against poetry to argue for proportionality. 'We do not resort to the sword to oppose the pen. Rather we resort to peaceful means as much as we can.'[47]

At the prompting of the presenter, Qaradawi explained when one may resort to violence and the conditions that apply to such a situation. With reference to a Prophetic hadith, he said that one could resort to violence against those in power only when there was 'unequivocal disbelief (*kufr bawāḥ*) for which one has a clear proof from God.' He explained this by adding that if there were people who wished to eliminate Islam altogether from the umma, then the umma had to resist this. But even here, Qaradawi adds the crucial condition of having the power (*qudra*) to do so. 'All of this is predicated on possessing power.' In this connection, he cited a hadith from the collection of *Ṣaḥīḥ Muslim* in which the Prophet states:

> There was no Prophet that God sent to a community before me except that he had helpers and companions who would practice his sunna and follow his commands. Until there came after them successors who would say that which

> they would not do, and do that which they were not commanded. Thus, whoever struggles against these people with his hand (*jāhadahum bi-yadih*) is a believer, and whoever struggles against them with his tongue (*bi-lisānih*) is a believer, and whoever struggles against them with his heart (*bi-qalbih*) is a believer, and beyond this, there is not even a mustard seed's worth of faith.[48]

Qaradawi pointed out how this hadith was related to the better known 'three modes' hadith of Abū Sa'īd al-Khudrī discussed above: 'Whoever among you sees something reprehensible (*munkar*), let him change it with his hand; and if he cannot, then with his tongue; and if he cannot, then with his heart, and that is the weakest level of faith.'[49]

These two hadiths present two related principles, Qaradawi argued, that clarify the umma's obligations. One was 'jihad against oppressors and those who deviate from the Prophetic way' (*jihād al-ẓalama wa-l-munḥarifīn*), and the other was 'changing what is reprehensible' (*taghyīr al-munkar*). The umma is not permitted to simply resign itself to the presence of the reprehensible (*munkarāt*), he averred. In keeping with the hadith, he argued that one first had to try and change things for the better with one's hands. Thereafter with one's tongue, i.e. through sincere counsel (*naṣīḥa*). In this connection, Qaradawi cited the Qur'an (Q. 103:3) to highlight the duty of using one's tongue to advocate for change. The verse describes the believers as people who 'exhort one another to the truth, and exhort one another to steadfastness.' No one, he insisted, was beneath exhorting and advising their fellow Muslim towards good; conversely, he declared, no one was above being given an exhortation. Exhorting and advising one another, and commanding right and forbidding wrong, were duties of the entire umma.

He continued to ground these assertions in scripture by next citing the Qur'an (Q. 3:104): 'Be a community that calls for what is good, commands what is right, and forbids what is wrong: and those who do this are the successful ones.' He contrasted this with what is reported in the Qur'an using similar language regarding the state of the Children of Israel (Q. 5:78–9): 'Cursed were those who disbelieved among the Children of Israel by the tongue of David and of Jesus, the son of Mary. That was because they disobeyed, they persistently overstepped the limits, they did not forbid each other from doing wrong.' Qaradawi insisted that the Muslim umma had to avoid such pitfalls by upholding the banner of commanding right and forbidding wrong.

In terms of the approach taken to the incipient Arab revolutions at the time, Qaradawi argued that protests, strikes, and civil disobedience were all appropriate approaches to the revolutions that were supported by the Sharia, and that this was better than people using weapons. Indeed, he argued in the coming days that the approach taken to these protests had to always remain peaceful. He called on the regimes in the Arab world to permit peaceful demonstrations rather than compelling people to take up arms, and he lamented that tyrants (*ṭawāghīt*) did not permit such civil means: 'They do not permit people to speak. They do not permit people to protest peacefully. [Rather they respond with] live bullets, as we saw in Tunisia.'[50] We will see in Chapter 4 that the notion of being compelled to rebel finds an unexpected and ultimately ephemeral parallelism in Hamza Yusuf's blog on the Egyptian revolution from a few weeks later.

A little later in his discussion, in response to the presenters asking why God allows tyrants to go unchallenged for so long, Qaradawi would argue that 'everything has its time.' Citing a popular Arabic phrase, he said God 'gives time [to tyrants], but does not ignore [their deeds]' (*yumhil wa-lā yuhmil*). With reference to the Qur'an, Qaradawi argued that tyrants would ultimately receive their just deserts: 'We shall lead them on [to punishment] in ways beyond their knowledge; and I will give them time. Indeed, My plan is firm' (Q. 68:44–5). The tyrants would have their day of reckoning, he declared, and God would not be prevailed upon because of our impatience to rush things. But when their time came, there would be neither delay nor hastening (Q. 7:34). He added, however, that the umma should mature so that it was deserving of God's victory. The umma had to do something in the way that the Tunisian people had done in removing their tyrant. This, he asserted, was because the Tunisians came forward to make major sacrifices. In keeping with his religious message, he presented the revolutions as a religious act: 'they did not care that [their] lives were being lost in the path of God, nor did they despair.'[51]

'I am just following orders'

In the course of his Al Jazeera show, Qaradawi alluded to the Qur'an's criticism of people who did nothing to resist tyrants, and thus did not deserve God's support against them (Q. 43:54). However, this would lead on to a more serious discussion about the moral corruption that manifests among armies that are allied to autocrats (Q. 28:8). Qaradawi would note that army officers serving autocrats often justified their religiously condemned behavior with the assertion that they were simply following orders. But there was no such 'following orders' defense, Qaradawi retorted. Addressing such officers directly, he insisted: 'You have intelligence! Can a Muslim kill another Muslim when the latter has not perpetrated any crime that calls for killing him?! Even if one is commanded to kill, [...] this must be rejected.' Qaradawi added, 'The supporters of tyrants are with the tyrants in the Hellfire.'

To back this point up, he mentioned a well-known if historically uncertain story from the imprisonment of the notable scholar Aḥmad b. Ḥanbal (d. 241/855) during the *Miḥna* (inquisition) in Abbasid Baghdad in which he was tortured severely. Qaradawi related how a jailer asked Aḥmad, who was one of the leading scholars of hadith of his time, whether the hadiths regarding those who support tyrants (*aʿwān al-ẓalama*) were authentic. After Aḥmad responded in the affirmative, the jailer asked whether he would be considered such a supporter of tyrants. Aḥmad reportedly responded in the negative, explaining that the supporters of tyrants are those who took care of the jailer's needs by washing his clothes, preparing his food and the like. He concluded: 'As for you, you are one of the tyrants themselves!'[52] Qaradawi commented on this narration by adding that there are many who act as minor tyrants alongside the major tyrant. It is through them that the tyrant is able to sustain his tyranny. Citing the Qur'an, Qaradawi declared that such people would be with the tyrants in Hell. From the Qur'an, he quoted some of the people of Hell saying: 'Our Lord, we obeyed our chiefs and our elders, and they made us go astray from the path. Our Lord, give them twice the punishment, and send a curse on them, an enormous curse' (Q. 33:67–8).

The role of the ulama, Al Jazeera, and Qatar

Qaradawi also argued that the ulama had to play a role in supporting peaceful protests. In this connection, he referred to the notion of a 'silent satan' (*al-shayṭān al-akhras*) as referring to one who remains silent rather than speaking the truth in a time of need.[53] This, he noted, was better than a Satan who spreads falsehood. He added, however, that sometimes certain so-called ulama emerged—he gave an example of an 'insane' person, who he alleged had called for his assassination. Such people were examples, he asserted, of those the Prophet warned about in a hadith[54] found in the two most respected hadith collections in the Sunni canon, namely those of Bukhārī (d. 256/870) and Muslim (d. 261/875) in which the Prophet states:

> God does not take away knowledge by snatching it from the people. Rather he takes away knowledge by taking away the scholars, until when there is no scholar

remaining, the people take the ignorant (*juhhāl*) as their leaders. They are asked questions, and they give fatwas without knowledge, losing their way and misguiding others.[55]

Qaradawi argued that such people as the one he mentioned cannot be considered true ulama (*al-ʿulamāʾ al-ḥaqīqiyyūn*). Rather, he characterized true ulama, drawing on the Qur'an (Q. 33:39), as 'those who deliver God's messages and fear only Him and no one but God.' The verse he cited was originally addressed to Prophets, and was understood in this manner by early commentators, but Qaradawi took the characteristics mentioned in it to apply to 'true ulama' as well.[56] In contrast with such scholars, Qaradawi asserted that tyrants would utilize what he would later call the 'scholars of the sultan' (*ʿulamāʾ al-sulṭān*) as a means of opposing 'those speaking the truth.' In this connection, he offered the example of Tunisia—a state that once promoted the most aggressive form of state sponsored secularism in the Arab world. He asserted that for many years, Islamic scholars and writings were banned from entering the country. He then noted, with a sense of satisfaction, that the rise of satellite television in the region meant that shows like his own *al-Sharīʿa wa-l-Ḥayāh* had been able to enter Tunisia despite the best efforts of the government to limit Islamic voices. After saying this, Qaradawi took a moment to express his gratitude to Al Jazeera for taking up the cause of the Tunisian Revolution by closely following it and showing it to the world. He added that there were other channels that have followed the revolution, but that Al Jazeera had been the most important of the channels to provide support to the revolutions.[57]

This is a revealing remark on the part of Qaradawi, who as a channel insider and as its most respected religious voice at the time, noted that the revolutions were being actively supported by the channel, and that this was something he considered religiously praiseworthy. Al Jazeera's importance in the early revolutionary period was observed at the time by the international media, as well as by early participants in the revolutions, but it is noteworthy that, even before the Arab revolutions really took off, Qaradawi articulated an outlook that is probably reflective of at least some of those working within Al Jazeera at the time. As he put it, 'The Al Jazeera channel is a thorn in the side of tyrants, oppressors, and the enemies of Islam. They hate Al Jazeera, but Al Jazeera will stay strong despite them, God-willing.'[58] Of course, Al Jazeera is a Qatari state-owned media organization that is headquartered in a part of the world in which most of the media operates under heavy state direction.

Critics argue, for example, that Al Jazeera 'serves as an arm of its host nation's foreign policy.'[59] Yet, when compared with obvious state mouthpieces like the Saudi-owned Al Arabiya channel, Al Jazeera appears to represent an alternative model to such aggressively state-controlled media. However, it inevitably must work within certain constraints given the very serious political implications of its work, at a cost to its reputation for independence.

As I discuss briefly in Chapter 9, from 2017 till 2021, neighboring autocracies attempted to place considerable pressure on Qatar because of Al Jazeera's activities during the Arab revolutions, which are viewed by the neighboring United Arab Emirates and Saudi Arabia as threatening their stability. It appears immaterial to such states that Qatar is not a democratic state, and that it is clearly possible to create a relatively open media environment in which a scholar like Qaradawi can promote democratic values without automatically threatening the host autocracy with collapse. Such openness is, however, viewed as a dangerous slippery slope towards autocratic collapse by Qatar's much more populous neighbors. Qatar's tiny indigenous population coupled with its massive per capita GDP ensure, for now, that the populace will likely not seriously threaten the monarchy with democratic demands.[60] It is also worth bearing in mind that it may have been Qaradawi's personal relationship with successive Qatari heads of state that may have contributed to creating a more open culture in Qatar allowing a scholar like him to strongly advocate for democracy in the region.[61] Although some observers cry foul that Al Jazeera promotes democracy abroad while remaining silent about autocracy domestically, active democracy promotion abroad is still obviously a bridge too far for neighboring autocracies fearful of democratic 'contagion.' Presumably, the 'threat' of democracy could also face Qatar in the future. The country's democracy promotion means that it also opens itself up to questions of democratization and accountable governance in the long run even if it has been able to insulate itself from such questions for the time being.[62] Qatar's willingness to create such a climate is what had set it apart from counter-revolutionary autocracies throughout the region, most notably the UAE and Saudi Arabia.

On granting safe haven to tyrants

In the later more interactive portion of the show, the presenter relayed a question that had been sent in by a viewer asking Qaradawi about 'protecting oppressors and granting them safe haven.' Qaradawi responded by stating that this was impermissible, but then cautiously suggested that the questioner, who was from Tunisia, may have been inquiring about the fact that Saudi Arabia provides such protections to tyrants, as they had just done with the fleeing Ben Ali two days earlier on 14 January. Qaradawi's comment was perhaps illustrative of his recognition of certain restrictions upon him given the presence of Qatar's imposing neighbor, Saudi Arabia, which had in the 2000s objected to Al Jazeera's coverage and banned its reporters.[63]

He thus began by somewhat unpersuasively trying to argue that Saudi Arabia did not in fact 'protect oppressors' in a blameworthy fashion, since they stipulated upon such tyrants to whom they granted safe haven the condition that they could not involve themselves in politics of any kind. This is what was reported at the time regarding Saudi King Abdullah's grant of asylum to Ben Ali.[64] Qaradawi noted that this was like being a prisoner for these people, 'just like they themselves used to imprison the innocent.' By way of indirect criticism of Saudi Arabia, however, he added that he would have hoped that Saudi Arabia would purify itself (*tataṭahhar*) of these people and not permit them to enter the country. He concluded, with the carefully worded remark, '[To answer] the question, in general: it is not permissible for a person to protect an oppressor. It is not permitted for him to grant safety to an oppressor or conceal his faults or serve him in any way whatsoever.'[65]

'Rulers are kept in the dark'

As the program neared its conclusion, the presenter asked Qaradawi to address one last objection: some argued that the problem was not actually the leaders, but that the individuals and institutions around him were the ones actually responsible for the tyranny and corruption that one finds in these societies. The leaders, according to this line of argument, were distant from the masses and did not know the depths of corruption that the populace was experiencing. The presenter asked whether such leaders could be excused for such a state of affairs. Qaradawi responded to this question by highlighting the fact that these claims contradicted the claims that these leaders themselves made. Such leaders, he pointed out, claimed that they were of the people, loved by the people, and were intimately aware of the people's needs. This was hardly an excuse, he asserted, citing a couplet of poetry:

> If you were not aware, then that is a calamity.
> And if you were aware, the calamity is even greater![66]

Qaradawi went on to describe these rulers as evil examples, contrasting them with exemplary rulers like the second caliph, ʿUmar b. al-Khaṭṭāb (d. 23/644). The latter, he reported, was once brought very valuable war spoils by his army whom he praised as fulfilling their trust for doing so faithfully, rather than misappropriating any of it. In response, ʿUmar was reportedly told, 'O Commander of the Believers, you showed integrity and thus they showed integrity. Had you lived a life of extravagance, they would have done the same.'[67]

Conclusion

In the foregoing, we have seen Yusuf al-Qaradawi's response to the apparent success of the Tunisian revolution of 2011. Being a noted Islamic scholar, he built his energetic support for the revolutions on extensive invocations from Islamic scripture in the form of Qur'anic verses and hadith reports from the Prophet which he directly related to events that were unfolding in the region. In this regard, it is worth highlighting that a recent study of the persuasiveness of a fatwa ranked five components of a fatwa that were deemed to inspire most confidence among modern Muslims. The two most important factors were found to be: (1) the issuing authority, and (2) the citation of relevant verses and hadiths in support of the fatwa.[68] Qaradawi's authority as a noted Azhar scholar with a long track record of scholarly output alongside his extensive invocation of relevant scriptural citations likely made his pronouncements authoritative for many observers. It is also interesting to see his citation, albeit infrequent, of less well-attested hadith reports. As Jonathan Brown has noted, the invocation of weak hadiths—those whose attribution to the Prophet was considered doubtful by experts—was widespread in premodern Sunnism.[69] In the modern period, this has changed, with those I have referred to as Salafis and Islamists both adopting a more stringent approach of rejecting weak hadiths. Indeed, Brown points out that Qaradawi is one of the modern scholars who advocates such an approach.[70] As we have seen and will continue to see in the next chapter, however, he occasionally appears to cite poorly attested reports, though most of the Prophetic reports he cites are better attested. We will see that this contrasts with the Neo-traditionalist scholars we will meet in later chapters who largely maintain the premodern Sunni tendency to invoke weak hadiths without hesitation.

The preceding pages provide an overview of Qaradawi's initial response to the Arab revolutions in an interview given before the Egyptian revolution had taken place. His enthusiasm was palpable, and his religiously grounded encouragement for further *peaceful* protest in the region was argued in a robust and reasonably systematic fashion at the outset of what would soon be referred to as the Arab Spring. In his eyes, the importance of these revolutions in some sense excused the Tunisian street vendor whose self-immolation sparked them. Despite his commitment to political freedom and opposition to tyranny, however, Qaradawi advocated moderation (*wasaṭiyya*) which meant eschewing violence, despite his own recognition that the authorities were liable to respond to peaceful protests with live fire. Yet clearly, in his judgement, the risk of being killed by the state was outweighed by the possibility that the protests could bring about real change in a region that often suffered from severe political repression. Despite his advanced age in January 2011, it would turn out that Qaradawi was only getting started with his advocacy for revolution.

In the next chapter, we will consider Qaradawi's response to the upheaval in his home country of Egypt, which would start a few days after his interview. We will find that he was easily able to extend the foregoing arguments about the Tunisian revolution to the Egyptian case, at times by way of straightforward repetition. We will also briefly consider the limits of Qaradawi's approach, as exemplified by his lack of support for the revolution in Bahrain for fear of an apparently non-existent Iranian threat. By the time the revolutions reached Egypt, however, the stakes were much higher. Egypt is the most populous country in the Middle East. Through its long history, it has been one of the most important centers of culture in the Muslim world, housing the millennium-year-old Azhar of which Qaradawi was one of the most globally recognized graduates at the time of the revolutions. It is also home to the world's oldest Islamist movement of which Qaradawi is a member. It is hardly a surprise, then, that he would be particularly concerned about the Arab Spring's impact on that country. It is to Qaradawi's response to the Egyptian revolution of 2011 that we shall now turn.

2

QARADAWI AND THE EGYPTIAN REVOLUTION

(JANUARY–FEBRUARY 2011)

Yusuf al-Qaradawi was one of the most prominent Islamic scholars in the Middle East to enthusiastically celebrate the Tunisian revolution early on. As we have seen, he dedicated an episode of his weekly *al-Sharīʿa wa-l-Ḥayāh* show on Al Jazeera Arabic to it on 16 January 2011, two days after the revolution successfully ousted Tunisia's long-time dictator. In the next episode of his show, entitled '*Firʿawn wa-Āluhū wa-Afʿāluh*' (Pharaoh, His People, and His Actions) which aired on 23 January, Qaradawi continued on the theme of the revolutions with vigor. He may have been aware that Egyptian activists had designated 25 January as a day for a 'peaceful uprising against torture, poverty, corruption and unemployment in Egypt.'[1] If he was, then the title of the episode could be viewed as a deliberate if oblique attempt to encourage Egyptian protests since, as he notes in the course of the episode, Pharaoh (*Firʿawn*) was the historical title of the tyrannical ruler of Egypt. The tenor of the episode can be generalized to much of the Arab world, however.

The present chapter examines Qaradawi's engagement with the Arab revolutions in the lead up to, during, and following the Egyptian revolution that ousted long-time strongman Hosni Mubarak in early 2011. In his Al Jazeera show, Qaradawi will be seen to continue on the theme of confronting tyranny by drawing extensively on the Qur'an and hadith. Although Qaradawi generally supported peaceful protests against autocracies, we will also briefly consider his opposition to the Bahrain uprisings of March 2011 that would mar his reputation for independence according to at least one scholar. Over the course of his show prior to the Egyptian uprising as well as during one aired immediately after the successful ouster of Mubarak, Qaradawi would again demonstrate an impressive mastery of the Qur'an and hadith in order to argue against tyranny and in favor of peaceful protest. Even with Mubarak's successful removal, Qaradawi showed himself to be an active participant in Egypt's revolution by continuing to make demands of the Egyptian army that was now in control of the country. He would also critique the fatwas of scholars who supported the regime and opposed the revolutions alongside responding to hadiths that suggest acquiescence to tyranny. In the chapter's conclusion, I will briefly consider some of the ambiguities in the Islamist discourse on democracy that scholars like Qaradawi uphold and which perhaps contributed to the failure of the democratic experiment in Egypt in 2013.

'Pharaoh, his people, and his actions'

A week after his show celebrating the Tunisian revolution, Qaradawi was back on Al Jazeera addressing the problem of tyrannical government explicitly. He began addressing the topic of this episode of his weekly show by noting that Pharaoh was originally a title for the rulers of Egypt, just as Caesar (*Kisrā*) was the title of the ruler of Rome. However, he noted, the Qur'an often used it as a proper noun to refer specifically to the ruler of Egypt in the time of Moses.[2] Qaradawi next turned to the symbolic significance of Pharaoh in portraying oppression (*ẓulm*) and arrogance (*istikbār*). He noted that in the Qur'an Pharoah represented qualities of tyranny (*jabarūt*) and repression (*'uluww*).[3] Citing the Qur'an (Q. 28:4, 44:31, 10:83, 23:46), he argued that Pharaoh's arrogance led him to repress his people and look down upon them. This was made more explicit in a separate verse he cited (Q. 43:54: *fa-stakhaffa qawmahū fa-aṭā'ūh*), highlighting Pharaoh's disdain for his own people. Additionally, he highlighted that the Qur'an portrays two types of people who work alongside Pharaoh in the persons of Korah (Qārūn) and Hāmān. For Qaradawi, the first of these represented, in a transhistorical sense, 'exploitative capitalism' and 'feudal oppression.' He expressed wonder at the Qur'an pointing out that Korah was actually an extremely wealthy individual from the Children of Israel (Q. 28:76) who was co-opted by enemies in the form of Pharaoh and his people. Qaradawi described this as Korah betraying his people and joining their enemies because of certain mutual interests (*maṣlaḥa*).

According to Qaradawi, the second of these individuals, Hāmān, represented the political elite who have 'sold their souls' to arrogant rulers who regard themselves as virtual deities (*al-mustakbirīn al-muta'allihīn*). Such people acted as political strategists (*siyāsiyyūn*) at the service of Pharaoh's oppressive rule. This, he said, forms a ruling triumvirate of tyranny: the self-deifying ruler, the oppressive capitalist, and the politician all working together against the interests of the people.[4] It is an elegant theory in its simplicity that is informed by a Qur'anic worldview, yet intelligible to contemporary observers. Qaradawi was implicating the political and business elites in the entrenchment of autocracy in the Middle East. But his theory has obvious echoes of leftist critiques of neoliberal democracies in the early twenty-first century, possibly because comparable ideas were widespread in mid-twentieth-century Egypt where Qaradawi came of age intellectually.

Qaradawi next outlined certain features of what the presenter referred to as Pharaonic politics, which Qaradawi said characterized all tyrannical rulers and autocrats everywhere.[5] The foundation of such politics, he asserted, was tyranny (*ṭughyān*), as indicated in certain Qur'anic verses (Q. 20:24, 20:43, 79:17). The verses all say the same thing: 'Go to Pharaoh, for he has truly become a tyrant.'[6] The fact that Moses is given this as his first command after God makes him a Prophet indicated, according to Qaradawi, that the first thing that divine revelation seeks to address is confronting tyranny. Thus, he concluded, the primary feature of Pharaonic politics is tyranny and transgressing against people. The next feature he highlighted was dividing the people of a single land into factions. He cited a verse in the Qur'an (Q. 28:4) which reads: 'Pharaoh had become high-handed in the land, and had divided its people (*ahl*) into factions.' The land here, he noted, was Egypt, in which Pharaoh divided the people into Egyptians and Israelites, whereas the Qur'an considered the latter to be people of this land (*ahlahā*). While the Israelites were outsiders who came to Egypt, they had arrived with the consent of the people. They were not occupiers, he added, in a possible reference to his long-standing opposition to the modern Israeli occupation of Palestine. Had they been so, he argued, they would have been considered outsiders even if they had stayed hundreds of years. Rather, they had come hundreds of years earlier in the time of Joseph, when he had been elevated to a high office in Egypt at a time when he would save Egypt and its environs in a time of famine. The point of this presentation is, of course, not to examine the historicity of the exegetical reports Qaradawi is drawing on, but to explore his conception of Pharaonic politics.

According to Qaradawi, the entry of the Israelites into Egypt and their staying there for 'hundreds of years' was why the Qur'an considered them 'people of Egypt.' Qaradawi put this in contemporary terms by saying that they were deemed by the Qur'an to deserve the country's nationality (*jinsiyya*) and have the right to be treated as indigenous to those lands. However, according to his second principle of Pharaonic politics, such people were unjustly divided into factions. In another respect, Qaradawi deduced from the Qur'anic narrative that Pharaonic tyrants were always fearful of their people who they needed to factionalize in this manner. They feared that if their subjects were unified, they could be the cause for the tyrant's downfall. The just ruler, by contrast, did not fear their people. In this connection, Qaradawi related a popular but possibly apocryphal story from the time of the second Caliph 'Umar in which a messenger from the Persian ruler came to Medina to convey a message to the Caliph, only to find him sleeping under a tree without any guards. The messenger is reported to have remarked to the awakened Caliph: You were just, hence you were safe, hence you slept (*'adalta fa-aminta fa-nimta*).[7]

A third principle of Pharaonic politics that Qaradawi mentioned was the ruler insulting his people's intelligence and pulling the wool over their eyes. He repeated the Qur'anic verse regarding Pharaoh, which he had earlier cited in relation to Tunisia (Q. 43:54). In it, the Qur'an describes Pharaoh as prevailing over his people (ironically) by belittling them. Pharaoh expressed his overweening arrogance by boasting to his people about his great wealth and power relative to the Israelites (Q. 28:38, 43:52–3). In the process, Qaradawi argued, Pharaoh was able to delude Egyptians into supporting his persecution of the Israelites. Qaradawi added that Islam thus placed some of the responsibility of legitimating these tyrants on the shoulders of the masses that followed them. They operated through distraction and diversion to make their actions appear reasonable.

On simply following orders

Reiterating ideas from a week earlier, Qaradawi highlighted the role of the army in perpetuating dictatorship, declaring that 'the Qur'an makes armies responsible for the repression of tyrants because they are tools in their hands.' He dismissed the excuse that they were simply following orders. 'Who ordered you?' he asked rhetorically. 'A created being like yourself.' Qaradawi cited the Qur'an (Q. 28:8) to argue that such excuses were simply unacceptable: 'Pharaoh, Hāmān, *and their armies* were wrongdoers.' He then recited another set of verses in quick succession (Q. 28:40–1):

> We seized him and his armies and threw them into the sea. See what became of the wrongdoers! We made them leaders calling [others] only to the Fire: on the Day of Resurrection they will not be helped. We made a curse pursue them in this world, and on the Day of Resurrection they will be among the despised.

In an excursus on this point, Qaradawi highlighted how the security forces were not under any circumstances permitted in the Sharia to obey rulers who command them to kill protestors. 'The police are meant to be serving the people. The police are not meant to kill the people!' Using teargas was conceivable in his view, but Qaradawi was outraged by the suggestion that they would use live fire in kill shots. 'This is impermissible. Whoever does this bears its responsibility [before the Law and before God].'[8]

These remarks were, of course, made before major protests broke out in Egypt and the rest of the Arab world leading to vicious crackdowns characterized by precisely this kind of mass killing on the part of the security forces. However, reports from Tunisia where security forces had used live ammunition with fatal consequences were already available around the time that Qaradawi was speaking, likely informing his commentary.[9] As I will discuss further in later chapters, some pro-autocracy ulama would actually go on to encourage this kind of state violence. As we will see on the part of Ali Gomaa in the context of the Egyptian coup two years later, one finds the approach, seemingly exceptional among the ulama but empowered by the state, of actively encouraging the killing of unarmed protestors using the pretext that they were in fact armed. In contrast, Qaradawi was enthusiastic about peaceful protests and calling for the people's right to freedom of expression to be respected, but he was also the most vocal of scholars in protesting the violence of the state.

Qaradawi on Bahrain

The notable exception to this stance for Qaradawi would emerge during the Bahraini revolution that he would refuse to support, declaring it a 'sectarian revolution' that pitted Shia against Sunni. According to David Warren, Qaradawi's image as politically independent would suffer due to this choice, although given the highly polarized and sectarianized context of the post-Iraq War Middle East, Qaradawi's problematic sectarian response to the Bahraini revolution was hardly exceptional in the region.[10] Alongside Islamists, Neo-traditionalists and Salafis had become increasingly anti-Shia in tone in the years prior the Arab revolutions given the widespread perception of Iranian influence through much of the Arab world in the wake of the Iraq War of 2003. In the range of Sunni attitudes towards the Arab revolutions of 2011, however, Qaradawi's general reputation as an enthusiast for the uprisings and his vocal opposition, with the exception of Bahrain, to their violent suppression by autocratic states was clear early on. It is in this connection that he would highlight what he called 'a deceptive and poisonous culture' regarding following orders among the state security forces.

In his *al-Sharīʿa wa-l-Ḥayāh* episode aired two days before the Egyptian revolution began, Qaradawi repeated his excoriation from a week earlier of an attitude that rationalizes murderous violence in the name of 'following orders.' He called for this attitude to be overturned through a recognition of something that he considered obvious—that murder was unacceptable. Killing on the part of the state, he insisted, could not take place without a fair judicial process in which a judge could only issue capital judgements against people who genuinely deserve it. The bar was already remarkably low in Qaradawi's context in 2011. He found himself appealing for the basic semblance of the rule of law. It is tragically ironic that the floodgates would be opened to far worse than he had witnessed in the coming months and years.[11]

In his show, Qaradawi summarized Pharaonic politics as being based upon oppression (*ẓulm*), dividing people into mutually hostile groups (*tafriqa bayn al-nās*) and deceiving the people (*taḍlīl al-nās*).[12] On the last point, he elaborated further by citing the Qur'an (Q. 40:26): 'Pharaoh said, "Leave me to kill Moses—let him call upon his Lord!—for I fear he may cause you to change your religion, or spread corruption in the land."' Qaradawi argued that Pharaoh was using deception here to declare Moses to be the one who was spreading corruption, whereas Pharaoh described himself as directing his people 'to the right path' (Q. 40:29). Such deception, he averred, led to the tyrant's rendering his people deaf, mute, and blind.

'As you are, so will your rulers be'

The presenter next relayed the question of a viewer who was asking about the reasonableness of the saying, occasionally reported from the Prophet, but whose Prophetic provenance is questioned by experts that may be translated,

'As you are, so will your rulers be' (*kamā takūnū yuwallā ʿalaykum*).[13] Qaradawi asserted that the statement was sound inasmuch as tyrants were products of their people. He related an Egyptian proverb: 'O Pharaoh, what made you Pharaonic?' Pharaoh's response was: 'No one stopped me.' Qaradawi asserted that had the people confronted such Pharaohs by highlighting their human frailty and mortality, they would not become Pharaonic.

> People must not surrender to Pharaohs. These Pharaohs are only human like them. Tyrants are people like us. The Qur'an places the responsibility [for tyranny] on peoples who genuflect and bow their heads before tyrants, and become their loyal followers, groveling at their doorsteps. This is the heart of the problem.[14]

Similarly, he argued that both the followers and the followed were to blame. He cited the Qur'an (Q. 34:31–2) which says:

> If you could only see how the wrongdoers (*ẓālimūn*) will be made to stand before their Lord, hurling reproaches at one another. Those who were oppressed will say to the oppressors, 'If it were not for you, we would have been believers.' The oppressors will say to them, 'Was it we who prevented you from following right guidance after it had reached you? No! You yourselves were sinners.'[15]

Qaradawi added that while both groups blame each other, the Qur'an punishes both as noted in another verse (Q. 7:38) with an analogous message: 'Every one of you will have double punishment, though you do not know it.' By making both groups responsible, Qaradawi argued that the Qur'an gave every individual agency. He asked the followers: 'Who has made you sell your soul to these people?' He demanded that people recognize their agency and not simply render themselves blind followers of others. 'God has created [the human] as a leader (*raʾs*) not a follower (*dhanab*).' He also cited the fourth Sunni Caliph, ʿAlī b. Abī Ṭālib (d. 40/661) who reportedly advised his son: 'My dear son, do not render yourself someone else's slave when God has made you free.'[16] Summarizing his thoughts on the saying, 'As you are, so will your rulers be,' Qaradawi noted it was equally true that, 'As your rulers are, so will you be' (*kamā yuwallā ʿalaykum takūnū*)—rulers influenced the people, but at the same time, the people were the ones who produced their rulers. 'The oppressive ruler is the product of the society. A healthy society (*al-mujtamaʿ al-ṣāliḥ*) does not produce an evil ruler.' Qaradawi thus concluded that this meant the entire society was liable for its tolerance of tyrants.

He cited two hadiths to drive home this point. The first, which we have already seen, is narrated by the Caliph Abū Bakr who relates a hadith in which the Prophet says: 'If the people see a tyrant and do not restrain him, God is on the point of overwhelming them all with His punishment.' The second is one that Qaradawi characterized as 'a great hadith in educating and guiding people,' namely one in which the Prophet exhorted his followers: 'Support your brother whether he be an oppressor or an oppressed person.'[17] Qaradawi pointed out that this was a saying of pre-Islamic times and was understood literally to justify a tribal mentality—supporting one's tribe whether they be right or wrong, oppressive or oppressed. The Companions of the Prophet intuited that this could not be the Prophet's intention. Qaradawi notes that they responded to the Prophet's statement by seeking clarification—they could understand supporting the oppressed, but how would they support an oppressor? The Prophet responded: 'Restrain him from oppressing people. That is how you support him.' Qaradawi added that this is what a Muslim society should do. Qaradawi's Qur'anic anthropology is arguably one that empowers individual agency in a way that paves the way for a democratic citizenry. This fits well with his own democratic sensibilities, as well as the Islamic conception of democracy he has been actively preaching since the late twentieth century.[18]

How to confront modern 'Pharaohs'

Qaradawi next turned to the question of how to confront today's tyrants. The presenter pointed out in this connection that Moses had been guided and supported by no less than God Himself. Qaradawi responded that modern Muslims had to follow the example of Moses in confronting Pharaoh. He and his brother Aaron were told, as related in the Qur'an (Q. 20:44): 'Go, both of you, to Pharaoh, for he has exceeded all bounds. Speak to him gently so that he may take heed, or fear [God].' Qaradawi highlighted that they were told to approach Pharaoh with gentleness, calling him to God with a beautiful exhortation (*maw'iẓa ḥasana*) as also enjoined in the Qur'an (Q. 16:125). Elsewhere, he noted, the Qur'an (Q. 79:17–19) says: 'Go to Pharaoh, for he has exceeded all bounds, and ask him, "Would you like to purify yourself [of sin]? Would you like me to guide you to your Lord, so that you may hold Him in awe?"' The style advocated by the Qur'an, Qaradawi argued, was remarkably gentle, and this should generally guide even those who are addressing tyrants.

Qaradawi also added that in the Qur'an (Q. 20:45–6) the two prophets, Moses and Aaron, expressed fear for their safety in confronting Pharaoh, but

God responded by telling them: 'Do not be afraid, I am with you both, hearing and seeing everything.' Extrapolating from the verse, Qaradawi averred that God supports everyone who stands up for justice and confronts tyranny. 'Every person who stands up to a tyrant should know that God is with them and that no one can reduce his lifespan by a single moment, nor reduce his worldly provision (*rizq*) by a single morsel of food or a penny. [...] Why then should he fear anyone?' Qaradawi then went even further in encouraging people to confront tyranny by giving strategic advice. The people, he said, 'should work together in resisting oppressors.' This is what he said allowed the people of Tunisia to succeed in their revolution nine days earlier. He reiterated his belief that the man who sparked the revolutions, Mohamed Bouazizi, should not have committed the major sin of suicide, but he also reiterated his prayers for the man's forgiveness hoping that the perpetrators of injustice against him would ultimately be held responsible for his death.

But he noted how the people of Bouazizi's region began to protest in anger at his mistreatment, and thereafter other regions followed one after another, providing a united front of peaceful protests against the tyrant. When people are thus united, Qaradawi asserted, the tyrants are unable to neutralize them. It is only when they are divided and therefore weak that tyrants can maintain their hold on power. Invoking the Qur'an (Q. 61:4) which speaks of God loving those who fight as though they were a solid wall, Qaradawi encouraged people to work together to combat tyranny by joining forces. In such a scenario, the tyrants would be forced to respond to demands for rights and just treatment. Qaradawi highlighted the need for people to mentally prepare themselves to confront tyrants. He offered the example of the Prophet Moses who God assisted in preparing himself to confront Pharaoh. Qaradawi suggested that people had to consider the example of such preparation on the part of Moses and similarly mentally prepare themselves to stand up for the truth.

This was doubtless assisted by the likes of Qaradawi providing much spiritual and ideological hope and support. In a sense, he did this with his closing remarks to the episode. He expressed a conviction that while God gives tyrants respite for a while, they will ultimately see divine justice, citing the Qur'an with respect to Pharaoh (Q. 54:41–2): 'The people of Pharaoh also received warnings. They rejected all Our signs so We seized them with all Our might and power.' Ultimately, Qaradawi said with characteristic optimism, tyrants will receive their comeuppance. He concluded by quoting a hadith found in the two canonical Sunni collections of Bukhari and Muslim that conveyed this message as clearly as he could hope for. In it the Prophet says: 'God gives a tyrant free reign for a time, but when he seizes him, he has no escape.' Then [the Prophet] recited: 'Such is the punishment of your Lord when he seized the towns in the midst of their sins: His punishment is terrible and severe' (Q. 11:102).[19]

Qaradawi in Cairo during the Egyptian revolution

Intriguingly, Qaradawi and a number of globally recognized scholars were due to visit Egypt on 24 January, the day after his weekly show aired, to attend a conference at the Azhar as important guests. At this stage, the Azhar's leadership had not yet commented on the Tunisian revolution or the social media chatter regarding the protests planned in Egypt for the following day, and it was not definitively clear which side they would take. Perhaps in an effort to reach out to the Azhar establishment, Qaradawi was effusive in his praise of the Azhar leadership and the Shaykh al-Azhar Aḥmad al-Ṭayyib, in particular, in remarks on both the Al Jazeera broadcast, and at the conference at the Azhar the following day. As we will see, these cordial relations radically changed in a few short weeks' time.[20]

Five years later, an elderly Qaradawi would reminisce in an interview with Azzam Tamimi, a British–Palestinian Islamist academic and broadcaster, about his early encounter and support for the protestors in Egypt.[21] He remembered visiting Tahrir Square, which his hotel was in the vicinity of, in the late afternoon on 25 January and meeting enthusiastic youths whom he encouraged to keep up with their protests. He noted that he remained at the hotel for two days and witnessed the youths coming to the square each day while the police tried to prevent them. On Thursday 27 January, the day he was due to leave Cairo, Qaradawi said he sought out a venue where he could speak in support of the protests and was given the opportunity in an interview by the *Shurūq* newspaper, which was published the following day.[22] In his 2016 reminiscences, he noted that he expressed his support for the revolutionary youths but added that they were not to engage in violence or vandalism and had to ensure safety and order. He also said that he directed remarks at the police who he said were not to use gunfire against protestors who are unarmed.[23]

His recollections are accurate if incomplete. The *Shurūq* interview records a short but incisive message of enthusiastic support from Qaradawi for the protests, which he saw as holding much promise for the future of Egypt.

He called the protests 'the blessed uprising of the Egyptian people' which he hoped would spur much needed change and allow the people to achieve their 'rights (*ḥuqūq*) in the form of freedom (*ḥurriyya*) and dignity (*karāma*).' He saw the protests as a transnational phenomenon which started with the 'great lesson' of the Tunisian revolution, 'which must be repeated and change the Arab nations for the better.' Despite his long historical relationship with the MB, he was non-partisan in this interview. He argued that these youths were not protesting at the behest of any political party or force, but rather represented all of Egypt in its desire for freedom, dignity, a decent standard of living and 'a better tomorrow.'[24]

In the interview, he also criticized the killing of four non-violent protestors by the security forces and gave a fatwa prohibiting firing on non-violent protestors and enjoining insubordination to commanding officers who demanded this. The blood of these four martyrs had not been spilt in vain, he declared, and would only serve to spur on the protests. Similarly, Qaradawi expressly prohibited protestors from any form of vandalism of public or private property, or attacks on the police. On a conciliatory note, he declared, '[The policemen] are part of us, and we are part of them, and their blood is inviolable. They may well be suffering as we suffer, and were they to be given the opportunity, they would join the people [protesting].' Qaradawi concluded by calling on the authorities to heed the call of the populace for their own good.[25]

Shifting allegiances in the Arab Spring

Yet, in an intriguing coincidence on 24 January 2011, quite literally the eve of the Egyptian revolution, Qaradawi was seated next to Shaykh al-Azhar Aḥmad al-Ṭayyib at a major Azhar conference focused on theological unity.[26] The conference's rather long title was: 'The Sunnis are the Ashʿarīs, Māturīdīs, and the Ahl al-Ḥadīth: A Call to Unity and Tolerance and a Rejection of Disunity and Extremism.' The banner behind the speakers arrayed seventeen photos of the senior scholars in attendance from around the Arab world. It illustrates how, just a day before the Egyptian revolution, there was apparently a remarkable degree of inter-denominational concord among the ulama of the Middle East on what had been historically sensitive issues going back centuries. This in turn illustrates the extent of the rupture experienced within the ranks of the ulama as a consequence of the Arab revolutions and the subsequent counter-revolutions.

Of the scholars emblazoned on the banner, at least eight could be characterized as Islamists in some sense. They are: Yusuf al-Qaradawi, Muḥammad ʿImāra, ʿAbd al-Majīd al-Najjār (b. 1364/1945), Ṭāriq al-Bishrī (d. 1442/2021), Salīm al-ʿAwwā (b. 1361/1942), ʿIṣām al-Bashīr (b. 1376/1956), Aḥmad al-Raysūnī (b. 1372f./1953), and Salmān al-ʿAwda (b. 1376/1956). Between the images of Qaradawi and ʿAwda one finds Abdallah bin Bayyah, who at this stage had an ambiguous reputation, coming from a Neo-traditionalist heritage but having closely associated with Islamists like Qaradawi for many years. Thus, by one reading, a majority of the conference's speakers were Islamists or their sympathizers.

Curiously for a conference that was meant to be calling for a rapprochement with Salafis who are, likely deliberately, referred to by the more premodern label of Ahl al-Ḥadīth, there only appear to have been two scholars who would fit this paradigm, namely Salmān al-ʿAwda whose Islamist leanings have just been alluded to, and al-Sharīf Ḥātim al-ʿAwnī (b. 1385/1966), a moderate Salafi scholar who was developing a reputation for being critical of Salafism. The noteworthy Neo-traditionalist scholars in attendance form, with the benefit of hindsight, a Who's Who of counter-revolutionary ulama, many of whom we shall meet in later chapters. We have already noted the presence of Bin Bayyah, and Aḥmad al-Ṭayyib served as the host of the conference as shaykh al-Azhar. But besides them, there was the prominent Syrian scholar, Muḥammad Saʿīd Ramaḍān al-Būṭī (d. 1434/2013) and Ali Gomaa. All of these scholars became noteworthy, in the course of the weeks, months, and years that followed, as the most prominent defenders of the autocratic regimes of the Middle East, drawing on a distinctive reading of the Islamic tradition to religiously justify, directly or otherwise, vicious crackdowns against overwhelmingly unarmed protestors throughout the Middle East. They can be contrasted with the Islamists above, most of whom were religiously grounded enthusiasts for the popular revolutions that were sweeping the region. As the counter revolutions consolidated, a number of these scholars, perhaps most notably Yusuf al-Qaradawi, emerged as targets of smear campaigns on the part of counter-revolutionary states, most notably the UAE, Egypt, and Saudi Arabia.

As we shall see in later chapters, counter-revolutionary scholars would present a figure like Qaradawi, and the institution of the IUMS he presided over, as fomenting civil strife or fitna. In their view, the problem in the Middle East was emphatically not, as a figure like Qaradawi saw it, the repression of long-standing dictators and their ruthless security apparatuses that severely curtailed freedoms in the region, monopolized wealth, and robbed people of their basic human rights and dignity. While counter-revolutionary scholars would sometimes allude to the need for greater justice and less corruption in their countries and/or the wider region, for them the main problem arose from the chaos that was being fomented by protests and dissent against the existing regimes.

The (initial) success of the Egyptian revolution

As we have seen, Qaradawi was clearly following closely the events of the Egyptian revolution from its start. Fortuitously, he happened to be in Egypt when the first protests broke out on 25 January 2011. He had voiced his support for the protests in interviews with journalists and often lengthy comments on Al Jazeera Arabic news programs. He had also articulated his encouragement of them in Friday sermons. Once again, his prominence on the Arab world's most popular and influential news channel arguably cements his position as the most influential Islamic scholar who supported the Arab revolutions from its beginning. In this respect, he began supporting the revolution before the inevitably more cautious official MB leadership who began officially supporting the revolutionary uprising on 27 January.[27] Qaradawi's comments on Al Jazeera over the period of the Egyptian revolution also included criticism of establishment scholars such as the shaykh al-Azhar whom we will consider in greater detail in the next chapter. In this section, however, we will briefly consider Qaradawi's reaction to the success of the Egyptian revolution in ousting Mubarak on 11 February 2011. On 13 February, Qaradawi would be on his weekly Al Jazeera show. The episode on that day was inevitably dedicated to the apparent success of the Egyptian revolution after the army removed Mubarak.

Qaradawi opened the episode by reciting the praise of God and citing verses in the Qur'an that encouraged people to rejoice at God's mercy and generosity (Q. 10:58) and others that highlighted God's agency in the removal of tyrants (Q. 6:45, 11:102, 17:80–1). The tenor of his message was emphatically one of gratitude to God. He also characterized the behavior of the youths who participated in protests as resembling the Ansar, the Medinan members of the early Muslim community who received and supported the Prophet's small community of believers as they left Meccan hostility to their message to find a new home in Medina. Qaradawi spoke of these youths' willingness to make sacrifices for the sake of others in need.[28] Such 'exceptional youths,' Qaradawi insisted, would confront the armed thugs of the Egyptian state peacefully 'without any weapons besides their tongues.' It is true that numerous observers have pointed out that violent protestors were part and parcel of the uprisings, but Qaradawi may have been unaware of this and in any case, forcefully advocated only peaceful protests as we have seen. Focusing on these peaceful activists, Qaradawi congratulated these youths but then urged them to recognize that the revolution was ongoing. He also enjoined them to stay united and put forward representatives who could convey their demands to the army. The comment was prescient in some ways, but in other respects quite obvious.

Qaradawi then moved on to address the army directly.[29] He first praised the army for declaring early on that they supported the right of the youths to express themselves. In particular, he reiterated with approbation the declaration of the army that they did not and would not attack the youths directing the protests.[30] The army made this remark on 31 January, and with the benefit of hindsight, given that the army were a major force behind crushing the revolutions in 2013, their stance in 2011 has been understood by some observers to have likely been an effort to strengthen their own hand vis-à-vis Mubarak in his twilight years.[31] Qaradawi's remarks at this point may be viewed as an attempt to maintain relations with an institution that had not yet seemed implacably opposed to the democratic openings appearing in Egyptian society in early 2011.

Yet, even now, Qaradawi did not simply praise them but had demands that were aligned with the revolutions. In a sense, his announcing these demands from his Al Jazeera show allowed them to be made before an audience of millions around the world and continued mounting the pressure for reform in the region. In this regard, Qaradawi was an active participant in the revolutions of 2011. Specifically, he demanded that the army release all the youths who had been imprisoned or disappeared in the course of the Egyptian revolution. Indeed, Qaradawi went further:

> We want the release of all political prisoners who have been sentenced by unjust military tribunals with sentences they did not deserve. That era is over. It is an obligation (*yajib*) to release those who have unjustly spent years in the dungeons of the prison; as well as the Egyptians in exile who cannot return because there is a sword hanging over them—the sentences that these military tribunals have passed over them. I also demand that they implement what they have promised by annulling the state of emergency. They said they would annul the state of

> emergency as soon as these circumstances come to an end. The circumstances have come to an end! Why is the state of emergency not over? [This state of emergency] has shackled Egyptian society for thirty years! The whole world lives a normal life except us. We are ruled by a state of emergency. It is time for the Supreme Council of the Armed Forces to give the Egyptian people the good news of ending the state of emergency—ending this nightmare that has suffocated Egyptians for so many decades. This is my message to the army.[32]

Anti-revolutionary fatwas and scholars

At the presenter's prompting, Qaradawi next addressed the fact that a number of religious figures had described those engaged in the revolutions, the same people praised so profusely by Qaradawi, as being rebels, using the highly charged religious term, Khawārij.[33] The term is the Arabic plural form of the word Khārijī and refers to an early Islamic sect that rebelled against the fourth Caliph ʿAlī b. Abī Ṭālib, with one of their number eventually assassinating him. In order to do this, they developed the doctrine that anyone who had, in their estimation, committed a major sin (*kabīra*) had thereby apostatized, and therefore could be killed with impunity. ʿAlī had, in their view, apostatized because he had ceased hostilities with Muʿawiya (d. 60/680). Early Muslims also transmitted reports from the Prophet prophesying the emergence of such extremists as the Khawārij. Indeed, their name derives in part from reports in which the Prophet says that they would leave (*yakhrujūn*) the religion like an arrow that goes straight through hunted game.

The verb related to their name, *kh-r-j*, in addition to meaning 'leave' also means 'to rebel against political authority,' a sense that may have developed in response to the historical context of the early Khawārij. In a somewhat ironic twist, rebellion against a just ruler is considered a serious sin in Islam, although the Khawārij could always circumvent this problem by declaring the rulers in question unjust, thereby legitimating their rebellion, at least in their eyes. Most later Sunnis, as we briefly considered in the last chapter, limited the idea of legitimate rebellion against even unjust rulers to those who a group of rebels could militarily unseat without precipitating major social dislocation leading to even worse outcomes for the society.[34] In such a case, they would not be considered Khawārij in a theologically problematic sense, but only in the linguistic sense of having rebelled against an unjust incumbent. This makes the theologically loaded label Khawārij especially compelling as a term of vilification. As Jeffrey Kenney notes, 'comparing someone in the modern period with the Kharijites is not a neutral, descriptive assessment; it is normatively and politically weighted against rebellion and in favor of the ruling authorities. The violence perpetrated by someone who is a Kharijite is by definition extremist, unlawful, and intolerable.'[35] As well as suggesting that these people are leaving the religion, the term also casts them as violent rebels against a *just* ruler who is owed allegiance according to Islamic teachings, and rebelling against such a ruler is a grave sin.

Considering those against whom such a label is made to stick, things are in fact even worse. Multiple canonical hadiths report that the Prophet sanctioned killing people with certain characteristics that the early Muslims saw in the Khawārij, most notably their anathematization of other Muslims and perpetration of deadly violence against them. The Prophet legitimated their killing even though they exhibited rigorous devotion in prayer and fasting.[36] The Khawārij have thus nearly universally been condemned by Muslims in all eras, given that the Khawārij considered all non-Khawārij to be disbelievers who could be killed with impunity. Consequently, non-Khārijī Muslims considered fighting and even killing Khawārij to not just be justified but praiseworthy. It is important to note, however, that the early Muslims did not take this as a license to seek them out to kill them, but rather as a means of legitimating self-defense against their aggression, even if it resulted in deaths among the Khawārij.

The term also appears to be used in Islamic legal discourse to refer to rebels more generally, while carrying the opprobrium of association with the early Khārijīs. Indeed, there were debates in early Islam regarding whether they were considered Muslims at all, with a minority of notable Companions and scholars declaring them infidels.[37] The use of such a term is thus quite provocative. In later chapters, we will consider the ideas of some of the scholars who have used such language and arguments in the course of the Egyptian revolution to vilify peaceful protestors. In the present chapter, however, we will mainly consider Qaradawi's reaction to such scholars.

Qaradawi responded to the presenter's question by expressing his deep sadness at this state of affairs:

> There are people who claim an affiliation with (*yantasibūna ilā*) the religion and religious knowledge for whom truth has become confused with falsehood to the point that they accused these youths of being rebels (*khārijūn*). The [historical] Khārijīs had certain characteristics among which was their declaring all Muslims besides themselves to be disbelievers. Everyone besides them was deemed a disbeliever. They also deemed licit people's lives and property. Everyone besides

> them was deemed licit. To the point that they made licit the blood of the first son of Islam, the Knight of Islam and the Sage of the Umma, ʿAlī b. Abī Ṭālib, God be pleased with him. They rendered his blood licit [by killing him...]. Do these youths excommunicate anyone? Do these youths render people's blood licit? How can anyone say they are rebels (Khawārij)?[38]

In this regard, Qaradawi proceeded to accuse the figures making such accusations, characterizing them as 'affiliating themselves with the ulama' of pursuing ambiguities in the revelation while setting aside matters that are definitive.

In speaking of such 'ambiguities,' Qaradawi was making a reference to a Qur'anic verse (Q. 3:7) which refers to two types of verses in the Qur'an. The verse reads:

> It is He who has sent this Scripture down to you [O Prophet]. Some of its verses are definite in meaning—these are the cornerstone of the Scripture—and others are ambiguous. The perverse at heart eagerly pursue the ambiguities in their attempt to make trouble and to pin down a specific meaning of their own: only God knows the true meaning. Those firmly grounded in knowledge say, 'We believe in it: it is all from our Lord'—only those with real perception will take heed.

Qaradawi thus implied that such scholars as Ṭayyib, someone he had praised only weeks earlier, and his Azharī colleague, Ali Gomaa, exemplified deviation and interpretive perversity. In addition, he suggested that they did not follow appropriate interpretive methodology more generally and had thus profoundly misused language. He gave the example of calling these protests rebellion (*khurūj*), pointing out that the word *khurūj*, when used in Islamic law, referred to armed rebellion. As I note in Chapter 7, this stance is ironically upheld by Gomaa in an interview after the Rabaa massacre two years later. In the 2011 interview, Qaradawi asked: 'Were any of these [youths protesting in 2011] carrying anything? No. They were not carrying any weapons. [...] They only had their tongues. They were speaking out.'[39] Like many outside observers, Qaradawi appeared to have been unaware that some protestors had indeed engaged in violence, though as he made clear from the outset, he was opposed to such behavior.[40]

Others, Qaradawi said, deemed these protests to be a religiously reprehensible innovation (*bidʿa*).[41] It is not clear who held this to be the case in the Tunisian or Egyptian revolutions, and it may simply be a reference to past questions that Qaradawi has addressed in this connection. In the fourth volume of his collected fatwas, published in 2009, he includes a fatwa in which the questioner asks Qaradawi his opinion regarding the view of some scholars that protests and demonstrations are a reprehensible innovation.[42] Qaradawi strongly disagrees with this characterization and proceeds to provide an extensive religious justification for protests that are seeking to uphold legitimate demands. In his 2011 remarks on Al Jazeera, he was quite possibly echoing his fatwa rather than confronting a more proximate claim that protests constituted *bidʿa*.

Qaradawi argued on his Al Jazeera show that the concept of *bidʿa* pertains to strictly religious issues and that protests regarding rights were not a strictly religious issue. Speaking as though he were uttering a general principle, he noted: 'religious issues are built on strict adherence, while worldly issues are built on innovation' (*umūr al-dīn taqūm ʿalā al-ittibāʿ wa-umūr al-dunyā taqūm ʿalā al-ibtidāʿ*). As Michael Cook points out, this attitude is well-grounded in the Islamic tradition, perhaps most famously articulated in a hadith in which the Prophet says to a group of farmers, 'You are more knowledgeable in your worldly affairs.'[43] It is, of course, worth pointing out that Qaradawi's conception of religion differs significantly from popular modern Western conceptions of this idea. What is most relevant to the present discussion, however, is that Qaradawi rejected the notion of *bidʿa* being argued for by some modern Muslim scholars. He pointed out that modern Muslims adopt many Western norms and institutions such as parliamentary government. These are all tools and means, he argued, that could legitimately be adopted from non-Muslim sources just as the early Muslims did. He noted that the second Caliph, ʿUmar b. al-Khaṭṭāb, adopted the *dīwān*, ostensibly a record keeping system used in his administration, and other administrative techniques used by his Caliphate from neighboring empires. None of this had any precedent among the Muslims of the time, and none of it could be considered *bidʿa* according to Qaradawi.

In fact, Qaradawi went further to argue that the Companions had themselves also engaged in protests after ʿUmar b. al-Khaṭṭāb entered the fold of Islam. They formed a procession in Mecca of two lines, one led by ʿUmar and the other by Ḥamza b. ʿAbd al-Muṭṭalib, as a means of showing their strength to the hostile Meccan leadership. It is noteworthy that he did not comment on the strength of the report, given that some scholars regard it as extremely weak in its attribution to the Prophet.[44] Its weakness arguably did not, however, undermine the more general legal arguments he presented in favor of peaceful protests. In keeping with this, he argued that modern scholars who prohibit such protests were guilty of 'distorting the meaning of revelation' (*yuḥarrifūna al-kalim ʿan mawāḍiʿih*), a severe rebuke that the Qur'an directs at some Jewish rabbis in a few instances (Q. 4:46, 5:13, 5:41).

Mildly contradicting himself, Qaradawi expressed deep distress that some 'great scholars' (*ʿulamāʾ kibār*) had accused these youths of misguidance, apostasy, and stirring up fitna. Earlier he had described those putting forward this narrative of claiming an affiliation with knowledge—an expression typically used to belittle a person's learning. It is likely that the 'great scholars' he was speaking of were the likes of the Shaykh al-Azhar Aḥmad al-Ṭayyib who had invited him to speak in Cairo three weeks earlier and whom he had praised in his speech. However, as we will explore in greater detail in the next chapter, Ṭayyib had come to oppose the protests as constituting fitna or civil strife—a fact that Qaradawi had criticized on an Al Jazeera news interview while the protests were still ongoing.[45] Hence, Qaradawi's extempore criticism of the anti-revolutionary perspective struggled to balance his attempt to show respect to the shaykh al-Azhar while severely criticizing Ṭayyib's perspective.

Islam's opposition to tyranny

In defending the right of Egyptian youths to protest in the Egyptian revolution, Qaradawi presented a short but powerful defense of the principle of confronting tyranny as being central to Islam by citing verses and hadiths to that effect in quick succession from memory. In two and a half minutes, he cited four verses and six hadiths to convey his message. While he was mostly recapitulating citations from earlier interviews, his obvious command of the scriptural sources, constantly on display in his live Al Jazeera show, served to reinforce his religious authority given that it demonstrated his mastery of the Islamic scholarly tradition. Responding to the aforementioned accusations regarding the youths who had participated in these protests, he expressed his incomprehension that such allegations could be directed at youths who were protesting tyranny (*qāmū yarfuḍūn al-ẓulm*). Qaradawi continued:

> I do not understand how the verses and hadiths that reject tyranny (*ẓulm*) are lost on these [ulama]. Hundreds of verses in the Holy Qur'an reject tyranny, curse tyrants, express hatred of tyranny and its perpetrators, and that God does not love tyrants, that he does not guide people of tyranny, and that tyrants are never successful, etc. This is not all. [God declares:] 'Do not incline towards those who have committed tyranny lest the Hellfire touches you' (Q. 11:113). Simply inclining towards tyrants necessitates the touch of Hellfire—God grant us refuge!—'and then you will have no one to protect you from God,'—you will

be deprived of God's protection—'nor will you be helped'—you will be deprived of God's help. Furthermore, The Qur'an says: 'Pharaoh, Hāmān, and their armies were wrongdoers' (Q. 28:8); 'so We seized him and his armies and threw them into the sea. See what became of the wrongdoers!' (Q. 28:40); 'We made Our rejection pursue them in this world, and on the Day of Resurrection they will be among the despised' (Q. 28:41). [...][46]

Islam teaches us to stand in the face of tyrants, and the hadiths of the Prophet are many in this regard: 'The best jihad is speaking the truth before an oppressive authority (*sulṭān jā'ir*);'[47] 'The master of the martyrs is Ḥamza b. 'Abd al-Muṭṭalib, and a man who stands up to a tyrannical ruler (*imām jā'ir*), commands him [to do what is right] and forbids him [from wrong], so he kills him;'[48] 'Indeed, when people see a tyrant (*ẓālim*) and do not restrain him, God is at the point of subjecting them all to His punishment;'[49] 'If you see that my umma fears addressing a tyrant with the words 'O tyrant!,' then they have been bidden farewell.'[50]

There are many such hadiths. The Prophet once mentioned tyrannical rulers and said: 'Whoever struggles against them (*jāhadahum*) with his hand is a believer, and whoever struggles against them with their tongues [by speaking out against them] is a believer, and whoever struggles against them with his heart [by hating their actions] is a believer. Beyond that, there is not even a mustard seed's worth of faith.'[51] [He also said:] 'Whoever among you sees a wrong, let him change it with his hands. If he is unable to, let him change it with his tongue. If he is unable to do even this, let him change it with his heart, and that is the weakest level of faith.'[52] These [youths] are changing with their tongues. They did not carry swords, nor explode bombs, nor did they aggress against anyone.[53]

Qaradawi was clearly demonstrating that the Islamic tradition could be used to legitimate such protests quite effectively. There are plainly plenty of scriptural sources that could be invoked to justify protests against tyrants. However, he did not address numerous hadiths that suggest the contrary—that one should remain patient in the face of tyranny.[54] It is thus fitting that the first phone-in question from a viewer asked Qaradawi how one was to respond to such hadiths which, as the presenter pointed out, include ones deemed authentic by hadith experts.

Hadiths enjoining patience

One hadith in particular that is recorded in the canonical Sunni collection of *Ṣaḥīḥ Muslim* was mentioned by a caller who highlighted that scholars opposed to the revolutions prohibit 'rebelling against the ruler' (*khurūj 'alā al-ḥākim*) because this hadith included the phrase 'hear and obey the ruler even if your back is struck and your wealth is taken.' Qaradawi responded by noting that protests do not constitute rebellion. Rebellion, he pointed out, was necessarily armed, and what was impermissible was engaging in armed rebellion on the part of those who did not have the ability to do so—that is, those who could not unseat an incumbent tyrant by force of arms and replace them with a just ruler while causing minimal disruption to the social order. Rebellion and protest were frequently and, it seems, deliberately conflated by opponents of the protest movements that formed the early Arab revolutions. Since Sunni scholars are generally opposed to armed insurrection as discussed in the previous chapter, because it often results in civil strife, conflating unarmed protests with armed rebellion is a potentially effective strategy in delegitimizing the former by association with the latter.

Qaradawi noted that he had argued for three methods of changing governments in modern times—methods we considered in the previous chapter. In this 2011 broadcast, he provided only a brief description of each method with a changed order of the first two. Thus, he first suggested democratic means and secondly mentioned change undertaken by an army.[55] He noted that most Arab countries had governments that emerged militarily through a process that premodern jurists referred to as gaining power by force (*taghallub*). Given his critique of regnant Arab regimes, this remark would suggest that Qaradawi was less enthusiastic about this method of change. The last method he mentioned was, of course, popular revolution (*thawrat al-sha'b*). In his Al Jazeera interview, he explicitly linked this to the 1979 Iranian revolution in which the populace partook in overthrowing the Shah and bringing Khomeini to power. While the army initially sided with the Shah and trying to crush the revolt, Qaradawi argued (perhaps with undue generalization) that armies cannot persist indefinitely in quelling such revolutions because armies were constituted by the people. After a period, the Shah's army had to stop, and the revolution was successful through the people (*intaṣarat al-thawra 'an ṭarīq al-sha'b*). Similarly, he asserted, Tunisia and Egypt had succeeded through the people.[56]

Qaradawi contended that this third method did not in fact constitute rebellion. Instead, he argued that a genuinely popular revolution that expresses the will of the people constituted a pledge of allegiance (*bay'a*) that symbolized the transference of political legitimacy to a new order. Qaradawi's theory located political authority in the people, and hence their genuine preference was what ultimately mattered.[57] Clearly, in Qaradawi's conception of political legitimacy it would simply be incomprehensible for a peaceful popular revolution against a tyrannical despot to constitute a rebellion. Hence it is no surprise that he expressed incredulousness that 'those of intelligence' (*alladhīna ʿindahum baṣīra*) could see things any other way in the context of Egypt in early 2011. He asked such religious critics of the revolution:

> Will you side with these people who are demanding what is right (*ḥaqq*) and rejecting what is wrong (*bāṭil*), who are calling for justice (*ʿadl*) and rejecting tyranny (*ẓulm*)? Will you side with these people or with the tyrant (*ẓālim*) who has misappropriated the wealth of the country, plundered fortunes, created corruption, tortured people to death, and perpetrated terrible crimes? Will you be with these people or their opponents?! I am astounded by these religious people who pretend to knowledge![58]

Qaradawi next turned to the hadith in *Ṣaḥīḥ Muslim* that was the basis for the viewer's question. He began by pointing out that this Prophetic report was not in fact one of the foundational hadiths of Muslim's collection. He explained that the collection had two types of hadiths, those that were foundational (*aḥādīth al-uṣūl*) and supporting hadiths (*mutābiʿāt*). In the supporting hadiths, Qaradawi averred, Muslim was not as rigorous as he was regarding the foundational ones. Clearly prepared for this question, Qaradawi read from a paper in front of him the criticism leveled at this hadith by the noted hadith expert Dāraquṭnī (d. 385/995). Qaradawi, following Dāraquṭnī, argued that this hadith was not in fact authentic, despite being in Muslim's collection. This, he noted, was because great hadith experts such as Dāraquṭnī, Mizzī (d. 742/1341), Ibn Ḥajar (d. 852/1449) and others point out that the narrator from the Companion of the Prophet who relates the hadith never in fact met the Companion in question, and thus there is a break in the chain rendering the hadith *mursal* in the technical terminology of hadith studies.

Qaradawi was not the only scholar to dismiss this hadith on the basis of such arguments. As I note elsewhere, however, one can also find scholars who argue that the hadith is sound but did not apply to the Arab revolutionary context.[59] Qaradawi argued that this hadith 'which many rely upon' to justify silence in the face of tyranny could not be appealed to in the face of the Qur'anic condemnation of tyranny and many other hadiths that do the same. He argued that the way to reconcile these apparent contradictions was through the exercise of *fiqh al-muwāzanāt* (i.e. understanding how to balance competing legal considerations) alongside *fiqh al-maqāṣid* (i.e. understanding how a concern fits into the overall aims and purposes of the Sharia), and finally *fiqh al-awlawiyyāt* (i.e. understanding how to order priorities in fiqh). These are juristic tools that Qaradawi develops across his oeuvre and pertain to addressing the concerns of modern Muslims. Ultimately, he would express with great passion how he was convinced of the Islamic legitimacy of the Egyptian revolution, and it was his combination of passion, scholarly authority, and systematic juristic argumentation on the basis of the Qur'an and hadith that rendered him such an important figure in the early period of the Arab revolutions.

The prohibition against harming protestors

In his Al Jazeera show, Qaradawi also addressed the question of the state apparatus harming protestors. He stated that one who has been killed by the state for peacefully protesting was unquestionably to be considered a martyr (*shahīd*), a sanctified station in the Islamic tradition. Becoming a martyr is considered a highly meritorious act in Islam, with several Qur'anic verses and hadith reports that encourage people to make the ultimate sacrifice for a just cause.[60] Qaradawi was arguing that protesting against tyrants was such a just cause. By contrast with the martyr, Qaradawi severely condemned those members of the state security forces who killed peaceful protestors of whom many hundreds had died during the Egyptian revolution of 2011.[61] He pointed out that those who had killed protestors were guilty of the severest of major sins (*kabīra min akbar al-kabā'ir*), namely murder. Qaradawi's argument was a moral one, given his appeals to otherworldly punishment rather than worldly penalties. But for his devout audience, such warnings would have likely carried much weight. Whether it would have any impact on the presumably less devout Egyptian security forces seems quite unlikely.

The moral force of his argument was backed up by a partial citation of the Qur'anic verse prohibiting murder: 'If anyone kills a person—unless in retribution for murder or spreading corruption in the land—it is as if he kills all mankind' (Q. 5:32). Qaradawi asserted that those who had been killed by the security forces had neither committed murder themselves nor spread corruption. Rather they had been 'calling for justice, waging war against tyranny (*ẓulm*), and working towards the interests of their nation.' Qaradawi went on to argue that the following verse applied to such people: 'If anyone kills a believer deliberately, the punishment for him is Hell, and there he will remain: God's wrath is against him, He has cursed him, and has prepared a tremendous torment for him' (Q. 4:93). He further cited a Prophetic hadith that states: 'The end of the world is less grave than the wrongful killing of a Muslim.'[62]

Returning to the theme of following orders, he reiterated that no one was permitted to obey a command to sin, paraphrasing well-known hadiths of the Prophet to the effect.[63] Addressing army officers directly, Qaradawi said: 'If you are commanded to kill someone, do not proceed with it because there is no law or constitution or anything that permits the killing of people for nothing.'[64] He concluded on a severe note, declaring those who had engaged in such killing to be 'people of the Hellfire—God save us!' Importantly, he added that he did not consider such a person a disbeliever, unless they considered such an act to be licit, in which case they would be considered a disbeliever, since they would thereby have rejected a prohibition that was not open to doubt for a believer, i.e. the prohibition of murder. This is a standard Sunni criterion for judging infidelity on which Qaradawi had written a short work in the 1970s.[65]

Conclusion

As we have seen above, Qaradawi was a deeply anti-authoritarian figure in 2011, in keeping with his long career. But his advocacy of democracy would have been colored by his religious identity in the eyes of many observers. For many Egyptians, from self-professed 'liberals' to establishment religious figures, for very different reasons, such calls to democracy would come to be seen with deep suspicion by 2013, as we shall see through the counter-revolutionary ulama's eyes in later chapters. A major challenge for Islamist advocates of democracy is the normativity of liberalism in the global order. In this context, the invocation of non-liberal forms of democracy are seen with considerable hostility. As Shadi Hamid and Andrew March have recently illustrated, the Islamic democracy promoted by Islamists like Qaradawi, while still not an extensively elaborated discourse, cannot and does not claim to be liberal.[66] Liberal anxieties concerning the Islamist democratic project have been expressed well by March thus:

> because this Islamic democratic vision of self-rule involves a very deep kind of consensus about metaphysical truths and the ethical purposes of human life, it does not escape the possibility that such deep moral agreement is no longer likely

> in the contemporary world, at least without the kinds of coercion and limitation on freedoms of conscience and speech that Islamic democrats claim to reject. What if moral pluralism is here to stay?[67]

Advocates of Islamic democracy like Qaradawi have not engaged this liberal concern in any detail, giving rise to considerable misgiving among liberals both within and outside the Arab world about the long-term implications of the Islamic democratic project. At times, Islamic democrats suggest that there is greater moral consensus in the region than there actually seems to be, and at others they simply put off addressing these concerns until a future point at which they become a more pressing concern. Neither approach assuages such liberal anxieties. For their part, Egyptian liberals and some of their Western counterparts would not be coy about expressing their opposition by supporting the violent ouster of the Islamists from power. But the unexplored tensions between liberal democracy and Islamic democracy doubtless did not help make a case for Islamists' democratic bona fides in the face of what Shadi Hamid has characterized as an irrational fear of Islamists on the part of Egyptian liberals.[68] Ultimately, most Egyptian liberals and members of the (liberal) Obama administration would directly or indirectly support the removal of MB leader turned President of Egypt Mohamed Morsi in 2013.[69] As I will discuss further in the conclusion of the present work, the concern that March raises is complicated by the fact that various aspects of liberalism similarly (and somewhat ironically) cannot be upheld in the region without 'the kinds of coercion and limitation on freedoms of conscience' that liberals similarly claim to reject. Such a form of liberalism is increasingly manifesting in Europe as 'muscular liberalism,' but it has its echoes in the early history of liberalism as Uday Mehta has noted.[70]

At the beginning of the Arab revolutions, however, the Egyptian revolutionary opposition to Mubarak distracted from these and other fundamental disagreements. Opposition to the Mubarak regime was a unifying factor sufficient for overcoming any mistrust between the various Egyptian groups, even if it would ultimately be short-lived. Qaradawi's active involvement in the Arab revolutions during this period would continue through his weekly Al Jazeera show alongside his regular Friday sermons and occasional commentary on current affairs in other forms. His passion for the Egyptian revolution never waned throughout 2011 and 2012. It is only after August 2013, after the Egyptian coup and the Rabaa massacre that followed it that his show was taken off the air by pressure placed on Qatar by its Gulf Cooperation Council (GCC) neighbors who had, by this time, developed into a veritable counter-revolutionary force led by the UAE and Saudi Arabia.[71] He also stopped giving Friday sermons from March 2014 after a sermon from the previous month in which his criticism of the UAE led to the country summoning the Qatari ambassador to protest Qaradawi's 'insolent remarks.'[72] Prior to this, for years, if not decades, his sermons had been aired on Qatar's national channel on a weekly basis. Of course, given Qaradawi's advanced age, being eighty-four at the start of the Arab revolutions of 2011, there were also spells of absence due to ill health and medical treatment which prevented him from giving sermons and participating in his show.

Between 2011 and 2013, however, he regularly engaged debates around the Arab revolutions. His ideas from this period are spread across countless lectures, interviews, and writings. It is naturally not possible to engage in an exhaustive assessment of these here. However, the foregoing gives us a clear idea of his zeal for the Arab revolutions and for the possibility of democratic and accountable government in the region replacing long-standing and often extremely brutal dictatorships. Qaradawi never lost his enthusiasm for the revolutions. Indeed, his animosity towards the region's dictatorships seems only to have intensified with the passage of time and the relentlessness of the counter-revolutions. In later chapters, we will have occasion to see his scholarly reaction to the Egyptian coup of 2013 which brought to a violent end the country's brief experiment with democracy, and also inaugurated a dark period in the history of the MB and their supporters who were systematically targeted and crushed by the coup regime of Abdel Fattah al-Sisi. As we will see, Qaradawi would continue to passionately argue for the religious illegitimacy of the coup while still calling for peaceful protests rather than a turn to violence in the face of the bloody massacres faced by supporters of the ousted President Mohamed Morsi.

Qaradawi's contribution to the early period of the Arab revolutions was probably as the single most influential and authoritative religious voice calling for peaceful protests against military dictatorships in the Arab world. In addition to being a vocal supporter of the revolutions, he also had, over many decades, produced a large body of scholarship that attempted to develop a coherent Islamic discourse that was adapted to modern conditions and which crucially included the indigenization of democratic norms into Islamic political and legal thought.[73] He thus combined qualities that allowed him to play a supporting role in the early Arab revolutionary period that was perhaps more important than any other scholar in the Arab world in 2011.[74] In the next chapter, we will consider three establishment scholars, two of whom would eventually emerge as the most significant counter-revolutionary religious voices of Egypt in 2013. It is to their early opposition to the Egyptian revolution of 2011 that we shall now turn.

3

ALI GOMAA, AḤMAD AL-ṬAYYIB, AND ALI AL-JIFRI

THE EARLY OPPOSITION TO THE EGYPTIAN REVOLUTION (JANUARY–FEBRUARY 2011)

In the last two chapters, we considered the statements of Yusuf al-Qaradawi whom I have characterized as the most prominent early scholarly supporter of the Arab uprisings of 2011. Although a number of scholars would adopt such a stance, there were also several scholars who were opposed to these revolutions. The present chapter considers three such scholars in the Egyptian context. Two were senior scholars of the Egyptian establishment and a third was a younger Yemeni preacher. The most senior of these scholars was Aḥmad al-Ṭayyib, the rector of al-Azhar University, also known as the shaykh al-Azhar. Next in seniority was Ali Gomaa, who in 2011 was the grand mufti of Egypt, the next most senior post in the modern Egyptian state's religious hierarchy after the shaykh al-Azhar. Finally, there was the much younger Ali al-Jifri, a charismatic scholar based in the UAE who was a student of Gomaa and who would frequent Egypt; he had (and continues to have) a prominent presence in Egyptian media and social media more generally. All three scholars emerged as critics of the protests against then Egyptian strongman Hosni Mubarak, who had ruled Egypt before his ouster for nearly thirty years. In what follows, we will examine the sorts of juristic arguments deployed by these scholars asking protestors to desist from their opposition to the Mubarak regime.

The statements of scholars against the revolution are more difficult to place temporally than those of a scholar like Yusuf al-Qaradawi. In part, this may be because the relative unpopularity of the positions they adopted meant that they may not have wanted them advertized after the revolution succeeded. Unlike with Qaradawi, one does not find a book in which Gomaa or Ṭayyib have collected their statements concerning the revolutions of 2011. But this absence is probably also a function of the fact that the Egyptian media does not include an institution like Al Jazeera that would systematically document these statements and make them easy for researchers to study.

The present chapter begins by considering Ṭayyib's opposition to the revolution, which reached its crescendo just hours before Mubarak's ouster. Wielding his religious authority as the shaykh al-Azhar, he would characterize the protests as fomenting anarchy (*fawḍā*) and constituting rebellion (*khurūj*) while making what seemed to be references to Qaraḍāwī's 'false and mendacious fatwas.' Yet, he would swiftly adapt to the new reality after Mubarak's ouster. Gomaa's trajectory was similar to Ṭayyib's. He too would seek to defend the Mubarak regime by casting the protests of early 2011 as constituting rebellion against a legitimate ruler. Finally, Jifri's opposition, relayed over a phone call on a satellite TV show, is the shortest of the engagements considered in this chapter. Jifri's intervention, coming from where he was based in the UAE, was noteworthy for presaging Gulf tensions between the petro-monarchies since he leveled a frontal attack upon Qatar and Al Jazeera. All three scholars did in fact express some praise for the revolutionaries and their desire to reform the country, but as we shall see, such sentiments were outweighed by the scholars' increasingly severe condemnations of the uprisings. The chapter concludes with a brief comparison of the approach of these scholars to the Egyptian revolution with that of Qaradawi.

Opposition from the shaykh al-Azhar

The earliest statement on the part of Shaykh al-Azhar Aḥmad al-Ṭayyib concerning the uprisings appears to be from Monday 31 January 2011, six days after the protests began. This happens to be the same day that the Egyptian armed forces, controlled by the Ministry of Defense, shocked the Mubarak regime by issuing a statement declaring it had not and would not resort to force against the 'noble Egyptian people' and their 'legitimate demands,' while warning against creating insecurity in the streets.[1] This move by the armed forces may have signaled to Ṭayyib the boundaries within which he could express his support for the protests. He issued a carefully worded proclamation on the same day that gave similarly qualified support to the protestors' demands, though he additionally expressed confidence that Mubarak would resolve the crisis.

I have not been able to find Ṭayyib's actual statement, but only reports about it.[2] According to these reports, Ṭayyib called on protestors to ensure the safety and security of Egypt and avoid vandalism so that those who were 'sincere' among the authorities could 'wisely' address current circumstances. His call for calm and his demands of safety and security were arguably somewhat unusual coming from a state official. They came at a time when the police, under the charge of the Ministry of Interior, had withdrawn from the streets of Egypt over the previous two days in a move that some read as a deliberate attempt by the state to let the streets descend into chaos and looting.[3] It is possible that Ṭayyib was unaware of this situation, but his message still revealed his feeling that it was the protestors who bore the responsibility of maintaining peace in Egypt.

For a scholar like Yusuf al-Qaradawi, who appeared to better reflect the sentiments of the protestors on the streets of Egypt, the focus had been on making demands of the Egyptian state rather than of the protestors for whom he expressed far greater enthusiasm than Ṭayyib. Yet, Ṭayyib's statement did concede that the protestors had 'just demands of freedom, justice, and fighting poverty, unemployment and economic stagnation.' He also expressed 'his great sorrow and pain at the spilling of blood and infractions perpetrated by elements that do not fear God nor preserve the sanctity of the homeland.' Notably, he did not take sides between the security forces and protestors when lamenting loss of life. A couple of days earlier, Reuters had estimated that over 100 deaths had resulted from the first few days of protests.[4] It is reasonable to assume that the overwhelming majority of these would have been unarmed protestors given that months later a panel of judges spoke of 'police forces shooting protesters in the head and chest with live ammunition' in the course of the uprising.[5]

Ṭayyib's statement from 31 January ended on a less conciliatory note towards the protestors, nonetheless. 'However just the demands are, they cannot serve as a justification for anarchy (*fawḍā*) and aggressing against [people's] property and lives.' Alongside this statement, he was also reported as having spoken to Hosni Mubarak, reaffirming his support for the latter and expressing 'confidence in [Mubarak's] ability to get beyond the crisis and side with the people's demands.'[6] Ṭayyib seemed eager to hedge his bets by both justifying the protests and expressing confidence in Mubarak. The overall tone, given the anger in Egypt towards Mubarak, seemed indicative of the struggles of an establishment scholar responding to protests against a regime to which he had long been seen as a loyal member. In this connection, it is worth bearing in mind that the shaykh al-Azhar was also a long-time member of the National Democratic Party (NDP), the ruling party of Egypt lead by Mubarak, and 'a regime loyalist' according to an independent observer.[7] It was also reported that Ṭayyib had reluctantly resigned his NDP membership only because Mubarak wished to appoint him shaykh al-Azhar, a post that required its holder to have no formal affiliation with a political party.[8]

The next time we have a report of Ṭayyib's comments about the Egyptian protests, the comments, once again, do not come directly from their putative source but rather can be gleaned through a remark made by Qaradawi on 2 February. Given Qaradawi's contrasting enthusiasm for the protests, one should be circumspect about his characterization of Ṭayyib's remarks, but they are still useful in seeing how an enthusiastic supporter of the protests would have perceived such a statement. On 2 February, Qaradawi appeared on Al Jazeera Arabic expressing support for the protests in Egypt in the face of a series of events that would come to be referred to as the Battle of the Camel (*Mawqiʿat al-Jamal*).[9] On that evening, the Egyptian security forces unleashed armed men on camels and horses to attack protestors killing five and injuring over a thousand according to Egyptian officials.[10] In his Al Jazeera appearance, Qaradawi condemned these actions and called for all Egyptians to support the protests, making especial note of the 'religious scholars' (*ʿulamāʾ al-dīn*).

He added that he had called on the shaykh al-Azhar and sent him a message (*risāla*) calling on him to 'stand with the people and not stand with the enemies of the people.' Qaradawi lamented, however, that Ṭayyib had made a statement (*taṣrīḥ*) that day censuring the protestors. In Qaradawi's assessment, the shaykh al-Azhar was 'condemning the tyrannized (*maẓlūmīn*) and not condemning the tyrants (*ẓālimīn*). He says those who call to these protests do not have even an atom's weight of [religious] faith in their hearts.' Qaradawi predictably remonstrated at such a characterization arguing that the protestors were only seeking 'some' of their rights. He continued: 'They seek to live through licit earnings, they seek freedom (*ḥurriyya*), and they seek dignity (*karāma*). Is this forbidden to the people?!' Yet, I have not been able to independently verify Qaradawi's report of shaykh al-Azhar's statement.

Despite an extensive search, I have only found a version of the statement on a chat forum from the following day which seems to be out of step with Qaradawi's portrayal of Ṭayyib's remarks.[11] Similarly, the former's characterization does not quite tally with Ṭayyib's own description of his comments a couple of weeks later in a press conference, which we shall consider below.

After the revolution had successfully ousted Mubarak, Ṭayyib highlighted passages from his statements from previous weeks that illustrated his support for the revolutions, carefully eliding the critical comments we have seen above. This included what he described as the 'first statement' from the Azhar on 2 February from which he read out the sentence: 'Indeed Islam affirms rights (*ḥuqūq*), protects freedoms (*ḥurriyyāt*), rejects tyranny (*ẓulm*), and stands with the people in their legitimate demands regarding justice, freedom, and a dignified life.' The version of the statement I have found online does indeed contain these words, though in his press conference immediately after Mubarak's ouster, he omits mention of the praise he directed in it towards Mubarak.[12] In addition, one might view the tardiness with which Ṭayyib issued his 'first statement,' nine days after the revolutions started, as signaling less enthusiasm for them than Qaradawi, for example.[13] Another statement of Ṭayyib's from roughly 4 February is similarly ambiguous. In it, he described the protestors as being 'sincere patriots' and having 'legitimate demands' but who were also liable to be exploited by foreign interference in Egyptian domestic concerns.[14] While Ṭayyib is most explicit about Iranian interference in an arguably sectarian tone, he also targeted 'regional fatwas' from 'notable religious figures' in what may have been an oblique reference to Qaradawi.

Fatwa on the day of Mubarak's fall

Besides the foregoing, during the revolutionary period prior to Mubarak's ouster, there appears to have been one more public statement from Ṭayyib. This statement, which is the lengthiest and also the most critical of the protests, may be found in an Egyptian news clip from 11 February, and was aired less than five hours before Mubarak's resignation was announced.[15] In his statement, speaking 'in the name of Islamic law' (*bi-ism al-Shar'*) as well as the Azhar, with its thousand-year history of Islamic religious prestige and scholarly authority, Ṭayyib asserted that the protestors had gained what they sought, in that the President's powers had been delegated a day earlier on 10 February to his deputy in what Ṭayyib described as a 'miracle' (*al-mu'jiza*). Accordingly, he argued, the protestors had to return home.

Ṭayyib's statement, though well-aligned with the Mubarak regime, was dramatically out of step with the sentiments of the protestors in the streets of Egypt who had received the news of Mubarak's delegation of powers, rather than his resignation, with anger and disbelief.[16] In sharp contrast with this widespread sentiment, Ṭayyib asserted that further protests were 'meaningless' after such concessions had been made and had lost all their 'legal and rational justification.' He also presents himself as having been in favor of the protests from the start, but adds that at this point, continued protests were not just irresponsible, but effectively a call to anarchy (*fawḍā*) and thus Islamically prohibited (haram). He thus called on the protestors to go home becoming thereby 'an example for the youths in all the surrounding countries.'

This is a telling remark. It may be taken as illustrating the fear of the potential 'contagion' faced by the region's autocratic regimes in the face of such protests. In a region that shares a common language, religion, and youthful demographic, it is quite understandable that political elites like Ṭayyib would be fearful of the potential for the spread of such protests against autocracy as was exemplified by the Arab revolutions and amplified by media organizations like the Qatari-owned Al Jazeera channel to which Ṭayyib would make an oblique reference as we shall see a little later. He further added that before they had achieved the 'gains' of Mubarak's delegation of his powers, the protests had been Islamically justifiable (*kān lahu mubarrir Sharʿī*). As we have seen, despite his lukewarm attitude towards the protests more generally, in his earlier statements he certainly acknowledged that the demands made by the protestors could be seen as legitimate.[17]

In his broadcasted message, Ṭayyib contrasted the message he presented as his and the Azhar's previous view that these protests had been legitimate with those who had died being deemed martyrs, with his and the Azhar's current view that:

> today, it is prohibited (haram) for you to be in the protests. Today the protests are haram because they constitute rebellion (*khurūj*) against the state (*dawla*), the order (*niẓām*), the people (*nās*), and the multitudes (*jamāhīr*). Furthermore, I am certain that those outside Tahrir Square do not support these protests [...]. [Those supporting these protests] have most unfortunately exploited (*sakhkharū*) the religion and betrayed (*khānū*) [religious] knowledge. They have exploited false and mendacious fatwas (*al-fatāwā al-maghlūṭa al-kādhiba*) to serve the [foreign] policies of their countries and their own base desires. We have [already] drawn attention to this.[18] [...] God will not ask them about others... God will only ask them on the Day of Resurrection about what is taking place in their [own]

> countries, and they will respond with the silence of the dead. The Prophet warned us against such people and drew our attention to the fact that among those who call (*du'āh*) are callers to fitna and callers at the Gates of Hell (*du'āh 'alā abwāb jahannam*), whoever obeys them or listens to them are cast into It.[19]

There is much to unpack in these brief but revealing extempore remarks from the hours before Mubarak's resignation on 11 February 2011. Firstly, they appear to illustrate poor coordination between the organs of the Egyptian state. The head of its religious arm was here defending the Mubarak regime on national television just hours before its dominating military arm removed Mubarak from office. But beyond this, Ṭayyib's remarks represented an escalation in the sharpness of the religious rhetoric he was willing to use against the protestors by describing the continuation of protests as *khurūj*, a term in Islamic law that refers to armed rebellion that is typically responded to militarily. Given that these remarks do not appear to have been coordinated with the state's military arm, they did not in fact presage a brutal state crackdown against protestors in the way that was witnessed two years later at the Rabaa massacre, as we will consider in Chapter 5. However, the severity of Ṭayyib's language bears a further comment.

Condemning 'mendacious fatwas'

Without referring explicitly to the scholars giving fatwas in support of these protests, Ṭayyib reiterated his earlier condemnation of foreign meddling through 'false and mendacious fatwas.' The likely target of these comments is Yusuf al-Qaradawi whose outspoken support for these protests and his explicit criticism of Ṭayyib we have already seen. However, while Qaradawi castigated Ṭayyib by stating that he was supporting a tyrant against the tyrannized, Ṭayyib arguably upped the ante by referring to such scholars as political mercenaries serving foreign interests, and more pointedly, as 'callers at the Gates of Hell' who were only calling on protestors to be cast into Hell.[20] It is worth remembering that less than three weeks earlier, these two scholars were seated next to each other at a conference at the Azhar hosted by Ṭayyib. Qaradawi was treated with great honor by the shaykh al-Azhar, being seated next to the latter. Qaradawi had praised him generously in his speech and a day earlier in his Al Jazeera show. Yet, the two swiftly found themselves opposed to one another in the wake of the Egyptian revolution.

Ṭayyib's comments are interesting in another respect. It arguably marks the tension between a commitment to the logic of the autocratic nation state and religious principles that could be seen as standing in tension with such 'provincialism'. So while Ṭayyib condemned foreign interference in his country's internal affairs, a stance that makes sense in his capacity as a senior official in the bureaucracy of the Egyptian nation state, as a figure of Islamic religious authority, he had to contend with the fact that concerns of Muslims for other Muslims wherever they may be was embedded within Islamic scriptures.[21] In this particular instance, Ṭayyib may be seen as giving precedence to his national and political allegiances over considerations of a more religious nature. By contrast, Qaradawi, who was also Egyptian, but simultaneously a naturalized Qatari operating from within Qatari state-owned institutions like Al Jazeera, arguably prioritized the religious imperative of what might be called 'umma-patriotism' to override arguments about nation state sovereignty.

However, even by modern norms of international relations, Qaradawi appeared to be on a firmer footing. The modern norm of state sovereignty is an ideal that is not seen to be undermined by the criticism of a state's actions by another state or the latter's citizens, especially if the former state is also not backed by its people. Thus, autocratic states are routinely criticized, if tolerated in practice, in the contemporary international order. Here it is worth reiterating that Qaradawi is also a supporter of democracy. In this context, we may view the disagreement between Qaradawi and Ṭayyib as blending both religious and political considerations. The religious dimension is addressed extensively by Qaradawi, as we have seen, who justified his position at great length. Ṭayyib contrasted with his older colleague early on by simultaneously suggesting that the protestors' demands may be legitimate while impugning the intentions of those, like Qaradawi, who were supporting them.

By the day of Mubarak's ouster, Ṭayyib was simply asserting the religious illegitimacy of the protests as we have seen without providing much by way of religious justification. As for the political dimension, it is worth bearing in mind that Qaradawi would likely object to a sharp separation between the religious and the political, although Ṭayyib, as a faithful official in the modern Egyptian state, was arguably operating within the logic of such a distinction.[22] In this respect, Qaradawi was more out of step with the norms of the secularizing modern state than Ṭayyib. Ṭayyib's approach is thus more understandable from within the paradigm of a political subordinate in a modern secularizing autocracy, while Qaradawi's approach appears to reflect the space available to a politically active religious scholar in the relatively freer and more Islamically oriented autocracy of Qatar. The public sphere in

Qatar had been deeply influenced by Qaradawi's presence for half a century, and Qaradawi could speak with remarkable frankness regarding his religio-political views including his forceful advocacy of democracy when compared to other Arab autocracies.[23]

In this context, Ṭayyib's thinly veiled condemnation of Qatar is interesting. As we have seen, the Qatari state-owned Al Jazeera Channel was a significant player in fanning the flames of revolutionary fervor in the streets of Egypt.[24] In this respect, Al Jazeera was reflecting the Qatari state's own enthusiasm for most of the revolutions, although this was not a case of complete congruence. Famously, Al Jazeera Arabic remained more closely aligned to the Qatari state in its lack of support for the Bahraini revolution, while months later, and after the fact, Al Jazeera English aired an award-winning and highly sympathetic documentary that showed the world how the revolution was crushed with the collective support of GCC states including Qatar.[25] There is an irony to Ṭayyib's comments too of course, for those he was attacking could have leveled similar accusations at his own behavior. The accusations he made of the exploitation of religious knowledge and 'mendacious fatwas' for political ends 'to serve the policies of their countries' seem to be an odd choice of phrase for a state-appointed mufti who was a member of Egypt's political elite.

His next remark was similarly ironic. He asserted that such people would be asked on the Day of Resurrection about what was taking place 'in their [own] countries.' Of note in this connection is that Qaradawi has been willing to publicly criticize Qatar, at times with severity. He credibly claims to have done so on more than one occasion.[26] Similarly, Al Jazeera, on both its English and Arabic channels has, admittedly infrequently, aired pointed criticisms of Qatar, including in an interview of its foreign minister.[27] The extent to which it can attack its own funders is, however, undoubtedly constrained by the norms of a region where Al Jazeera has been viewed as a threateningly open space for debate.[28] The irony of Ṭayyib's aforementioned remark was that he was himself unwilling to criticize the Egyptian state and those who control it, but more than happy to attack foreign ones with his authority as the shaykh al-Azhar whose fatwas, in theory, would find adherents worldwide.

The immediate aftermath of revolution

Once the revolutions had succeeded in removing Mubarak, the shaykh al-Azhar noticeably changed his tone, although his enthusiasm for the revolution continued to be somewhat muted. Speaking at a press conference around 16

February, less than a week after Mubarak stepped down, he began by stating that the Azhar was a religious institution above revolutionary matters—'its history supersedes the history of revolutions and governments.'[29] Yet he then proceeded to obliquely praise the protestors he had been describing as rebels scarcely five days earlier. It is clear, however, that his praise was strategic. He proceeded to say: 'God be praised, by virtue of what the youths of 25 January have proffered, we live at the start of a phase in which we hope that freedom and democracy will preserve the right of difference of opinion.'[30] Such a comment appears to have been aimed at pre-empting critics of his earlier stance of support for the Mubarak regime and his outright hostility towards the protestors. He now characterized this as a matter of 'difference of opinion.' His appeals to democracy and freedom inevitably sounded somewhat contrived in this context, coming as they did from an ancien régime official who had resisted the displacing of an order to which his allegiance was clear till the very end.

Having made such appeals to democracy and freedom, he proceeded to declare that no one could claim to outdo the Azhar in its support for advocates of liberty. This statement seems to be directly contradicted by his explicit opposition to the protests from five days earlier, as we have just seen, but Ṭayyib was attempting to forestall such a criticism. He did this by denouncing the critics as failing to recognize that the Azhar's, and by extension, his own stances were both grounded in two countervailing concerns, one regarding the protestors' physical safety and a second concerning the social breakdown of the nation leading to unmitigated anarchy. This latter point is arguably the standard defense of authoritarianism: the authoritarian, whether Mubarak, The Supreme Council of the Armed Forces (SCAF), or Sisi, sees themselves as necessary because only they can prevent social breakdown. The logic of this argument makes sense in the absence of any conceivable alternative to authoritarianism. But a moment earlier, Ṭayyib had referred to the new era of democracy and freedom that he claimed they now enjoyed, arguably undercutting his assertion. Clearly an alternative was not only conceivable, but Ṭayyib was familiar enough with its discourse to be able to appeal to it without difficulty.

Ṭayyib's message thus illustrated the adaptation of Egypt's most important religious institution to a seemingly brave new world. Conveniently for him, his messaging during the uprising, and that of his institution, was ambiguous enough for him to be able to selectively cite statements from the revolutionary period that showed him as supportive of the youths who led the revolution.

Ṭayyib next cited sections from 'the first statement of the Azhar' originally published on 2 February—a statement that would have been issued with his blessing as the head of the institution. He proceeded to read out the following passage from that day, the first part of which we briefly saw above: 'Indeed Islam affirms rights, protects freedoms, rejects tyranny, and stands with the people in their legitimate demands regarding justice, freedom, and a dignified life.'[31] He continued, pointing out that the statement also praised the army for siding with the protestors, thereby mirroring Qaradawi's praise for them during this period. Ṭayyib further added that the Azhar had also declared at the time that any action that caused the shedding of blood was prohibited in Islamic law (*muḥarram Shar'an*), and a crime before God.

Ṭayyib's statement then became particularly hostile towards his critics. He declared:

> Indeed the Azhar preceded all of the voices that are only now jumping on the bandwagon and plying their trade through appeals to religion and ethics, and grasping this opportunity to pour out their hate and evil poison on the Azhar and its noble ulama. The Azhar preceded all of them when it sought the right of 'all political forces, without exclusion, in the conducting of a dialogue that seeks to contain the crisis and bring about reconciliation,' and I place a red line under the expression 'without exclusion.'[32]

Ṭayyib continued with reference to the second statement issued by the Azhar which we saw earlier criticizing foreign meddling in Egypt's affairs, highlighting that it deemed the youths who had died to be martyrs. He then went on the offensive:

> The Azhar said this openly at a time when hypocrites (*munāfiqūn*) were liberally dissembling in support of the regime (*niẓām*) and forming their positions in whatever direction the wind was blowing. These [statements demonstrate] the stances of the Azhar which stood up for the truth, and did not temporize, as is claimed now by some profiteers, opportunists, and those seeking a role in the new era. I assure you—and you can go back to the statements of the Azhar—I assure you that the Azhar did not ingratiate itself (*yatamallaq*) with the presiding authorities at that time, and it will not ingratiate itself with the presiding authorities now. [...] This is the Azhar which adopted these stances on the basis of the enduring principles of the umma and the ultimate interests of Egypt, and on the basis of its responsibility in expressing the conscience of the Islamic umma and the pain and hopes of the Muslims in the East and the West. This honorable Azhar is not a timeserving opportunist (*imma'a*) that says: 'I am with the people, if they do good I will do good, but if they do evil, I will

> do evil.' Rather it affirms what it believes to be right and correct and declares it openly.[33]

Ṭayyib went on to call for elections as part of a civilian democratic order within six months as had been announced by SCAF. He also called on the establishment of a number of values including those of knowledge/science (*'ilm*), justice (*'adl*), and freedom (*ḥurriyya*). On this latter value, he pointed out that:

> it liberates [people's] energies, builds civilizations, and breaks the shackles of ignorance, repression (*qahr*), and dictatorship (*istibdād*) which kills talent (*yaqtul al-malakāt*), incites to hypocrisy (*yughrī bi-l-nifāq*), sows fear and doubt, and implants feelings of cowardice and egotism. All of these are fatal diseases and illnesses that destroy the individual and society, and annihilate nations and civilization.[34]

Ṭayyib had more to say, but the above suffices in providing an example of his general approach. The post-revolutionary Ṭayyib sounded much like the revolutionary Qaradawi we saw in the last chapter and bore little resemblance to the Mubarak-era alim who had expressed confidence in a dictator's ability to rule and could be seen as attempting to pour cold water on the revolutions by suggesting that they were being exploited by foreign interests. No such references to foreign powers were present in Ṭayyib's post-Mubarak statement. Rather he was content to commend the Azhar's, and metonymically, his own commitment to democratic norms and religious values that more 'hypocritical' individuals and institutions might play fast and loose with. Not the Azhar, however, in Ṭayyib's telling. Unlike such people, the Azhar was never a 'timeserving opportunist' that behaved sycophantically towards power. The self-assuredness of the performance was impressive. With the benefit of hindsight, most notably in the form of the events of 2013 we shall consider in later chapters, one can recognize that its sincerity was perhaps questionable. The same would apply, a fortiori, to the next scholar we will consider.

Mufti Ali Gomaa and the revolution

As I hope to have made clear above, the Shaykh al-Azhar was a partisan of the Mubarak regime during the uprisings of 2011, and even after the revolution succeeded in removing Mubarak, his reception of the new order appeared defensive. Yet, in his actual pronouncements prior to Mubarak's ouster, Ṭayyib did not appear to be as forcefully and passionately opposed to the protestors as his more charismatic junior colleague, the then grand mufti, Ali Gomaa. The office of the grand mufti (*muftī al-diyār al-Miṣriyya*) is in practice the second-highest-ranking post in the modern Egyptian state's religious hierarchy after the office of the Shaykh al-Azhar, and it is the man who held the role of grand mufti of Egypt in 2011 who was undoubtedly the most forceful anti-revolutionary scholar in the country. Once again, it is sometimes difficult to place his statements with temporal exactitude, but he appears to have made at least three relatively lengthy statements aired on Egyptian television channels during the revolutionary period. Gomaa's tone regarding the protests seemed more measured in some of his statements and bordered on the inflammatory in others.

Perhaps his earliest remarks were made in live telephone comments broadcast on 2 February 2011,[35] where he may be seen as praising both the protestors and President Hosni Mubarak, who was at the time still in power. Mubarak would receive the lion's share of praise, given his statement from the previous day which was 'filled with dignity and nobility' according to Gomaa. In it, he had 'responded to the hopes of the people, and reduced their pain.' It is worth noting that Mubarak's comments from the previous day may have set the parameters for what Gomaa would say in the same way that the remarks of the military spokesperson on 31 January may have done so for Ṭayyib. Perhaps following Mubarak's lead, and that of the military a day earlier, Gomaa issued a message that balanced apparent praise for 'noble youths' exercising their 'rights to peaceful protest' and an openness to 'dialogue' with an offer of no substantive concessions. The appealing rhetoric he used did not find a receptive audience among the protestors who may have been skeptical that the dictator of nearly forty years would have had a sudden change of heart or modus operandi in his twilight years. Mubarak's promise that he would not run in the next elections that were set for September of that year fell considerably short of the demand that he step down.

Given that the youth's demand for Mubarak's resignation had not been met, Gomaa's remarks arguably demonstrated prevarication rather than a meaningful attempt at dialogue. This was hardly surprising. The brief message provided a foretaste of the direction in which Gomaa would travel over the coming days, and indeed years, to become revolutionary Egypt's fiercest pro-autocracy alim. Given Mubarak's concessions, Gomaa asserted, the youths had to now go home so that the tribulation (*miḥna*, fitna) could come to an end. Thus, the praise of the youths was coupled with describing their behavior as instigating fitna, a word which can be glossed chaos, anarchy, or social breakdown, thus counterbalancing the earlier praise. Gomaa immediately followed this with the citation of several Prophetic hadiths including a non-canonical one that states: 'fitna is dormant, God damn (*la'ana Allāh*) those who rouse it.'[36] A second hadith he cited reads: 'There will be fitna that is deaf, mute and blind. Whoever witnesses it, it will come upon them. Verbal utterances in [those times] will be like the striking of the sword.'[37] Both of these hadiths are of highly questionable authenticity according to Sunni hadith experts, but Gomaa used them to castigate the protestors in remarkably severe terms. His citation of the first hadith suggested that God's curse was upon the protestors, and the second suggested that even peaceful protests could amount to murder.

Having made reference to such hadiths and Qur'anic verses, Gomaa proceeded to praise Mubarak for opening the door to dialogue in his statement from the previous night. Gomaa characterized Mubarak as having 'responded to the demands of the people,' and while he praised the 'youth' protesting in the streets of Egypt for 'energizing [the nation's] political life,' he followed this with the demand that they return home immediately, since their demands had been met. He called them all to leave their protests and let the legitimacy (*shar'iyya*) of Mubarak's regime resolve the problems they faced. Gomaa was thus able to confidently declare the legitimacy of Egypt's long-standing strongman in religio-legal terms while invoking an array of verses and hadiths that suggested a blistering condemnation of the protestors against Mubarak. He also added a theme that appears in the discourse of subsequent counter-revolutionaries we will meet in later chapters, namely that 'the absence of political authority can only lead to destruction. We want change, not destruction.' These apocalyptic prophecies would not quite come to pass, although another kind of destruction did ensue—the fall of the Mubarak regime nine days later. But his portentous prognostications did serve to illustrate Gomaa's willingness to defend dictatorship with all the considerable religious charisma he could muster. Though he was not successful in this particular instance in preventing the fall of a dictator, he would be far more successful in his anti-Morsi advocacy two years later, as we will see in Chapters 5 and 7. Gomaa concluded his remarks in the news interview by declaring that 'rebelling (*khurūj*) against legitimacy is haram, haram, haram by the agreement of all Muslims, East and West, past and present.'[38]

Both in terms of language and tone of voice, Gomaa was the most forceful of the ulama who supported Mubarak before his ouster. But of particular note was his use of arguably inflammatory language against the protestors that rendered his apparent praise for them unconvincing. Firstly, his short-lived praise of the youth of the revolution was followed by a thinly veiled imprecation against them, and a subsequent characterization of their behavior as 'rebellion' (*khurūj*) against a legitimate ruler. As noted in the last chapter, the term *khurūj* is highly charged in Islamic legal and historical discourse. In Islamic law, it is typically used to characterize groups engaged in armed rebellion, and for such groups, who could at times be considered the equivalent of 'terrorists,' the most gruesome punishments in the Qur'an were sometimes suggested (Q. 5:33).

But in addition, rebellion of this kind was historically associated with the early Islamic group considered briefly in the previous chapter known as the Khawārij. We will see this term used several times in the coming pages as Gomaa repeatedly resorted to it in his support for autocratic rule in both 2011 and 2013. Gomaa's language and fatwas from the period of the Egyptian coup in particular leave no doubt that his two years of post-revolutionary life did nothing to blunt his enthusiasm for autocratic government, despite his continued ability to function as a public figure in Egypt during the post-revolutionary period. In fact, it appears to have enthused him towards authoritarianism even more than before, as we shall see when we consider his 2013 support for the coup in later chapters.

Gomaa's next interview

On the following day, 3 February, Gomaa appeared via live phone call on an Egyptian TV show called *Wāḥid min al-Nās* (One of the People) on the Dream channel.[39] During the phone call, which lasted nearly twelve minutes, he began by praising the youth involved in the protests and disavowing any accusations that he was opposed to them. He stated that he considered them to be engaged in the scriptural duty of commanding right and forbidding wrong (*amr bi-l-maʿrūf wa-l-nahy ʿan al-munkar*) and the duty of giving advice (*naṣīḥa*) to those in authority. He also praised the 'popular committees' (*lijān shaʿbiyya*) formed to preserve order in the streets, while eliding any reference to the police having vacated their posts leading to the security vacuum necessitating such committees.[40]

Then came Gomaa's praise of pro-Mubarak protestors. Gomaa argued that the world media was unaware there were two perspectives on the streets of Egypt. The presenter immediately responded by concurring with this point. In this connection, one must bear in mind that in Egypt even private satellite channels like Dream were generally beholden to the regime rather than being independent since they were owned by politically connected businessmen.[41] Furthermore, the portrayal by Gomaa and the presenter of pro- and anti-Mubarak protestors as equally representative of Egyptian popular sentiment was highly tendentious, given that pro-Mubarak protestors in Mustafa Mahmud Square, despite having state backing, numbered in the low thousands as opposed to anti-Mubarak protestors who numbered in the hundreds of thousands.[42] While Gomaa proceeded to assert that he wished no harm to come to the protestors in Tahrir, citing a hadith regarding the gravity of killing even a single Muslim, he quickly moved on from this point to call on protestors to return to their homes. Recognizing that they feared arrest, he declared a general amnesty for the protestors who returned home, on behalf of himself and the Shaykh al-Azhar. If anything happened to the protestors after this, he declared, there would be 'a revolution from us.'[43] By his own subsequent admission, it was unlikely that anyone heeded the grand mufti's call.[44] But his declaration may also have been unfulfillable given comments Gomaa made after Mubarak's ouster, in which the mufti claimed that he had tried his best to communicate with the organs of the state but that he had found no channels of communication available to him.[45] In his own telling, the declaration was an effort to limit bloodshed by stopping protests, but in addition to his admission that he could not in fact ensure the safety of protestors from the security forces, such a move was also necessarily a commitment to the status quo of dictatorship and repression that had caused these protests to begin with.[46]

Returning to his interview from 3 February, Gomaa next referred to the so-called Battle of the Camel from the previous day, concerning which *The New York Times* reported that Mubarak 'unleash[ed] waves of his supporters armed with clubs, rocks, knives and firebombs in a concerted assault on thousands of antigovernment protesters.'[47] Unlike the *Times*' report from the same day, which was based on information from their journalists on the streets of Cairo, Gomaa, in an indirect attempt to exonerate the Mubarak regime from responsibility for it, made the vague claim that investigations would prove that there was a 'devil' (*shayṭān*) responsible for it. By contrast, independent observers like *The New York Times* journalist David D. Kirkpatrick, who lived in Egypt through the revolutionary period, made a point to describe the Battle of the Camel as a 'government crackdown.'[48]

Next, the presenter asked the mufti about his view on Qaradawi's calls for protestors to come out on Friday (i.e. 4 February) in their millions. Gomaa responded in a condescending tone, stating that Qaradawi was simply being fed information by Al Jazeera, and did not actually know what was going on in the streets of Egypt. As was the case with Gomaa's claims about the Rabaa massacre which we will see in later chapters, physically being in Egypt did not actually help him get accurate information about the happenings within his own country, perhaps in part due to the extreme biases of the country's media. In contrast with Qaradawi's encouragement to protest, Gomaa declared that Egyptians could legitimately leave off the usually obligatory Friday prayers, thus reducing the numbers of people on the streets. He stated that the permissibility of such an action was a matter of agreement among all Islamic schools of law (*jamīʿ al-madhāhib*) in cases of fitna when people feared for their well-being.

In an instance of apparent balance, he added that both pro- and anti-regime protestors should not do anything to hurt each other and should remain peaceful, citing Prophetic authority for his position. However, thereafter he returned to characterizing pro-Mubarak protestors as people who 'want[ed] to crown the hero of war and peace, want[ed] to crown the legitimate ruler, want[ed] to stand up for the Constitution, and want[ed] to stand up for stability.' On the other side, he conceded that there were those who wish to object to the high levels of unemployment, corruption, and the like, which he accepted as legitimate concerns.[49] Overall, Gomaa was clearly critical of these protests, but occasionally came across as supportive of the protestors' cause.

Against 'fitna' and 'rebellion'

What was perhaps the severest of Gomaa's statements from early February 2011 is difficult to date with precision.[50] Since the broader discussion in the clip was about clashes between pro- and anti-Mubarak protestors on the streets of Egypt,[51] a likely date seems to be Wednesday 2 February, i.e. the day of the Battle of the Camel, but it is also possible that it was from a later date.[52] In a six-minute clip broadcast on the Nile News channel (*al-Nīl*), Gomaa made his most passionate and provocative religious pronouncements yet. As with the interventions we saw earlier, he cited the non-canonical hadith 'fitna is dormant, God damn those who rouse it' and the other poorly authenticated hadith that warns against fitna in which verbal utterances are compared with the striking of the sword. He added other hadiths such as one in which the Prophet reportedly stated, 'Control your tongue, keep to your house, and weep over your sins,'[53] and 'Whoever among you wakes up in the morning secured in his dwelling, healthy in his body, having his food for the day, then it is as if he has been given the whole world.'[54] These hadiths spoke for themselves in Gomaa's view. To them, he simply added that he was astounded that people should 'rebel against [Mubarak's] legitimacy (*shar'iyya*).'[55]

Gomaa could here be contrasted with Qaradawi in that the former was citing hadiths in a way that appeared to ground the acceptance of authoritarian rule in Islamic sacred texts while assuming that Mubarak was the legitimate ruler of Egypt. Unlike Qaradawi, Gomaa did not have a lengthy television show to elaborate his stance at length in this particular instance. When he was at liberty to do this, we find that his responses were still relatively spare in terms of religious justification as we will see in later chapters. With respect to the present discussion, the hadiths that were chosen were open to interpretation in ways contrary to Gomaa's assertions. For instance, there was no necessary contradiction between controlling one's tongue and speaking out against injustice. Nor could the Prophetic exhortation to stay in one's house have been an unqualified directive.

In the interview, Gomaa declared that the consequence of rebelling against Mubarak's political legitimacy, if successful, would be a 'deaf, mute, and blind fitna' that would ultimately result in civil war.[56] He provided some putative examples to back up his assertions, including the case of Tunisia. He asked rhetorically: 'Has Tunisia succeeded in achieving anything through this chaotic situation?' The fall of the Tunisian dictator a few weeks earlier was not an achievement in Gomaa's view. After the brief comment on Tunisia, Gomaa highlighted the pro-Mubarak rallies with the assertion that, if all of these people were members of Mubarak's NDP, then the NDP was 'really the party of the majority,' and if they were not members, they were average Egyptians who were 'glorifying their great leader, the hero of war and peace.' By subtle sleight of hand, he had transformed the majority of protestors in the streets into pro-Mubarak protestors despite the actual numbers showing the opposite.

He also added that Mubarak had called to dialogue and reform, but that the anti-Mubarak protestors had rejected this offer out of hand. The obstinacy of the protestors, in Gomaa's telling, threatened the very gains that had been made since 25 January. After criticizing these protestors, he praised the soon to be ousted dictator with the words: 'I take this opportunity and salute

President Mubarak who offered dialogue and responded to the demands of the people.' This was followed by praise for the youths in a manner similar to his other interviews for their reviving of political life and the popular committees for helping to preserve order. But this praise was immediately followed by a declaration that it was an obligation (*yajib*) for them to end their protests and affirm the legitimacy (*shar'iyya*) of the regime, 'for indeed rebelling against legitimacy is haram, haram, haram.' Quite clearly, Gomaa had intended to wield his Islamic legal authority with this pronouncement. The youths, he was asserting, were perpetrating a crime not only against the state, but a crime against God.

With the next remarks, Gomaa began to display a more dangerous rhetorical repertoire. He reiterated that the protests demonstrated that 'the people are with Mubarak, and the majority are with Mubarak, and this is the [political] legitimacy that we are commanded to adhere to.' He also reiterated the hadith regarding God damning those who rouse fitna, but crucially this time, he paraphrased part of a short hadith that would become an important pillar of his religious pronouncements in the Egyptian coup two years later that is worth quoting: 'If you are all agreed on a single man [as your ruler], then someone comes in rebellion against him, then kill him, whoever he may be.' Gomaa realizing how such a hadith could be understood as justifying murder immediately added, as though he was catching himself, 'We do not wish to say this in these fitnas because He also prohibited us from killing and fitnas, but we wish to remind people of God.' As we shall see in Chapters 5 and 7, when Gomaa chose to lend his support to the 2013 Egyptian coup, he was no longer constrained by such concerns, leading him to provide a full-throated religious justification for the military-led massacres that followed the coup of that year, an exceptional occurrence for a religious scholar of his standing.

Gomaa and Ṭayyib were probably the two most significant pro-regime scholars in Egypt and remain important today, but as noted above there were a number of international figures who also chimed in during the period of the revolutions. These figures are of interest as they show us that the kind of thinking found among the pro-regime ulama is found among Muslim scholars around the world. This is therefore not simply a case of anomalous thinking among Egyptian ulama aligned with the autocratic regime. Rather these commitments appear deeper and more meaningful than simply a commitment to Mubarak or Sisi.[57] I next consider a younger Yemeni scholar who resembled the counter-revolutionary scholars considered above, and who was, appropriately, a protégé of Gomaa based in the UAE.

Ali al-Jifri's intervention

The first non-Egyptian figure we will consider is the junior colleague of Ali Gomaa, and an intriguing figure in himself, namely Ali al-Jifri.[58] Jifri is by far the youngest scholar considered here. He is sometimes characterized as a preacher (*dāʿiya*) rather than a scholar—many of his published works are more popular in nature than those of Ali Gomaa, whom Jifri held in high regard as his shaykh. But his political and intellectual precocity were perhaps in evidence in his establishing the Tabah Foundation in 2005, when he would have been thirty-three or thirty-four years old. The Tabah Foundation is a UAE-based non-profit organization whose website suggests that it is a religiously authoritative think-tank backed by some of the world's most recognizable religious figures. In fact, its 'Senior Scholars Council' could be viewed as a Who's Who of the senior scholars of Neo-traditionalism at the time of the Foundation's establishment.[59] Two of the three living members of the council are included in the present study, namely Gomaa and Bin Bayyah.[60]

That the Saudi-born Yemeni Jifri was able to set up such an institution in the UAE and maintain a charismatic presence in multiple forms of media for nearly two decades illustrates his talent as a public figure.[61] This may owe something to his father's career as an 'aristocratic' Yemeni politician with Saudi citizenship who served as 'a key Yemeni front man for Saudi Arabia' during the country's fractious politics in the late twentieth and early twenty-first centuries.[62] It is possible that the younger Jifri's political heritage had a bearing on his political orientation. As we will see, Ali al-Jifri would consistently make religious arguments in the post-Arab revolutionary public sphere that were in the interest of the UAE–Saudi counter-revolutionary, anti-democratic alliance and hostile to the Qatari-Islamist pro-revolutionary alliance of the period.

Jifri was and remains to this day very well-known in the West, with a considerable following and a number of students and colleagues who ensure his invitation and promotion in the West on a regular basis. He is also a frequent guest on Egyptian and Arab satellite channels, although there is no shortage of televangelists in the region. But it is his close relationship with Gomaa, alongside the Egyptian television show host, Khayrī Ramaḍān, that is of particular note for our purposes here. His treatment of Ali Gomaa both in his presence and absence was with the utmost respect and reverence. During the period we are concerned with, however, this translated into an apparently unconditional commitment to the positions of his shaykh. As we shall see in Chapter 7, this would be of particular interest in 2013. For the present chapter, however, I will consider his remarks on a television show with the aforementioned Khayrī Ramaḍān from 10 February 2011, the day before Mubarak's ouster.[63]

The day before the Egyptian revolution succeeded in removing Mubarak, Jifri's message was one of apparent conciliation. He did not come out strongly in favor of either the supporters of the revolution, nor those against it. But he warned that the outcome in Egypt would be one that affected the entire region. He praised the sincerity of the youth who were frustrated with the system and wished to change it. But he immediately added that no one should impugn the loyalty of others (*yanbaghī an nughliq bāb al-takhwīn*). Whose loyalty he had in mind can be garnered from what he said next. He asserted that there is 'an honorable group' (*fi'a ṭayyiba*) that had become active. He appears to have been referring to some of the protestors, though he did not make this explicit. Similarly, there was 'an honorable group responding from within the regime' whom he described as also sincere in their attempts to redress these legitimate grievances.

By way of showing that he was not a partisan of the Mubarak regime, Jifri revealed that he had himself been prohibited from entering Egypt for seven years by 'the iniquitous forces' (*al-fi'a al-sayyi'a*) within the regime, despite, as he put it, not engaging himself in any 'political activity (*nashāṭ siyāsī*), near or far.' He then revealed publicly 'for the first time' the regime's reasons for banning him, which he said he was made privy to after being permitted to re-enter Egypt. He summarized them in three reasons: that he was very active (*shadīd al-nashāṭ*) in the public sphere, that he was influential (*shadīd al-ta'thīr*), and that he was high-handed in his dealings with the security establishment. Jifri did not comment on the first two, which are in any case complimentary of him, but denied that he was ever high-handed with the security establishment. These remarks, he suggested, made him someone who was well-placed to comment on the ongoing crisis in Egypt, but they are revealing in what they indicate about Jifri's political orientation.

Firstly, his holding that his disavowal of any kind of political activism exonerated him from accusations of being a 'problematic' actor in Egypt or the wider Middle East implicitly affirmed the authoritarian model of a politically repressive public sphere as normative. Similarly, his comments disavowing any disrespect on his part towards the security apparatus tacitly affirmed, or perhaps more accurately, avoided the question of whether such institutions ought to have the right to conduct themselves in a manner that was in keeping with the status quo in a place like Egypt, with all the unchecked systemic abuse of power that this entailed. Despite the popular outrage at the authoritarian regime's abuses over many decades, like his mentor Gomaa, Jifri appeared to come to the defense of the regime by arguing that there was an honorable group that had begun to respond positively to the protestors from within the regime.

But then he went on the offensive. In opposition to these honorable groups, he asserted, there was a demagogic group (*fi'a ghawghā'iyya*)[64] in Tahrir Square who were beyond the control of the more sensible people in the Square. He highlighted how depraved this group was, while stressing the positive forces within the regime, whom he described as representing 'a struggle for change within the regime.' Jifri stated this after nearly three weeks of the Mubarak regime violently responding to the protestors, which received no specific mention in Jifri's comments. Instead, he mentioned some of the protestors' excesses. In these circumstances, he highlighted the importance of building bridges, a fact that seems indicative of his preference for the Mubarak regime.

Jifri against Qatar and Qaradawi

In his message on the show, Jifri next said that he had two messages to state publicly. Apologizing that he was about to name names, he said that circumstances compelled him to do so. He then proceeded to attack Al Jazeera, a channel that had been instrumental in promoting the revolutionary wave in early 2011, as being a channel with highly questionable motives (*'alayhā alf istifhām*). This, he said, was not just about Egypt, but more about what he asserted was Al Jazeera's contextual hypocrisy. He noted that it was a channel highly critical of Israel, and America's involvement in the region, and its long-term relationship with the Egyptian military for the security of its strategic partnership with Israel. Despite this, Jifri noted, Al Jazeera is only a few miles from the Qatari desert where one can find the 'largest American military base outside [the United States],' referring to the Al Udeid (al-'Udayd) Air Base and Camp As Sayliyah (al-Sayliyya). This base in fact only became the largest military base in the region as of 2015, four years after Jifri made his remarks, and it remains the largest prepositioning base of the US military outside the US.[65] However, in terms of physical size, it is relatively small, and cannot even be included in the top fifty American bases outside the USA.[66]

The polemical nature of Jifri's remark could be illustrated by the fact that his country of domicile, the UAE, also hosted several US and NATO bases at the time, and that Abu Dhabi, the particular emirate in which Jifri resides to this day, hosted two of these.[67] The presence of US military bases in and of themselves were thus not a problem for him. Jifri continued, claiming 'it is said that Israel [and the Iraqi occupation] are funded from within [the Qatari US base].' Such a remark is at once unevidenced and implausible. By using the phrase, 'it is said,' Jifri did not need to worry about attribution or accuracy, placing some distance between himself and the idea while simultaneously allowing his authority as a religious figure to back the allegation. As we shall see in Chapter 7, Jifri would be overcome by righteous indignation in 2013 when his own teacher Gomaa was accused of what he considered inaccurate reports. We will see that he would remonstrate about the urgency of verifying such dubious reports, which in fact happened to be accurate.

By contrast, in 2011, Jifri proceeded to excoriate Al Jazeera in impassioned tones for being, 'a channel that claims to speak the truth, and is willfully blind concerning these facts [regarding the American military base].' Additionally, he cast thinly veiled aspersions on Yusuf al-Qaradawi. He proceeded by referring to 'a certain scholar whose past contributions all of us esteems and respects, who speaks in the name of "uttering the truth,"[68] and in a fashion that is direct (*ṣarīḥ*), clamorous (*ṣārikh*), and provocative (*muḥarriḍ*).' For such scholars to be consistent, he argued, they also had to confront the kind of iniquity entailed in Qatar's hosting a US airbase and supporting Israel. Jifri appeared to be unaware of Qaradawi's public criticism of this base as well as the Qatar-Israeli bilateral relationship on BBC Arabic in February 2010.[69] Qaradawi stated in that interview that he had criticized the presence of the base publicly, and everyone including the Emir of Qatar knew this.

With respect to Israel, when the deputy prime minister at the time, Shimon Peres, visited (referring to his high-profile visit in 2007), Qaradawi stated that he gave a Friday sermon on the issue.[70] In it he shockingly, by regional standards, declared that those who had shaken Peres' hand should wash theirs seven times, one of them after rubbing one's hands with dirt—this being the Prophetic guidance for cleaning utensils for human use that have been in contact with the saliva of a dog.[71] Considering that Qaradawi's Friday sermons had traditionally been aired on Qatar's national television channel, which is also broadcast around the region via satellite, this could have been grounds for a major diplomatic incident. This shows that the portrayal of Qaradawi as a 'mouthpiece for the al-Thani family,' in Courtney

Freer's words, cannot be taken at face value.[72] Given the restrictive nature of most Arab regimes with respect to their subjects airing disagreements with their policies, the foregoing statement is also an indication of a degree of latitude that is afforded to a scholar like Qaradawi in Qatar that is beyond the general norm of the region. It is not clear to me whether Qatar has afforded this degree of freedom to others within its borders.

For his part, the apparently uninformed Jifri was extremely suspicious of the 'pure provocation' of the calls that were coming from the shaykh and Al Jazeera. He further criticized Qaradawi, again without mentioning his name explicitly and while affecting a derisive tone, as one who had 'set himself up to speak in the name of the scholars of the umma,'[73] while suggesting that senior scholars of the Azhar were responding to the revolutions in bad faith. We have already seen above that Qaradawi publicly castigated the Shaykh al-Azhar for not supporting the revolutions. Although Jifri had left Qaradawi unnamed, this would have done little to conceal the identity of the figure he was attacking. 'This is unacceptable,' he declared in response to Qaradawi's critique of senior Azharīs. The remark was ironic. While Jifri was clearly angered by Qaradawi's criticism of the much younger Shaykh al-Azhar over a political disagreement, the thirty-nine-year-old Jifri felt no hesitation in similarly castigating Qaradawi, a much older Azharī, for the same reason.

Jifri then added another argument which resembles one we have seen already from Ṭayyib. He pointed out that a part of promoting democracy and liberty was to create an environment of entertaining views of those with whom one disagreed, even in times of intense disagreement such as were arising in early 2011. Yet, this appeared to be the invocation of democratic culture on the part of a scholar who did not himself seem to have a strong commitment to such values. Unlike Qaradawi, for instance, Jifri did not appear concerned about holding the regime to its word in its claims that it would accede to the demands of the protestors. Nor did he seek accountability for the large number of deaths caused by the security forces over the course of the uprisings.[74] This leaves one with the impression that Jifri was more interested in castigating those calling for political accountability rather than seriously thinking about political reform.

In observing his criticism of Al Jazeera and Qaradawi, one must bear in mind Jifri's personal context in the Emirates, which has historically been hostile towards Qatar's Al Jazeera for its free criticism of the countries within the region, including, on occasion, the UAE. Jifri was probably not working at the behest of the UAE government at this stage, just as a scholar like Qaradawi had probably never worked simply at the behest of the Qatar government, but these scholars probably resided, and indeed were welcomed in these countries, because their politics were broadly in alignment with the states in which they resided.

Conclusion

The three scholars considered in this chapter adopted a similar approach to the 2011 revolutions, one which contrasted sharply with the approach of Qaradawi seen over the previous two chapters. Qaradawi viewed the revolutions as an opportunity for major political change in a region that suffered from the scourge of autocracy; these three scholars viewed the revolutions as a threat to the very notion of order itself, and therefore saw them as a call for unmitigated anarchy. For Qaradawi, the threat of tyranny needed to be confronted by introducing accountable government; for these scholars, the threat of anarchy needed to be confronted by fiercely defending and perhaps consolidating the existing order. It was as though the holders of these two divergent perspectives lived in two alternative realities.

For Qaradawi, there seemed almost nothing redeemable about the tyranny of the thirty-year-long Mubarak regime, while for Ṭayyib, Gomaa and Jifri, words like 'tyranny' and 'oppression' were entirely absent from their discourse. For the latter scholars, the order was not tyrannical, and thus the revolutions appeared incomprehensible. This may explain why their main response to the revolutions was to complain about anarchy (*fawḍā*) and social strife (fitna) that was being instigated, for no apparent reason, against Egypt by a state like Qatar and its Al Jazeera network. The absence of tyranny in Egypt, in their view, led them to seek explanations in the hostility of foreign states and 'dishonest' ulama (like Qaradawi) who were gratuitously attacking a completely innocent state like Egypt for no apparent reason. The 'opportunistic' Qaradawi and his Qatari sponsors, according to this reading, were simply exploiting the fact that there were some people in Egypt who happened to be receptive to their propaganda.

Such a reading renders the response of these scholars more comprehensible. For them, the revolutions were an irrational response on the part of the Egyptian populace to a foreign attack. There was no such thing as an oppressive Mubarak regime, and so these scholars recognized that such 'baseless' accusations could not be countered through reasoned argument, for anyone who was 'taken in' by them could not be reasoned with. Thus, Ṭayyib resorted to warning against 'callers to Hell,' and both he and Gomaa warned that 'rebelling against [Mubarak's] legitimacy' was unequivocally haram. For his part, Jifri tried to show that those advocating for these revolutions from abroad were hypocritical opportunists. None of these scholars directly responded to Qaradawi's extensive scriptural justifications for peaceful protest, unlike Qaradawi who, as we have seen, attempted to respond directly to many of the counter-claims of these scholars in some detail.

But this significant divergence of perspective also meant that there was no real chance to bridge the gap in perception between the two poles of disagreement among these scholars. While I consider Qaradawi's engagement with the scriptural and juristic traditions to be far more substantive, rigorous, and cogent than that of the scholars sampled in this chapter, his arguments could not bridge the divide between those like himself, who perceived the Middle East as marred by politically unaccountable dictatorship, and those who simply did not see any such problem as existing in the region. Arguably, this inability to bridge this gap in perception is one of the reasons behind the fact that these revolutions have so far failed to take the region's politics in a less authoritarian direction.

We shall have occasion to return to the activities of these scholars in later chapters, especially in relation to events in Egypt in 2013. For now, we will transition to two other internationally recognized scholars who have come to support autocracy in the wider Arab world. Both these scholars are somewhat anomalous in that they arguably started off supporting the revolutionary side to a greater or lesser degree. By the time of the Egyptian coup, however, their commitment had reoriented, and they had begun speaking and acting in accord with autocratic powers in the region, although, like Gomaa and Ṭayyib, they likely would characterize their orientation as reflecting a commitment to order. These two scholars are Hamza Yusuf and his shaykh, Abdallah bin Bayyah, and it is to a consideration of their gradual transformation of outlook that we shall now turn.

4

HAMZA YUSUF AND ABDALLAH BIN BAYYAH

FROM SUPPORT TO OPPOSITION (JANUARY 2011–FEBRUARY 2013)

Innumerable scholars commented on the Arab revolutions as they erupted in early 2011. The past three chapters have shown the engagements of a selection of prominent scholars, both mainstream Islamist and Neo-traditionalist, towards the revolutions. We have seen that the Qatar-based Yusuf al-Qaradawi enthusiastically supported the revolutions from the very beginning. He was one of many mainstream Islamist scholars to do so. We also saw that two leading scholars in Egypt and a prominent Yemeni preacher opposed the revolutions. In the present chapter, we consider two scholars who represented a less clear-cut position on the revolutions, namely the Saudi-based Mauritanian Abdallah bin Bayyah, and his Californian student Hamza Yusuf. Both held what could be considered ambiguous positions in 2011, although as we shall see, by 2014, they firmly sided with the counter-revolutionary stance towards the Arab revolutions. Hamza Yusuf had much more to say at the outset of the revolutions, whereas Bin Bayyah would express himself in greater detail from the later months of 2011 onwards.

The present chapter thus begins with Yusuf's solicitous response to the Tunisian revolution in January 2011, which would give way in the following days to his passionate support for Egyptian efforts to overthrow Mubarak. Within months, however, he would appear on Arab media arguing against democracy and signaling an apparent change of heart, which I will argue below was in fact a reversion to type. A curious aspect of his aversion to democracy explored below is his explanation as to why monarchy was preferable to it. Something similar to Yusuf's move towards more active support for autocracy was also discernable in the statements of his teacher, the respected Mauritanian jurist Abdallah bin Bayyah. Bin Bayyah, while never a vocal enthusiast for the Arab revolutions, was not a vocal opponent of them in 2011 either. His long-time association with Yusuf al-Qaradawi may have suggested that there was some degree of political alignment between the two scholars. The Arab revolutions would, however, show Bin Bayyah to harbor profound misgivings about protesting against one's rulers. While initially cautiously optimistic about the revolutions, as we shall see later in this chapter, by 2013 he had developed jurisprudential reasoning to rationalize political absolutism in Islamic terms. In the conclusion of the chapter, I will briefly compare Yusuf and Bin Bayyah's ideas with those of the scholars considered in earlier chapters.

Yusuf on the Arab revolutions

Hamza Yusuf is an American Islamic scholar who converted to Islam in 1977 before pursuing Islamic studies with the ulama in several countries across Europe, the Middle East, and Africa. His most important stint of study in his early career would take place in the deserts of Mauritania with the noted Bedouin scholar Murābiṭ al-Ḥājj wuld Faḥfū (d. 1439/2018). In his later career, however, he would become the most important Western student and disciple of Abdallah bin Bayyah. A charismatic speaker, by the early 2000s Yusuf had become Neo-traditionalism's most influential voice in the English language.[1]

During the Arab revolutions of 2011, Hamza Yusuf provides the intriguing case of someone who changed his views from being pro-revolutionary to avowedly anti-revolutionary in a few short months. Yusuf's transformation may have taken place through the influence of his shaykh, Abdallah bin Bayyah. Bin Bayyah appears to have experienced a change of allegiances during this period, most strikingly in the wake of the events in Egypt in 2013. Prior to this, Bin Bayyah had been a long-time colleague of Yusuf al-Qaradawi, and until his resignation shortly after the 2013 Egyptian coup, his vice president at the IUMS. Bin Bayyah is thus a complicated figure whose political stances I will have occasion to discuss in detail later in this chapter.

Yusuf's initial response to the Arab revolutions may be found in a blog post he wrote in late January 2011 about the self-immolation of the Tunisian street vendor Mohamed Bouazizi a month earlier that led to his eventual death, sparking the Arab Spring. In a post published on 29 January 2011, two weeks after the revolution successfully ousted Tunisia's long-standing dictator, he sympathized with the desperate state of the young man, Bouazizi, who despite his best efforts to lead a dignified life was treated with contempt by the Tunisian state leading him to self-immolation. Yusuf had harsh words for non-monarchic Muslim tyrants and their cronies who brought revolution upon themselves due to their corrupt practices. His predilection for monarchy is something we shall see more of below.

Yet even in this first written commentary on the Arab Spring, Yusuf's wariness regarding revolution was on display. He noted that the lesson bequeathed by past 'revolutions and coups' was that '[w]ith rare exceptions, they bring in new governments that are as bad or worse than the ones they ousted.'[2] Yusuf's wariness, however, blurred the distinction between rebellion and the largely peaceful protest that had characterized the early days of the Arab revolutions. Yusuf's assimilation of such protest to rebellion was intriguing in light of his own Californian upbringing, especially given that he would often highlight his own family's credentials as political activists advocating for African Americans in the US.[3]

In his blog on the Tunisian revolution, Yusuf's next remarks offer insights into his conception of legitimate forms of rule. In it, he highlighted that past revolutions in the Arab world had removed monarchs who:

> practiced the tradition of benevolence. They were not always benevolent but were raised with the understanding that they were there to serve the people. These pathetic Arab rulers who overthrew those monarchs practice the worst types of cronyism and nepotism, placing their sons on their 'thrones,' and they thrive in an environment that is driven by family and tribal allegiance.

In Yusuf's opinion, there was something inherently noble about monarchy, a viewpoint he made explicit in an interview he gave later that year which we shall consider below. Even when they were not benevolent, he appeared to maintain that their behavior was informed by an ethos of service as opposed to the rapacity of the upstarts who overthrew them in much of the Arab world in the twentieth century. I am not aware of any instance in which Yusuf has attempted to ground his belief of the virtue of monarchy in scripture or tradition. However, such a stance does help us understand his wholehearted embrace, by 2014, of the counter-revolutionary Arab monarchy of the UAE.

Yet, such a perspective can also give rise to aporias, for monarchs are also susceptible to pressures that arise from the 'family and tribal allegiances' he viewed as problematic in 2011. Indeed, monarchy is nepotistic by definition, and nepotism and cronyism are often intimately related. Yusuf provided no reason for his readers to believe these tensions were resolvable in his conception of monarchy. Consequently, his understanding of the history of premodern monarchy appeared rather romanticized. One could ask where the monarchs for whom he had such high regard came from. They had presumably also overthrown some past ruler on the basis of military superiority. Yusuf concluded his blog post on Tunisia with the pessimistic if prescient comment regarding the 'flames' of revolution having 'spread to Egypt, and we watch with fear and trepidation for the well-being of our Egyptian brothers and sisters, hoping and praying for their future and that of Egypt, the heart of the Arab world, which now is engulfed in the bonfire of revolution.'[4] Within days, however, we would find him appearing to almost wholeheartedly embrace the ongoing Egyptian revolution in February 2011.

The Egyptian revolution

On 7 February, fourteen days after the Egyptian revolution began, and four days before it would result in the ouster of long-time autocrat Hosni Mubarak, Hamza Yusuf wrote a short essay in support of the Egyptian revolution which he published on his blog. Scarcely a week after his circumspect piece on the Tunisian revolution, Yusuf appeared to be overtaken by revolutionary fervor in a piece published on his blog on Egypt.[5] After an epigraph drawn from the American Declaration of Independence, he opened his piece with the exclamation, 'America, where are you?' Given his prior and subsequent exhortations regarding the general ills of revolution, Hamza Yusuf appeared out of character in calling on the US government to intervene in the Egyptian revolution to facilitate its success. He declared: 'it behoves America to lend a helping hand to Egypt's people at this crucial moment,' and called out 'President Obama and Secretary of State Clinton' as 'apparently missing in action' while 'Hosni Mubarak [was] unleashing his thugs on innocent protesters and journalists.'

How are we to understand Yusuf's apparent about face from conservative to revolutionary in the face of the Egyptian revolution, and then to conservative once again some months later? How was it that he held that revolutions almost always ended badly, but when it came to the Middle East's most populous nation, he enthusiastically called for American (political) intervention into the affairs of a region in which the Iraq war remained a painfully fresh memory? It seems difficult to reconcile these apparently mutually irreconcilable positions. In the case of the Egyptian revolution, there was by Yusuf's own account a revolutionary fervor in the reporting of the events by Western media from Tahrir Square and perhaps he too was simply carried away by those extraordinary moments of euphoria. Whatever the case, Yusuf would write forcefully for the need for accountable government. As his piece on Egypt argued:

> Since the American and French Revolutions, it is increasingly accepted that leaders must only lead when they have the support and the confidence of their people. If leaders breach the social contract of popular consent of the governed through abuses, they not only lose legitimacy but they must relinquish their mandate to govern. There can be no doubt—if there ever was—that Hosni Mubarak has lost his legitimacy with his people despite the apparent legality of his rule, whether it be cloaked in constitutional or Islamic principles.[6]

Yusuf was thus drawing on historic Western revolutions to argue that a ruler had to possess a popular mandate. He may have been unfamiliar with Islamist arguments for the same that drew on hadiths that speak of a prayer leader, and by extension, a political ruler, also needing to enjoy their people's approval.[7] Yusuf thus asserted that Egypt's autocrat had lost his legitimacy in 2011 because of 'abuses' and consequently demanded that he relinquish rule.

Yet this blog post appeared strikingly at odds with Yusuf's later approach to a host of issues, including issues that addressed the concerns of justice more generally beyond the Arab revolutions. One example may be taken from remarks he made regarding anti-black racism in the United States. In his 2011 essay championing the Egyptian revolution, he argued:

> The Egyptian people, many for the first time in their lives tasting the inebriating wine of political freedom, are challenging their government, courageously defying the fear factor so ruthlessly cultivated in the belly of the bestial state security apparatus. This mirrors what happened in the 1960s when African Americans lost their fear of a brutal system that had kept them in check for centuries and after much *rebellion and rioting* resulted in a freer and more enfranchised society.[8]

Five years later, Yusuf would court considerable controversy in the United States by speaking dismissively of anti-racism movements and appearing to minimize the existence of systemic racism in the country.[9] He subsequently apologized for these remarks, but as one observer commented, the apology was undercut by accompanying comments that the crises facing the African American community were largely of their own making.[10]

On the point of rebellion as well, Yusuf would argue some years after supporting the Egyptian revolution that the notion of opposing one's rulers was completely rejected by the Islamic tradition.[11] As we have seen, this was at odds with his apparent acceptance of the necessity of 'rebellion and rioting' on the part of African Americans in the 1960s in their pursuit of justice which ultimately 'resulted in a freer and more enfranchised society.' One way to understand this apparent but unexplained transformation would be to assume that Yusuf experienced a profound change of heart towards the revolutions after seeing how 'rioting and rebellion' destabilized post-revolutionary Arab countries in the later months of 2011. Seeing things this way, he reverted to a discourse that emphasized the obligation of obeying one's rulers. In this connection, it should be noted that Yusuf's later anti-revolutionary discourse did not make a distinction between rebellion and peaceful protest, a feature we shall also see in Bin Bayyah's statements below.

Yusuf on Ali Gomaa

Yusuf's piece on Egypt, 'When the Social Contract is Breached,' also offered some thoughts concerning the role scholars should play in these revolutions. He began by enjoining the ulama to take a firm stand against the regime of Hosni Mubarak before it was too late. If they did not, he argued, they risked being shown up as regime stooges:

> These are indeed times that try men's souls, and the scholars of Egypt need to offer good counsel to their people. If the scholars are to have any relevance when the dust settles, they must take firm positions now. If they merely wait to see what happens, they lose the very thing that empowers them: the people's trust. [...] Scholars need to guide and not be dictated to by the puppet masters of power who cut their strings as soon as their usefulness is over, leaving them in the paralysis of paltriness.
>
> The need for resolute positions of solidarity with the Egyptian people in their pleas for political change is undeniable. I personally feel that the scholars, inside and outside of Egypt, have a responsibility to stand with the Egyptian people in

> their pleas for reform in Egypt. While scholars have a right to their own opinions on this and other matters, my personal opinion is that in order to stop further conflict and prevent more blood from being spilt, the scholars of Egypt should call for an immediate change in the government of Hosni Mubarak.

Yet, writing on 7 February, Yusuf was clearly aware that Ali Gomaa had taken a resolutely oppositional stand to what he was advocating. Arguably contradicting what he had just said, in the next paragraph, Yusuf described Gomaa as an 'honorable and pious man' who understood 'the complexity of the situation.' As Yusuf put it:

> I believe we should maintain a good opinion of the scholars who either take a position or choose to remain silent—a valid option during fitnah. We must recognize that personal ijtihad in difficult times is to be respected. The Mufti of Egypt is an honorable and pious man; he understands the complexity of the situation, the dangers of instability, and the tragedies that can quickly arise when conflagrations take a life of their own. [...] While some may not agree with his opinion, Muslims should respect religious authority, acknowledge a scholar's right to it, and not assume we know anyone's intentions. God alone is the Judge of men's hearts.

It is not clear then, whether Gomaa had lost 'the people's trust' in Yusuf's view, since he exhorted the same people to respect and acknowledge the 'religious authority' of scholars like Gomaa. One could perhaps read these paragraphs as applying to different audiences—the former two to scholars, and the latter to the layperson, but their juxtaposition was nonetheless jarring.

Yusuf's enthusiasm for the revolutions in the piece also uncomfortably juxtaposed two other statements that range from the unusual to the misinformed. Firstly, he argued against democracy in Egypt as it was likely to become a 'destabilizing factor' in the country. Yusuf proposed no alternative. Presumably he did not want a reversion to Mubarak-era autocracy. However, what exactly he was advocating in its place was unclear, perhaps because he did not have any substantive suggestions. Instead, he expressed himself thus:

> In fact, the world's problems are solved daily in the cafes of Cairo with creative solutions coming from the waiters as well as the waited upon. What is lacking in Egypt is a reasonable living standard that enables average wage earners not to succumb to the necessity of graft, a government that serves the people, a sound judicial system relatively free from corruption, and, most importantly, basic human dignity—the right to be respected in your own land.

Besides this, he also made the remarkable claim that there is no lack of freedom of expression in Egypt. Writing in February 2011, Yusuf asserted that Egypt had 'the freest press in the Muslim world.' Such a view is, however, not backed up by the evidence. Reporters without Borders who publish the global Press Freedom Index noted around the time that the attacks on journalists that began under Hosni Mubarak's crackdown against the revolution caused Egypt's place on the index to fall from the unfavorable starting point of 127 out of 179 countries in 2010 to 166 for 2011/2012.[12]

Yusuf's peroration also read as out of step with his subsequent transformations. In the final paragraph of the blog post, he highlighted how the historical tendency of 'traditional scholars' to side 'with stability in order to prevent bloodshed' tended to create 'worse situations than the ones being opposed.' He continued:

> in an age where peaceful protest is the only rational means of a people to redress the wrongs of their government, the scholars should not only support but acknowledge this change in the world. The situation in the Middle East is intolerable, and as John F. Kennedy rightly remarked, 'If we make peaceful revolution impossible, we make violent revolution inevitable.'

Yusuf here showed that he appreciated that times had changed in modern political culture that recognized the role of 'peaceful protest' as a means of political reform. As noted previously, this resembles Qaradawi's remarks from a few days earlier when he expressed concern that suppressing peaceful demonstrations could compel people to take up arms. Indeed, both Qaradawi's remarks and Yusuf's citation from Kennedy were prescient given the direction many of the Arab revolutions would take, illustrating that the logic of these statements applied to these contexts all too well, as we will see in later chapters. Yet, Yusuf's subsequent change of heart regarding the revolutions, which he would soon come to oppose as inevitably destructive and contrary to Islamic teachings, show that his commitment to any notion of protest ultimately proved ephemeral.

Precisely when Yusuf experienced his change of heart is difficult to pinpoint. Even a month later in March 2011, Yusuf was still beating the drum of revolution in the region in a blog post entitled 'On Libya.'[13] Once again, he praised the 'benign monarchies of the old Muslim world' who had been 'replaced by malevolent dictators.' Of particular interest was his support for a scholar he described as follows:

> My friend and teacher through his works, Shaykh Sadiq al-Ghiryani, who in my opinion represents the highest example of a scholar-warrior with his intrepid statement on al-Jazeerah [*sic*], chose to speak the truth despite being in Tripoli, hence putting his life on the line. He is now in hiding and posting videos from his hideout to encourage the resistance. I recommend watching his post to see a true scholar fulfilling his duty. This is indeed the greatest jihad: to speak the truth in the presence of unjust tyranny. May God reward and protect him and his family during these trying times.

Ghiryānī is a respected Islamic jurist who was closely aligned with and actively supportive of Libyan Islamists. Even then, scholars opposing tyranny were to be celebrated as fulfilling the duty of commanding right and forbidding wrong as praised in a hadith.

A change of heart

By early August 2011, however, Yusuf had begun to shift dramatically from his revolutionary orientation. It was perhaps not a coincidence that this shift was articulated in remarks made in Abu Dhabi, a place destined to become the nerve center for counter-revolutionary activities throughout the region over the coming years. Indeed, it does not appear accidental that the UAE-based Saudi presenter himself, Turkī al-Dakhīl (b. 1393/1973), would within a few years be revealed as intimately involved in the counter-revolutionary machinations at the highest levels of the Saudi and UAE states, the two states leading the charge against the Arab revolutions. In particular, he would become notable for his involvement in advising the Saudi crown prince, Muhammad bin Salman, on how to deal with the pro-revolutionary *Washington Post* journalist, Jamal Khashoggi.[14] Muhammad bin Salman would eventually be held by a CIA assessment to be responsible for the journalist's assassination in 2018 in Turkey, and Dakhīl would write an article threatening the West against any adverse action against the crown prince.[15]

Of course, the young prince was in many ways the protégé of the far older and more experienced crown prince of the UAE, Muhammad bin Zayed, the main driving force behind the Arab counter-revolutions.[16] The trust placed in Dakhīl by the closely coordinating de facto leaders of the UAE and Saudi Arabia is illustrated by the appointment of Dakhīl as the Saudi Ambassador to the UAE in 2019.[17] Yusuf, who was interviewed by Dakhīl in September 2011, could not have known of the sorts of activities that his interviewer and the rulers of the UAE were going to be engaged in over the years that followed. But the coincidences are noteworthy nonetheless.

Around September 2011, Dakhīl interviewed Yusuf on his show *Iḍā'āt* on the pan-Arab UAE-based Saudi-owned news channel, Al Arabiya, which was developed by Gulf monarchies as a counterweight to the influence of Al Jazeera in the region.[18] In his interview, Dakhīl asked Yusuf about a lecture he gave on 3 August 2011 in Abu Dhabi in which Yusuf said: 'patriotism (*ḥubb al-waṭan*) is important and foundational in our religion,' and that 'it protects Muslims from evil and unrest. If Muslims understood patriotism then we would not see the scenes that we witness in many countries.' Additionally, Dakhīl cited Yusuf as saying: 'among the obligations of the religion is for us to be loyal to those in power and not to pray against them even if they are tyrants (*jā'irīn*).' In light of these remarks, Dakhīl asked whether Yusuf accepted the doctrine of obeying one's rulers (*ṭā'at walī al-amr*). Yusuf responded by asserting that 'exalting the ruler (*ta'ẓīm al-sulṭān*) is the foundation of society.' However, he arguably clarified what he meant in his next sentence: 'If the government is not respected and [its authority] infringed upon, how can a person feel security.' If one were to read his remarks about 'exalting the ruler' as referring to showing them the respect they are due by way of generally following the laws instituted by a government, then this is uncontroversial. This basic level of respecting ruling institutions is fundamental to the integrity of any system of governance. If this was his intent, then his initial turn of phrase, namely 'exalting the ruler' was less than ideal, but the idea of respecting governmental authority in principle is hardly exceptional.[19]

Yusuf further interjected that rulers also had great responsibilities. Some, he pointed out, plundered more than they provided to their people. Such pressures, he noted, could lead to 'explosions.' Using the language of the Islamic tradition, he argued that just as the 'subjects' (*ra'iyya*) had to respect the rights of the ruler (*sulṭān/rā'ī*), similarly the ruler had to respect the rights of their subjects. 'If the shephard (*rā'ī*) is a wolf who devours the sheep, then how can the sheep feel safe?' The regnant conditions of the region, in his view, served as a warning to rulers. Yet, this warning only extended to certain rights, as Yusuf made clear from the comments that followed. He pointed out that the Emirates, where he was giving his interview, provided excellent public infrastructure and services. 'The rulers here serve their people and you can feel this. When you enter the country, you feel whether the people are served or humiliated.'

The oil-rich Gulf states have some of the highest per capita income levels in the world. Their ability to provide services and infrastructure was obviously no indication of whether these countries' citizens enjoyed any political freedoms. Such freedoms did not appear to find a place in Yusuf's understanding of the relevant services that were to be rendered to a people, as his subsequent comments made clear. In response to the presenter's interjection as to how one could reconcile the need to exalt one's rulers with a situation in which the ruler was not serving his people, Yusuf's response was an articulation of his political conservatism. He would signal his reliance on authority in his prefatory remark by highlighting that the political values he was about to articulate were ones that he had learnt from his teachers.[20] This refrain in his discussions of the topic of political reform signals a deep-seated reluctance to question the norms he had inherited from his unusually politically 'quietist' tradition of Islamic learning. In accord with the doctrines that he had inherited from his teachers, he noted that reform came from within the individual since 'as you are, so will your rulers be.' This is the same idea that Qaradawi had addressed some months earlier on his Al Jazeera show, as we saw in Chapter 2. Yet, while Qaradawi took this to mean that the people were to some degree responsible for the corruption of their rulers, and that in recognizing that responsibility, they had to attempt to instigate political reform, Yusuf's approach was diametrically opposed to such a reading.

The individual had to blame themselves for the corruption of the rulers rather than seek to reform or replace the ruler. Yusuf complained that too many in the Muslim world felt that their problems would disappear if they got rid of their rulers. 'This is not true. History belies it.' He continued by pointing out that when Gaddafi came to power through a coup, people were dancing in the streets but their hopes were subsequently dashed. To drive his point home, Yusuf cited a verse from the Qur'an: 'God does not change a people until they change their selves' (Q. 13:11). He highlighted that God did not say 'their government' but rather 'their selves.' He pointed at his heart, declaring: 'the revolution starts here.' He then concluded by invoking the authority of his teachers and stating: 'this is what we have learnt.'

Yusuf's stance contrasts pointedly with that of Yusuf al-Qaradawi. Qaradawi had explicitly cited the same verse that Hamza Yusuf would subsequently cite in September 2011. Qaradawi invoked this verse in the course of his Friday sermon given in Tahrir Square on 18 February, less than a week after Mubarak's ouster, and roughly seven months before Yusuf would invoke the same verse to argue for the opposite of what Qaradawi had argued.

Qaradawi's invocation of the verse is worth citing in full to give a sense of the contrast in the two readings:

> God Most High says: 'God does not change the condition of a people until they first change that which is in their selves' (Q. 13:11). Change what is in your self, and God will change your situation and your condition. The people changed, so God changed their condition! The people endured, they were put to the test, they made sacrifices, they were determined, and the fear was removed from them. The pharaohs, in the past, made people fear, they used to gain victories by frightening them, they used to throw fear into the hearts of people. But people did not care about Pharaoh, nor about Korah (Qārūn), nor about Hāmān, nor about the State Security, nor about torture, nor about the camels, the mules, the horses, nor about the snipers, nor about any of these things. They were determined, the people were determined, the youth were determined, the youth of the revolution were determined to continue, and God realized their hopes, God realized their goals.[21]

We thus find the exact same verse being invoked in completely contrasting ways by two influential scholars, although Qaradawi's global footprint at the time was more significant than the much younger Yusuf who was at a relatively earlier stage in his public career. In his interview on Al Arabiya, Yusuf still asserted that the ulama had a duty to stand up to tyranny.

> The problem is that unfortunately many of those who are affiliated with the religion are more covetous of what is in the pockets of the rulers than warning them of their faults. [...] It is true that [scholars] have a right to remain cloistered, this is a [legitimate] option, but this is not for everyone. Some of them must undertake to admonish their [rulers].

Yusuf also placed some blame on a ruler's entourage that would persuade them that the masses loved them. But ultimately, he noted, the ruler would stand before God as the verses of the Qur'an declare. Yusuf added, however, that the admonishing of rulers had to be gentle, tactful, and strictly in private. It was not to be conducted in front of other people, such as going on TV and calling the ruler evil. This was a very different approach to the one we have seen from Qaradawi. The latter, it is true, did argue for a ruler to be corrected gently and tactfully as a general principle. This was reflected in the indirect manner in which he expressed disapproval of the Saudi tendency to grant safe haven to ousted autocrats. But he also did not hesitate to severely castigate long-standing autocrats like Hosni Mubarak and Ben Ali as we have seen. Yusuf would likely approve of the manner in which Qaradawi addressed his disagreement with the Saudi authorities but would not find the castigation of Mubarak or Ben Ali acceptable, at least as he portrayed his approach in this interview.

Yet, it is worth recalling that in the early months of the Arab revolutions Yusuf had explicitly and by name castigated the long-time rulers of Tunisia, Egypt, and Libya. Whether describing them as tyrants, or 'conniving, mutant, dark, and absolutely cruel,' it is clear that Yusuf did not feel that rulers could not be criticized in practice, despite what he held in theory. Clearly, certain types of injustice did merit open criticism, even according to Yusuf. As he suggested in his blog on Hosni Mubarak, the social contract between the ruler and the ruled entailed certain obligations on both sides. If broken through systematic abuses on the part of the ruler, it would fail to be binding as a social contract upon the populace. Presumably, a normal state of affairs would entail rulers providing certain services in return for the loyalty of the ruled. If the ruler provided the means for a dignified existence for the ruled, then the ruled had to respect the ruler's authority and not publicly criticize them.[22] However, if the ruler failed to uphold their side of the contract, then Yusuf's blog suggested that public castigation was no longer out of bounds. Yet, this was not entertained in his interview from mid-2011 or in his public statements thereafter. His revolutionary fervor, it would appear, had worn off by this point.

The incorruptibility of kings

The new, some might say renewed, Hamza Yusuf no longer wished to place any limits on the power of political authorities. In this context, the presenter asked Yusuf whether he felt that the culture of political engagement predicated on governmental accountability in Western democracies should not be applied to the Muslim world. In response, Yusuf expressed his preference for 'constitutional monarchy' over democracy as a system of government. However, as he made clear, he was not referring to the form of constitutional monarchy found in a number of European countries in which the monarch is largely ceremonial. Rather he wished for the monarchs to possess real power. His reasons for this were quite extraordinary:

> Firstly, kings are incorruptible (*ghayr qābil li-l-fasād*) unlike those who do not possess great wealth. [Presenter interjecting: 'Like the nouveau riche?'] Yes, like that. Such a person can be [corrupted]. As for a king, he is satiated (*shab'ān*). He has everything. He does not need anything.

It is not clear on what basis Yusuf believed kings to be incorruptible. He provided no justification for this highly unusual claim. He had himself cited the Prophet's warning about the corrupting influence of power over humans in general in his blog post on Egypt earlier in 2011:

> The Prophet, God bless and grant him peace, warned that 'Governance is great remorse on the Day of Judgment. Power is a luxurious wet-nurse and a terrifying weaner.' Scholars interpreted this saying to mean that once a man tastes the perks of power, he finds it difficult to give up, but death comes to us all, and at that point, the crisis of having failed in one's duties to the people will turn into great remorse.

One could also cite a similarly canonical hadith in which the Prophet Muhammad reportedly said: 'If a son of Adam were to own a valley full of gold, he would desire to have two.'[23] The Qur'an (Q. 3:14) also speaks of man's propensity to desire the things of this world without excepting monarchs: 'The love of desirable things is made alluring for men: women, children, gold and silver treasures piled up high, horses with fine markings, livestock, and farmland.' Yusuf himself quotes the famous remark of Lord Acton in a work of the former from 2010, 'Power tends to corrupt, but absolute power corrupts absolutely.'[24] In the same work, which we shall have occasion to explore in greater detail presently, Yusuf argues, drawing on the Qur'an (Q. 42:27), that 'oppression is largely driven by power and wealth.'[25]

The counterpoint to Yusuf's assertion, namely that non-monarchic heads of state are more liable to be corrupt is, like his claims about Egypt's apparently free press, not substantiated by the evidence provided by global rankings of corruption by state. Although Transparency International's Corruption Perceptions Index (CPI) is focused on the public sector of a state as a whole, Yusuf's claim about the relative incorruptibility of monarchs would suggest that monarchies would be overrepresented at the top of the CPI, while the bottom would be dominated by non-monarchic states. In fact, there are no true monarchies in the top ten states in the CPI.[26] Rather all the countries aside from Singapore have been fully fledged democracies in recent years.

The above notwithstanding, in his 2011 interview Yusuf made clear his predilection for monarchy. Indeed, when asked by the presenter about reforms that the King of Morocco had instituted because of pressures resulting from the Arab revolutions, Yusuf expressed his dissatisfaction at the apparent concessions.[27] In his view, the King should have retained as much power as possible, especially in light of the state of crises pervading the region after the Arab revolutions. In this context, Yusuf argued, there was a need for a monarch to be able to make 'quick and decisive decisions,' rather than engage in processes that hamper such swift decision-making.

The foregoing provides an idea of Yusuf's journey from enthusiasm for the Arab revolutions to what I have characterized as a reversion to a politically quietist Islamic conservatism. In the remainder of the present exploration of Yusuf's ideas from this period, I wish to demonstrate that this was indeed a reversion to a past orientation of Yusuf's that was only briefly interrupted by his zeal for the Arab revolutions. This can be illustrated with reference to the relatively lengthy introduction Yusuf wrote to a prayer book he published in 2010 entitled, *The Prayer of the Oppressed*.

In his introduction, Yusuf is most concerned with diverting the gaze of those who wish to confront tyranny away from the typical targets—'[t]he tyrant who lives in the palace' or 'the bully on the street corner'—to the more subtle 'tyrant within our own souls.'[28] It is to this problem that Yusuf wants his reader to divert their attention. Later on in the introduction, he speaks of 'the gift of powerlessness' which he almost appears to celebrate:

> Most of the Muslim world is now experiencing a state of powerlessness, and therein lies a great opportunity. The loss of state power, military might, sovereignty, and control is not the end of Islam but a new beginning. It may be the end of political Islam, but it surely portends the resurgence of spiritual Islam.[29]

A little later, Yusuf cites with approval a passage from the British anti-imperialist Wilfrid Scawen Blunt (d. 1341/1922) that celebrates the Ottoman loss of political power as it would bestow upon Islam a more 'religious' and 'spiritual' rather than political character. In the context of considerable territorial losses to European imperial powers, Yusuf cites Blunt's remarks with approval. He also adds what might be perceived as an Orientalist observation, namely that '[Blunt] had first hand experience and knowledge of the levels of corruption to be encountered at all strata of Muslim society.'[30] Imperial subjugation, and one might say, by extension, tyrannical subjugation, turns out to be a good thing in Yusuf's view, as long as one views it with a spiritual lens. In this connection, he adds:

> Until Muslims learn and internalize the sunnah of powerlessness, we will not be worthy of assuming the responsibility that comes with power, and for God to give it to us before we are ready and prepared would be an abandonment of His providence for this community.[31]

Doubtless, the ability to turn a negative into a positive has its benefits, but one can also see why such a quietist doctrine that redirects all of one's moral energies to reforming the self would prove appealing to authoritarians. In other words, Yusuf may not wish to serve autocracy, but his doctrines as articulated in this work recommend themselves remarkably well to such uses. We should perhaps thus view his enthusiasm for the Arab revolutions in early 2011 as an out-of-character interregnum that soon gave way to his reverting to type by late 2011. As we shall see later, Yusuf is quite understandably co-opted by the UAE regime as part of its ambitious foreign policy agenda. The most important scholar the UAE would go on to appoint, however, would be Yusuf's learned teacher, the Saudi-based Mauritanian Islamic jurist, Abdallah bin Bayyah, whose similarly equivocal response to the Arab revolutions we shall briefly consider in the remainder of this chapter.

Bin Bayyah and the revolutions

Unlike his student turned colleague, Hamza Yusuf, Abdallah bin Bayyah's stance towards the revolutions was never one of enthusiasm. In this regard, he also contrasted sharply with his senior colleague at the IUMS, Yusuf al-Qaradawi. At the same time, he did not vigorously oppose them like the Egyptian establishment scholars we met in the previous chapter. It is worth remembering that Bin Bayyah was a founding vice president at the IUMS where Qaradawi, a scholar with whom he had worked closely since before the IUMS' establishment in 2004, was the founding president. Rather than vocally oppose the revolutions, Bin Bayyah quietly published an old video on YouTube in early February 2011 that seemed to signal his disquiet at the revolutions. On 2 February, after the protests had persisted for over a week, Bin Bayyah uploaded a video of a lecture he gave in London in 2007 with live translation by Hamza Yusuf entitled 'From Protest to Engagement.' This was a lecture given at a conference with the same title that had been organized by a broad-based network of community activists known as 'The Radical Middle Way' who were funded by the UK government for the purpose of counter-radicalization in British Muslim communities.

Its publication on Bin Bayyah's YouTube page, after no videos had been published on it for over a month, was very likely as a response to the ongoing protests in Egypt. As its title suggested, the lecture argued that Muslims needed to engage more constructively with their interlocutors rather than adopt a posture of opposition and criticism.[32] It is intriguing that Yusuf, who always described his teacher with the utmost reverence, should have published the opposite message to Bin Bayyah less than a week after the latter had published this video on his YouTube channel. It indicated that the two did not coordinate a shared message on political matters during this period. Some weeks later in March, Bin Bayyah published a shorter clip from this lecture that, especially with Yusuf's English translation, evinced concern at the dangers inherent to the activities of the uneducated masses—the 'ignorant' and the 'foolish' in Yusuf's translation—who needed to be restrained by a society's elites to prevent disaster.[33]

Both videos strongly suggested Bin Bayyah's antipathy towards the Arab revolutions. This was further underlined in a lecture from late April 2011 that Bin Bayyah gave on a panel on the Arab revolutions with other senior IUMS scholars, including its then president, Qaradawi, alongside other prominent Islamists. Unlike the enthusiasm of the other scholars on the panel, Bin Bayyah's presentation was tepid about the revolutions and his concern for the future was palpable.[34] However, in terms of the Islamic legitimacy or otherwise of these revolutions, his first detailed engagement with the issue may be found in an interview given in October 2011 on an Egyptian satellite channel CBC on a show, *Momken* (*mumkin*), which had a presenter who enjoyed a particularly close relationship with Ali Gomaa as we shall consider in later chapters. Indeed, he was the same presenter, Khayrī Ramaḍān, who hosted Jifri's phone call in February 2011, which we considered in the previous chapter.

In October 2011, Bin Bayyah was interviewed for roughly forty-four minutes regarding his thoughts on the Arab revolutions.[35] Ramaḍān, in keeping with the tenor of Egyptian media after the 2013 coup, would become a cheerleader of especially polemical anti-MB commentary. For now, however, he welcomed Bin Bayyah, a vice president of the IUMS, an institution closely associated with Qaradawi, to discuss the Arab revolutions. Ramaḍān revealed in the course of the interview that he had been able to watch a recording of a private discussion of Bin Bayyah's in which the latter had refused to pronounce in favor of such protests—the language used by Ramaḍān was 'rebelling against the ruler.' Ramaḍān may have been drawn to Bin Bayyah precisely because of his, until then, private reservations regarding the question of protests. For while Bin Bayyah may have signaled his discomfort at the protests through previous statements, his apparent refusal to afford any of them Islamic legitimacy after their success in ousting two long-standing dictators, and in the face of widespread euphoria at these successes, suggests a particularly deeply felt antipathy towards even relatively peaceful revolution. Some of this was doubtless a result of the fact that some of the revolutions had resulted by this point in civil wars, notably in Libya, Syria, and Yemen.

Whatever Ramaḍān's intentions in inviting Bin Bayyah to the show, he succeeded in coaxing Bin Bayyah to publicly pronounce his juristic reservations regarding the revolutions with greater clarity than he had done at any time I am aware of since the beginning of the protests almost a year earlier. In a series of questions about the Arab revolutions, Ramaḍān's inquiry regarding when one may 'rebel' against one's rulers is of particular interest to the present study. Ramaḍān noted that at the outset of the Arab revolutions, many scholars held that 'the default position (*al-aṣl*) was the prohibition of rebelling against one's ruler (*'adam al-khurūj 'alā al-ḥākim*)'. This framing reflects the persistence of the juristic paradigm of 'rebellion,' a violent form of political intervention as opposed to 'peaceful protests' (*al-muẓāharāt al-silmiyya*), which was the preferred language of scholars like Qaradawi in places like Egypt. Yet, there is no doubt that by this point in time, some of the revolutions had devolved into fully fledged civil wars, which could perhaps be construed as rebelling against one's rulers. Ramaḍān continued by pointing out that after 'rebellion' did take place, and its 'evil consequences became apparent' (*ẓaharat al-mafāsid*), the scholars needed to reconsider the matter. He noted to Bin Bayyah that he was aware of the latter's deferral of pronouncing any new fatwas on the matter of rebellion. Presumably Ramaḍān was referring here to fatwas that would contradict 'the default position.' Ramaḍān asks why Bin Bayyah had deferred his judgement on the matter.

Bin Bayyah's response was circumspect. He noted that the question was complicated (*mu'aqqada*). He argued that the *bay'a* or pledge of allegiance given to the ruler, which he likened to Jean Jacques Rousseau's notion of a social contract (although his description of the contract was closer to the understanding of Thomas Hobbes as articulated in the *Leviathan*) was a pledge that is binding (*mulzima*) on both the ruler and the ruled. If there was a failure to live up to the requirements of the contract, Bin Bayyah argued, certain processes needed to be initiated. 'Rebellion is not immediate, but rather there should be other means, such as calling to dialogue and consultation (*shūrā*) to bring things back to normality.'

Taking the long view

Bin Bayyah next articulated a second concern using the Arabic term *ma'ālāt*, which may roughly be translated as longer-term consequences. He described this as the 'most important problem that has arisen in the context of these revolutions.' He asked what the possible consequences of these revolutions would be:

> Is it the case that the ruler surrenders, and consequently, there is no bloodshed and people are saved from evil with only small losses, or will the ruler resist and consequently the losses will be significant and many will die, as we have seen in Libya, Syria and Yemen? [...] These losses are what have caused many to refrain from giving fatwas to encourage these revolutions.[36]

He added that once the revolutions are underway, the rulings may be different. He gave the example of Syria where he said that if people were told to stop rebelling once the rebellion had started, they would have been annihilated. Though he did not say so explicitly, the violent aggression of the Syrian Assad regime necessitated that civilians arm themselves and engage in a full-blown military conflict. He noted that the divergent circumstances necessitated a different legal ruling. Ultimately, he argued, the ruling would depend on weighing benefits (*maṣāliḥ*) against harms (*mafāsid*) and considering longer-term consequences (*ma'ālāt*). It was disagreements over these that were at the heart of the legal differences of opinion on these matters, he added. He also noted that the main Sunni position was not to rebel against one's rulers, though he noted that there were dissenting voices, such as the Andalusian Mālikī scholar, Ibn 'Aṭiyya (d. c. 541/1147), who Bin Bayyah cited as stating that a ruler had to be removed if he did not engage in Qur'anically mandated consultation (*shūrā*).[37]

Despite being an accomplished jurist, Bin Bayyah appears to have conflated a number of distinct legal issues in his discussion. Firstly, he appeared to assume that the revolutions had entailed legal 'rebellion' (*khurūj*) from the start. Bin Bayyah did not justify this rather unusual position—one that was contradicted not only by pro-revolutionary scholars like Qaradawi, but would also go against the position of an anti-revolutionary figure like Gomaa.[38] As noted earlier, Yusuf al-Qaradawi, Bin Bayyah's senior colleague at the IUMS, had argued that peaceful protests did not constitute rebellion. Though Bin Bayyah did not say so explicitly, the arguments he presented assume that peaceful protests were equivalent to what is referred to as *khurūj* in the Islamic legal tradition. That is to say, Bin Bayyah appeared to assume that peaceful protest was equivalent to armed insurrection in Islamic law. He provided no justification for this operative assumption in his thinking.

It is also the case that in some respects, his ideas seemed out of step with political realities in the region. When he referred to breaches of the social contract not justifying immediate rebellion, but rather that certain processes of dialogue needed to be engaged in, one wonders how he perceived the Arab public and political spheres. For many decades in Arab autocracies like Saudi Arabia, Egypt, Libya, and elsewhere, the public sphere had been characterized by repression. Attempts at calling for dialogue and political openness, let alone political accountability for breaches of the social contract had routinely resulted in the repression of those attempting to make such calls. Under such circumstances, which Bin Bayyah was undoubtedly aware of as a retired politician, one wonders what to make of his suggestion that protest should not have been engaged in, but rather that there should have been calls for dialogue. Either he was cynically using such discourse to provide cover for authoritarian regimes, or more likely in my view, he had internalized authoritarian normality to such an extent that he could not understand why people living under such circumstances would require significantly more freedoms than the few they already enjoyed. Indeed, his invocation of the Hobbesian social contract is noteworthy in this respect. He argued that the *bay'a* was equivalent to the European social contract tradition in which the individual traded certain freedoms with the ruler for the sake of security. He did not specify what these freedoms were, but it would seem that, like Hobbes, Bin Bayyah believed that almost all of one's freedoms could be curtailed. His discussion of long-term consequences seemed similarly one-sided, as we shall see in greater detail below.

In form, however, his arguments appeared quite reasonable. He noted that the benefits of these political questions had to be weighed by the Islamic jurist against the potential harms. He added that the jurist had to be scrupulous, God-fearing and had to avoid appeasing either the masses or the ruler. He further noted that the jurist could also be unaware of all the pros and cons of a given action. He pointed out that when the revolution started in Egypt, it was not clear what the outcome would be. Bin Bayyah said that he asked some people what they expected would be the outcome in Egypt, and their response was 'it's unknown, it's unknown!'[39] He added to this:

> God forbid, had there been a greater massacre, the results would have been different [...]. There would have been more victims. Therefore, we must not make light of (*nastahīn*) the killing of people. I cannot countenance the making light of (*istihāna*) killing people. I am not one who countenances making light of killing people. But given the public interest upon which legal rulings are based, and the fact that much of the Muslim world lives under tyranny (*ẓulm*), dictatorship (*istibdād*), and corruption; and that it is necessary to try and prevent this tyranny, especially when a peaceful approach to the revolutions was proposed, all of this may, it *may* in principle or logically, prevent tyranny without significant losses. Consequently, it was a sound point of entry, as whoever peacefully seeks to command and forbid, as has been mentioned in the hadith—[the Prophet said:] '[The master of the martyrs is Ḥamza b. 'Abd al-Muṭṭalib and a man who stands up to a tyrant and] commands him to right and prohibits him from wrong, and so he kills him'—this point of entry is sound when considering the benefits (*maṣāliḥ*).
>
> Despite this, we must not denigrate the views of others who have considered the long-term consequences (*ma'ālāt*). We must not denigrate the views. We must not accuse them [of evil intent]. Just as Shāfiʿī (d. 204/820) said, 'I do not accuse anyone [of evil intent].' As long as they are within reasonable limits, we should say, by God, these people may have been frightened and worried by the long-term consequences that might result from [the revolutions]. As a result, they may have either remained silent, or they may have given fatwas, perhaps timidly in some cases, and in others, may have ridden the wave with the ruler to a great extent. Thus the matter is complicated; it is complicated. There are a number of possible [interpretations] we must take into consideration.[40]

These comments are telling in that they illustrate that Bin Bayyah's ideas were still inchoate at this stage of the revolutions. His repeated remark that he could not countenance making light of killing people is particularly interesting in its not making explicit who was engaged in killing. In some respects, it reflected an embrace of powerlessness in the way we have seen Yusuf express above. Bin Bayyah seemed effectively to be arguing that fatwas that had permitted revolutions had made light of the mass murder that had occurred in their wake. It appeared immaterial that pro-revolutionary muftis like his colleague Qaradawi were forcefully advocating peaceful revolutions except in cases of ongoing civil wars. Indeed, Bin Bayyah's position on self-defense in the context of civil war was not dissimilar to that of Qaradawi at this stage. As we have seen, Bin Bayyah recognized that in Syria, where the state response to peaceful protests had been a military crackdown, protestors were forced to take up arms. Yet, he also seemed to suggest that by initially peacefully standing up to a murderous state, the protestors had 'made light of killing people.' The argument posited that such regimes were liable to be murderous, but additionally, it appeared to assume that it was the supporters of revolutions who were responsible for a tyrannical regime's murder of even peaceful revolutionaries. Bin Bayyah seemed to argue that such regimes' ability and willingness to deploy firepower against unarmed protestors acted as a trump card against any counterargument. To presage Bin Bayyah's mature position, he seemed to be saying that if one had power, one could not be questioned.

Interestingly, he was still willing to suggest that tyranny and corruption were undesirable and that confronting them peacefully may be reasonable. But the powerless had to recognize their limits, and in particular, those who called for protests were not to criticize those scholars who criticized them by condemning protests, nor those scholars who remained silent when the powerless tried to confront tyrannical power, because such scholars were ultimately taking the long view, a stance that Bin Bayyah characterized as recognizing that these were 'complicated' matters. In this argument, he left unarticulated what was perhaps the underlying consideration, namely that the powerful authoritarians could very likely crush the relatively powerless protestors, and so siding with the powerful in such a case, or at the very least not criticizing them, may have proved prudential for the scholar. As noted earlier, Bin Bayyah did not explicitly critique the authoritarian state of affairs that allowed the powerful to commit mass murder with impunity. His arguments foreshadow what became a reality within a couple of years of the interview, namely that Bin Bayyah would remain silent while a repressive state engaged in mass murder during the Egyptian Rabaa massacre, which we shall consider in the next chapter. More surprisingly, by 2014, he actually chose to publicly and actively support what had perhaps become the Middle East's most aggressively counter-revolutionary state, namely the United Arab Emirates.

A worrying prognosis

Returning to his 2011 interview, the presenter's next question concerned Bin Bayyah's comments made in the private dialogue alluded to earlier, in which Bin Bayyah said he was awaiting the 'final results' (*al-natā'ij al-nihā'iyya*) that would show whether these revolutions had resulted in any good. If, on the other hand, they only resulted in greater anarchy, the fatwa of prohibiting rebellion would remain standing. Bin Bayyah's response to this question was, once again, quite instructive. He readily accepted the presenter's portrayal of his position, adding a reference to the American saying 'April showers bring May flowers.' He argued that he had seen 'showers of blood in April,' in likely reference to the ongoing struggles in Syria, Libya, and Yemen, but he was still waiting for the flowers.[41] Continuing on this theme, Bin Bayyah noted:

> We fear, in reality, that the consequence (*ma'āl*) of these revolutions will be disagreements, discord, and civil war. We do not belittle the significance of these revolutions. We do not belittle the significance of these youths standing up without protection for the sake of the interests of the country and for the sake of putting an end to this overwhelming danger and this nightmare that has weighed heavily upon the umma's chest for a long time. It did not permit it to express its freedom and creativity. This is a situation that is unacceptable. Yet, despite this, and alongside this, there is a fear that these revolutions will not reach the desired outcome. There is the wise person who says, 'Revolution is a bulldozer' it bulldozes everything before it. But it needs a construction engineer to undertake building thereafter. The revolutions are bulldozing, but where are these sensible people, these engineers who can build a new edifice which we hope will be an expansive edifice that will accommodate all the sons of the nation, in which there is no ostracizing of one group by another, in which there is no fighting about [one's] existence (*tanāzuʿ al-baqāʾ*). Let me say that existential fights result in annihilation. Thus we propose to people that they work towards coexistence, work towards building.[42]
>
> We are in need of a sensible mind to lead the revolution. Hope and confidence is placed in those who engaged in the revolutions, and in the Islamic peoples, and in these people who are the heart of the Islamic umma and the Arab umma, that the results will be good, and that the consequences will be glorious. But there may be some distance between hope and reality. It is not my place nor in my ability to assess this distance. Rather it is only my place to warn (*an uḥadhdhir*) and present some advice which I will call values, or the building blocks of the future of these revolutions—tolerance (*tasāmuḥ*), dialogue (*ḥiwār*), humility (*tawāḍuʿ*)—a set of values which we consider necessary to prepare our minds for building what follows the revolutions. If we permit our emotions and our egos to rule, then the revolutions will not achieve their goals, and consequently a man may one day say—and I hope he will not and I do not think he will say such a thing: 'many a day I cried about, but when I reached another day I cried over [the former's] passing.'[43]

Bin Bayyah's concerns appeared reasonable in isolation, but as with his earlier remarks, they reflected a particularly narrow conception of moral agency. Notably, the protestors were moral agents and had to be attentive to the moral dilemmas of revolution, however peaceful they may have been. The state, the security forces, and the rulers, were amoral agents in Bin Bayyah's framing. Bin Bayyah did not appear to have much to say to them besides appearing to indirectly criticize them by referring vaguely to 'this nightmare' that presents 'overwhelming danger,' as though it were a natural law that by that very fact could not be reformed by humans. Consequently, in sharp contrast with Qaradawi, Bin Bayyah extended no exhortations to the security forces to not fire on unarmed protestors, nor called on tyrants to change their tyrannical behavior in line with global democratic norms which a scholar like Qaradawi had spent many years arguing was far more closely aligned with Islamic norms than authoritarianism. In contrast with his general silence regarding how authoritarian states should behave in revolutionary contexts, Bin Bayyah did have plenty of advice for revolutionaries. Unlike the authoritarian state, revolutionaries had to reflect on the long-term consequences of their actions. They, rather than the military and security officials responsible for the deaths of hundreds if not thousands by this point in the revolutions, had to embody the moral values of tolerance, dialogue, and humility. It is they who had to be 'sensible' and avoid 'ostracizing' other groups by being the engineers who construct an expansive and accommodating new reality for the nation.

Of course, during this period, and for nearly the next two years, Bin Bayyah remained associated with the IUMS. He did not dissociate from them until September 2013, shortly after the Rabaa massacre that defined the Egyptian coup of that year. Thus, Bin Bayyah was able to publicly countenance that opinions differed on these questions, and pointed out that Yusuf al-Qaradawi, a scholar nearly a decade his senior, and whom he referred to in the interview as his shaykh, had already started to develop new legal ideas in the realm of popular protest. As noted in Chapter 1, Qaradawi had been developing these ideas systematically in his writings well before the Arab revolutions. Bin Bayyah added, however, that at the time he was himself exploring other concepts that he believed had to precede the development of Islamic legal doctrines pertaining to revolution. To this end, he was researching the notions of *taḥqīq al-manāṭ* and *fiqh al-wāqiʿ*. In his own distinctive reading, the classical jurisprudential concept of *taḥqīq al-manāṭ* concerned studying and 'understanding [modern] reality' (lit. *fiqh al-wāqiʿ*) in order to know when it was appropriate to apply Islamic legal rulings. He argued that jurists could differ due to the differing levels of their grasp of modern realities. The concept of *taḥqīq al-manāṭ* would play an important role in Bin Bayyah's subsequent thought in which it was used to rationalize authoritarianism on an Islamic basis, as we will see in preliminary outline at the end of this chapter.

Bin Bayyah on Al Jazeera

Before we explore Bin Bayyah's novel juristic formulations, however, we should briefly consider the trajectory of his thought from late 2011 until early 2013 as it will provide context for his response to the Egyptian coup of 2013 and the subsequent massacres in Egypt which one may argue, given Egypt's significance in the Arab world, served as the most important indicator of the health of the Arab revolutions. Two other Al Jazeera interviews of Bin Bayyah, both on Qaradawi's show *al-Sharīʿa wa-l-Ḥayāh* which would occasionally invite other senior scholars to be interviewed instead of Qaradawi, are worth alluding to in this connection. The first took place in early November 2011, a couple of weeks after Bin Bayyah's CBC interview. In it, he repeated a point already mentioned above, namely that while the revolutions were supposed to be peaceful, one had to recognize that those which had not been peaceful had often become violent because they had been compelled to violence. He mentioned the Libyan case as exemplifying this, but then added an interesting caveat. He noted that Libyans were threatened with mass extermination, but then noted 'at least this is what we have heard, or what appears to be the case.'[44] Similarly, when asked to comment on the violence perpetrated in Syria, he demurred. He stated:

> In reality, I would like to say to you [i.e. the presenter] that if I have not lived in a situation, I cannot comment on it in detail. I hear that blood has been spilt, as far as I have heard, and that violations have been perpetrated, and thus everyone who is able to stop this bloodletting should do that, either with his hand, or his tongue, or his heart, and that is the lowest level of faith. However, despite that, I acknowledge that the people of Syria are more aware of their circumstances than we are. We only hear through the media, through what we see, and also by talking to some Syrian brethren concerning shameful circumstances, disgraceful circumstances. Circumstances unbecoming of humanity. Barbaric circumstances. We see a fight for survival, what I once called an existential fight that leads to annihilation. Thus it is a futile situation and a profitless war that is almost a kind of extermination, a kind of recklessness with people's blood. I thus join my voice to other voices to call those who rule that country to end this war and to expend

every effort possible to return security to the country by way of bringing the people of this country to mutual reconciliation and contentment.[45]

In a sense, at the beginning of this passage, Bin Bayyah was pleading ignorance about the conditions that were being invoked to justify revolutionary action. The theme of pleading ignorance would also become important in Hamza Yusuf's thought concerning the Arab revolutions some years later, and he would explicitly invoke his mentor, Bin Bayyah, to make the case of its relevance in responding to the revolutionary context.[46] Besides this, Bin Bayyah also made explicit earlier in his 2011 Al Jazeera interview that he did not encourage revolutions.[47] 'Firstly, and I wish to say this in a personal capacity, I am not a caller to revolution. I am a caller to reform (*iṣlāḥ*). I believe that the rulers (*ḥukkām*) and the ruled (*maḥkūmīn*) must reform their situation so that they are not impelled towards revolution.' To my knowledge, this was the first time Bin Bayyah explicitly abjured revolution. As with his earlier comments, he appeared to place the responsibility of reform on both the rulers and the ruled equally. Bearing in mind his earlier acknowledgement that many people in the region were living under dictatorship, it is noteworthy that in calling both the rulers and the ruled to reform themselves, he continued to present the responsibility of reform equally upon dictators and those living under their repression. Given that his earlier comments would suggest that dictators were deserving of moral disapprobation, it is not clear why he was calling on repressed and disempowered populations to reform their situation on an equal footing as those he held to be the agents of their repression.

A year later, Bin Bayyah was once again on Al Jazeera's show *al-Sharīʿa wa-l-Ḥayāh* addressing the rather topical issue for the Arab revolutions of how to change what is wrong in society (*fiqh taghyīr al-munkar*). Towards the end of the episode, the presenter asked Bin Bayyah how to engage a ruler who had perpetrated something wrong and needed to be corrected. Like Qaradawi's response to a similar question which we saw in Chapter 2, Bin Bayyah invoked the Qur'anic story of Pharaoh and God's exhortation to Moses and Aaron to suggest that they speak to the ruler gently at first. Bin Bayyah noted that advising the ruler (*naṣīḥat walī al-amr*) is unlike advising other people. But interestingly, Bin Bayyah, alive to the democratic experiments that were ongoing in places like Egypt and Tunisia as he spoke, highlighted how norms might differ in these contexts:

Of course, there are now what are called democracies, and democracies have created a new situation that realizes the legal purpose [of giving advice]

> (*yuḥaqqaq fīhi al-manāṭ*). The president in these democracies has come [to power] through a particular agreement in a specific way, and so people may address him as they address anyone else through newspapers and television, as long as that is in a respectful manner, as long as that is in an Islamic way. The way of denouncing and defaming does not yield benefit.[48]

These comments are particularly interesting because they showed Bin Bayyah's willingness to accommodate himself to democratic norms in a way that starts to reverse markedly after 2013. He argued that democracies provide structures that legitimate certain forms of accountability of the ruler that may take place in the public sphere. There was also an implication, however, that in non-democratic circumstances such public accountability did not need to be, or perhaps, ought not be observed.

The principled legitimation of authoritarianism

Bin Bayyah's legitimation of executive absolutism was more manifest in February 2013, a few short months after his Al Jazeera interview, at the beginning of a fateful year for the Arab revolutions. It is worth remembering that Bin Bayyah had expressed significant reservations regarding democracy for many years, and so in some sense his predilection for authoritarianism had a longer history.[49] Between 18–20 February that year, at a conference in Kuwait organized by Bin Bayyah, he addressed a technical jurisprudential discussion regarding the concept of *taḥqīq al-manāṭ* we saw earlier. His presentation contained an argument that appeared to mark a significant departure from the Islamic legal tradition by asserting that in certain areas of governance that intersected with Islamic law, the ruler was to be empowered over and above all Islamic jurists to decide how Islamic law applied in practice to such questions given that the modern reality, the *wāqiʿ*, as Bin Bayyah would refer to frequently, had rendered certain historic Islamic practices controversial.[50] In a room full of eminent Islamic jurists, this doubtless raised some eyebrows, and consequently in the ensuing discussion some queries regarding his argument were articulated.

The very first comment, from the distinguished Azharī jurist, Ḥusayn Ḥāmid Ḥassān (d. 1442/2020), reflected this concern.[51] As he put it respectfully to Bin Bayyah, 'The fact of the matter is that revelation came to change the reality (*al-wāqiʿ*).' Indeed, as he understood his younger colleague, an understanding of which he would shortly be disabused, Bin Bayyah could not possibly be claiming that 'we should render the [sacred] text subservient to the reality—the Shaykh never countenanced this.' Ḥassān further argued that *taḥqīq al-manāṭ*, as he conceived of it, could be an act of developing rulings that helped 'change reality' (*taghyīr al-wāqiʿ*), but he resolutely rejected the suggestion that *taḥqīq al-manāṭ* should simply be an expedient tool for adapting the Sharia to create 'new rulings because the reality imposes this upon us.' Rather, he argued, if the Sharia ruling obligates an act, 'then we must change the reality' so that the ruling may be applied. He balanced this statement with a recognition that the Sharia naturally had numerous mechanisms and principles to help accommodate changing realities, such as the principles of facilitation (*taysīr*), gradualism in the application of laws (*tadarruj*), and recognizing exigent circumstances (*ḍarūrāt*).

Specifically on the issue of Bin Bayyah's placing absolute Islamic legal authority in the hands of the ruler in matters of the public interest, Ḥassān argued that this could not be an unqualified prerogative. Rather, the ruler possessed executive authority (*al-tanfīdh*), but the ulama were the ones with the prerogative to define the context in which the law applied since it was a matter of ijtihad. What might be called 'the classical Islamic conception of the separation of powers' here articulated by Ḥassān serves to underline the exceptional nature of the absolute empowerment of the executive that Bin Bayyah was attempting to justify. To use modern terminology somewhat anachronistically, Bin Bayyah's argument was effectively a means of rolling the three branches of government, the legislative, the judicial, and the executive, into one. Indeed, Bin Bayyah's response to his slightly older colleague made clear that Ḥassān had underestimated the former's determination to empower the executive branch in absolute terms.

Bin Bayyah acknowledged that he did not wish for pernicious realities (*al-wāqiʿ al-wabīl*) to define Islamic law. But he pushed back against Ḥassān by slightly misrepresenting the latter's argument. He asserted that there was 'great danger' in claiming that 'every reality must be changed' by Islamic law. Bin Bayyah provided examples from the second Caliph ʿUmar who did not apply certain laws in cases in which there were extenuating circumstances. He also appealed to the Ḥanbalī jurists, Ibn al-Qayyim (d. 751/1350) and his teacher Ibn Taymiyya (d. 728/1328) to argue that under certain conditions, it was not possible to change a bad reality. What was of note in the examples he cited was that they were all circumstances in which the legal judgement was being articulated by a jurist. By contrast, Bin Bayyah did not require the ruler to have any juristic qualifications in deciding whether or not to apply Sharia-based laws to modern contexts. This is arguably a significant innovation on his part.

In his response to Ḥassān, he also pointed out that a jurist was not a judge such that they could appoint someone to execute their ruling. Once again, Bin Bayyah's point was not to argue that some jurists should be empowered to become judges, as was historically the norm in Muslim lands. Rather, he made clear that it was up to the ruler to decide when the law applied. To use the language of modern governance, this made it even clearer that Bin Bayyah wished to place all of the powers of the legislative and judicial branches in the hands of the executive. The emergence of these ideas in the context of the Arab revolutions was particularly opportune or dangerous depending on one's viewpoint. The ideas Bin Bayyah expressed in early 2013 were the most sophisticated Islamic arguments put forward thus far to ratify authoritarian government. And the authoritarians were clearly listening. Bin Bayyah's Kuwait conference concluded on 20 February. Three days later, UAE Foreign Minister Abdullah bin Zayed visited Bin Bayyah's home to discuss 'the state of the umma and the possibilities of its revival.' Bin Zayed tweeted an image of the meeting, praising Bin Bayyah as a Renewer (*mujaddid*), a Prophetic concept that referred to the most important Islamic scholar of a given century.[52] Bin Bayyah's website also shared an image of this tweet.[53] As we will see in later chapters, Bin Zayed would soon become the patron of Bin Bayyah's religio-political ideas.

Conclusion

In early 2011, the responses of both Hamza Yusuf and Bin Bayyah fell somewhere between the poles of enthusiasm and hostility towards the Arab revolutions displayed by the scholars explored in previous chapters. In the foregoing, we considered how Hamza Yusuf's response to the uprisings over the course of 2011 seemed to reflect a genuine change of heart, and hence his positions on Egypt and Libya were later directly contradicted by his embrace of (ostensibly) benevolent authoritarianism, though to my knowledge he never explicitly disavowed his earlier positions. Bin Bayyah's response was far more systematic in keeping with that of his reputation as a noteworthy jurist. He initially appears to have avoided adopting a clear stance towards the revolutions and openly expressed his uncertainty regarding their legal status. At this stage, he was willing to respectfully recognize Qaradawi's viewpoint as that of an authoritative jurist without adopting it as his own. Subsequently however, he began to systematically theorize his justification for authoritarian absolutism. As noted earlier, this appears to be an unprecedented innovation in Islamic jurisprudence which has historically required rulers to adhere to the rule of Islamic law as developed by independent jurists.[54]

While Yusuf was content to rely on the authority of his teachers like Bin Bayyah, the latter clearly did not feel bound by precedent. In this regard, Bin Bayyah's thought resembled that of Qaradawi who similarly had developed novel juristic arguments about responding to tyrannical government. Where the two jurists differed was in their conclusions. Qaradawi argued against absolutism in favor of democracy though he only legitimated peaceful means of realizing that goal under normal circumstances. By contrast, Bin Bayyah argued for absolutism and would subsequently make explicit his opposition to the Arab revolutionary call for democracy. As we will discuss in Chapter 9, by 2014, he would plainly state that in the Middle East, 'the call for democracy [was] essentially a call for war.'[55] Thus, while he did not start out sharing the perspective of the counter-revolutionary scholars we saw in the last chapter, he would eventually join their ranks while offering a more sophisticated and substantive legal justification for autocracy than his younger colleagues were able to muster.[56] Before briefly considering developments in 2014 towards the end of the present work, however, we must study how the other scholars responded to the intervening period. The next chapter thus considers Ali Gomaa's counter-revolutionary activism after 2011 culminating in the fateful events of Rabaa in the summer of 2013.

5

ALI GOMAA AND THE COUNTER-REVOLUTIONARY MASSACRES

(JUNE 2012–AUGUST 2013)

The foregoing chapters mainly considered the ulama's public responses to the Arab revolutions from their outset, with much of the emphasis placed on the early days of the Egyptian revolution. The present chapter returns our focus to Egypt, but chiefly considers the activities of Ali Gomaa, the scholar whose interventions and the reactions they elicited will in many ways be the defining concern of the remaining chapters. Given their initial opposition, it was not surprising that the establishment ulama of Egypt like Aḥmad al-Ṭayyib and Ali Gomaa would have been dissatisfied with the country's attempted democratic transition. These two scholars, who had actively discouraged protests against Hosni Mubarak, arguably also tried to hobble the transitional order. It could not have helped that that order had witnessed the MB, towards whom both Ṭayyib and Gomaa were reportedly unsympathetic or even hostile, gain a plurality of seats in parliament and subsequently, the presidency of Egypt in the country's first ever free and fair elections. As Masooda Bano has noted, Shaykh al-Azhar al-Ṭayyib was 'openly critical' of the Morsi presidency of 2012 to 2013 and demanded that political freedoms be protected in a way that he never demanded under the Mubarak regime or under the coup regime that ousted Morsi in July 2013.[1] Shortly after Morsi's election, for example, Ṭayyib actively opposed Morsi's attempts to appoint a Salafi scholar to the post of minister of religious endowments by coordinating with the SCAF to undermine Morsi and force him to put forward a different candidate.[2]

While I will briefly consider the important activities of Aḥmad al-Ṭayyib in the present chapter, specifically his justification of the Egyptian coup of July 2013 in religio-legal terms, Gomaa's more prolific interventions will receive most of the attention. The two main engagements that will concern us will be Gomaa's opposition to the presidential candidacy of the Muslim Brother Mohamed Morsi in the summer of 2012, and more significantly, his public and private support for the Egyptian military coup of that year. That support culminated in him vocally backing the Rabaa massacre of August 2013, the largest and most deadly of several crackdowns that took place after the coup. This chapter will mainly consider his private backing for violence against opponents of the coup offered prior to the Rabaa massacre while Chapter 7 will consider his support for the military's heavy-handed approach after Rabaa. The present chapter will culminate with a narration of the events of the day of the massacre.

Gomaa: from Mubarak's ouster to the coup

Given that Ali Gomaa was the most vocal scholar defending Hosni Mubarak's legitimacy in 2011, it is not altogether surprising that he would offer his support to the military's preferred candidate in Egypt's mid-June 2012 election run-off between the MB member Mohamed Morsi and former Egyptian Air Force commander and Mubarak's last Prime Minister, Aḥmad Shafiq. In a Friday sermon from 8 June 2012, roughly a week before the run-off election between Morsi and Shafiq, Gomaa spent most of the sermon arguing for Shafiq over Morsi as president. Aired live through the Egyptian satellite channel, CBC, he did not explicitly mention the names of either of the two candidates, but observers knew who he was referencing, and Egyptian media at the time reported the sermon as an attack on Morsi.[3]

Gomaa also uploaded the sermon to his semi-official YouTube channel the following day.[4] Consequently, in the next few days, as the election approached, a number of third parties, mostly hostile to Morsi and supportive of Shafiq, uploaded shorter versions of Gomaa's inexplicit criticism of Morsi and praise of Shafiq to their YouTube channels, garnering tens of thousands of views by the time of writing in 2019.[5] The most popular of these videos with nearly 300,000 views, however, was from an anti-Gomaa, anti-Shafiq YouTuber who interspersed his video with scornful written commentary in Egyptian dialect describing Gomaa as part of the 'same team and gang' as the SCAF. Shafiq was clearly the SCAF's preferred candidate and would doubtless have received considerable surreptitious support from the so-called Egyptian deep state. After these clips, the YouTuber inserted clips of Gomaa's defenses of Mubarak in 2011 which we saw in an earlier chapter.[6]

The deep state's support manifested in myriad ways, but at its heart were the military and security forces. The media establishment would presumably have been taking orders from these arms of the state, directed as to what kinds of narratives had to be purveyed in news stories and talk shows.[7] Similarly, they coordinated closely with business tycoons who led Egypt's crony capitalist economy that helped enrich the political classes and created a small coterie of businessmen who worked symbiotically with the political and military establishments. An example of a business tycoon in this system was Ahmad Bahgat; part of Bahgat's empire is the Dream Channel which we saw in an earlier chapter hosting a call-in from Ali Gomaa.[8] Gomaa enjoyed excellent relations with a number of these channels, both privately and publicly owned, whose hosts would typically maintain close ties with the security state and its intelligence services. The messaging of these media outlets was closely aligned with that of the deep state, and Gomaa would soon become an important voice in the coup regime's propaganda war, sometimes through the 'military's propaganda arm,' namely the Department of Moral Affairs (DMA).[9] It is thus unthinkable that Gomaa did not also enjoy close ties with the security state. Indeed, he suggests as much in his remarks in 2011, cited in Chapter 3, when he declared on behalf of himself and the shaykh al-Azhar that they could grant protection to any youths who go home and withdraw from the protests on the streets of Egypt.[10] This is also hinted at by one of Gomaa's colleagues at the Azhar's Council of Supreme Scholars, Muḥammad ʿImāra, whose comments we will consider in Chapter 8.

It is thus quite possible that Gomaa's Friday sermon on 8 June 2012, in the days leading up to the election run-off between Shafīq and Morsi, was given at the behest of the state security apparatus so as to encourage people to vote for Shafīq and dissuade them from supporting Morsi. The sermon was a remarkable display of political theater. After the customary recitation of prayers, Gomaa launched straight into a discussion of the tribulation that had beset the country which had led to a 'crossroads from which only God can save us,' an apparent reference to the upcoming election run-off. Within two minutes, he made this explicit. He stated that at the very beginning of the election campaign, he made known his decision to remain publicly neutral regarding the candidates as a matter of principle. He took pride in this stance declaring in the sermon: 'I am a scholar for all. I explain to them God's religion. I do not intervene in party politics in any way whatsoever, or under any pressure.' He thus asserted that he was above partisan politics of any kind. 'I have only made the words of God, "Do what is good so that you may prosper," as a light for whomever seeks God's path.'[11]

After speaking of the Prophet's coming to spread peace (*salām*), he lamented its absence in public discourse in recent days. Rather, he asserted, public debates had been characterized by the arrogant presumption of claiming to know God's decision (*al-ta'allī 'alā Allāh*) regarding the elections. This was the central theme of the sermon as highlighted in the very title of the sermon on YouTube. In the context of the elections, and without mentioning his name, Gomaa claimed that the Muslim Brother Mohamed Morsi had effectively stated that God would make him win when he was asked how he would react if his opponent, the military-backed Aḥmad Shafīq, won the elections. Morsi was said to have replied: 'It will never happen.' Gomaa responded to this by declaring: 'Who dares to arrogate to themselves the knowledge of God's decision?' The Arabic phrase he uses, *man dhā alladhī yata'allā 'alā Allāh*, doubles as a citation of a canonical hadith. His more learned audience members would have been familiar with the hadith as referring to a man who did just this by swearing by God that God would never forgive a certain person's sins. God responds in the hadith by saying: 'Who dares to arrogate to themselves the knowledge of God's decision that I will not forgive so-and-so? Indeed, I have forgiven him, and rendered your good deeds worthless.'[12]

Having condemned Morsi's stance, Gomaa reasserted with great passion his claims to impartiality:

> I have no connection with either [candidate]. I am only relaying to you the Prophet's stance when such matters were presented to him! He would respond: 'Who dares to arrogate to themselves the knowledge of God's decision?' It is a great calamity (*muṣība*) and tribulation (*baliyya*) for us to be ignorant of our religion to this degree! [The candidate] declares, 'It is impossible!' Where is the impossibility in this? Does he not know that God does whatever He wills? And that nothing exists in the universe except that which He wishes? Does he not know that the future is in God's hands?[13]

Here we find a righteously indignant Gomaa transforming Morsi's defiance of the military candidate who was perceived as threatening the

Egyptian revolution into a sin against God and Islamic theology. Morsi was doubtless making a political statement rather than a theological one, but Gomaa was misreading it to cast doubt on Morsi's religious integrity and suitability for public office. In this connection, he upped the ante against Morsi with what he said next. After asking the questions above, he continued by inquiring, 'What did the other candidate [i.e. Shafīq] say, and did they ask him this question?' Gomaa reported that Shafīq was indeed asked the same question and responded, 'I will go home and congratulate him.' In the culmination of his sermon, Gomaa declared: 'Therefore, this person [i.e. Shafīq] is closer to God than that person [i.e. Morsi].' Gomaa followed by saying that this was not a defense of either candidate. Rather it was a defense of Prophetic values that should not be forgotten.

Yet, less than three minutes later, Gomaa reasserted that he was maintaining impartiality so that people could vote as they see fit without undue religious influence.[14] In a brief digression, Gomaa next targeted a major charitable institution closely affiliated with the Azhar known as al-Jamʿiyya al-Sharʿiyya, which forms one of the largest and oldest Islamic charitable and missionary institutions in modern Egypt.[15] In recent weeks, after the first round of elections had resulted in a run-off between the MB's Morsi and the military's Shafīq, the influential al-Jamʿiyya al-Sharʿiyya had endorsed the former over the latter.[16] In his sermon, Gomaa proceeded to lambaste the Jamʿiyya for what he portrayed as political partisanship. This, he declared, was contrary to the principle of non-partisanship upheld by the Jamʿiyya's Azharī founder, Shaykh Maḥmūd Khaṭṭāb al-Subkī (d. 1352/1933). Gomaa asserted that, in contrast with the Jamʿiyya's stance, the Azhar, its Islamic Research Academy (*Majmaʿ al-Buḥūth al-ʿIlmiyya*) and Dār al-Iftāʾ, the affiliate institution Gomaa presided over in his capacity as grand mufti, had upheld this just principle. Gomaa did not seem to consider that the partisan comments he had made a few minutes earlier would contradict his claim that Dār al-Iftāʾ had remained non-partisan.

Continuing on this theme, Gomaa added:

> Does the Jamʿiyya violate proper procedure except in pursuit of its blameworthy desire (*hawā*)? We say to them, you have made a mistake! Your officials have made a mistake. Turn back to God! You have contradicted all of the founders! They never did this! You have contravened justice and the covenant that we would all maintain a [non-partisan] distance [from all parties], and [in doing so] we do not fear any criticism, for the sake of God. [...] I say this so that God does not look upon us in anger. I say this so that God sees truthfulness in us, and so He is True

> to us, that He conceals [our faults], grants us success, shows us mercy, responds to our prayers, and places in power whoever is best. [...] I say this, without any desire for this world, without fear of any place. Rather, I fear the Lord of the Worlds. [...] O servants of God, this is religious counsel, so whoever's heart is opened by God to accept it, let them convey it to others.[17]

The remainder of the sermon concluded with conventional prayers. Overall, Gomaa presented himself as non-partisan with such self-confidence, and was so consummate a master of religious homiletics and prayer that it would have been quite understandable if many people were persuaded by his performance.

Given Morsi's subsequent success at the polls, however, Gomaa's exhortations did not have their desired effect, and Morsi was duly sworn in as Egypt's first genuinely democratic president that summer on the basis of a relatively thin but unmistakable electoral majority. However, Morsi's presidency was destined to be a short-lived one. In a tumultuous year following his election, a series of missteps and miscalculations, alongside the active hostility towards him and the MB on the part of the institutions of the state, culminated in a popular coup a year later on 3 July 2013 led by General Abdel Fattaḥ al-Sisi, who had been appointed defense minister by President Morsi some months earlier. In this phase too, the official ulama were to be intimately involved, though as we shall see in the following sections, no one played quite the role of Ali Gomaa. Gomaa's pro-military posture in response to the 2013 coup left no doubt that his enthusiasm for the Egyptian security establishment alongside his animus towards the MB had few limits.

The Egyptian coup of 2013

On 3 July 2013, General Sisi would bring an end to the Morsi presidency with a military coup. In a carefully choreographed event, Sisi announced the suspension of the constitution and the removal of the president flanked by a number of prominent public figures. These included the former Egyptian diplomat popular with the West, Mohamed ElBaradei, and the secretary general of the Salafi Al Nour Party, Jalal Murra, who appears to have been more of a Salafi politician than a religious scholar.[18] Similarly, the Egyptian Coptic Pope Tawadros II endorsed Morsi's removal by the general. Sisi was clearly cognizant of the importance of co-opting religious voices that represented the breadth of Egyptian society to ratify his coup. However, none of the aforementioned figures, including the religious figures, were scholars in the way that Aḥmad al-Ṭayyib was. Jalal Murra is described in public statements as an engineer, and the Coptic Pope was, intriguingly, a pharmacist with apparently limited theological training.[19] The only serious religious scholar to be involved in Sisi's declaration removing Morsi was Ṭayyib. His contribution to the process, besides his presence alongside Sisi, was to give a short speech of less than two minutes justifying the removal of Morsi. Given its brevity, it is worth translating in full. Ṭayyib stated:

> In the name of God the Beneficent, the Merciful. The great Egyptian people, may the peace, mercy, and blessings of God be upon you. To proceed: it has become eminently clear from [our] gathering that Egypt stands before two options, the best of which is bitter. The worst of the two bitter options is the [social] breakdown of the Egyptian people and that their pure blood should stream onto the ground. For this reason, in accord with the law of the Islamic Sharia which says that perpetrating the lesser of two evils is a Sharia obligation; and in an attempt to get out of this political crisis into which the Egyptian people have fallen, between the supporters of the [current] order, and those opposed to its continuity—both holding firm to their opinion, refusing to budge—for all these reasons, I have supported the conclusion at which those gathered have reached, namely the holding of early presidential elections in which the people will arbitrate at the ballot box. [Its] transparency will be ensured by the great Egyptian judiciary, the heroic men of the armed forces, and the intrepid police forces. I ask God, the Exalted, that through this choice, this opinion, and this plan, He reconcile between two opposed groups who live on the same land and drink from the same Nile. And may the peace and mercy of God be upon you.[20]

Given its brevity, this two-minute speech could not offer any detailed scholarly justification for the coup, and its invocation of the Islamic legal principle of committing the lesser of two evils was vigorously critiqued by numerous scholars outside of Egypt, including, predictably, Qaradawi and his colleagues at the IUMS. Other scholars throughout the region and beyond publicly expressed their dismay at the ouster of Egypt's first Islamist democrat, some of whom we will meet in Chapter 7. To my knowledge, Hamza Yusuf and Bin Bayyah did not comment on the coup or its aftermath. On the other hand, Ali Gomaa was just about to commence his aggressive pro-coup advocacy as we shall see shortly. In contrast with Gomaa, however, Ṭayyib's support for the new regime did have its limits. In particular, the massacres that followed the coup, culminating in the one at Rabaa, which we will consider in the section that follows, proved too bloody even for Ṭayyib.

He responded to the massacres by speaking of the sanctity of blood in brief public comments.[21]

Immediately following Rabaa, he issued an even briefer statement lamenting the loss of life, disavowing any prior knowledge of the massacre, and calling on 'all sides' to prevent bloodshed.[22] As we shall see later in the chapter, only one side was armed. His disavowal of prior knowledge of the massacre was also somewhat unusual, since there was a public effort by the coup regime to legitimate mass bloodshed in the days leading up to the massacre.[23] What he may have meant was that he had not been involved by the security forces in the planning or justification of the clearing of anti-coup protests throughout Egypt which, many observers recognized, was likely to be violent. In a separate statement three days later, in the context of ongoing violence, he tactfully asked the security forces to avoid harming peaceful protestors, while accusing the MB and foreign regimes of responsibility for the violence.[24] Ṭayyib's approached contrasted sharply with that of Gomaa who would emerge as the coup regime's most ardent enthusiast. It is to a more detailed consideration of Gomaa's support for the military regime's bloody interventions that we shall now turn.

Ali Gomaa after the coup

After the dramatic events that culminated in the coup of 3 July 2013, Gomaa's involvement with the military gradually came out into the open far more visibly, marking a departure from his previously more discreet approach. As we shall see in greater detail below, in the early weeks of the coup, he gave a recorded lecture to the army's propaganda arm, the DMA, providing religious justification for the coup and the killing of anti-coup protestors whom he portrayed as armed rebels threatening Egypt as a whole. He also gave Friday sermons to the armed forces with Sisi in attendance, and in other instances, gave Friday sermons in praise of the Egyptian army after a fashion that may be characterized as religious legitimation for the coup. In these lectures, he lionized the Egyptian army in the lead up to the Rabaa massacre.

These were followed by a lecture given to senior military cadres shortly after the Rabaa massacre extolling their work of recent days. Gomaa's post-coup lecture to the Egyptian army's DMA prior to the Rabaa massacre, and his lecture to the security forces' top brass after Rabaa may be read in full translation in the Appendices. In the remainder of this chapter, as well as in Chapter 7, I will consider his overall argument for supporting the Egyptian army and legitimating the Rabaa massacre both before and after the army had undertaken this remarkably brazen act of mass murder in full view of the international media. The present chapter will consider his pre-Rabaa support, while Chapter 7 will consider his post-Rabaa support. These engagements marked only the beginning of his career as the 'Army's Mufti,' as Yusuf al-Qaradawi would disparagingly refer to him after the Rabaa massacre. As we will see, this was not far off the mark. In the months and years following the massacre, Gomaa would continue to give sermons and lectures to the military with Sisi in attendance, and effectively act as a religious spokesperson for the military regime.[25]

Gomaa's most significant post-coup engagement prior to Rabaa was a lecture given to camera and recorded by the military's DMA.[26] It is not entirely clear when this lecture was recorded, but internal references to the month of Ramadan mean that it would have been sometime between 9 July and 7 August 2013.[27] The lecture was leaked shortly after the Rabaa massacre on 14 August. Until that point, Gomaa's message was accessible only to the security forces. As we shall see in his public appearances prior to these leaks, his public persona had not yet revealed the full extent of his support for a crackdown against the MB. That support began to show in this recording, although his involvement reached its crescendo in the lecture that he gave to the Egyptian security forces a few weeks later on 18 August, as we will consider in Chapter 7.

Gomaa's pre-Rabaa private recording for the security forces

Gomaa began his presentation by praising the 30 June protestors against the Morsi presidency.[28] He claimed that 'all of the aerial observations, and international observers, state that the crowds are more than thirty million.' This was one of the inflated figures purveyed in the pro-coup media at the time, and a few weeks later Gomaa would claim that it was actually a crowd of thirty-two million.[29] However, as Neil Ketchley and others have shown in careful studies of the crowds and an assessment of the physical capacity of the major squares of Cairo, these numbers are wildly exaggerated, with some of these being uncritically reproduced in international media.[30] Rather than millions, which would have been physically impossible, hundreds of thousands were more likely to have protested. Ketchley places the 'plausible' upper limit on crowds against Morsi as reaching a million protestors.[31] He notes that studies show that 'no more than 5 percent of a national population mobilizes at any one time' in such protests.[32] Gomaa was doubtless aware that the crowd sizes he was citing made little sense, requiring a third of Egypt's population to be on the streets. Instead, he called those questioning these numbers to be denying the 'plain reality.'

In this context, he also was willing to argue that the Sharia sanctioned the removal of a ruler in keeping with the principles of commanding right and forbidding wrong. He now held the protestors to indicate the ruler's lack of political legitimacy declaring that the true possessors of power were the people.[33] In saying so, he did not sound dissimilar to Yusuf al-Qaradawi who argued this at the beginning of the revolutions. Gomaa now adapted the line from the famous revolutionary poem of Abū al-Qāsim al-Shābbī (d. 1353/1934) that Qaradawi cited in his Friday sermon at Tahrir Square a week after Mubarak's ouster.[34] Also like Qaradawi in 2011, Gomaa was now citing the second Caliph 'Umar who encouraged those he ruled over to correct him, even if it were with their swords. Gomaa, as we have seen, eschewed such references during protests against Mubarak whose legitimacy he continued to uphold till the very end. With Morsi, however, he clearly felt differently.

Consequently, he emphatically abjured the term coup. 'This was not a coup' he insisted, because the army was only responding to the cries of the populace to save the nation. It did so for selfless reasons, Gomaa insisted. It is worth remembering that this was addressed to officers in the security forces, some of whom may have felt moral qualms about the army's role in the coup. For such moral qualms, the DMA found Gomaa to be a charismatic figure who would justify the army's cause. Gomaa drew on several non-canonical reports from the Prophet and his Companions, mostly of dubious authenticity according to Muslim scholars, to craft an narrative that had the Prophet singling out the modern Egyptian army as invincible by virtue of divine protection.[35] The absurdity of this claim was picked up by some hadith scholars in Egypt at the time, but this was arguably overcome by Gomaa during the immediate post-coup period by the constant state-sanctioned repetition of these narrations in a variety of forms in the climate of fear of MB 'terrorists' that had been cultivated by the military regime.[36]

Fighting the Khawārij

Another theme that ran through Gomaa's post-coup discourse was the casting of the MB as Khawārij, a historical term with highly charged religious resonances that proved especially potent in providing religious legitimation for the mass slaughter and incarceration of MB members and sympathizers. As discussed in Chapter 2, the Khawārij formed a politico-religious schism from early Islam by rebelling against the political authority of the fourth Caliph, 'Alī b. Abī Ṭālib, with one of their number ultimately murdering him. Gomaa now applied a Prophetic report about the Khawārij: 'Blessed are those who kill them and are killed by them,' to the overwhelmingly unarmed protestors against the coup.

According to other hadith reports, the Prophet called them 'dogs of the Hellfire,' a phrase we will see Gomaa use repeatedly to refer to protestors against the coup.[37] Indeed, a minute into this lecture, he referred to those who would deny the outpouring of 'thirty million' protestors as 'our own people who speak our language,' citing a hadith of the Prophet that was traditionally understood to be a reference to the Khawārij.[38] The systematic use of such language was found throughout Gomaa's discourse, but its use this early in his presentation suggests that the casting of anti-coup protestors and MB members as Khawārij was a deliberate and carefully calculated effort on Gomaa's part. In addition to the religio-historical resonances of the term, the word can be viewed as analogous to the term 'terrorism' in the modern War on Terror context. This word is highly emotive and allows governments who use it to flout the rule of law with remarkable impunity. It is no accident, therefore, that both these terms were frequently invoked in the post-coup context by the security forces and those at their service, like Gomaa.

Indeed, Gomaa proved exceptionally effective at interspersing his discourse with constant references to the hadiths about the Khawārij, and after the coup he was often seen on Egyptian television shows emblazoned with the words 'Egypt Fights Terrorism' written in English on the screen, as we shall see. When his first post-coup message to the military was recorded, the primary referent for his use of the word 'Khawārij' were the anti-coup protestors in Rabaa Square. The square was populated by members of the MB and their sympathizers who wished to see the restoration of Egypt's first democratically elected president. While the sit-in was peaceful, we will see that the security forces, who would violently clear it in August 2013, were told that the sit-in was in fact heavily armed. Similarly, Egyptian media spent the weeks before the Rabaa massacre repeatedly claiming that the sit-in was well-armed and posed a clear and present danger to Egyptian society.[39]

The discourse of the War on Terror combines a fear of violence with otherizing of perceived terrorists in a variety of ways. One notable weapon in the war is the exclusion of perceived terrorists from the conventional rights of citizenship. They are excluded from the usual rights of freedom and privacy through arbitrary detention, the search and seizure of their property, and even cruel and unusual punishment. In extreme cases, they are stripped of their citizenship and rendered stateless, even though this is of questionable legality under international law. In the context of Egypt in 2013, Gomaa also tapped into these more modern streams of otherizing. Indeed, he explicitly assimilated his premodern reservoirs of otherizing through appeals to discourses about Khawārij with the modern discourse about terrorism when he said that what the Khawārij did in the past is referred to 'in modern language as terrorism.'

In otherizing the protestors who were against Morsi's ouster as Khawārij and terrorists, Gomaa was able to effect a subtle sleight of hand in talking about 'the sanctity of Egyptian blood' while excluding these protestors (who were also Egyptian) from benefiting from such claims of inviolability. Indeed, he was working in concert with the coup regime's media propaganda in this regard. That media had presented the Rabaa sit-in as being heavily populated by non-Egyptians. The state-sanctioned xenophobia that had characterized Egypt's airwaves in those days had meant that Syrians, Palestinians, and other non-Egyptians were viewed with deep suspicion in Egypt at the time and accused of making up a large contingent of the sit-ins.[40] By excluding the protestors from the Egyptian nation, something he made more explicit in his post-Rabaa lecture, Gomaa legitimated treating them as enemies without legal protections in Egypt in keeping with the possibilities provided by the logic of the modern nation state. In a sense, Gomaa's conceptual framework melded the Islamic religious tradition and the norms of the modern state to create a hybrid that was well-suited to his authoritarian sponsors in the Egyptian military.

Gomaa's performance was striking when he stated, without any hint of irony, that:

> There are those who incite; and this incitement, in reality, is incitement to civil strife and the Prophet says regarding fitna, 'The statement of the tongue in such cases is like the striking of the sword.'[41] Incitement against the Muslims, incitement against the Egyptian people, incitement against the security of society, incitement against social peace: all of these things are like the strike of a sword. The individual is using his tongue, but God will judge him for it as though he used a weapon. He is figuratively killing people, but God will judge him for it as though he has killed a human being.
>
> Consider the Prophet when he says to the Kaaba, 'How great is your sanctity before God, but the blood of a Muslim has greater sanctity before God than you

> have.'[42] He also used to say, 'For the Kaaba to be destroyed, and taken apart stone by stone, is less grave to God than killing a believer.'[43] And he said: 'The human is the edifice of the Lord. Accursed are those who destroy the edifice of the Lord.'[44] Listen to the Messenger of God, and do not listen to impassioned emotional rhetoric that is deceptive. Rhetoric that incites against the Muslims. Rhetoric that uses words that they do not believe in to begin with, like the word 'legitimacy' and 'democracy,' etc. And they do not even believe in them! Then you will realize who is deceiving and who is deceived.[45]

Gomaa stated the foregoing with such self-righteous confidence that his audience might have missed that this severe judgement could have applied to Gomaa's statements in the course of this recording, addressed as they are to an army that was seeking to reassert its authority through the threat of violence. References to democracy also made clear that his target was the MB members and Morsi sympathizers who had been protesting the coup. It is also noteworthy that a number of hadiths he cited are deemed by Sunni hadith scholars to be either weak in their attribution to the Prophet or outright forgeries.

Gomaa's lecture to the military reached a climax when he cited a hadith in which the Prophet gave encouragement to people who were unified under a leader and who were then confronted by someone who wished to sow dissent among them. 'Kill him whoever he may be,' the Prophet exhorted. He portrayed the coup as bringing about unity under the leadership of Sisi, and thus the MB were the ones sowing dissent in Gomaa's view. As we will see in Chapter 8, Qaradawi would counter that this hadith would apply better to Sisi and the army who were sowing dissent regarding the leadership of Morsi. Gomaa, however, was unequivocal. This hadith gave the army the license to kill those who objected to the military takeover, overriding hadiths that spoke of the 'sanctity and seriousness of shedding blood.' Gomaa's forceful exhortation to the army officers to 'yield' to their commanding officers and render them their 'obedience' may have been an indication of dissension in the ranks in response to the use of live fire to kill large numbers of protestors in the week after the coup. It is quite possible that the army enlisted Gomaa's support to help put to bed any moral disquietude in the ranks of the army officers. This may explain why the second half of his lecture, lasting nearly twenty minutes, was focused in the main on the legitimacy of killing opponents of the coup as well as the great sin of desertion.

Gomaa provided a fairly detailed justification for killing those opposed to the coup in the remainder of his lecture. He began by drawing on Islamic law. Having earlier asserted that the anti-coup protestors were Khawārij who had 'raised weapons against the Muslims,' and who intended to 'kill Muslims,' he noted that Islamic law permits the killing of such aggressors, as this would constitute self-defense. The security forces would not be liable for such deaths, as they were simply 'a type of suicide,' and in any case, these people were destined for Hell. Gomaa's comments had a macabre prescience to them, given how hundreds of protestors murdered weeks later by the security forces would be written off as suicides. In this lecture, likely given some weeks earlier, Gomaa argued that 'the killer is the one who aggressed' against the security forces and brought about his or her own death at their hands.

Gomaa also asserted that the rules of engagement provided by the security forces to their officers upheld 'human rights, the Sharia, the law, and justice.' These guidelines, which he presented himself as being closely acquainted with and perhaps even involved in developing, also legitimated killing anti-coup protestors, since they were not peaceful, but murderous. Gomaa claimed to have 'seen and heard the soldiers, while they [were] fasting, being aggressed against by these vile enemies, and they massacre[d] and kill[ed] them while they were fasting. Those who survived among them [said], as they killed us they were calling us disbelievers.' I have found no independent evidence backing up such a claim, and Gomaa's personal testimony cannot be viewed as reliable. However, to much of his audience, such remarks coming from a senior Azhar scholar and former grand mufti would doubtless have appeared compelling. It is also noteworthy that Gomaa once again highlighted accusations of the protestors engaging in anathematization, reinforcing his argument that these protestors were Khawārij and so could be killed with Prophetic sanction. He immediately labelled them as such, citing Prophetic statements to justify killing the protestors: 'They are dogs of the Hellfire [...] blessed are those who kill them!'

Once again, he blurred the line between the peaceful protestors of the MB and groups like al-Qaeda and the insurgents in the Sinai who were inspired by the latter group. He further claimed that these protestors were suicidal in their orientation. 'This is why you see them commit suicide, and put explosives on themselves and blow up people.' His apparent condemnation of 'suicide bombing' is quite striking as Gomaa has shown himself to be one of the most extreme religious proponents of 'martyrdom operations' in the past, albeit restricted to the Palestinian context, as I discuss further in the Epilogue. On one occasion, Gomaa asserted that those who rejected 'martyrdom operations' were to be excommunicated.[46] Yet, here he was vilifying 'suicide bombing' as a practice of terrorists who were 'trying to exploit the religion of Islam.'

To the above, he added Qur'anic justification. Such people were to be killed because 'God [had] commanded it' when He said:

> 'If the hypocrites (*munāfiqūn*), those in whose hearts is disease, and those who spread lies to cause fitna (*al-murjifūn*) in Madina do not desist, we will incite you against them. Then they will not remain your neighbors except for a short time. They are accursed; wherever they are found, they are to be seized and completely massacred.' (Q. 33:60) The explicit text of the Qur'an with respect to those who spread lies states that God has permitted his Prophet to kill them.

It is true, Gomaa noted, that the Prophet did not act on this, but God in His wisdom provided this Qur'anic dispensation for later peoples so that they could use it in the sorts of circumstances Egypt now confronted. Gomaa's exhortations thus culminated in his drawing on the Qur'an to encourage the 'massacring' of protestors by the Egyptian military. But these were accompanied by a warning directed at soldiers harboring doubts about killing protestors with which Gomaa concluded his nearly forty-minute lecture. These soldiers had to recognize that desertion was one of the greatest sins one could commit, he asserted, and God may never forgive them for it. In other words, if they deserted the army in this time of need, they may go to Hell for desertion.

Gomaa's incitement of the Egyptian army to massacre the anti-coup opposition was still, at this stage, only known to the army. In public, his discourse remained indirect and inexplicit in his advocacy and justification of the use of deadly force by the Egyptian army. In fact, he occasionally seemed conciliatory towards the MB. In this regard, Gomaa was clearly playing a double game. The foregoing lecture to the army and another post-coup lecture that will be discussed in the next chapter only appeared in the public domain after the Rabaa massacre—in one instance, many weeks later. By that time, Gomaa's public persona had also embraced a more incendiary discourse in its hostility towards the anti-coup protestors. Prior to the massacre, however, he made a number of public interventions that are worth examining before we consider his post-Rabaa discourse in Chapter 7 in order to illustrate the differences between his public persona and his private work with the security forces.

Gomaa's public discourse prior to the Rabaa massacre

During the month of Ramadan that year, when Gomaa would have recorded his lecture for the armed forces, he made many more public appearances. His YouTube channels were constantly uploading more conventional religious lessons of his, most of which did not really discuss current events. However, some of them did touch on events in Egypt at the time. Four of these are briefly worth considering, alongside a sermon he gave on Eid al-Fitr, that is, the first day after the month of Ramadan which corresponded with 8 August 2013.

On 15 July, Gomaa gave a sixteen-minute recorded presentation, speaking only to a camera, talking about 'terrorism' (*irhāb*) on an Egyptian channel as part of a regular program that appears to have been aired throughout Ramadan. In this particular episode, he spoke about modern groups engaged in perpetrating violence in the name of religion who he compared to the Khawārij.[47] It is an interesting presentation—he appeared to describe the terrorists in a way that resembled groups like al-Qaeda, but he used many of the same references in lectures he gave to the military around this time to characterize the unarmed protestors at Rabaa. In this more public-facing recording, unlike the private lecture to the security forces we have just considered, he did not explicitly link the hadiths about the Khawārij to the MB.

In some respects, the key themes of this discourse went back some years, although in the past, they appeared to be used exclusively to refer to groups like al-Qaeda. The innovation he introduced after the coup was to transform this Islamic anti-extremist discourse into what might be described as anti-MB propaganda given that the MB's religious values had been studiously non-violent for several decades. To take one example, Gomaa gave a fiery sermon on 7 October 2011 entitled 'The Constitution of Jihad in the Way of God' (*Dustūr al-Jihād fī Sabīl Allāh*) with some military personnel in attendance.[48] It may have been a response to an insurgency in the Sinai against which the Egyptian army had recently launched an offensive against jihadists, with some soldiers losing their lives in the process. This sermon had many of the same tropes as the private Ramadan lecture to the armed forces, showing that Gomaa's anti-extremist scriptural citation repertoire was fairly well developed before the MB emerged on the scene as the most prominent political player.

In some sense, in 2013 Gomaa was refashioning his religiously grounded counter-terrorism narrative so that it could be used by the coup regime to religiously justify attacks on the MB. Indeed, as early as 2 June 2013, some people were aware of the utility of weaponizing Gomaa's discourse against the MB. The YouTube channel of a weekly Egyptian newspaper, *Miṣr al-Maḥrūsa*, uploaded a four-minute clip from the 2011 sermon that passionately criticized the 'Khawārij' confronting the Egyptian army in 2011, but the title of the YouTube video told a different story that was more suited to the time of its being uploaded in the summer of 2013.[49] It read: 'Dr Ali Gomaa: the sellers of religion (*tujjār al-dīn*) are the Khawārij of [our] time and are dogs of the Hellfire.' 'Sellers of religion' had emerged as an effective slur against the MB that summer, and over a month prior to Gomaa's exhorting the army to kill the 'dogs of the Hellfire,' (i.e. the anti-coup protestors) some people had recognized the utility of Gomaa's anti-militant discourse for targeting the MB.

On 19 July 2013, Gomaa gave what seems to be his first post-coup sermon to the military. With Sisi seated in the front row, and virtually all the attendees in uniform, the sermon was broadcast live on the private satellite channel CBC as well as the state-run Egyptian Channel 1, as can be gathered from the onscreen watermark. The video of the sermon was uploaded to Gomaa's semi-official YouTube channel, on the same day it was recorded, with the title: 'The sermon on the western army which is granted victory by God.' As mentioned earlier, Gomaa was using a hadith of dubious attribution to the Prophet that mentions a western army and which Gomaa claimed was referring to the army of the modern Egyptian state.[50] The choice of the title was apparently a part of Gomaa's concerted effort at providing religious legitimacy to the Egyptian coup at a time when it was perpetrating mass killings of protestors on the streets of Cairo. The content of the sermon was similar in its praise of the army as Gomaa's other lectures during this period, but there was no explicit incitement to kill protestors unlike the private recording we have discussed. Gomaa's appeal to hadiths that experts considered to be fabrications was the object of refutation and ridicule among other scholars around this time.[51]

Then around 23 July, Gomaa was broadcast speaking on a recorded rather than live TV show in Cairo entitled al-'Āṣima (The Capital) to discuss recent events in Egypt. The two halves of the interview were aired on 23 and 24 July, although Gomaa uploaded both parts of the interview, totaling fifty minutes, to his YouTube page on 12 August.[52] Once again, his tone appeared almost but not quite conciliatory towards the MB. Some of his more conciliatory public remarks directly contradicted his more incendiary private remarks, for he asserted that he could not claim that the leaders of the MB would not reach Paradise before him. 'Might they not enter Paradise before us?' It is not clear how one could reconcile this with privately referring to the MB as Khawārij and 'dogs of Hell.' The relatively conciliatory tone notwithstanding, he still argued for the legitimacy of the military coup and the lack of legitimacy of Morsi's presidency. Given that his message to the Egyptian army was recorded by the DMA around this time, it would suggest that Gomaa was consciously engaged in double-dealing.

A few days later, on 26 July, Gomaa gave another Friday sermon, although this time it appears to have been recorded by the Azhar's YouTube channel, 'Azhar TV,' and there seemed to be no military officers in attendance. The short clips of the camera panning at the beginning and the end of the sermon showed only civilians present. Once again, it was uploaded to Gomaa's semi-official YouTube channel, although this time it was a few days after it was recorded, having been uploaded on 12 August, just two days before the Rabaa massacre. The title given to the video was interesting because it did not appear to reflect the actual sermon which seems to have had a more general theme. Its title on YouTube was: 'Sermon of a Message of Support for the Egyptian Army.'[53] Many of the same reports that Gomaa had been citing over the previous days and in the private recording for the army concerning avoiding fitna and the sanctity of blood appeared in this sermon, but he said nothing inflammatory. Rather, his intent was clearly the opposite of incitement. Towards the conclusion of the short sermon, Gomaa was particularly emphatic, and apparently quite emotional, about avoiding killing anyone in a time of fitna, even if it meant sacrificing one's own life by refusing to defend oneself. Under no circumstances, he exhorted, were people to reach for:

> a metal object [as a weapon], because metal [weapons] are manufactured for another purpose, and they have their own specialists who know how and when to use them. Metal [weapons] are not for you, rather they are against you. Even if [you use them] by way of threatening, intimidation or in jest. Even if it is [in jest].

This remark, which fits well with remarks he made in the private recording for the military, appears to explain the irenic tone of this sermon. Gomaa was addressing a civilian rather than military audience. Since his ultimate aim was to support the military in gaining control over Egypt, even in the face of civilian opposition, we can view this sermon aimed at a civilian audience as intending to dissuade civilians from resisting military rule. This was the flip side of his military address. In that lecture, he informed the military that 'if someone comes in jest brandishing a knife before his brother, and the knife ends up in [the aggressor], there is no compensation due to him. Rather this person has died in vain, and this is a type of suicide.'[54] However, his aim was not to cause needless deaths, but rather to support the military by: (a) justifying their right to exercise lethal force; and (b) dissuading civilians from resisting their effort to gain complete control of the Egyptian public sphere. It is possible that Gomaa believed that to realize this noble end, the double-dealing he was engaged in was actually necessary for the greater good.

Gomaa's final pre-Rabaa public engagement with the military seems to have been his Eid al-Fitr sermon which he gave in the early hours of 8 August at the 'Air Force Mosque' with a number of senior military and political figures appointed by the military after the coup in attendance. They included then General Sisi in uniform, Interior Minister Muhammad Ibrahim, President Adly Mansour, Vice President Mohamed ElBaradei, and Prime Minister Hazem El Beblawi. All were seated next to one another in the carefully choreographed center of the front row.[55] Also in the front row, further to the left, were two of Gomaa's Azharī colleagues. One was his successor as Egypt's Grand Mufti, Shawqī 'Allām (b. 1381/1961), and the other was the coup-regime appointed minister of religious endowments, Muḥammad Mukhtār Jum'a (b. 1385f./1966).[56] 'Allām would subsequently prove a loyal supporter of the coup regime, and he was noted for signing off on its innumerable death sentences against MB leaders and members in 'sham' trials.[57]

Gomaa's sermon was broadcast live on Egyptian television in the early morning, but was posted to his YouTube page on 12 August, two days before the Rabaa massacre. In the customarily short Eid sermon of nine minutes, Gomaa mostly recited generic prayers and did not explicitly mention the MB or praise the Egyptian army. In this short recording, his messaging was more indirect. His praise for the army could be read into his obvious closeness to them as displayed visually, and his indirect criticism of the MB could be read into a short remark made in the middle of his homily in which he said: 'Some people are like this, they harm their neighbors and cause their children to carry their burial shrouds. Some people are like this. They think that they are doing good, but God is their judge.'[58]

Once again, it is notable that in all his public statements before the Rabaa massacre, Gomaa appears to have carefully tempered his language to avoid the perception that he was actively goading on the military to massacre the protestors in post-coup Egypt. In fact, he had not yet reached his personal crescendo, publicly or privately, of encouraging the military to engage in mass slaughter. His remarks were still, as will become clear, quite measured, even when he privately suggested to the soldiers that the protestors were 'dogs of the Hellfire' who it was virtuous to kill. The crescendo would be reached four days after the Rabaa massacre left over a thousand civilians dead at the hands of the Egyptian security forces. When we consider that lecture in Chapter 7, we will find an Ali Gomaa who exults in the blood flowing in the streets of Egypt. But to better understand what exactly he was endorsing, we must first direct our attention to the actual Rabaa massacre in greater detail.

The Rabaa massacre

In the weeks following the coup of 3 July 2013, Egypt would witness a series of massacres of anti-coup protestors that would culminate in the atrocities of 14 August on the streets of Cairo that left well over a thousand people dead in a single day. Human Rights Watch (HRW), which conducted an extensive study of the massacres following the Egyptian coup, called its report *All According to Plan* to indicate the premeditated nature of the mass killings perpetrated by the Egyptian security forces under Sisi's leadership in the weeks following the Egyptian coup.[59] Among other evidence, HRW pointed to the fact that many of the protestors who had been killed by the security forces had been struck with sniper fire aimed at the head and upper torso, that is to say with kill shots. This was no accident. The estimates of the leaders of Egypt's own security forces were that several thousand would be killed in the clearing of the Rabaa sit-in on 14 August.

Their own later admission that roughly a thousand people had been killed on that day was described as almost certainly an underestimate by David Kirkpatrick, an American journalist who had been in Rabaa on the day of the massacre.[60] Egypt's interior minister later stated that only fifteen guns had been found, confirming the fact, widely reported in international media, that the tens of thousands going in and out of Rabaa over the past several weeks were overwhelmingly unarmed.[61] According to the assessment of aerial photos from 2 August by HRW, there were 'approximately 85,000 protesters at the Rab'a sit-in' on that day.[62] It was also the case that state-supporting media propagated narratives that characterized the sit-ins as being heavily populated by terrorists armed to the teeth and that the casualties were only a result of soldiers being fired upon and watching some of their colleagues fall. As a general claimed in an uncorroborated narrative purveyed on Egyptian media, only after many hours enduring such attacks from the armed protestors at Rabaa did the soldiers strike back to avenge their fallen. For him, the death of only a thousand illustrated their restraint. 'If we had kept firing shots, everyone there would have died.'[63] We will see in Chapter 7 that this narrative was also purveyed by Ali Gomaa. It bore no relation to the truth.

Rather, as innumerable witnesses corroborated from within Rabaa, including independent Western journalists, soldiers set upon the sit-in participants in the early morning with unrestrained firepower. HRW reported security forces firing on protestors 'a little after 6 am.' Snipers had been seen 'fortifying their defenses' through the night, and 'began firing from the first minutes of the dispersal.' No audible warning was provided regarding the impending assault, nor was there any safe passage provided to protestors. According to witnesses interviewed by HRW:

> Security forces [...] besieged demonstrators for most of the day, attacking from each of the five main entrances to the square and leaving no safe exit until the end of the day, including for injured protesters in need of medical attention and those desperate to escape. Instead, in many cases security forces fired on those who sought to escape[.][64]

In his book on the Egyptian revolution, Kirkpatrick of *The New York Times* describes '[h]undreds of riot police with Kalashnikovs,'[65] a deadly assault rifle used in wartime with the potential to discharge a hundred rounds per minute, setting upon protestors from the early morning. Throughout the weeks that followed the coup, the use of snipers using kill shots was also systematic on the part of the coup regime. HRW's specialist analysis of photos and witness evidence concluded that 'precise, fatal wounds to the head such as those sustained by several of the dead indicated that they had been deliberately targeted, with stabilized fire and the assistance of optical sights, both of which require expertise.'[66] Trained snipers using advanced weaponry were being deployed by the regime with the intent to kill virtually unarmed protestors. They were placed on rooftops, and according to dozens of witnesses, they were also firing from helicopters in the case of the Rabaa massacre. Rabaa was the most violent assault by far, according to HRW. As they note in their detailed report:

> Human Rights Watch researchers documented the dispersal of the Rab'a sit-in and found that security forces opened fire on protesters using live ammunition, with hundreds killed by bullets to their heads, necks, and chests. Human Rights Watch also found that security forces used lethal force indiscriminately, with snipers and gunmen inside and alongside APCs [armored personnel carriers] firing their weaponry on large crowds of protesters.[67]

At least a thousand people are thought to have died at Rabaa according to independent estimates, while the MB asserted that 2,600 had been killed.[68] It is not clear on what basis they made this assertion, but it is certainly clear that the Egyptian Health Ministry's claims of anything from 288 to 638 deaths were hardly credible and contradicted by statements of the interior minister at the time, Muhammad Ibrahim, and the prime minister, Hazem El Beblawi.[69] El Beblawi said in a newspaper interview that the clearing of protestors in Cairo's squares on 14 August resulted in 'close to 1,000' deaths. The interior minister on the other hand, who more closely oversaw the massacres, claimed that 'thousands' of protestors lost their lives at Rabaa. Recognizing that Rabaa had 'more than 20,000' attendees, he estimated that '10 percent of the people' were killed by Egyptian security forces.[70] This would place the number of deaths closer to the figure claimed by the MB. HRW's estimates were based on deaths they were able to confidently verify. However, given the atmosphere of intimidation created by the coup regime and its security forces which included forcing hundreds of family members to declare that their relatives who died in the anti-coup sit-ins had committed suicide, or in some cases, the regime's bulldozing and incinerating the dead bodies at Rabaa, the figures may be closer to those suggested by the interior minister and claimed by the MB.

The deaths were also inevitably far fewer in number than the many thousands who had been injured. The trauma suffered by a section of the Egyptian people, which had been cheered on by large numbers of their fellow Egyptians, would leave a mark on the Egyptian psyche whose repercussions will likely reverberate for generations. David Kirkpatrick, who himself survived the Rabaa massacre from the inside of the sit-in provides valuable insights into how the coup regime approached the clearing of Rabaa. His findings from investigations conducted over many years and reported in his clear-eyed and incisive book on the Arab revolutions are worth citing in full below, despite their length. After citing the enormous death toll of the massacre, he recounts HRW's conclusion that '[t]he indiscriminate and deliberate use of lethal force resulted in one of the world's largest killings of demonstrators in a single day in recent history.' He continues:

> Rabaa surpassed the Tiananmen Square massacre in China in 1989 and the Andijan massacre in Uzbekistan in 2005.
>
> Families and human rights groups told me that government coroners were forcing families to accept falsified death certificates to hide the real death toll (a common practice to lower riot statistics in many Arab autocracies).

> 'About three hundred deaths were written off as suicides,' Khaled Amin, the former brigadier general in the police, later told me. 'As though everyone just decided to kill themselves that day! Hospitals and morgues were pressured to do it. They told the families, "Call it a suicide or you don't get your kids."'

Kirkpatrick notes that for several years he sought out soldiers or policemen who had participated in the massacre so that he could hear their side of the narrative. They either 'refused or backed out' with Kirkpatrick being told that some were afraid of being caught discussing the massacre with a Westerner. He continues:

> The official story was a variation of the one that the Egyptian police have told many times to explain excessive violence: The demonstrators fired the first shot. The security forces, enraged by a noble zeal, avenged their fallen comrades. 'They started shooting and three martyrs fell from our side in less than forty-five minutes,' a police general insisted in a television interview a few days later. 'So how can we deal with gunfire? We can't just say, 'Be quiet." He maintained that the police had restrained themselves as best they could. 'If we had kept firing shots, everyone there would have died.'
>
> Then he added, even less plausibly, that most of the dead civilians were killed by 'friendly fire' from other Islamists anyway.
>
> None of this, of course, was ever remotely corroborated.
>
> Amin later told me that the security forces had used their standard procedure for any major operation. The senior officers 'charged up' the rank and file before the clearing of Rabaa ever began. The commanders reminded the troops about their friends and colleagues who had been killed in the past by violent Islamists and warned that the Rabaa sit-in was heavily armed. Prepare for fierce, violent resistance, the commanders instructed. The Islamists inside wanted the blood of the police.
>
> 'They really pump them up,' Amin said. 'The message is, 'They killed your friends, they have guns, they will kill you, they are scary.' The officers manipulate you emotionally and charge you up, so you can fire on others.'
>
> Amin had retired at the beginning of that summer, but he stayed in touch with his colleagues. 'No one talks about it because it is unforgivable,' he told me years later. 'Those who regret it are too scared to talk, and those who don't regret it are quiet.'[71]

Conclusion

This chapter illustrates the lengths to which counter-revolutionary ulama were part and parcel of the effort to bring to an end Egypt's short-lived democratic experiment in the summer of 2013. Specifically, it considered the efforts of two of Egypt's most senior scholars, the shaykh al-Azhar, Aḥmad al-Ṭayyib, and its former grand mufti, Ali Gomaa. Ṭayyib's activities were instrumental in legitimating the Egyptian coup, but he was not prepared to support the military regime's actions unconditionally—a tendency that would cause him to have much-publicized disagreements with Sisi in the years that followed, which ironically earned him a reputation for being something of a dissident despite his having been instrumental in bringing about the Sisi regime.[72] The role of offering unconditional fealty to the state would instead be taken on by Ali Gomaa. Indeed, Gomaa's counter-revolutionary activism, perhaps at the behest of the state's security forces, preceded the Egyptian coup by over a year with his sermon against candidate Morsi. By the time of the summer of 2013, he would be deploying his religious knowledge both publicly and privately to legitimate the Egyptian coup. However, going considerably further than his colleague Ṭayyib, he would also actively develop juristic arguments drawn from the Qur'an and hadith to legitimate the killing of protestors, ostensibly in self-defense. As we saw by the end of the present chapter, the Egyptian security forces would unleash deadly force against the anti-coup protestors throughout that summer culminating in the Rabaa massacre. I have argued in the foregoing that Ali Gomaa's intervention in this process was to provide religious legitimation for this use of violence.

As we will consider in Chapter 8, the Rabaa massacre would elicit an outpouring of condemnation from several anti-coup ulama besides Qaradawi, some of whom we will meet in the next chapter. However, as already alluded to, Gomaa had not yet articulated his most unequivocal endorsement of the massacre. This would be made most explicit in a private lecture he would give to the military four days after the Rabaa massacre as we shall consider in Chapter 7, which would only be leaked to the public two months after the mass killings. Towards the end of Chapter 8, we will consider the responses of pro-revolutionary ulama to these leaked recordings. Before we consider these post-Rabaa responses of the ulama, however, in the next chapter I will discuss the opposition of several Azharī ulama to the Egyptian coup and the smaller massacres that followed in July 2013. It is to their public rejection of the overturning of democracy by the coup that we shall now turn.

6

AZHARĪS OPPOSED TO THE COUP AND COUNTER REVOLUTIONS

(JUNE–JULY 2013)

Several prominent scholars took to the airwaves around the time of the Egyptian coup of 2013 to voice their opposition to the actions of the military that had put an end to Egypt's democratic transition. As might be expected, the most prominent of these was Yusuf al-Qaradawi who would turn eighty-seven that year. Despite his advanced age, the Egyptian scholar, from his adopted home of Qatar, had been an active observer, commentator, and participant from afar in debates about the Egyptian revolution. Besides Qaradawi, the present chapter will consider the responses of two other senior Azharīs to the Egyptian coup and the early post-coup massacres, namely Ḥasan al-Shāfiʿī and Muḥammad ʿImāra (d. 1441/2020). Shāfiʿī and ʿImāra were both senior Azharīs who sat on its Council of Senior Scholars (CSS) of which Qaradawi was also a member until the latter's resignation in December 2013 in protest against the shaykh al-Azhar and his support for the Egyptian coup.[1] Many other scholars, both in Egypt and beyond, publicly expressed their opposition to the coup and their horror at the massacres that followed. The sampling of views in this chapter, which will proceed chronologically as events unfolded in the summer of 2013, will hopefully be representative of these other scholars.

The present chapter begins by considering how Qaradawi and the IUMS responded to the major Egyptian protests planned against the Morsi presidency on 30 June and which paved the way for the coup of 3 July. Next, we will briefly study Qaradawi's fatwa against the coup. This will be followed by an exploration of Ḥasan al-Shāfiʿī and Muḥammad ʿImāra's respective condemnations of the coup and the smaller-scale atrocities that the military had perpetrated in its immediate aftermath. As noted earlier, we will consider the responses of these scholars to the Rabaa massacre in Chapter 8. As we shall see, in striking contrast with the pro-autocracy scholars, many of the objections of these ulama were grounded in their concern for the end of Egypt's democratic freedoms. The final section of the chapter considers the responses of these scholars to the escalating violence that the country was witnessing by the end of July. I conclude the chapter with a brief reflection on the political divergences exhibited by the arguments of the pro-democracy and pro-autocracy scholars in their early reactions to the coup.

The build up to the coup

As David Kirkpatrick has documented, the events of that summer had been planned long in advance with a good deal of funding and strategic support coming from the Gulf states of the UAE and Saudi Arabia.[2] By 30 June that year, when the UAE-funded and military-backed Tamarod (*Tamarrud*) movement had called for nationwide protests on the first anniversary of Morsi's term in office, the re-emergence of the military regime was all but a fait accompli. In the lead up to the protests, on 19 June, Shaykh al-Azhar Ṭayyib issued a fatwa declaring the protests legitimate, apparently in response to certain extreme voices who had declared joining them to constitute disbelief.[3] But Ṭayyib, it would seem, had an ulterior motive. Within days of issuing the fatwa, he would be in the company of General Sisi giving his blessing, as Egypt's most senior religious official, to the coup that removed Morsi, as we saw in the previous chapter. By contrast with Ṭayyib's fatwa supporting the protests, on 25 June Qaradawi, in his capacity as the President of the IUMS, issued a statement co-signed by the IUMS secretary general, ʿAlī al-Qaradāghī (b. 1368/1949), a prominent Azharī jurist in his own right, warning against the destabilization of Egypt and calling for the preservation of democracy.[4]

The protests, organized as they were with the logistical support of the Egyptian security forces and the deep state, perhaps inevitably proved some of the biggest in modern Egyptian history, although as noted earlier, Neil Ketchley and others have pointed out that the figures cited in the media, both domestic and international, were considerably overstated. On the same day as the protests, Qaradawi issued a plea on Al Jazeera's Egyptian sister channel, Mubasher Misr that lasted almost half an hour and was directed towards the Egyptian people.[5] In his plea he explicitly abjured partisanship and tried to call for the unity of all Egyptians against those who would divide them. Recalling his address to all the diverse groups in Egypt in his Friday sermon on 18 February 2011, a week after Mubarak's ouster, he plaintively asked:

> Did we not all partake in a single revolution? Were we not all victims of a tyrannical repressive regime? It stole our wealth, plundered our resources, deprived us of all of our rights, casting many of us into prison, oppressing many of us. But then God finished them off for us through our united revolution. Why don't we once again reunite? What is it that is separating us from one another? My dear brethren, I believe we must come to a mutual understanding among ourselves [...]. There is no such thing as a problem without a solution. All problems have their solutions.

Qaradawi recognized that the protestors were protesting against the presidency of Mohamed Morsi, but for Qaradawi, as was the case for the other scholars we shall see, what was ultimately at stake was the potential loss of the democratic order, and the reassertion of the police state that had dominated recent Egyptian history. He pointed out that it was perfectly reasonable to critique President Morsi, since for Muslims only God and His Prophet are above such criticism. He acknowledged the right of the protesting youths, who had sacrificed so much, to be heard by Morsi, but he adds that there needed to be a willingness to listen on all sides. In saying so, Qaradawi was acknowledging the severe polarization that had come about in Egyptian society, much of it engineered, it would later turn out, by pro-military media outlets in league with a deep state with apparently limitless funding—'a free-flowing spigot'—from counter-revolutionary Gulf states.[6] Qaradawi was thus fighting a losing battle in the counter-revolutionary war led by the UAE and Saudi Arabia. Three days after his address on Al Jazeera, on 3 July 2013, General Sisi finalized the coup through his declaration annulling the constitution and removing Morsi.

Qaradawi's fatwa against the coup

Qaradawi's opposition to the coup was declared forcefully in a detailed fatwa published on his Facebook page three days later on 6 July in which he asserted that it was an Islamic obligation to support Morsi and uphold the Egyptian constitution of 2012 so as to preserve democratic legitimacy.[7] He asserted that many of the ulama of the Azhar and ulama throughout the Arab and Islamic world joined him in this fatwa. Being the head of the IUMS at the time, he could perhaps claim to speak on behalf of many scholars around the globe, and this fatwa, though only authored by him, shared the sentiments of other scholars as we shall see in this chapter. Some of the arguments that Qaradawi presented in this fatwa appeared to be protesting a lost cause at this point but are still worth considering as reflective of principles of governance and Islamic law that he was passionately committed to. He argued that the appointment of Morsi in Egypt's first ever free and fair elections represented a commitment akin to a binding contract that meant that people had to accept him as their leader for the duration of his term. Notably, in Qaradawi's view, this applied to General Sisi who had given a pledge of allegiance to the president but was now usurping the latter's authority. Such an act, Qaradawi noted, was both in breach of the constitution and Islamic law.

At the heart of Qaradawi's protestations was his commitment to Islamic democratic constitutionalism that he had over many decades of scholarship incorporated into his understanding of Islamic law. For him, upholding Islamic democracy constituted upholding Islamic law and vice versa. More specifically on the Islamic legal side of the divide, he highlighted the obligation of rendering obedience to one's legitimately appointed rulers so long as they did not command to sin or commit an act of explicit disbelief (*kufr bawāḥ*). In both cases, Qaradawi insisted, Morsi had been faithful to Islamic law.

Qaradawi also took aim at Aḥmad al-Ṭayyib. Sisi's claim to be acting on behalf of the Egyptian people was belied by those who he picked as their representatives in his coup declaration. Qaradawi declared:

> The Grand Imam Dr Aḥmad al-Ṭayyib, President of [al-Azhar's] Council of Senior Scholars of which I am a member, did not consult any of us, nor did we give him a mandate to speak on our behalf. He is wrong to support rebellion (*khurūj*) against the country's legitimate president. He has gone against the consensus (*ijmāʿ*) of the umma and has not based his stance upon the Qur'an or the Sunna. In fact the entirety of the Qur'an and Sunna is in support of Morsi. [Ṭayyib] has gone against the ulama of the Islamic umma who do not sell their knowledge for the sake of anything of this world. All Ṭayyib referred to was: 'the perpetration of the lesser of two evils.' Whoever said that removing the legitimate president, rejecting the constitution which roughly two-thirds of the people consented to, and casting the country into a desolate wilderness that God only knows, is the lesser of two evils? Indeed, it is the greater evil that the Qur'an, Prophetic hadiths, and the

> teachings of the ulama have all warned against. If only Dr Ṭayyib had dealt with Morsi in the way that he dealt with Hosni Mubarak before him! Why the double standard? This is the ruination of the role of the Azhar which always stands with the people, not with despotic rulers.

Qaradawi's appeals to consensus may need a little explanation. He was not arguing that opposing Morsi in itself constituted a break with consensus—an argument that does not make much sense in Islamic legal terms. Rather the consensus being contravened was the *ijmāʿ* concerning the prohibition of rebelling against a ruler who was both legitimate and did not behave tyrannically. As noted in Chapter 1, rebellion was generally opposed in Sunni jurisprudence even against tyrannical rulers unless there was a virtual guarantee that such a rebellion would cause less fitna than would be entailed by the persistence of the tyrant. Where there was no tyranny or injustice involved, as Qaradawi held to be the case for Morsi's rule, rebellion was prohibited as a matter of juristic consensus. This was the consensus that Qaradawi now accused the shaykh al-Azhar of breaking with. Of course, Tayyib did not discuss the question of rebellion in his own short intervention backing the coup. Rather he argued that the removal of Morsi was the lesser of two evils, and here too we see that Qaradawi was unpersuaded.

Ultimately, Qaradawi feared the re-emergence of autocracy which he was witnessing with his very own eyes. As he viewed it, the recrudescence of state repression would only cause Egyptians to suffer and prevent Egypt's long-term development. He was even willing to appeal directly to Sisi in his fatwa, 'with great love and sincerity,' to do the right thing and reinstall Morsi in power. Clearly, before the massacres began, Qaradawi appeared to believe that Sisi could still be reformed. Qaradawi also extended a hand to the Coptic community, something he had done in the past, saying that Pope Tawadros did not speak in their name, thereby absolving them of association with the coup. Some weeks later, after churches were burnt in the wake of the Rabaa massacre, he would also condemn these attacks.[8] Indeed, Qaradawi's relationship with the Coptic community is worth exploring in a separate study. During the early post-coup period, Qaradawi made overtures towards Egypt's Christians on several occasions. In his interview on his Al Jazeera show, *al-Sharīʿa wa-l-Ḥayāh*, on 21 July 2013, he argued that not enough had been done to make Copts feel safe in Egypt by their Muslim compatriots.[9] He had made similar comments in the past.

In the peroration to his fatwa, he declared:

> I call from the depths of my heart upon the entire Egyptian people whom I love and would give my life for, without the desire for any reward or thanks, but only for the sake of God alone. I call upon them in Upper Egypt, on the coast, in the cities and villages, in the desert and the countryside. I call upon [all of] them: men and women, young and old, rich and poor, office workers and laborers, Muslims and Christians, liberals and Islamists, to stand as a single united front for safeguarding the gains of the revolution: freedom, democracy, and liberation from all dictatorship. We must not abandon it to an absolute ruler, military or civilian, for this is what some nations fell into, thereby losing their freedom which they did not regain for years—and there is no power except through God.

But Qaradawi's pleas fell on deaf ears and came too late to have any impact on political realities in Egypt. As Kirkpatrick documents, the Egyptian deep state had played its cards strategically from the very beginning. Its leaders had never supported the Morsi government. Indeed, many of Morsi's officials had actively sought to undermine him while ostensibly serving him. By the time Qaradawi had published his fatwa, the coup regime was preparing to embark on its massacres. Within two days, on 8 July, Egyptian security forces carried out their first massacre by opening fire on overwhelmingly unarmed anti-coup protestors at the Republican Guard headquarters in Cairo where Morsi was thought to be held—a fact later confirmed.[10] Official state figures put the number of deaths at sixty-one.[11] Qaradawi and his colleague Qaradāghī would issue a statement on behalf of the IUMS that day condemning the massacre and calling for 'the wise people (*ḥukamā'*)' of Egypt to intervene to prevent more bloodshed, but the writing was now on the wall.[12]

Ḥasan al-Shāfiʿī's statement

The Republican Guard massacre was an event that also elicited an extensive response and plea from another of Egypt's highest-ranking scholars, Ḥasan al-Shāfiʿī, who also sat on the Azhar's CSS. Shāfiʿī was a professor of theology and philosophy, and a scholarly practitioner of Sufism, but he was also notable as an official advisor (*mustashār*) to the shaykh al-Azhar, a fact featured prominently on-screen by Al Jazeera when they published his remarks. In a twenty-five-minute statement broadcast by the channel, Shāfiʿī condemned both the massacre of that day and the coup that preceded it.[13] In it, he referred to his youth when he served prison sentences in 1954 and 1965 enduring 'torture of a kind we have never read the likes of in the history books.' He had been imprisoned as a member of the MB. Although he appears to have had no formal affiliation with the organization for decades, a MB website describes him as a regular student of the organization's founder Ḥasan al-Bannā when Shāfiʿī was in his teens.[14] In the course of his statement, Shāfiʿī highlighted that he had no involvement in party politics and that for over fifty years he had not been a member of any political party or group, signaling that he had not been a formal member of the MB for more than half a century.[15]

Shāfiʿī's statement was in two parts, the first of which he said he wanted to publish two days earlier on 6 July, which would have corresponded with Qaradawi's fatwa that was critical of the coup and calling Egyptians to demand Morsi's reinstatement.[16] As we shall see, in many respects, Shāfiʿī's statement bore a similar message presented more diplomatically, perhaps in part because of the risks of forthrightness in the post-coup Egyptian context. In it, Shāfiʿī indirectly characterized the events of 3 July as a military coup against a constitution that had been prepared by a 'balanced elected body' and was approved by the popular will in a free and fair referendum according to independent observers. He also suggested that there had been subversive coordination between arms of the state and the military that ultimately led to the coup, even though it had been 'brought out in an elegant and civilian garb, with caution and secrecy, and with careful calculation.' In saying so, Shāfiʿī was taking a considerable personal risk, since the coup leadership and its powerful supporters in the media were casting those who called it a coup as potentially seditious.

Addressing the coup leadership directly, asserting the right of the average citizen to do so, he pointed out that despite the media blackout in Egypt, they were doubtless aware through their sources that there were 'millions' in the squares of Egypt protesting about the coup. These included protestors both for and against the coup, he reminded the coup leaders, and asserted that they were all Egyptians. 'You have announced that the army and the police would not harm any citizen expressing his opinion peacefully without breaking the law. Have you then considered how you will return these millions [*sic*] protesting the [coup] to their homes and their work?' Shāfiʿī then mentioned the reports in newspapers that were actively supportive of the coup that demonstrated the use of force against protestors. Official figures put the deaths at over fifty, he noted, and the injured at over a thousand. 'Are these not protected souls the killing of whom God has prohibited? Are the current authorities not responsible for protecting all of these people?'

Shāfiʿī's questions illustrated the level of the crisis in Egypt which would only worsen in the coming days. It was unclear to him how the coup regime could assert its authority in the face of anti-coup protests without potentially using deadly force. He also suggested that the calls to national reconciliation were meaningless in a context in which people faced the real possibility of death at the hands of the regime. If they were serious about reconciliation, he argued, they had to release all political prisoners, 'including Mohamed Morsi.' Yet Shāfiʿī was still pragmatic. Throughout his statement, he showed deference to the coup regime by not leveling accusations too directly towards its leadership. In this context, he proposed a possible solution, namely that a committee for reconciliation (for which, he noted, he had been suggested as a potential member) should undertake a genuine initiative to effect reconciliation among the aggrieved parties. As an advisor to the shaykh al-Azhar, he suggested that the shaykh al-Azhar's involvement could also facilitate this reconciliation.

Shāfiʿī also called for the reinstatement of Islamic satellite channels and opposition newspapers that had been closed down after the coup. He pointed out that during the past year that Morsi had been in power,

> political parties, newspapers, satellite channels, and cartoonists had continued to disparage Dr Mohamed Morsi, his children, and his family, attributing to him every fault, and [accusing him of] being an American agent. Despite that, he did not close a newspaper or take a journalist to court.[17] Is this then the freedom that exists today, as some courageous journalists have asked?

He noted the absence of the loud voices in unions of media workers and creative artists who had clamored about freedom of speech, freedom of thought and human rights during Morsi's era. He implied the existence of a double standard given their silence after the coup.

Shāfiʿī next addressed what was arguably the core of his message, the importance of the 2011 revolution. He praised the revolution for realizing 'major victories' among the most important of which he characterized as 'breaking the barrier of fear' (*kasr ḥājiz al-khawf*) that prevented people from speaking out against the repression that had characterized the politics of Egypt for decades. Breaking down this barrier, the revolution 'spread the feeling of freedom and democracy once again.' These achievements, Shāfiʿī added, required public officials to learn patience so that they could endure the criticism of some of their fellow citizens as an inevitable but ultimately positive cost of living in a free society. Another achievement he highlighted was the fact that all political and ideological trends in Egypt were brought out into the open, something that he described as a 'major gain for Egyptian political life.' He continued:

> The 25 January revolution will not be abrogated or changed. [...]. It will always remain standing, by God's will, in the hearts of its believers (*al-mu'minīn bi-hā*) among the Egyptian peoples. The only people who rebelled against it were the corrupt and opportunists who waged war against it with every weapon. It is political foolishness, indeed it is disgraceful for a revolutionary to work with the likes of such people, or protest alongside them, or call them back to the political arena. Anyone who permits himself to appear alongside these symbols [of the ancien régime], who are well-known to the Egyptian people, is only gambling with his own future, and harming himself rather than the revolution.

Shāfiʿī's endorsement of the 2011 revolution was clearly enthusiastic, belying the suggestion that Azhar officialdom and Neo-traditionalism more generally were opposed to the revolutions and were consistent in siding with the coup regime. Rather there was clearly a tug-of-war within the Azhar between what Mohammad Fadel has called 'authoritarian' and 'republican' ulama—that is, ulama who supported autocracy as Islamically legitimate and opposed political freedoms versus ulama who embraced political freedom and opposed absolute autocracy.[18] In other words, and at risk of stating the obvious, the Azhar is a diverse institution with both Neo-traditionalist and Islamist ideas ensconced at the highest echelons of the institution and, at times, within the same individual, without this being perceived as a contradiction.

Returning to Shāfiʿī's statement, he next made a more conciliatory gesture by expressing his 'love for every Egyptian soldier because [each of them] protects me and defends my country. [...] But I cannot accept for our armed forces to become entangled in politics and governance.' Rather, Shāfiʿī argued for a state run by civilians with the army obeying the civilian authorities. With this, and with a reminder to his Muslim listeners that they would have to answer to God for their actions in the next life, Shāfiʿī concluded his longer first message. The second message was written in response to the Republican Guard massacre that took place early that morning. This message was a stern warning of the Islamic scriptural condemnation of murder. He noted that nearly fifty protestors had been killed that morning—though as we have seen official figures put the numbers of dead even higher—and several hundred had been injured all while they were praying dawn prayers.[19] Official reports, he added, claim that this was the work of terrorists, but this was contradicted, Shāfiʿī says, by ten eyewitnesses. Still, as with the rest of his statement, he never directly leveled an accusation at the coup regime. Rather he argued that even if one were to assume the accuracy of official reports, the security forces have a duty to protect peaceful protestors. He asked:

> Is this not an obligation of the political authorities? That they do not distinguish between their citizens and do not neglect their duties? Is this how low we have fallen in disdaining people's sacred lives and blood? Does Egypt not have freedom and revolution? Who will condemn these catastrophic calamities?

Shāfiʿī's careful balancing of indirectness and directness, and his willingness to entertain official propaganda (about 'terrorists') while trying to convey a rebuke, was arguably a sign that the coup regime had successfully been able to re-instill fear among Egyptians. Given that the regime had shown itself ready to use lethal force, it is understandable that people would not wish to voice their opinions more explicitly by challenging their murderous behavior more directly. In closing, Shāfiʿī noted the risks he faced in speaking out but vowed to continue to speak the truth with God's help. Ultimately, his message sounded more plaintive than threatening. Sadly, he would end up making similar statements in the weeks that followed in response to ongoing atrocities, likely at very great personal risk to himself given his prominence in the Egyptian establishment and his advisory relationship vis-à-vis the considerably younger shaykh al-Azhar. However, Shāfiʿī was not the only senior Azharī to speak out in the way he did. His prolific colleague on the Azhar's CSS, Muḥammad ʿImāra, also exemplified an alim with many decades at the heart of the Azhar establishment who would not shy away from speaking out against the coup and the massacres that followed, as we shall now see.

Another Azharī's statement: Muḥammad ʿImāra

The late Muḥammad ʿImāra was perhaps the most prolific author in Egypt in the early twenty-first century. With over 200 published works, he was also one of the most prolific Islamic scholars in the world. As well as serving on the CSS until his death in 2020, he had long been a member of the Azhar's Islamic Research Academy as the editor-in-chief of the Azhar's official scholarly journal. Yet, he was also one of the world's leading (mainstream) Islamist ulama with extensive writings in the area of political jurisprudence and political philosophy, despite never having been a member of the MB. Once again, his presence over many decades at the heart of the Azhar establishment illustrates that mainstream Islamism is not alien to the Azhar but rather part and parcel of its diversity. Qaradawi, who until December 2013 also sat on the CSS, is another example illustrative of this fact.

It should come as no surprise then that ʿImāra resolutely opposed the coup of 2013. His reasons are characteristically systematic as outlined in a concise 'statement to the people' that he read out on 13 July, ten days after the coup and in the wake of some of the massacres that the security forces had perpetrated.[20] It read as follows:

In the name of God the Beneficent, the Merciful

I had thought that my stance did not require announcement, but in light of questions from some quarters, let me say:

1. What took place on 3 July 2013 is a military coup against a democratic transition whose path had been opened by the revolution of 25 January 2011, whose form had been fashioned in the new constitution [of 2012] which specified the rules regarding the peaceful transition of power by way of the ballot box, as is the practiced norm in all democratic states.
2. This military coup turns back the clock in Egypt more than sixty years when the repressive police state was established which relied on a policy of ostracizing the opposition until it reached a point at which the entire Egyptian people were politically marginalized. Its will was falsified, and it had to endure being terrorized by a security apparatus.
3. The path that this coup has opened not only harms the democratic transition of the umma, but also harms the armed forces because of [politics] diverting it from its original role. The military defeats that we suffered under the police state are a warning for those who reflect.
4. What makes this coup even more dangerous is that some desire to enact a coup against the Islamic identity of Egypt which has been established and deeply rooted through history. This would open the door to sectarian fitna (*fitna ṭāʾifiyya*) which we alert people to and whose evil consequences we warn against.
5. The constitution which was submitted to a popular referendum has become a social, political, legal (*qānūnī*), and religious (*sharʿī*) contract. In accord with this contract, the democratically elected president has a legal and religious agreement (*bayʿa*) with the nation, four years in length. The people, according to the law (*qānūn*) and the religion (*sharʿ*) are bound by their contracts. On this basis, his removal by a military coup is null and void according to the law and the religion, and everything that is built on an invalid basis is also null and void.

May God protect Egypt from the dangers of this coup, and grant it a way out of its ordeal.

Dr Muḥammad ʿImāra[21]

Like his Azharī predecessors Qaradawi and Shāfiʿī, ʿImāra called the removal of Morsi from the presidency a coup at a time when such statements coming from a scholar residing in Egypt placed him at risk of being targeted by the authorities. Like his colleagues, he considered the 2011 revolution to have been a much needed opening for Egyptian society and Egyptian politics, bringing it into the modern world by establishing a democratic constitution. Indeed, ʿImāra was the author of a short work published in 2011 in response to the revolutions entitled *The 25 January Revolution and the Breaking of the Barrier of Fear* (*Thawrat 25 Yanāyir wa-Kasr Ḥājiz al-Khawf*). In this work, he spoke about the instituting of Islamically inflected democratic norms that brought the political sphere out of the repressive norms of dictatorship and towards greater freedom and democracy while preserving Islamic values. For all of these ulama, unlike the authoritarian scholars such as Gomaa and Jifri, dictatorship was completely antithetical to Islamic values; democracy however, while being a political technology developed by non-Muslims, could, like other technologies, be adapted to Islamic norms as ulama like ʿImāra and Qaradawi had attempted in their scholarly writings on the subject.

For ʿImāra, the possibility presented by the Egyptian revolution of 2011 of transforming these theoretical writings into practice now looked to be undermined, thus taking Egypt backwards by 'sixty years' rather than forward towards the possibility of a genuinely Islamic society. Instead, Egypt now faced a renewed police state that would, once again, with absolute authority, crush any opposition, a view that would be vindicated in the years that followed. ʿImāra, like Shāfiʿī before him, also signaled a threat that these scholars perceived, which was directed towards Egypt's Islamic identity, given that its Islamic satellite channels were shut down and its largest Islamist organization was cast as the enemy. He warned that this could result in sectarian fitna. In some respects, this is a useful conceptualization of Islamists. While there is no doubt that ʿImāra is not advocating for casting Islamists as a sect in any pejorative sense, as I have suggested in the Introduction, the Neo-traditionalism of scholars like Ali Gomaa should be seen as a denomination that is in competition with other Sunni denominations, in which I include Islamism. In using the term denomination, I deliberately eschew the more problematic term 'sect' and its derivatives to discuss intra-Sunni groupings. In this context, ʿImāra's warnings about 'sectarian fitna' may be recognized as a warning against intra-denominational disagreements between Islamists, Neo-traditionalists, and other political groupings in the Egyptian public sphere devolving into bloodletting, something that would unfortunately come to pass in the massacres of Islamists and their pro-democracy sympathizers in the weeks that followed.

Repression would force Islamists underground which, as Shāfiʿī signaled in his statement and which scholars like Qaradawi had written about as long ago as the 1970s, had the potential to give rise to extremism. In his 1978 work, *Ẓāhirat al-Ghuluww fī al-Takfīr*, Qaradawi speaks of the deviant tendencies that are begotten by repression that forces debate underground rather than allowing it out in the open. Extreme ideas had the opportunity to take hold in conditions of repression, he argues, in a way they never otherwise could.[22] In fact, the Egyptian security forces might even have desired such an outcome, as it would justify their own existence. As the American Rabaa protestor and human rights activist Mohamed Soltan has noted of his time when incarcerated in Egypt, Egyptian authorities would appear to deliberately allow ISIS members to freely recruit among inmates.[23] The existence of groups like ISIS provides the perfect pretext for authoritarian states everywhere to maintain their tight grip on power. It does not appear beyond the realm of possibility that their existence, within certain limits, would almost be encouraged by authoritarian states like Egypt.[24]

ʿImāra concluded his statement in more legal terms. When it came to the law, both secular, in the form of the *qānūn*, and religious, in the form of fiqh, ʿImāra argued that the constitution symbolized a contract that was binding on the populace given that the populace had assented to it in the form of a referendum. Accordingly, the election of Morsi represented a bilateral contract between the people and the president, which was to last four years and could not be annulled unilaterally. Concomitantly, ʿImāra averred, the coup and all its consequences had no standing before the law, be it secular or religious. In essence, he lamented that there was no more rule of law in post-coup Egypt, but rather only rule by force.

On 15 July, in a phone interview with the London-based Islamist-oriented al-Ḥiwār channel two days after his statement was published, ʿImāra once again pointed out the illegal nature of the coup.[25] This time, he indirectly pointed out the inconsistency of the shaykh al-Azhar's position by noting that 'the Azhar' had issued a fatwa shortly before 30 June stating that non-violent protests were a protected right of citizens. He pointed out that the self-same fatwa described armed rebellion (*al-khurūj al-musallaḥ*) against a legitimate ruler (*al-ḥākim al-sharʿī*) as a great sin and transgression.[26] How then, he asked, can we describe a coup led by the armed forces, repeating the word 'armed' (*musallaḥ*) three times to emphasize that this obviously constituted an armed rebellion, against 'a ruler who was democratically elected in a free election' with a mandate to rule for four years. He directed this question to all citizens including those in the armed forces, potentially at great personal risk.[27]

Over the course of the next month, all of these prominent Azharī scholars would continue to vocally express their opposition to the coup in a variety of media. Qaradawi would speak on his Al Jazeera show only once during this period, on 21 July, but would appear several times on Al Jazeera Mubasher to make lengthy statements against the coup regime's actions. In his show on 21 July, he spent the lion's share of the time discussing Egypt, reiterating his opposition to the coup and calling for Morsi's reinstatement.[28] He also stated that the opponents of the coup were not to use violent means to voice their opposition, a point he insistently reiterated even after the Rabaa massacre, as we shall see in Chapter 8.[29]

Sisi's mandate to confront 'terrorism'

The next major event in Egypt would take place on 24 July. The coup regime's leader, General Sisi, called on the Egyptian people to grant him a mandate by joining a protest in Tahrir Square on 26 July so that he could confront 'terrorism,' a thinly veiled reference to anti-coup protestors who had gathered in several squares in Egypt, most notably in Rabaa Square in Cairo. In response, several of the scholars who were mentioned earlier in this chapter voiced their opposition to the call. Qaradawi and Qaradāghī immediately issued a joint statement on behalf of the IUMS declaring joining these protests, which they characterized as a call to civil war, to be religiously prohibited.[30] On the same day, Qaradawi took to Al Jazeera Arabic to make a twenty-minute statement to camera urging Egyptians not to support Sisi's call to protests in two days' time. He also condemned Sisi for characterizing those who were peacefully protesting against his coup as terrorists and thereby pitting Egyptians against one another as mortal enemies.[31] On the following day, in a telephone interview with Al Jazeera Mubasher, Shāfiʿī called on people not to attend the coup regime-sanctioned protests which he portrayed as an effort to legitimate violence against innocent lives whose loss every citizen would be asked about in the next life.[32]

Despite these calls, the pro-coup protests of 26 July went ahead with the full backing of the coup regime which used them as a pretext for a major escalation of violence against anti-coup protestors. The numbers of dead would now begin to rise steeply when the security forces intervened to break up anti-coup protests. It did not take long for the regime's ferocity to manifest. On the following day, the regime unleashed lethal force on demonstrators in Cairo with security forces on the street and snipers at a distance firing many kill shots aimed at the 'head, chest or neck,' according to HRW.[33] In all, official Egyptian figures put the numbers of dead at ninety-five, although HRW believed the actual number to be higher. All of the scholars cited earlier took to Al Jazeera Mubasher immediately to condemn the massacre of overwhelmingly unarmed protestors.

The scholars loudly condemned the deadly slaughter which, until that point, was the largest of the post-coup massacres. Qaradawi took to Al Jazeera Mubasher to denounce the coup regime in a message that lasted roughly half an hour.[34] Invoking Islamic scriptures and Islamic law, he called on the security forces to refuse to carry out orders to murder members of their own 'Egyptian family' in the month of Ramadan for fear of God's punishment. In language reminiscent of his similar calls from 2011, he insisted that being ordered to kill protestors would be no excuse before God. Qaradawi also issued a joint statement with Qaradāghī on behalf of the IUMS condemning the massacres in Egypt.[35] Ḥasan al-Shāfiʿī made a statement during an eight-minute interview on Al Jazeera Mubasher on that day as well. The sadness mingled with outrage in his voice was palpable. He conveyed reports of over a hundred deaths, insisting that 'not all of them were from the MB' and further that not everyone at Rabaa Square, from where the protest had emerged, were MB members. He also reported that roughly four thousand had been injured. Similar to what HRW would report a year later, Shāfiʿī declared that 'bullets were directed at heads and chests.' 'We have not seen the like [of this violence] even from colonialists.'[36]

Continuing, he stated:

> I speak as a member of the Council of Supreme Scholars of the noble Azhar with whom God has a covenant to speak [the truth] and not conceal it. God, Most High, says: 'Indeed, those who conceal what We sent down of clear proofs and guidance after We made it clear for the people in the Scripture—those are cursed by God and cursed by those who curse' (Q. 2:159).
>
> I address all the ulama of Egypt, at the head of whom is the esteemed shaykh al-Azhar who declared what the [Prophet] affirmed previously, that the blood of a Muslim is more sacred to God than the Kaaba, and that its destruction stone by stone is less grave than the spilling of innocent blood.[37] [...] I address the ulama of the entire Muslim world—in Saudi Arabia, the Gulf, Syria, Iraq, Pakistan, India,

> Malaysia, Indonesia, in the Maghreb (*al-Maghrib al-ʿArabī*), and Africa—I turn to address them all in this moment: 'O servants of God, four thousand injured and a hundred killed in a single hour or two in a battle that is not against the Zionists who have usurped the Holy Land, but rather with unarmed defenseless Egyptian Muslims?!'
>
> I call upon people of honor in the entire Muslim world whose human consciences cannot tolerate these repeated massacres—at the Republican Guard [on 8 July], at the Minaṣṣa Memorial [on July 27], at al-Qā'id Ibrāhīm Mosque in Alexandria [on July 26]—how can these events be characterized? When will the series of needless and vengeful mass killings end? What might those clutching rifle triggers do, those who are shooting at heads and hearts, as the head doctor at the field hospital has stated. Let them shoot at feet and legs if we are craving blood! We have never witnessed anything like this, even in the severest eras of dictatorship. [Gamal] Abdel Nasser never killed protestors against him in 1967. In the history of Egypt, the death of one or two people was sufficient to end a ministry and change a harsh ruler. How then can we characterize those who kill their own people en masse in the Arab world by those who are portrayed as pious and devoted to the Qur'an.[38]

Shāfiʿī concluded with a prayer beseeching God to put an end to this episode. He also called on people to speak out against these outrages (*ankir al-munkar*) in the spirit of commanding right and forbidding wrong, citing the Arabic proverb: 'one who fails to speak out for the truth is a mute devil.' He criticized the silence of ElBaradei 'who said after a single person had been killed during Morsi's tenure, "he has lost his legitimacy!"' He concluded with a prayer asking God to absolve his own weakness in his old age due to which he was unable to confront the actions of the coup regime more effectively and bring an end to the turmoil. Shāfiʿī's statement, being aired on Al Jazeera could not have reached a great deal of Egyptians at the time, vilified as it was by pro-coup media as a mouthpiece for the MB. But it did illustrate the overwhelming sense of horror felt by one of Egypt's most respected Islamic scholars in the face of the Egyptian coup. It could not contrast more strikingly with that of Shāfiʿī's younger colleague, Ali Gomaa, who had both publicly been championing the coup's legitimacy and privately been encouraging such slaughter.

In addition to the above scholars, Muḥammad ʿImāra also made a statement in a public gathering in Cairo that was broadcast on Al Jazeera Mubasher.[39] Like Shāfiʿī, he referred to a darkness in Egypt that had not been witnessed even in the days of colonialism. In keeping with his earlier statement, he lamented the loss of a promising democratic transition (*al-*

taḥawwul al-dīmuqrāṭī) which had been the 'primary gain' of the 2011 revolution. Like his earlier statement, he also highlighted that the greatest harm of this coup would be to the Egyptian military itself. 'When the army became preoccupied with politics and governance [in the 1950s] it resulted in its greatest defeat in modern history [in 1967 at the hands of Israel].' The historical consequences of the police state, he pointed out, had been dire. He thus concluded:

> For this reason, we wish to return, not to a particular individual or to a particular political party, but rather to the democratic transition which was the primary gain of the 25 January revolution. Therefore, in the midst of this innocent blood that has been spilt in a manner without precedent in this noble country, we want the return of the [political] legitimacy, the legitimacy of the democratic transition by way of the constitution that was subject to a popular referendum [...], a constitution we take pride in. It [also] contains means of amendment, since it is not a Qur'an or a holy book.[40]

The scores of deaths and the shocked protestations of these scholars notwithstanding, Egypt had not seen the worst of the massacres of that summer. That would come on 14 August at Rabaa square, as we have already seen, when the regime, with some assistance from Ali Gomaa, was gearing up for 'one of the world's largest killings of demonstrators in a single day in recent history.'[41] In the days following the 27 July massacre, most of the scholars we have met in this chapter do not appear to have made any public statements as Egypt remained quiet for the remainder of Ramadan that year. The only exception was the most senior scholar among them, namely Yusuf al-Qaradawi, who gave a nearly hour-long homily on Al Jazeera Mubasher on 4 August, corresponding with the twenty-seventh night of Ramadan, a night that many Muslims believe to be the 'Night of Power' (*Laylat al-Qadr*) mentioned in the Qur'an (Q. 97).[42]

In his message, he praised those camped out in protest against the coup in the squares of Egypt as engaged in an unarmed but essential jihad for realizing their political rights and for a democratic future for Egypt. He exhorted them to remain patient and steadfast in their protest. Perhaps he felt that the greater their numbers, the less likely it was that they would be violently attacked when the entire world was watching. Unfortunately for the protestors, none of these things would matter on 14 August, when the massive slaughter only elicited handwringing from the international community and exultation from powerful voices within Egypt. These voices included one that we have already seen, namely Ali Gomaa.

Conclusion

The foregoing illustrates that although Egypt's most senior official scholars were supportive of the coup, the Azhar's internal response, even from its most important scholarly bodies, was not unified in the summer of 2013. While Shaykh al-Azhar Aḥmad al-Ṭayyib, the most politically powerful figure within the institution, supported both protests against Morsi and the military coup, other figures, including the advisor to the shaykh al-Azhar, were resolutely opposed to it. Their reasoning, in contrast with those of Ṭayyib, included closely argued engagements with the Islamic juristic tradition. In keeping with his opposition to rebellion in general, Qaradawi argued that the coup constituted rebellion against the ruler. Of course, Qaradawi's opposition to rebellion in favor of peaceful protests was voiced, as we saw in earlier chapters, in opposition to tyrannical rulers of questionable legitimacy. In the case of Morsi, Qaradawi was arguing that he was far from a tyrant and his legitimacy had been ratified in free and fair processes, both in terms of the presidential elections and the constitutional referendum. The same arguments were made by Ḥasan al-Shāfiʿī and Muḥammad ʿImāra. Thus, all three scholars argued that a rebellion had been undertaken against a legitimate ruler without just cause. As Qaradawi noted, this went against Islamic juristic consensus.

Ṭayyib may in fact have recognized this. After all, his argument for the coup, brief as it was, spoke of the lesser of two evils, and so he arguably recognized that the coup was an evil. In Ṭayyib's assessment, however, it was necessary to restore order. Quite why he considered this to be the case, he did not say, and it is possible, given his timorous objections to the atrocities that followed the coup that he may subsequently have thought that the evils of the coup were greater than a continuing Morsi presidency would have been. If he did have a change of heart, however, he never publicly acknowledged this. Under the coup regime, it would probably have done him no favors to do such a thing, even if he felt strongly about it. He was a senior official in a regime that had shown itself to be ruthless in crushing its opponents, and his own personal and sectoral interests (as shaykh al-Azhar) would arguably make it dangerous for him and the Azhar to object too strongly against the new regime. To be sure, there was no clear evidence that he felt that the coup was the greater evil.

Whatever the case may be, this chapter has sought to show that other senior Azharīs certainly did feel that it was. As we shall see in the next chapter however, unlike Ṭayyib, there was one scholar in Azhar officialdom who was willing to offer unconditional support for the coup regime. Specifically, we will be considering Ali Gomaa's celebratory response to the Rabaa massacre, both in its immediate aftermath as well as in the years that followed when he would periodically be asked about his involvement in it.

7

ALI GOMAA

CELEBRATING THE RABAA MASSACRE (AUGUST 2013–JANUARY 2017)

Two chapters ago, we saw Ali Gomaa's initial enthusiasm for the Egyptian coup manifest in the dual discursive strategy of playing up the nobility of the Egyptian army in public while encouraging the army in private to recognize its right to engage in violence to gain full control of Egypt. Not long afterwards, on 14 August 2013, the army embarked on violently clearing tens of thousands of peaceful protestors who had camped out for weeks in Rabaa Square in eastern Cairo in order to voice their opposition to the coup of General Sisi. It was a defining day in the history of modern Egypt and, indeed, the modern Middle East, marking the point at which the democratic aspirations of the most populous nation in the region were crushed. Jean-Pierre Filiu has suggested that the muted response of the international community to the massacres may have emboldened the Syrian Assad regime to perpetrate the devastating chemical attacks on opposition strongholds a week later, leading to nearly 1,500 deaths including that of 426 children.[1] As both Filiu and David Kirkpatrick have persuasively argued, the recrudescence of a rapacious military regime in Egypt ushered in a dark era for the Middle East that created fertile ground for the rise and spread of similarly violent entities throughout the region, most notably ISIS, as I will discuss further in Chapter 9.

The present chapter returns to the figure of Ali Gomaa and his statements, both private and public, after the Rabaa massacre. I begin with a presentation and analysis of his private post-Rabaa lecture to the security establishment, followed by a consideration of his public-facing support for it in a lengthy interview a few days later. In the latter part of the chapter, I consider Ali al-Jifri's forceful defense of Gomaa during the post-coup period, including after the Rabaa massacre. Towards the end of the chapter, I address the longer-term impact of Gomaa's support for Rabaa on his reputation. In the conclusion, I briefly reflect on how Gomaa's support for the massacres may affect Neo-traditionalism more widely.

As noted earlier, the atrocities at Rabaa and elsewhere on 14 August hardly marked the end of Gomaa's work alongside the military, despite some of his colleagues like Ṭayyib distancing themselves from the slaughter. However, denunciations of Gomaa started emerging in the days after Rabaa as clips of the private recordings of his pre-Rabaa message to the security forces began to emerge. These clips were deemed to constitute a fatwa legitimating the killing of protestors. The excoriation of Gomaa would appear to have reached a climax in October when his post-Rabaa lecture given to the security forces on 18 August, and which we shall consider presently, was leaked to the press.[2] Al Jazeera reported on leaked clips from Gomaa's lecture on 8 October, unleashing a firestorm of criticism directed towards him. In response, Hānī Ḍawwah, a media liaison working at the office of the Egyptian grand mufti, released the full video that had been recorded by the Ministry of Defense's DMA.[3] In the video description on YouTube where Ḍawwah had released the video on his personal channel, he complained that Gomaa's lecture had been misrepresented through cherry-picking certain snippets and taking them out of context. We shall have the opportunity to consider this charge below.

Ḍawwah's publication of the video once again illustrates the remarkably close relationship between official ulama and the military regime. Although it had been recorded by the DMA, it was released by the office of the grand mufti which had, until his retirement in early 2013, been occupied by Gomaa for ten years. Perhaps it is unsurprising that officials within Dār al-Iftāʾ would not hesitate to defend a scholar they had worked with for so long, no matter how apparently shocking the scholar's statements. The lecture, which is translated in Appendix 3, contains Gomaa's most deadly declarations against anti-coup protestors to this day, most infamously including his exhortations to the security forces to 'shoot to kill.' It is to an examination of this lecture that we now turn.

Gomaa's private post-Rabaa lecture to the security forces

On 18 August 2013, four days after the horrors of the Rabaa massacre had been carried out by Egyptian security forces, Ali Gomaa gave a speech at a large lecture theater with hundreds of uniformed officers in attendance. At the center of the front row sat General Abdel Fattah al-Sisi and Minister of Interior Muhammad Ibrahim. The topic of the lecture, doubtless carefully selected for the moment, was 'Islam's tolerance.' As unusual as the topic may seem after potentially thousands of Egyptians had been slaughtered in the streets in recent weeks, it was arguably a notion that needed to be reinforced in the eyes of any officers who felt that their actions were out of step with Islamic ethics. If they felt this way, it was Gomaa's task to disabuse them of this sentiment, a task he would embark on with a passion.

Opening his speech with customary prayers, he immediately singled out Sisi and Ibrahim for praise and prayer. The language he used draws from a Qur'anic prayer that was directed towards the Companions of the Prophet whose rank in Sunni Islam is greater than all subsequent generations of Muslims. 'May God be pleased with you, and may He please you.'[4] Among a litany of prayers he recited while addressing them along with the officers in the room was for God to guide 'their gunfire' (*saddada ramyakum*). 'Stand firm,' he exhorted, perhaps in the face of the intense criticism they had been receiving from around the world after the Rabaa massacre. 'Be patient collectively and individually, for God, Most High, is your Supporter,' he counselled. 'The [enemy] shall be vanquished, and they shall turn their backs [in retreat].' This sentence is a verse from the Qur'an (Q. 54:45) that was traditionally understood as referring to the disbelievers from the Quraysh, the Meccan tribe of the Prophet that had, for much of his Prophetic mission, been his fiercest enemies. In this instance, Gomaa was using it against other Muslims.

This is notable because it is something that he would condemn the Khawārij for doing less than fifteen minutes later in the same speech. In keeping with historical reports from Companions of the Prophet, one of the distinctive characteristics of the Khawārij, for which they were censured early on, was their tendency to invoke verses of the Qur'an addressing disbelievers to attack other Muslims. As Gomaa said a few minutes after appearing to do just this, 'They take verses that God revealed regarding the polytheists, and use them against the Muslims.' Gomaa would level this criticism at other groups he considered to be Khawārij, notably ISIS, in

2014.[5] Yet, he seemed to do precisely this when addressing the military in 2013. He was quoting a verse that was understood as a condemnation of the disbelievers from the tribe of Quraysh and using these verses to attack other Muslims. This was presumably not because Gomaa considered the Khawārij to in fact be disbelievers. As he makes clear elsewhere, he adheres to the mainstream Sunni position that deems the Khawārij to be Muslims, even if they were misguided Muslims.[6] It may have been an unintentional slip up, but it may also reflect his disregard of such principles in fashioning a private religious justification that served the military's needs of unifying its forces behind the extirpation of the MB from Egyptian society. As we have seen, in his more public discourse, Gomaa did not appear to use such a strategy to condemn the MB.

Gomaa's praise of the security forces continued in his speech: 'Know that you are in the right (*ḥaqq*). Let no one detract from the clarity of your vision. Let no one detract from your path, for you are traveling on the path of God. God is the destination of all of you.' Gomaa asserted that the Sharia sanctioned their actions in its guise as God's law, but additionally asserted that innumerable dreams had been seen by the righteous, both saintly Muslims (*awliyā'*) and descendants of the Prophet (*Ahl al-Bayt*), all in support of the actions of the security forces in recent days. Indeed, Gomaa claimed that in some of these dreams, the Prophet himself had been seen sanctioning the work of the army and police in recent days and weeks. Gomaa presented these dreams as spiritual vindication for the coup regime. If there happened to be any dissension in the ranks, he was declaring in his capacity as one of the Egyptian state's most senior religious figures that God and His Messenger were unequivocally supportive of the military regime.

He referred to some of the hadiths he had been referencing in previous weeks, notably the hadith concerning the 'western army,' which he again appealed to as applying to the modern Egyptian army, and specifically the forces he was addressing. He treated the hadiths as sound, despite hadith experts deeming them extremely weak in their attribution to the Prophet as noted earlier.[7] These hadiths would remain contentious for years to come and would remain an important part of the propaganda war waged by the religious front of the Egyptian state in justifying the legitimacy of the military regime. Thus, for example, Gomaa's student, the Yemeni Ali al-Jifri, would give a lecture to the armed forces in 2017 at a 'counter-terrorism' summit organized by the Egyptian army with General-turned-President Sisi and the military top brass in attendance. At the heart of Jifri's lecture would be the insistent if unevidenced assertion that these hadiths, which Gomaa had quoted in 2013 in support of the Egyptian coup, were authentic.[8]

Gomaa next pivoted to the events of recent days—the Rabaa massacre and the days that followed which entailed smaller scale massacres, perhaps most notably at al-Fatḥ Mosque in Ramses Square where anti-coup protestors had begun protesting after Friday prayers on 16 August. HRW reported witnesses saying that the crowd of pro-Morsi activists, 'including women and children, was in a festive mood, with people beating on drums and chanting slogans for freedom and democracy.'[9] Protestors were met with 'indiscriminate' gunfire from security forces resulting in at least 120 deaths on that day according to Egyptian authorities. Egyptian officials would have had incentives to minimize casualty figures, so this was likely a conservative estimate. According to HRW, many of those who had been killed or injured suffered wounds 'to their head, necks and chest' which suggests, once again, that a policy of 'shoot to kill' was in force.[10] In response to the onslaught, some protestors had sought refuge in the mosque which had been transformed into a makeshift hospital and morgue. Barricading themselves inside, and besieged by armed security forces, the standoff lasted until the following day. Gomaa would reference this standoff, which took place the day before he gave his speech to the security forces, later in his lecture.

However, Gomaa first reasserted his claim that these people were to be considered Khawārij, who the Prophet described as exhibiting great religious devotion in prayers and fasting as well as an ability to cite the Prophet's words. But Gomaa reminded the army what the Prophet said about them: 'Blessed are those who kill them and are killed by them! Those who kill them are more worthy of God than they are.'[11] He also repeated another hadith in which the Prophet described the Khawārij as 'dogs of the Hellfire.' He explained that this was because they perpetrated their acts in the name of religion, misrepresenting Islam to the world such that other Muslims might feel that these people were being truthful, given that they cited God and His Prophet, 'but in fact they are misguided,' Gomaa concluded. Gomaa also noted that the Prophet warned against people of *al-harj*. The Companions asked the Prophet to explain the meaning of the word *al-harj*, and he said that it meant 'lying and killing.' Gomaa declared: 'This is what we witness, with our own eyes, they lie and they kill.' Somewhat ironically, some of the arguments used by Gomaa could be, and were, invoked by his opponents as applying to him rather than the peaceful protestors, as we shall see in the next chapter.

Gomaa next gave an example of the alleged mendacity of the MB. He claimed that he had heard them saying for decades that they would advocate for democracy until they reached power, at which point they would end democracy so as to stay in power permanently.[12] He cited verses from the Qur'an (Q. 2:204–5) that are usually understood to be about hypocrites (*munāfiqūn*) to drive his point home before turning to the question of killing (*qatl*). On this issue, he repeated a distinction that he made in his pre-Rabaa private address to the army, namely one between killing (*qatl*) and fighting (*qitāl*). The former was the activity of low lives (*awbāsh*), he declared, while the latter was the activity of knights (*fursān*). Gomaa was not interested in examining the record over the past several days as reported in the international media which showed the security forces engaged in mass killings without regard for the defenselessness of the overwhelming majority of the protestors against the coup regime. Rather his declaration may be understood as a performative one that was designed to be a means of absolution for the state security apparatus for both past and future acts of mass slaughter. In this regard, Gomaa's entire performance is best understood as his endorsement of the massacres perpetrated by the Egyptian military regime.

Urging the soldiers to stand firm (*uthbutū*), he next addressed the disquiet that may have been felt by some of the security forces troubled by the bloodshed of recent days. He would quickly dismiss the bloodshed as the fault of the protestors, asserting that killing the protestors had ultimately reduced bloodshed. In this sense, he held it to be a pre-emptive act of mass slaughter designed to prevent a larger death toll. As he put it: 'I will kill 100 in order not to kill 1,000.' In case anyone continued to harbor unease, Gomaa later added that '[t]he Messenger of God supports you, in the exoteric (*fī al-ẓāhir*) and the esoteric realms (*fī al-bāṭin*).'

Calling Qaradawi a 'kāfir'

In a remarkable excursus on Yusuf al-Qaradawi, who Gomaa seemed to quite clearly allude to without explicitly naming, Gomaa appeared to call his senior fellow Azharī a disbeliever (*kāfir*) and trash (*awbāsh*). At the time, Qaradawi was still a fellow member of Gomaa's on the CSS at the Azhar, and the former grand mufti, nearly thirty years his junior, was a less prolific and less globally recognized scholar than his Qatar-based colleague. As we shall see in a moment, in his public remarks, Gomaa would appear to temper his criticism of Qaradawi, while still disparaging him repeatedly as a senile scholar, well past his prime, who was suffering from Alzheimer's. However, in his private post-Rabaa lecture to the military, he felt no such restraint.

We can be fairly confident that the target of his private and indirect remarks was Qaradawi for the following reasons. In his lecture, Gomaa described the unnamed scholar who he called a *kāfir* as having done three things. Firstly, he had disparaged the Egyptian army by saying that the Israeli army was less rapacious than it. Secondly, he had permitted Hamas to attack a mosque in Gaza in 2009 that had been occupied by militants. And finally, he had prohibited attacks on the mosques of Rabaa and Fatḥ in Cairo that had been attacked by the Egyptian security forces in recent days. I have found clear evidence of Qaradawi doing the first two things. On the third point, I have found nothing explicit. It is quite possible that Qaradawi had said something explicit about the sanctity of mosques in the days of the massacres at Rabaa and Ramses Squares where the two mosques in question were located, but I have not been able to identify such explicit remarks. However, it is quite conceivable that Gomaa is taking Qaradawi's general criticism of the security forces' attacks on Cairo's squares to imply a criticism of their attacks on the mosques within them. Whatever the case, it was entirely in keeping with the tenor of Qaradawi's statements at the time that he would have excoriated the Egyptian security forces for attacking mosques in which anti-coup protestors had taken refuge. I am thus quite confident that Gomaa's intended target was his older Azharī colleague.

In his private post-Rabaa lecture, Gomaa asserted that the Prophet had warned against every silver-tongued (*dhū lisān ʿalīm*) individual. The statement was a subtle reference to a hadith report in which the Prophet warned: 'What I fear most for my umma is every silver-tongued hypocrite (*munāfiq ʿalīm al-lisān*).'[13] Gomaa immediately followed this with a thinly veiled reference to Qaradawi, insinuating that he was a hypocrite—a category of individual that the Qur'an declares to be worse than disbelievers (Q. 4:145). But he did not finish there. He averred, 'This person who came out yesterday claiming that the army of the Jews is better than the Egyptian Army; he is a disbeliever (*kāfir*)!' Two days earlier, in the wake of the Rabaa massacre, Qaradawi had exclaimed in a news broadcast that even the Israeli army did not attack Muslims with the unrelenting ferocity that the Egyptian army had displayed in recent days.[14] Gomaa responded to this with the following declaration:

> He is a disbeliever in God's bounty (*niʿma*). In fact he is a disbeliever in God's intent (*murād*). In fact, I do not wish to say we should not pay attention to him,

> rather we wish to purify (*nuṭahhir*) our city and our Egypt of this trash (*hādhihī al-awbāsh*). They do not deserve our Egyptian identity. We are disgraced by our association with them.[15]

His attack on Qaradawi was not over yet. He related the story of a mosque in Gaza, which was attacked in a police raid by the Hamas government after a suspected affiliate of al-Qaeda had occupied it. Gomaa did not mention the full context, but simply describes the group occupying the mosque as Khawārij, adding wryly that this was a case of Khawārij attacking other Khawārij. This was another instance of the expedient blurring of distinctions between al-Qaeda and MB-affiliated organizations like Hamas. As noted earlier, the former anathematize the latter for accepting the democratic process.

The episode Gomaa described took place almost exactly four years earlier on 15 August 2009 when a heavily armed militant group calling itself the Army of God's Helpers (*Jund Anṣār Allāh*) had forcefully occupied a mosque in the Gaza Strip and declared it an Islamic emirate. Gomaa remarked that this 'disbeliever,' (i.e. Qaradawi) legitimated the attack on the mosque by the Hamas government, something the latter had indeed done.[16] By contrast, Gomaa noted, the same person had condemned the burning of the mosques of Rabaa and Fatḥ. In juxtaposing these two contrasting positions, Gomaa declared the latter view to be 'an outrageous falsehood.' He then addressed the unnamed Qaradawi directly with the words: 'O compulsive liar (*kadhdhāb*)! Know your place! For indeed God, Most High, has disgraced you before the world.' Returning to address his military audience, he advised them to pay no attention to this 'farce' whose words he characterized as the barking of a dog (*nubāḥ*).[17]

Gomaa's vilification of a senior Azharī with such unrestrained language is highly unusual in scholarly circles. As noted earlier, he did not appear to use such unrestrained language in public. Indeed, it contradicted his own avowed principle of condemning the excommunication of other Muslims—a principle that is a jealously guarded feature of mainstream Sunni orthodoxy in part because of hadiths that suggest that declaring a Muslim to be a disbeliever threatens one's own faith.[18] A canonical report from the Prophet states: 'Whoever says to his Muslim brother, "O disbeliever," that statement returns to one of them.'[19] As a consequence, Sunni scholars generally exercised great caution before making such pronouncements. For Gomaa to do so in regard to a high-ranking scholar of Qaradawi's stature seemed theologically reckless and appeared closer to the behavior of the Khawārij he so passionately excoriated.

'Shoot to kill'

In case his earlier remarks were not enough to make plain his support for the deadly dispersal of protests in recent days, Gomaa now made his advocacy of lethal violence explicit. Referring to the protestors as 'putrid' (*natina*) and presenting an Islamic legal basis for Morsi's ouster, he argued that the preservation of life dictated that: 'If a single shot is fired from these rebels (*bughāh*), Khawārij—whether it is from them, or from those who have joined them, but are not of them; or from their direction—if *a single bullet* is fired, then shoot to kill (*iḍrab fi-l-malyān*).'[20] He then added: 'Beware of sacrificing your members and soldiers because of these Khawārij.' Gomaa's official YouTube page years later remonstrated that people misrepresented his words and that he never encouraged the Rabaa massacre, given that these words were uttered after those events.[21] However, it is difficult to see his speech as anything but post facto legitimation for the deadly violence of the coup regime, alongside religious legitimation to proceed however it wished in future when confronting its opponents.[22] As noted already, Egyptian authorities would go on to state that a thousand or more protestors had been killed, while only a handful of weapons had been found, demonstrating that Gomaa's stipulation that protestors only be fired upon in response to their gunfire was not actually observed. But Gomaa never subsequently backtracked from his forceful justification of the military's massacre of largely unarmed protestors. Rather, he continued to justify his statements for years afterwards.

Returning to his post-Rabaa military speech, while he did spend less than a minute suggesting some qualifications to his 'shoot to kill' declaration, these seemed like an afterthought that he himself dismissed as already properly observed by the army. Specifically, he noted that the injured were not to be chased so as to kill them and that kill shots were to be avoided unless necessary. But such conditions were undercut by his prefacing them with the unevidenced claim that they were already being observed and his concluding with a declaration of the security forces' chivalry. The evidence to the contrary was, at this point, already widespread in independent media reports, and it only became clearer with the passage of time. But Gomaa was not interested in examining the record. Instead, he redoubled his asseverations of the officers' greatness in God's eyes: 'Do not be afraid of these claims of religion,' he exhorted,

> for the religion is on your side; God is on your side; His Messenger is on your side; the believers are on your side; thereafter the people are your supporters; and

> the Angels are supporting you from the Heavens. Stand firm! Let no one among you ever hesitate to do this for the sake of God. Stand before God on the Day of Resurrection and say, 'O my Lord, I prevented the evil of evil people and the corruption of the corrupt from reaching people.'[23]

The rest of Gomaa's lecture resembled the themes already presented. They provide an insight into how religious scholars serve the interests of political and military power in Egypt today, and no doubt, such service is richly rewarded. That Ali Gomaa is one of the most prominent ulama in the Egyptian public sphere, frequently featured in the media with lengthy shows dedicated to spreading his teachings, is doubtless a result of the symbiotic relationship between the political classes and religious officialdom in Egypt. A concrete example of the rewards he has received for his service may be seen in the Sisi regime awarding Gomaa control over the MB's massive Islamic Medical Association, which the regime had seized after the coup. The Islamic Medical Association was a charitable institution that served the healthcare needs of two million Egyptians at affordable costs. Gomaa's appointment as its chairman lead one patient to lament that 'the wolf now guards the sheep.'[24] As noted earlier, Gomaa's post-Rabaa lecture to the military would not be released until October, and in the days and weeks after Rabaa, Gomaa had developed a public discourse that was less extreme than his private post-Rabaa message to the military but which still served to justify its actions and vilify opponents of the coup regime.

Gomaa's public post-Rabaa support for the regime

On 23 August, a little over a week after the Rabaa massacre, and five days after his private lecture to the security forces, Gomaa would discuss the events of the past few days in Egypt with CBC's Khayrī Ramaḍān on the latter's show *Momken*. Ramaḍān's interview of Gomaa represents what was perhaps Gomaa's most comprehensive public apologia for his stance vis-à-vis the Egyptian coup of July 2013 and the massacres that followed.[25] CBC, in common with most other Egyptian channels during this period, enthusiastic as they were about the coup, had a graphic on one corner of the screen that read in English: 'Egypt under attack,' and in Arabic 'Egypt wages war against terrorism' (*Miṣr tuḥārib al-irhāb*). Ramaḍān himself would conduct a congratulatory interview of Interior Minister Ibrahim, one of the main architects of the Rabaa massacre, a few days later on 31 August.[26] Thus the setting could not be described as neutral, but its presenter's approach suggested an attempt to feign neutrality. Over the course of more than two hours, Gomaa discussed his support for the Egyptian coup alongside recent accusations that he had given a fatwa legitimating the killing of protestors. These accusations were based on leaked clips from his pre-Rabaa private recording to the military which we examined in Chapter 5. The clips were deemed sufficiently controversial for Gomaa to respond to them directly at this point.

Gomaa was welcomed generously by the host and proceeded to speak of the Prophet's foretelling of all that was happening in Egypt today, but lamented people's confusion regarding a matter that should have been clear. Repeating some of the hadiths that he had cited in past days and weeks, he emphasized the 'sanctity of blood' (*ḥurmat al-dam*) as being at the heart of the Prophet's teachings. He also highlighted the gravity of murder in those teachings. It was clear that he said this without the security forces in mind. As he had confidently proffered in his private messages, officers of the state were not liable for murder, since they were 'in the right.' In the CBC interview, he made this explicit as well. 'There is killing, and then there is killing for the right [reason].' He described the latter as being 'from God, by God's command (*amr*), and by God's rule (*ḥukm*).'[27] Gomaa additionally noted that people criticized him for not joining the revolution of 2011 with enthusiasm, accusing him of standing with the regime. Gomaa insisted that his reasons for refraining at the time were due to his deeply held concern for the sanctity of blood which he feared would be spilt as a result of the confrontation. 'I wanted to protect the youth from being killed,' he insisted, adding that he had no interest in politics, 'I'm just interested in young men not being killed.'[28] As we have seen, such a statement cannot be reconciled with the content of his private messages to the military from a few days earlier.

Gomaa also discussed the Rabaa massacre more explicitly, mentioning with apparent sadness that one of his students had died there.[29] He argued that the dispersal of the sit-in was justified as the security forces were acting on the basis of a legal ruling issued by a judge permitting the clearing. 'This is because the Islamic state [of Egypt] is a state based on the rule of law,' he added. At this point in the proceedings, the presenter interjected with a striking question that drew on an accusation found on an anti-coup website. With great reverence he asked:

> A number of things have been attributed to your esteemed self in recent days, among them, let me begin with what the website *Raṣd* has attributed [to you],

> namely that a police officer confessed to them that he listened to you, and that your esteemed self permitted to him the killing of these people because they are Khawārij. Consequently, he killed eighty of them. Then he felt pain and remorse, and so he contacted a shaykh who said that he had to confirm the matter with Shaykh Ali Gomaa. The shaykh then contacted your esteemed self and you said to him, 'Where is this officer? Bring him so I can kiss his head.' *Raṣd* narrated this on its websites, and it spread. Is there any truth—not that I am questioning your truthfulness, for I know your eminence very well—but how do you view a story like this?[30]

Gomaa denied the story as a fantasy (*mawhūma*) and a fabrication (*talfiqa*). He pointed out that he had recorded a message for the army's Department of Moral Affairs (*al-shu'ūn al-ma'nawiyya li-l-jaysh*) to provide advice to the officers. It was a short snippet from this recording, Gomaa claimed, that they used to accuse him of legitimating the killing of protestors. He then cited the Qur'an to emphasize the extent to which he considered his statements to have been misrepresented. God exhorts: 'Why do you mix truth with falsehood? Why do you knowingly conceal the truth?' (Q. 3:71) The MB leaders, he declared, would be consigned to the dustbin of history (*mazbalat al-tarīkh*) for misguiding the youths under their leadership. He also accused them of planning to assassinate him as, he asserted, had been reported in the press the previous day. I have found no evidence of such a report which seems to be highly unlikely as coming from the MB leadership.

In light of the earlier discussion, it is obvious that Gomaa was not being entirely honest about his support for killing protestors in this interview. Not only had he provided the basis for their killing, after the Rabaa massacre he also celebrated the success of the Egyptian army's slaughter of protestors and repeatedly insisted that they were right to do so. In his remarks in the CBC interview, five days after the lecture to the army in which he praised its violence against thousands of protestors, Gomaa was appearing to deny even permitting the killing of the protestors.

At this point in the interview, the short clip that was being disseminated about Gomaa from his pre-Rabaa private lecture was played. It included the following statement from that lecture:

> There are those who wish to divide the ranks, and the Prophet says: 'When you are all unified around a single man'—*all* of you, not just a single party—'*all* unified around a single man.' And this is what happened in the revolution of 30 June—the people came out in [support of General Sisi]; and this is why the army stood with them. Thus we are all unified around a single man. [The Prophet

> continues:] 'And there comes someone who wishes to create rifts among you, kill him whoever he may be!' Despite the sanctity and seriousness of shedding blood, the Prophet permits us to fight this rebel.[31]

Gomaa's response to the clip was defiant. 'By God, does *any* Muslim disagree with this [...]?! *No* Muslim disagrees about this! Namely that armed rebellion against a ruler (*al-khurūj al-musallaḥ 'alā al-ḥākim*) [justifies this...]. The meaning of rebellion (*khurūj*) is [necessarily] that it be armed rebellion.' Thus, while Gomaa earlier appeared to disavow allegations that he had justified the killing of protestors, he was asserting its apparent opposite about five minutes later. It is possible to reconcile the two positions somewhat by viewing the first as a disavowal of unqualified permission to shoot at unarmed protestors, while the second position permitted killing armed rebels.

Gomaa would face two problems with this line of defense, however. Firstly, the hundreds if not thousands of protestors who were killed by the security forces in Rabaa were overwhelmingly unarmed according to the security forces' own testimony. Minister of Interior Ibrahim claimed in a press conference after the Rabaa massacre that a total of fifteen firearms had been found at Rabaa.[32] Presumably the minister of interior—not a neutral party—reporting that fifteen weapons had been found among tens of thousands of protestors would indicate that the Rabaa sit-in did not constitute the 'armed rebellion' that could be confronted with the level of violence that would cause such a large number of deaths.

Secondly, Gomaa's continued defense of the pre-Rabaa lecture after he celebrated the security forces' killing of hundreds if not thousands of people indicated that adding such qualifications regarding gradual escalation did not reflect a genuine effort at reducing bloodshed on his part. His continued insistence upon these qualifications at this stage appeared contrived. Indeed, as the program wore on, he appeared less and less guarded, and sounded more and more like his post-Rabaa private lecture to the military, although he never quite reached the same levels of ferocity on display there.

Having earlier in his interview denied calling for the killing of protestors, then affirmed killing them in cases where they were engaged in 'armed rebellion,' he asked the following hypothetical question: 'If an individual wants to engage in armed rebellion (*arād al-khurūj al-musallaḥ*) against the army, what are we to do?'[33] He answered without hesitation: 'Kill him (*uqtulūh*). Let me say it again: the one who rebels (*yakhruj*) against the Egyptian army or the Egyptian police, what he deserves in the Sharia is to be killed (*ḥaqquhū fī al-Sharī'a al-qatl*).' Gone was the earlier restraint of shooting to disarm rather than kill. Surely if, as he said here, what they deserved in the eyes of the Sharia was to be killed, they actually had to be killed rather than disarmed by being shot in their arms or legs. It is difficult to reconcile his above categorical statement repeated twice for emphasis with his earlier suggestions in the same interview that killing was a last resort.

Later in the interview, he reiterated his position thus: 'Let me declare to the whole world: any bullet that comes from any group towards the chest of the Egyptian army and the Egyptian authorities, the Egyptian army and the Egyptian authorities are obligated (*wajaba*) to respond in the same manner (*bi-l-mithl*).' The presenter followed this by asking whether it needed to be an actual bullet, or simply bearing weapons (*mujarrad ḥaml al-silāḥ*)? Gomaa responded that the bearing of weapons by the protestors was sufficient cause to allow the security forces to shoot. Citing the Qur'an (Q. 49:9), he argued that this was not killing, but fighting. That is to say, in keeping with arguments he made in private to the security forces, he held that they would not be guilty of homicide but rather that any deaths could be written off as cases of self-defense.[34]

Some minutes later, he appeared to speak again of gradual escalation, arguing that killing was not to be resorted to if the attacker could be stopped some other way. But when the presenter interjected by asking whether it was still permitted to kill, Gomaa responded by laughing and saying in the first person, speaking as a soldier:

> Of course, what can I do? He is going to kill me! If I don't kill him, he'll kill me! [...] This is why we have said: if a single bullet comes from the direction of any group, then the Egyptian army and the Egyptian police must act in a manner that is pleasing to God, including shooting to kill.

These remarks appear contradictory. Gomaa spoke of the possibility of shooting to disarm the attacker without killing them, but then in the same interview claimed that one had no choice but to kill or be killed, and that 'shooting to kill' was 'pleasing to God.' I read this as Gomaa's recognition that, given the way in which the security forces had unleashed massive violence against the protestors a few days earlier, he needed to overemphasize rules of engagement that permitted killing and underemphasize the usual rules for fighting armed rebels, namely attacking them in a way that disarmed them short of killing them.[35] This was a means of providing some kind of religious justification for the massacres after the fact, however unpersuasive it may have appeared. Repeatedly insisting (contrary to the evidence) that the protestors were actually armed and actively aggressing against the security forces could then legitimate the high death toll at Rabaa.

'Alternative facts' concerning Rabaa

To give this otherwise unconvincing religious legitimation greater credence, Gomaa also presented a narrative of what happened in Rabaa that appeared to absolve the security forces of any guilt of the charge of using excessive force.[36] He claimed that at 3 am on the morning of the dispersal, bulldozers were brought to Rabaa in order to remove the barriers that protestors had placed around the camp and the protestors immediately 'fired upon them.' No independent news reports mentioned any such early morning shooting from the protestors. Gomaa next claimed that security officers came to Rabaa and waited there between 11 am until midday with orders that they not shoot at protestors, even though three of their number had been shot. Despite being shot at, he claimed, they did not reciprocate. According to Gomaa, the security forces responded that they were awaiting orders, and on their honor could not act without the approval of their commanding officers. They were 'knights' (*fursān*), Gomaa declared. Speaking in their voice, he says: 'We cannot shoot even if all of us die [because of our refusal to fire back]. We must receive orders.' Permission to approach the protests came at 1 or 2 pm, Gomaa claimed, and they were only to fire if first fired upon.[37] Accordingly, he asserted, they proceeded, were fired upon, and thus responded with fire. 'The number of martyrs among the police reached seventy-five,' he lamented, adding euphemistically, 'so they were simply forced to deal with this situation.'

As we saw in Chapter 5, this narrative bears no resemblance with how events actually unfolded in Rabaa. As multiple eyewitnesses reported, security forces began firing a little after 6 am without any prior warnings that could be heard by those at the sit-ins, and the automatic gunfire continued through much of the day. However, Gomaa's narrative did bear more than a passing resemblance with state propaganda from the time as we have seen. Gomaa's narrative can be viewed as just another variation on these stories.[38] David Kirkpatrick's comment after he relates the official story is worth reiterating in response to these claims: 'None of this, of course, was ever remotely corroborated.' What is worthy of note for our purposes, however, is the readiness with which a senior religious scholar, ostensibly among the bearers of the highest moral authority in Egypt, was implicated in purveying the falsehoods that allowed for the legitimation of the military regime and its considerable violence.[39]

Attacking Qaradawi

In contrast with his private post-Rabaa lecture, Yusuf al-Qaradawi was now a named target of Gomaa's attacks in this public interview, but his tone was much milder than the remarks of the lecture. Unlike his private lecture, Gomaa did not now publicly declare Qaradawi a disbeliever. It is worth remembering that even in that lecture, he made thinly veiled references to Qaradawi without explicitly naming him, although anyone familiar with the context of his references could deduce who he was referring to. This time, Gomaa was pre-empted by the host who mentioned Qaradawi by name.

Gomaa's strategy for discrediting him was thus to assert that Qaradawi had become senile (*kharifa*) and was suffering from Alzheimer's. 'He used to be good,' he added derisively, 'and then he got Alzheimer's.'[40] The presenter, continuing in his role as devil's advocate, interjected that Qaradawi had presented arguments based on religious evidence to which Gomaa responded: 'If someone says that the Jewish [i.e. Israeli] army is better than the Egyptian army, then we cannot accept it, so we can only say that he is suffering from Alzheimer's.' Gomaa did not even present the pretense of a meaningful argument. It seems that he was happy for this to be seen as a personal attack against his senior colleague on the CSS.[41] This public reference to Qaradawi's criticism of the Egyptian army vis-à-vis the Israeli army further reinforces my contention that in his private lecture from a few days earlier, Qaradawi was indeed the unnamed scholar Gomaa was anathematizing. His disparagement of Qaradawi continued for some time with the presenter joining in with the accusation, posed as the following question: 'Is it not possible that he is basing himself on jihadist ideas [...] like his calling on the world's jihadists to come to Egypt to save Islam?'[42] Here the presenter was reiterating a report that had been purveyed in Egyptian media after the Rabaa massacre.[43] Indeed, even careful Western scholars have not been immune to this propaganda about Qaradawi.[44] On cue, Gomaa responded to the presenter's remarks by averring that 'Qaradawi asked jihadists to come and kill the Egyptian people and the Egyptian army and thereby defend Islam.' Under such circumstances, Gomaa added, 'I claim that he has Alzheimer's.'

Gomaa thus held two very different positions on Qaradawi—one in private before the security forces and one in public. In private he insinuated that he was a disbeliever (*kāfir*), while in public, given the extreme nature of the former position, he asserted that Qaradawi suffered from Alzheimer's. In fact, Qaradawi appeared to be just as lucid as Gomaa, a man twenty-six years his junior, in his many public engagements in those years, and continued to be so for years afterwards. In an interview in early 2017 with Al Jazeera, Qaradawi appeared as lucid, though not as energetic, at the age of ninety as Gomaa appeared on the same day, when the latter would have been sixty-four.[45]

Later on in the interview, Gomaa entertained a third possibility that Qaradawi could be considered to be of the Khawārij because, as Gomaa alleged without any basis in fact, Qaradawi had encouraged armed rebellion against Muslims while leaving disbelievers in peace. The irony of this accusation from Gomaa, as has already been mentioned earlier, was that the qualities he attributed to the Khawārij, namely perpetrating violent attacks against other Muslims as well as declaring one's fellow Muslims to be disbelievers (*kuffār*), were both acts that he had himself engaged in or encouraged. He had called Qaradawi a disbeliever, and he had encouraged the killing of anti-coup protestors. However, Gomaa resorting to ad hominem attacks over facts and arguments in his response to Qaradawi—the response of the religious voice of the coup regime—did signal something important. It arguably demonstrated that Gomaa had no substantive arguments against those of Qaradawi. As we will see in the next chapter, the 'senile' Qaradawi had plenty of substantive arguments of his own and wrote extensive rebuttals of Gomaa's justifications for supporting the coup.

Ali al-Jifri: Gomaa's devoted defender

While many scholars in Egypt and beyond expressed shock at Gomaa's support for the coup regime and its massacres as we shall explore in the next chapter, Gomaa's dedicated student Ali al-Jifri stood firmly by his shaykh. Jifri deserves to be studied in depth in his own right, since his relative youth means that he will likely be an important player in supporting authoritarianism in the Middle East for decades to come. On the day of the Rabaa massacre, Jifri published a post on his Facebook page expressing his great sorrow at the loss of life in Egypt's fratricidal bloodshed. 'There is no victor in this battle according to those of spiritual insight,' he declared, while praying for God to put an end to the fitna and show mercy to those who had passed.[46] A week later on 21 August 2013, however, in the wake of rumors of Gomaa's complicity in the killings by virtue of the leaked pre-Rabaa private lecture footage, Jifri's tone had changed. In a short post on Facebook, he defiantly defended his shaykh as follows:

> All praise is due to God.
>
> I contacted our shaykh, the supremely knowledgeable Imam (*al-imām al-'allāma*), Ali Gomaa regarding what some newspapers of dubious [integrity] have been spreading about a fatwa of killing (*fatwā al-qatl*). He responded, as expected from someone of his virtue and knowledge, by saying: 'this is all a lie without any basis.'
>
> So how can we trust to champion this religion those who deem it permissible to fabricate lies regarding those who disagree with them?
>
> In the coming days, there may appear many rumors and fabrications of this kind. Therefore one must be attentive and assess the veracity [of such reports] in accordance with God's words: 'O believers, if a nefarious individual (*fāsiq*) brings you news, then clarify it, lest you harm a people out of ignorance, and later come to regret your actions.' [Qur'an 49:6]
>
> We seek refuge in God from the insolence of little people against the senior [scholars] (*taṭāwul al-aṣāghir 'alā al-akābir*); God help us.
>
> O God, grant us truthfulness with which we may rise to the rank of the Truthful (*ṣiddīqūn*), and reform us, and reform others through us. Repel tribulation (*fitan*), both apparent and concealed. And may God's peace and blessings be upon our Master, Muhammad, and his Family and Companions. All praise is due to God, Lord of the worlds.[47]

Jifri's comments would do little to quell the criticism he was witnessing in the wake of the release of Gomaa's pre-Rabaa private lecture, however. As we have seen already, sections of Gomaa's pre-Rabaa private lecture, while not as provocative as the post-coup lecture, still gave sufficient reason to view Gomaa as legitimating the use of deadly force against protestors, as with the short clip shown to Gomaa in his CBC interview. It was not then 'all a lie without any basis,' as Jifri reported. Although he was unwilling to tolerate any disparagement of Gomaa's integrity, Jifri was happy to impugn the integrity of others, characterizing those spreading supposedly malicious untruths about his shaykh as 'nefarious individuals' who were condemned as untrustworthy by God Himself in the Qur'an. Ironically, as we have already seen, Gomaa showed little concern in spreading false information about a senior scholar like Qaradawi, indeed going so far as to call him a disbeliever. As we will see shortly, however, Jifri was also capable of spreading dubious reports about senior scholars.

We should therefore not be surprised that after the full video of Gomaa's pre-Rabaa lectures had been released, and after his two-hour interview on

CBC on 23 August, Jifri again took to social media on 26 August to repeat his defense of Gomaa with even greater force. This time, rather than denying that a 'fatwa of killing' had been given, Jifri argued that the fatwa was entirely legitimate. Jifri's relatively short statement, still available on his Twitter page, translates as follows:

> All praise is due to God.
>
> [This is] a statement clarifying the reality of the lies being spread to cause fitna (*irjāf*) concerning the fatwa of the esteemed and supremely knowledgeable Imam, Ali Gomaa, may God preserve him and benefit [others] through him:
>
> 1. The esteemed scholar gave a fatwa [permitting] fighting those who rebelled against the people (*kharaja 'alā al-jam'*) 'bearing arms,' and this is a matter of legal consensus among all Sunni scholars, as well as in laws around the world.
> 2. People lacking in piety and weak in their religion spread rumors that the esteemed scholar had given a fatwa [permitting] the killing of the 'Muslim Brotherhood' in general, and 'peaceful' protesters, weaving around [the rumor] a story. I asked the esteemed scholar about this, and he declared the rumor a lie.
> 3. The esteemed scholar gave a lecture that was recorded by the Department of Moral Affairs of the Armed Forces, which was longer than half an hour '30 minutes' [*sic*] which bears the same import as the fatwa of limiting fighting to those who engaged in 'armed' rebellion. [This] was distributed to all the units of the army and domestic barracks.
> 4. Dishonest people spread lies to cause fitna (*arjafa ḍu'afā' al-amāna*) by publishing just '49 seconds' of a lecture that is more than half an hour—a selection cut off from its context—claiming that it was 'leaked.' And satellite channels of fitna broadcast this selective clip, and people pounced upon it, without undertaking the obligation of authentication and clarification. God help us.
> 5. The esteemed scholar clarified the reality of the situation in a televized interview [on CBC on 23 August], but the spreaders of lies (*murjifūn*) stubbornly persisted in their spreading falsehoods to cause fitna (*irjāfihim*). The reality is that however much people may differ, honesty and religion require sound reporting, and avoiding lies and misrepresentation. Indeed elevated ends do not justify ignoble means.
>
> Finally, this is the reality of [this] esteemed scholar's fatwa. And however we may agree or disagree with him in understanding the situation, honesty requires [this] clarification [...].[48]

Jifri's message was consistent with his earlier defense of Gomaa, but his language is even more assertive with righteous indignation. This may seem particularly odd in light of Gomaa's private post-Rabaa lecture to the military, but there is no evidence to suggest that Jifri would have been aware of its content at this point. Indeed, in the days after it was finally released in October, Jifri did not comment on the controversy, but rather chose to ignore it despite someone at the time publicly posting to his Facebook page a request that he address it.[49] Perhaps it was too obviously a call to mass slaughter for Jifri to openly defend it. Whatever the case may be, his other remarks just cited in his defense of Gomaa are informative in other ways.

In particular, Jifri's response to Gomaa's critics was to go on the offensive and describe them as people guilty of spreading lies to cause fitna. He used the verbal noun, *irjāf*, the verb, *arjafa*, and its pluralized participle form, the Qur'anic *al-murjifūn* (Q. 33:60), which was used by Gomaa in his pre-Rabaa private lecture to the military, as we saw in the last chapter.[50] The Qur'an uses the term in a highly charged reference to the treachery of the Hypocrites (*munāfiqūn*) who, as alluded to earlier, are elsewhere in the Qur'an characterized as destined for the lowest depths of Hell (Q. 4:145). The authoritative early Qur'anic exegete Abū Ja'far al-Ṭabarī, in his commentary on Q. 33:60, cites early exegetical authorities who identify the *murjifūn* with the Hypocrites.[51] As we saw in the last chapter, Ali Gomaa referred to this verse (Q. 33:60) in the course of his pre-Rabaa private lecture to the Egyptian Armed Forces to justify massacring 'those who spread lies.'[52]

Overall, Jifri's protestations rang hollow in light of what Gomaa had actually said, some of which was yet to be revealed to the public. What was already available, however, in the form of the pre-Rabaa lecture and the post-Rabaa CBC interview was sufficiently incriminating for independent observers of Gomaa, such as *The New York Times*, to portray him as calling for the indiscriminate killing of protestors, as they did a day before Jifri published his pronouncements.[53] By contrast, in this statement, Jifri suggested that Gomaa's CBC interview 'clarified the reality of the situation' and completely exonerated Gomaa. With regard to Gomaa's critics, even when they were senior scholars like Qaradawi, Jifri was much less charitable. A month earlier in July, Jifri had condemned what he alleged was Qaradawi's unprincipled approach to the Sharia. As could be seen preserved in the post of a Western admirer of Jifri's, the latter accused Qaradawi of applying 'double standards' when it came to the legitimacy of rebellion against a ruler.[54]

As we will see in greater detail in the next chapter, in response to the coup Qaradawi appealed to hadiths prohibiting rebellion in his opposition to the ousting of Egyptian President Morsi. In Qaradawi's view, Morsi had a legitimate right to the Egyptian presidency by virtue of his democratic election to power in Egypt's first ever free and fair presidential election. But where Qaradawi saw a contrast between Morsi's electoral legitimacy justifying calls for his reinstatement and Mubarak's lack thereof justifying calls for his removal, Jifri claimed only to see Qaradawi's hypocrisy. 'Is this the same man who goaded on the revolutions and rebellion against rulers throughout the past two years? Or does the hadith only apply to a ruler who is a member of the Group [i.e. the MB]?'[55]

This criticism disregarded the fact that Qaradawi's first choice for the Egyptian presidency was actually the ex-MB Islamist ʿAbd al-Munʿim Abū al-Futūḥ and that Qaradawi had only supported Morsi against Shafiq in the subsequent run-off between the two because Shafiq represented the military establishment. Indeed, Qaradawi had stated on his influential Al Jazeera show just days before the first round of elections that he would have preferred that the MB not field a candidate in opposition to Abū al-Futūḥ.[56] Jifri's accusations of partisanship are therefore a polemical misrepresentation of Qaradawi's position. In regard to Jifri's allegation of hypocrisy on Qaradawi's part, it should be noted that Qaradawi is a committed democrat, who alongside other Islamists had spent much of his later career developing an influential Islamic conception of democracy as an answer to autocracy. This is a conception that Qaradawi had defended in multiple forums over many years with the passion of a true believer. For him, this made clear the distinction between Morsi's legitimacy and the illegitimacy of the Arab world's long-standing autocrats.

For the Neo-traditionalist Jifri, working from within a religious framework that had for many decades recognized the political legitimacy of the regional autocrats despite their repressive excesses, such distinctions probably did not make sense and needed to be confronted as pernicious ideas to be rejected by the Islamic tradition. It should therefore not surprise us to learn that Jifri would soon follow the lead of his mentor Ali Gomaa and become a fully fledged supporter of the Egyptian army, giving lectures on its greatness at Egyptian military events, including in the presence of the coup-regime's president Sisi, as noted earlier in the chapter.

His attacks against Qaradawi would also continue after the events of that summer. As Walaa Quisay documents in her study of Neo-traditionalist networks in the West, Jifri visited the UK for a spiritual retreat in Nottingham in 2014.[57] In the course of one of his talks at the retreat, he made the unevidenced claim that during the clearing of protestors in the streets of Egypt a year earlier, images of 'burnt bodies' were purveyed with the suggestion that the army and police had been responsible. In fact, he claimed, the protestors had burnt these bodies 'to frame the Egyptian army.' Naturally, no corroborating evidence was presented alongside this shocking claim. Similarly tenuous was a grave accusation Jifri leveled at Qaradawi. Qaradawi, Jifri explained, had issued the fatwa that led to the assassination of Muḥammad Saʿīd Ramaḍān al-Būṭī, Syria's most high-ranking scholar in 2013, who was also an avowed supporter of President Bashar al-Assad (b. 1385/1965).[58] Another attendee of a UK retreat of Jifri's a year later in 2015 relayed a similar though more explicit statement from Jifri.[59] According to this attendee, Jifri referred directly to a sermon of Qaradawi's in which he declared it permissible to kill scholars who support dictators. Less than a week later, Jifri claimed, Būṭī was assassinated in a mosque in Damascus. According to the attendee, the inference of Qaradawi's fatwa causing Būṭī's assassination was 'very clearly being made.'[60]

In fact, there was no real evidence for Jifri's serious accusation directed at a senior Azharī. The alleged fatwa to 'kill' Būṭī a week before his murder was in fact a call on people to 'fight' all supporters of the Assad regime three and a half months before the assassination.[61] Earlier we saw Jifri complaining about 'the insolence of little people against the senior [scholars] (*taṭāwul al-aṣāghir ʿalā al-akābir*),' when people criticized Gomaa's fatwas in support of the coup regime. With respect to Qaradawi, Jifri did not feel the same way. Nor did he evince a concern for being 'attentive and assess[ing] the veracity [of such reports] in accordance with God's words (Q. 49:6).' In this regard, Jifri was truly a loyal protégé of his shaykh, Ali Gomaa, though unlike his teacher, Jifri could visit Western nations with impunity. Aside from the regular spiritual retreats he had attended in the UK over the years, he was a guest of honor at the Bradford Literary Festival in the UK as recently as 2019. By contrast, Gomaa's support for the post-coup massacres appears to have prevented his travel to the UK in 2014 for fear of arrest.[62] He would struggle to cleanse the blood of hundreds, perhaps thousands, of protestors from his reputation for years to come, as we shall now consider.

Gomaa after Rabaa

Gomaa's two-hour CBC interview was the first of his many denials that he ever legitimated the killing of unarmed protestors. He would have to defend himself against these allegations repeatedly over the years. This was despite the severe curtailment of free political debate in Egypt in the years following the Egyptian coup. Gomaa's support for the military more generally continued after August 2013, however, as well as his hostility towards the MB whom he continued to identify with jihadist groups. Such groups, most notably ISIS, emerged as major players in the region after the Egyptian coup, energized by the failed democratic transition of the region's most populous nation, a transition many believed had the potential to render such jihadist groups obsolete. Instead, jihadism reasserted itself with a vengeance in Egypt in the summer of 2013 leading to a steady and significant stream of deaths in Egypt down to the present. Such a state of affairs was predictably exploited by the military regime to justify ever greater repression in Egypt, and Gomaa was always available to give the regime his blessing.

An example of this may be seen in a sermon that Gomaa gave on 20 September, a little over a month after the Rabaa massacre. Broadcast live on the satellite channel CBC, it was attended by a contingent of security forces a day after a senior police officer, General Nabil Farag (Farrāj), was killed in the course of a security raid against the Egyptian town of Kirdasa in which militants who were hostile to the coup had attacked a police station and killed several officers on 14 August. The original attacks were mounted in retaliation for the Rabaa massacre, and Farag died a month later as the Egyptian state security forces attempted to mount its own attack on 19 September to reassert control over the town. Gomaa's YouTube channel uploaded his sermon on 20 September, giving it the title 'A Message to the Khawārij.' He was thus replicating his discourse of previous weeks that was used to legitimate mass killings of the overwhelmingly unarmed protestors at Rabaa.[63] In this particular case, the attackers appear to have been armed, which may suggest that they were not members of the MB but rather only sympathizers of the deposed President.[64] The Brotherhood had, in its official statements, resolutely refused to take up arms, and at this stage appeared largely able to enforce observation of this official stance, despite falling into relative disarray after the Rabaa massacre.

Two days after this sermon, on 22 September, Gomaa was verbally attacked by a group of students at Cairo University during a public thesis defense. Later that day, Gomaa gave a raft of TV interviews, one of which he uploaded to his YouTube page, with the other six uploaded by third parties.[65] Representing seven different Egyptian television and satellite channels, they are illustrative of the fact that the post-coup regime media remained well-coordinated in their anti-MB message into the autumn of that year.[66] In all cases, the titles given to these videos on YouTube are illustrative of an anti-MB PR strategy. In an interview with Egyptian Channel 1 news, Gomaa claimed, at most twenty or so 'Muslim Brotherhood youths' were involved, playing down the event.[67] It illustrated the extent to which people harbored hostility towards him in the wake of the Rabaa massacre.

The Channel 1 video uploaded to Gomaa's YouTube page continued the theme of referring to the MB as Khawārij. It was entitled: 'Prof Dr Ali Gomaa's message to the leaders of the Khawārij and to sensible youths.' Feigning incomprehension, the newsreader asked whether these youths were protesting the contents of the dissertation being defended, or 'for no reason?' Gomaa explained that they were objecting to 'what they called military rule.' He clarified further:

> They are objecting to Ali Gomaa who is standing with the Egyptian state, who is standing with the [political] legitimacy [of the state], who is standing with the Islamic law [we have] inherited, who is standing with the Azhar, standing with justice, who is against criminality, who is against the massacre that they perpetrated at the Kirdasa police station. It angers and enrages them. For this reason, I am sending a message to the leadership of the Brotherhood because the youths, the poor things, are finished. They do not have any one to guide them having reached a state of revolution and agitation, and so I do not blame anyone on their account except the leadership of the Brotherhood.
>
> I am sending a message to the leadership of the Brotherhood to say that you have failed to properly raise your children. Rather than teaching them good character traits, sound religion, and [rational] reflection, you have taught them anathematization (*takfir*), cursing, slandering, impropriety and indecency. You have corrupted these youths—God is our sufficiency and refuge from you! You must repent before you die and miss the opportunity. You must reassess your situation, and re-educate your children. The same children who teach your signs [*sic*] and promote your slogans: they curse, they imprecate, they anathematize. We have recorded all of it on video. I am [also] sending a message to the sensible youths that such [behavior] is the result of the education of the contemporary Brotherhood who do not belong to Islam, or to any country, or to any organization.[68]

Using disparaging language, Gomaa thus painted a picture that rendered the MB and their supporters as outlaws who were not just irrational and characterized by 'criminal' rage, but also ignorant of their religion, and effectively did not 'belong to Islam.' Playing along with the presenter's feigned perplexity at the youths' behavior, Gomaa referred to the supposed crime of the MB attacking the Kirdasa police station. As already mentioned, the date of the original attack was, in fact, 14 August. Although the militants who perpetrated the attack were unlikely to have been from the MB, residents told journalists that the attack took place because people from the town had been attending the anti-coup sit-in at Rabaa and were killed that day by security forces in the Rabaa massacre.[69] Thus, while Gomaa blamed the MB for the Kirdasa massacre that resulted in the death of fourteen policemen on 14 August, he carefully elided any reference to the killing of more than a thousand people by the Egyptian security forces at Rabaa earlier that day that served as the spur for the police deaths. Perhaps more to the point, he also elided his personal enthusiasm for, and encouragement of, the slaughter at Rabaa.

A few weeks later on 8 October, Al Jazeera reported on Gomaa's leaked post-Rabaa private lecture to the security forces, which was considered earlier in this chapter. With the full video released a couple of days later, recriminations began to make themselves felt once again. By 19 October, Gomaa was engaging in damage control after the controversy reached one of his mosque classes.[70] The short remarks translated in full below illustrate the understandable aftereffects of Rabaa on Gomaa's reputation. The video description provides background to the question alongside part of Gomaa's response, although the video itself includes only Gomaa's response, which is longer than what is transcribed in the description. The overall translation, merging both the description and the recording, and thus switching from the first person to the third person, is as follows:

> Peaceful protest is a right that is guaranteed for everyone protected by the state and the law. However, by the simple transformation of the peaceful protestor to a protestor bearing weapons so that he may kill and destroy, the state is obliged to confront him. The following exchange took place between myself and a student in which he asked: 'Why did you give a fatwa allowing the killing of protestors?' [Gomaa responded:] 'Have you heard this from me?' [The questioner replied:] 'No, I have not heard this from you, but....' [Gomaa cutting off the student:] 'Thus is the first calamity...' [Other attendees:] 'Allahu akbar!' [Gomaa continued:] '... that he did not hear it [for himself]. Muslim narrates in his *Ṣaḥīḥ*, on the authority of our Master [the Prophet], peace and blessings be upon him, "It is enough of a lie for a person to repeat everything he has heard."'[71]

Throughout this exchange, Gomaa's audience expressed their constant enthusiasm through pious exclamations for what Gomaa had to say in response to this perceived questioning of his integrity. Gomaa continued with his response as follows (with italics representing instances where he was raising his voice):

> [I asked:] 'Have you heard this?' He replied: 'No.' In that case, we are making a mockery of God and His Messenger. Are you slandering me because he did not hear? Of course I know that this boy's heart is pure. However, he has made a mistake. He is a good person, but he has committed a sin. [Namely] that he did not verify the truth of the matter. *Our entire religion* is built on verification. *Our entire crisis* is based on a lack of verification. *All of this pure and innocent blood that is spilt* is a consequence of a lack of verification. 'Indeed, this matter is [our] religion, so look carefully from whom you take your religion!' This was said by Shu'ba (d. 160/776), and said again by al-Sha'bī (d. c. 103/723), and a third time by Ibn al-Mubārak (d. 181/797), and so forth. '*Indeed, this matter is [our] religion*, so look carefully from whom you take your religion!' This statement [regarding killing protestors] is a blatant lie. I never said: 'kill the protestors.' I never uttered it. This is the lie of the Muslim Brotherhood on their websites, because they are planning to murder me. In order to provide a justification for this murder, they want to anathematize me (*yurīdūna takfīrī*); and in order to provide a justification for this anathematization (*takfīr*), they claim that I deem licit the blood of Muslims and wage war against Muslims. And that I am considered by them to be a hypocrite (*munāfiq*), *so kill him*! This is the arrangement.[72]

One of the attendees could be heard over the video exclaiming: 'God damn them! May their hands be cut off before they can reach you!' The comment rendered some of what Gomaa said next inaudible, and was followed by his concluding remarks in response to the question:

> Look at how these matters reach the people. You are a section of the people. But don't believe Facebook and Twitter, *especially if it comes from compulsive liars*. 'Does the believer lie?' [The Prophet] replied: 'No!' [... He also said:] 'Whoever attributes a lie to me deliberately, let them take their seat in the Hellfire!' *What a terrible matter! What a serious matter!* He prohibited us from bearing false witness (*shahādat al-zūr*), he prohibited us from slander (*iftirā'*), he prohibited us from lying (*kadhib*). Why? Because they cause fitna like this, and fitna is worse than killing.[73]

Gomaa was, of course, technically correct when he asserted that he never once uttered the phrase 'kill the protestors.' As we have seen, however, it was for very good reason difficult for him to avoid accusations of encouraging (and subsequently celebrating) the massacre of protestors in Egypt in the summer of 2013. This is because his extensive statements to the army seem to make his intent perfectly clear.

Gomaa's closeness to the army and Sisi also continued in the years that followed. On 14 March 2014, he gave a sermon at a military mosque, with Sisi in attendance, that was broadcast live.[74] Two other Azhar scholars in attendance were Grand Mufti Shawqī ʿAllām and Minister of Endowments Muḥammad Jumʿa. The theme of the sermon was the celebration of martyrs.[75] The sermon may have been requested in response to the killing of a soldier by a gunman on the previous day.[76] Gomaa also reiterated in the sermon his claims regarding the Prophet's alleged praise of the modern Egyptian army. He also attacked the MB in a sermon later that year, likely one of many such instances.[77]

Gomaa frequently appeared to give sermons to the army in the wake of militant attacks against the Egyptian security forces. On 30 January 2015, he gave a sermon after ISIS attacks on the previous day left several security officers and civilians dead in the Sinai.[78] Some members of the army and/or police were in attendance, and the onscreen watermark shows that the sermon was broadcast live at the time and had been uploaded to Gomaa's official YouTube channel on the same day. The title given to the sermon on YouTube was particularly belligerent, using a reference to a statement of the Companion of the Prophet, ʿUmar b. al-Khaṭṭāb (d. 23/644), who declared to the Meccan enemy at the Battle of Uḥud after the Meccans had succeeded in inflicting significant casualties on the Muslims, 'Our dead are in Paradise and your dead are in Hell!'[79] It is an interesting choice, as it once again applies a statement intended for hostile non-Muslims to Muslims, albeit extremist ones in this instance. In the course of the sermon, Gomaa prayed for the deceased and cast the ISIS militants as Khawārij which was, of course, the same term he had used to characterize non-violent pro-democracy protestors at Rabaa, once again blurring the lines between these two vastly different groups in a way that served the coup regime's interests.

Even in 2015, Gomaa could not escape the fallout from Rabaa despite the passage of time. He was asked, in one of his mosque classes uploaded to his official YouTube channel in March 2015, about his using the phrase 'shoot to kill.' The video is fifty-two minutes long. That he was still responding to this issue at such length nearly two years after the events in question shows that he was struggling to distance himself from his encouragement of the military to kill protestors in 2013.[80] The video also contained another attack against the MB. One new accusation he leveled against them was that the Brotherhood leader Muḥammad al-Biltājī (b. 1382f./1963) had been in league with the militants in the Sinai province who would more than a year later, in late 2014, ally themselves with ISIS. This was because of comments Biltājī made on 8 July 2013 saying that the militancy in the Sinai which he characterized as a 'response to the military coup' would cease if Sisi annulled the coup and returned Morsi to power.[81] A fuller eighty-five-second recording of Biltājī's statement, of which only fifteen seconds was promptly uploaded to YouTube by CBC Egypt, one of Gomaa's main media platforms, clarifies that the CBC clip misrepresented Biltājī's statement.[82]

In an interview a few days later, Biltājī described the shorter clip as 'a media and intelligence apparatus fabrication (*fabraka*)' that deliberately misrepresented his statements.[83] His assessment was entirely reasonable. The Egyptian media, in line with post-coup propaganda against the MB, clearly tried to portray Biltājī's statement as an admission that the MB controlled the militants in northern Sinai.[84] Gomaa was simply repeating such propaganda. As late as June 2019, state-owned media was still uploading the tendentious version of the Biltājī clip to YouTube alongside onscreen writing declaring 'Lest we forget,' and concluding the video with: 'We will never forget and we will never forgive. Sympathizing with those who kill the country (*sic*) is treason.'[85]

It is ironic that one of the protestations of Gomaa against the 'mendacity' of the MB was their misrepresentation of his words by publishing short clips that had been taken out of context. Indeed, in the March 2015 video description, as well as in the video itself, Gomaa counter-accused the MB of cherry-picking (*iqtiṣāṣ*) and fabrication (*fabraka*) in declaring that the phrase 'shoot to kill' had been used to incite the security forces to clear the Rabaa sit-in. The video description pointed out that this statement had been made on 18 August, while the clearing of Rabaa took place four days earlier, namely on 14 August. Therefore, it could not have been encouragement of the military to clear Rabaa. I am not familiar with any attempts by Gomaa's critics to portray this phrase as encouraging the Rabaa massacre specifically, rather than portraying the murderous behavior of Egyptian security forces more generally. As I have noted already, the lecture of 18 August may be seen as Gomaa's post facto vindication of the Rabaa massacre in the strongest terms.

A year later, after an apparent assassination attempt of Gomaa on his way to Friday prayers by gunmen on a motorcycle on 5 August 2016, Gomaa immediately accused the MB of being behind the attempt, although there was no evidence that this was the case. He uploaded a partial recording of his sermon from that day with the striking presence of a plainclothes security officer standing in front of the pulpit holding a gun as though he was ready to shoot at any potential attackers against Gomaa. The title of the video referred to the attackers as 'dogs of the Hellfire,' in keeping with his ongoing theme of referring to his enemies as Khawārij.[86] Gomaa took the opportunity of being interviewed after the assassination attempt to accuse the MB of being ultimately responsible.[87] He asserted that they were a single group with diverse manifestations including ISIS and al-Qaeda. None of these accusations were corroborated by him. He did nothing to explain how groups that anathematize the MB might be a manifestation of it. In any event, the attack was actually claimed by a little-known group calling themselves Hasm.[88]

The blending together of groups like ISIS and the MB was, as we have seen, part of the Egyptian state's strategy of legitimating violence and repression against the MB. Gomaa was a senior public figure in Egypt who reinforced such ideas at every opportunity, explaining his response to the attempted assassination. The logic of states like Egypt in fact resembled that of Islamophobic lobbies in the West in the context of the War on Terror that includes, at the Western governmental level, so-called policies for 'countering violent extremism,' a policy framework for dealing with terrorism that has frequently been criticized as racist for its targeting of Muslims. Without this broader paradigm, the Egyptian state's policies would not make sense, and concomitantly Gomaa's arguments would not persuade anyone. This is what has led some Western observers to argue that Arab autocracies are the 'most powerful Islamophobes' in the world.[89]

There are plenty of more recent examples of Gomaa's support for the Egyptian military regime as well as his attacks on the MB. A final example may be taken from 25 January 2017, a day after the deadliest non-state attack in modern Egyptian history was perpetrated against Sufis in the Sinai, killing more than 300 people, including twenty-seven children, all of whom were attending Friday prayers. While discussing extremism on a show on the channel MBC Egypt, Gomaa took this opportunity to reiterate his belief that the appropriate term for describing these murderous groups was 'Khawārij.' In doing so, he continued his effort to portray such extremism as having an affinity with the MB, whom he had for years by this point, also characterized as Khawārij.[90] This was made explicit in the course of the interview when Gomaa discussed a recently published book entitled *Mawqif al-Azhar al-*

Sharīf wa-ʿUlamāʾihī al-Ajillāʾ min Jamāʿat al-Ikhwān al-Muslimīn [The Stance of the Noble Azhar and Its Honorable Ulama Towards the Muslim Brotherhood]. The book, he claimed, showed that the ulama of the Azhar had been referring to the group as Khawārij since its very founding.[91] To the extent that he was referring to the Azhar's official views after it had been brought under state control by Nasser, this seems partially true. As Jeffrey Kenney notes, Azharī ulama were conscripted into Nasser's efforts at delegitimizing the MB.[92] But as Malika Zeghal and others point out, plenty of Azharīs have been sympathetic to the MB, or indeed MB members, over the course of the past century.

Conclusion

The foregoing is intended as a sampling of Gomaa's post-Rabaa activism as a religious scholar backing authoritarianism in Egypt in the years after the Rabaa massacre. As we saw, Gomaa's public persona was characterized by a remarkably close relationship with the autocratic Egyptian state and its supporting media apparatus. Gomaa provided religiously grounded ideological backing for the state justifying its extreme repression against dissident voices of both a peaceful and militant orientation. I have deliberately highlighted more of the former given that opposing militant opposition to a state's authority is less controversial. Gomaa's hostility towards civil society-based religious opposition was thus far more noteworthy. Such repression needed extra justification due to its controversial nature both domestically and internationally. Gomaa had shown himself willing to provide that justification in the service of the Egyptian coup regime of Abdel Fattah al-Sisi. In particular, we have seen how Gomaa's hostility towards the MB culminated in his support for the massacres against peaceful protestors in the summer of 2013. These, in turn, severely tarnished his reputation in the time since that summer.

We also briefly considered Ali al-Jifri's passionate defenses of Gomaa. It is noteworthy that the shaykh al-Azhar, Abdallah bin Bayyah, and Hamza Yusuf have never publicly commented on Gomaa's support for the Rabaa massacre, although as I have discussed elsewhere, Yusuf defended Gomaa's religious standing in a private exchange after Rabaa.[93] However, the silence of many leading Neo-traditionalists regarding one of their most recognizable voices globally is quite striking and arguably indicates a state of crisis within the denomination, a point I will explore further in the Epilogue. In the foregoing, we have only considered popular reactions to Gomaa's forceful pro-coup stance. Naturally, Gomaa also had many scholarly critics of his actions that summer, both in Egypt and beyond. As we turn to the next chapter, we shall consider some of the scholarly responses to both the Egyptian coup of that year and to the scholars who supported it.

8

THE REACTIONS OF ANTI-COUP ULAMA TO THE RABAA MASSACRE

(AUGUST–OCTOBER 2013)

Responses to the Rabaa massacre from anti-coup ulama were swift, mingling outrage with disbelief. The anti-coup protestors, both within and outside Egypt, had clearly underestimated the brutality the coup regime was capable of. The three most senior anti-coup Azharīs we met in Chapter 6 issued their immediate condemnations. Qaradawi responded in a sixteen-minute statement aired on Al Jazeera Mubasher by defiantly calling on all Egyptians to come out onto the streets in protest to express their rejection of the brutality. He declared this a religious obligation on every Egyptian who was able to do so. He also named the leaders of the coup regime saying that they would have to answer before God for this 'black mark' that had no precedent in the long history of Egypt. Appealing to international bodies to stand with the truth and 'call on these butchers to stop spilling Egyptian blood,' he also asked for Muslims around the world to engage in global protests on the upcoming Friday.[1]

Ḥasan al-Shāfiʿī also issued a short statement condemning the Rabaa massacre and highlighting that peaceful protest was a fundamental human right recognized by all and that the massacre went against all established religious principles and secular laws. 'Its perpetrators will be punished one day,' he asserted. He condemned the coup regime for its double standard in preserving the right to protest of pro-coup protestors but depriving anti-coup protestors of the same right in the most violent manner possible.[2] In a separate statement on the Ḥiwār channel, Muḥammad ʿImāra echoed Qaradawi's remarks by referring to 14 August 2013 as 'the darkest day in Egyptian history,' without parallel even in the colonial period. The perpetration of mass murder of its own population while the world witnessed live was a level of 'depravity without equal in the history of Egypt.'[3] He reiterated his conviction that these protests were not about the MB or Morsi, but about restarting the democratic transition. He said this was essential to stave off the possibility of Egypt descending into fully fledged internecine conflict. He also explicitly placed the blame for the massacre squarely at the feet of Sisi, asserting that all of the other so-called leaders of Egypt did not have any real power. Yet, far from despairing, he insisted that it was still possible for Egypt to step back from the brink.

Alongside these senior Azharīs, two other scholars' reactions are worth considering. They came from Aḥmad al-Raysūnī and Rajab Zakī (b. 1380/1960).[4] Aḥmad al-Raysūnī, a prominent Moroccan Islamist, features later in the chapter. In 2018, he would succeed Qaradawi to become the president of the IUMS, highlighting his global standing as a scholar. Rajab Zakī is a noted orator and student of the outspoken Azharī orator of an earlier generation, ʿAbd al-Ḥamīd Kishk (d. 1417/1996).[5] I will presently consider at length the sermon he gave two days after the Rabaa massacre. It was illustrative of the outrage an eloquent younger Azharī felt at the bloodletting of recent days and weeks. This chapter thus begins with a consideration of Rajab Zakī's sermon at some length. Next, I study Qaradawi's reaction to Ali Gomaa's pre-Rabaa private support for the coup regime. This would be aired on Qaradawi's Al Jazeera show nearly two weeks after the Rabaa massacre. As it would turn out, that episode would be Qaradawi's last. ʿImāra and Raysūnī would also briefly join the show to criticize Gomaa's remarks. By the time Gomaa's post-Rabaa video was made public in October, Qaradawi's and Raysūnī's responses would only be offered in written form. In the conclusion, I will briefly reflect on the relative powerlessness of moral arguments in the face of the Sisi regime and its mercenary scholars.

The sermon of Rajab Zakī

Arguably the most powerful rebuke of the coup regime after the Rabaa massacre from this period would come two days later in one of Cairo's many mosques. The slaughter at Rabaa took place on a Wednesday. On Friday, a blind Azharī scholar in his fifties by the name Rajab Zakī would take to his pulpit and deliver a fiery sermon directed not only at his congregation, but at the coup regime's leaders. Fulminating with righteous anger over the coup regime's scorn for the people it had mowed down in the streets in recent days, Zakī's stirring sermon was reminiscent of his one-time teacher, the outspoken blind scholar ʿAbd al-Ḥamīd Kishk. The congregation's loud weeping could be heard over the microphone during the brief intermission between the two parts of the Friday sermon.[6]

The shaykh began his sermon with the recitation of God's praise in numerous Qur'anic verses all of which began with the words *al-ḥamdu li-Llāh*, his sonorous voice being carried with clarity as he spoke into the pulpit's microphones. He then briefly raised his voice to a crescendo as he recited the testimony of faith: 'I bear witness that there is no god but God, alone without any partner.' Resuming a moderate volume, he interspersed verses from the Qur'an with his own speech as he reminded his congregation that it was God who ultimately had power over life and death:

> He is the One Who created death and life (Q. 67:2). He bestowed upon the human being the gift of life, and it is He, in His Glory, Who takes his spirit at the hour and in the moment that He has appointed; since there is no provider but He, no creator but He, nor can anyone grant or withhold aside from Him. No created being whatsoever [can claim] any of these [prerogatives].

Reaching a crescendo once again, he declared: 'For this reason, there is no one Who may be called in prayer except He, and no one Who may be turned to in hope of benefit except He, nor may anyone be feared, feel awe of, or be terrified by anyone but He!' The shaykh then sent customary salutations upon the Prophet. The Prophet was sent, he noted, in a time of widespread tyranny (*ẓulm*) and tribulations (*fitan*) in which the strong would take advantage of the weak. In this context, Zakī reminded them, God sent the Prophet to remind the people that 'they were born free.' Reaching a gradual crescendo once again, he asserted that no one could enslave (*yastaʿbid*) them—the only one deserving of their worship (*an yaʿbudūh*) was God, the only one who had power over their life and death.[7] With this introduction lasting roughly five minutes, Zakī next outlined the core theme of his sermon, namely his response to the massacres of recent days.[8]

Egypt and the Islamic umma more generally, he said, was going through one of its 'darkest periods' (*min aḥlak al-fatarāt*). Raising his voice to a crescendo of anger, he exclaimed: 'no one could have expected or even contemplated that matters would come to this.' Yet, he voiced his gratitude to God that nothing like this had taken place before these days, despite the tyranny (*ẓulm*, *ṭughyān*), repression (*qahr*), and corruption (*fasād*) that had been Egypt's lot in recent decades, unlike in communist Russia, for example, where the repression of Muslims was even more extreme. Recalling dark episodes from Islamic history, he noted that the Mongols and the Crusaders ravaged Muslim lands in the premodern era, but God ultimately brought an end to them. There were many such episodes in history, he pointed out. As he made these remarks, he affected cadences with his voice, periodically raising it to a crescendo before returning to his normal stentorian clarity with an impact on his audience that is naturally difficult to convey in writing. In the remainder of my description of his sermon, however, I will indicate instances in which he had raised his voice considerably by using italics in direct quotations.

Zakī noted how in the middle of the twentieth century, some of this repression against religious expression was even witnessed in Egypt, with the state imprisoning youths simply because they were attending prayers in the mosque. Some of these youths were 'buried alive' in prison, he exclaimed in anger. But then, Egypt began returning to its religious and spiritual roots. Before this took place, Zakī asserted, the humiliating defeat of Nasser in the war of 1967 was inevitable. In sonorous tones, he declared:

> May God show mercy to Shaykh Shaʿrāwī (d. 1419/1998) when he *prostrated in thanks to God* on the day of the *defeat in 1967* causing people to ask in astonishment, '*how can you prostrate*, O Shaykh, when God has vanquished Egypt and the Muslims at the hands of the Zionists? How can this be!' *He replied*, '*Had God granted us victory at the hands of these people*, He would have been a tyrant, and God can never be a tyrant.'[9]

Zakī then attributed the qualified 'victory' of Egypt's 1973 war against Israel to the Egyptian people beginning to turn back to God after the defeat of 1967. It is not my purpose to evaluate the historicity of these claims as much as it is to illustrate their articulation in response to the coup regime's perceived crushing of the religiously minded in ways that were reminiscent of earlier eras in modern Egyptian history.

Zakī portrayed the era of Mubarak, however, as little better than that of the mid-twentieth century. For thirty repressive years, he noted from his personal experience, no one was able to speak truth to power 'except for *the one who knew with religious certainty that God alone* was in control of everything.' In a brief aside, he asked God to bless the many 'virtuous, powerful, true men' among his teachers, 'who did not fear *anyone but God*, despite the ordeals and tribulations they were put through.' Mentioning some of his teachers including Muḥammad al-Ghazālī (d. 1416/1996) and 'Abd al-Ḥamīd Kishk, he declared, 'they would *speak the truth*, despite suffering imprisonment and incarceration. But God be praised: the tyrants came to an end and the memories of our ulama were upheld honorably because God is the one who elevated them, and abased their enemies.'

The shaykh next turned to the 2011 revolution in which, he highlighted, the people were united in their opposition to tyranny and repression. He praised God for the people's unseating of promoters of tyranny (*ẓulm*) and falsehood (*bāṭil*) in that revolution but noted that the fitna was only to return in a form that was more violent (*a'naf*), more severe (*ashadd*), and more abominable (*afẓa'*). Raising his voice to a loud crescendo, he exclaimed:

> *I had not contemplated that I would witness in Egypt, in my lifetime, that the first victory of its powerful army in forty years* would be against its own people, *for whatever reason! For whatever reason! That there be murder and incineration—incinerating a mosque, incinerating the House of God!*[10]

Lowering his voice, he asked: 'In whose interest is this? Let us disagree however much we like. We agree that there are differences of opinion, political differences and differences in perspective.' Raising his voice again, he continued: '*Say whatever you like! But there are people who covet power, and covet authority, and they are prepared to pay for it even with the blood of the entire populace.* All this is fine. These are desires (*shahawāt*). They exist. They rise and fall. They come and go.'

Raising his voice once again, he then cried out:

> *But for matters to come to the point of murder, premeditated murder with the most vicious of weapons, and instruments of war in the hands of the Egyptian army and police; then for Muslims to be incinerated* for no reason other than that they expressed their opinions! *I am free, my brother. Indeed, [Aḥmad] 'Urābī (d. 1329/1911) said as much, after 'Umar b. al-Khaṭṭāb did: 'How can you enslave people,* when their mothers gave birth to them as free!' Brother, we can have different opinions, but that the result of my differing with your opinion be that you kill me, just because you have weapons *and power! Then you kill me, then you incinerate me, and then you lie to the people. And then a servile and wicked media that knows no restraint, recognizes no one's rights, and whose controllers have no fear of God, and which many of the poor populace believe, and consequently they cheer on the evil, cheer on the burning, cheer on the oceans of blood that flowed on the earth!*[11]

Zakī's outrage at the curtailment of free speech and liberty may appear counter-intuitive to some readers expecting such exhortations to come from liberals rather than beturbaned Azharīs speaking out for the rights of the MB. For the shaykh, there was clearly no contradiction in these matters. In keeping with the discourse of this generation of Islamists, which is still unfortunately drowned out in much Orientalizing media coverage of mainstream Islamism, many are wont to forget that political liberties are at the heart of the contemporary Islamist project. Many of these ideas, promoted by Islamists in recent decades, have also permeated the thought of the ulama in institutions like the Azhar, necessitating the imbrication of mainstream Islamism and Neo-traditionalism in modern Sunnism. This would result in the ironic reality that many of the Islamist-sympathizing ulama in post-coup Egypt would show themselves to be more committed to political liberty than Egypt's so-called liberals, many of whom defended or even celebrated the slaughter and subsequent incarceration of tens of thousands of MB members and sympathizers.[12]

In his sermon, Zakī now returned to a quieter tone of voice, asking calmly: 'In the interest of whom [do these people act]? We have furnished *Israel* what it could not have dreamt of doing over many decades. With our own hands, we killed each other.' Zakī now returned to a raised voice:

> *I will now say something after which I may not ever say anything from this place again. It may be that I end up with the people in prison! I may be killed just as my friends and brothers have been killed!* I have no problem with that, because as I said at the beginning, *no one owns life (al-rūḥ) and sustenance (al-rizq) except God! But I must say something, or else: may my tongue be cut out if I stay quiet rather than speaking the truth in the darkest of times and circumstances. Let those who are pleased be pleased, and let those who are angered be angered. Let those who agree with me agree, and let those who disagree with me disagree. What is important is that I am absolved of guilt, as God says in the story of the People of the Sabbath,* 'when some of them asked [their preachers], "Why do you bother preaching to a people whom God will destroy, or at least punish severely?" [The preachers] answered, "To absolve ourselves before your Lord, and so that they may perhaps take heed"' (Q. 7:164). *I say these words to absolve myself before God, and perhaps one who hears me will fear God.*[13]

In a quiet voice, he added: 'For death is coming. Those who preceded us were also tyrannical. And where are they now? Many people were tyrannical and arrogant.'

Returning to a rising crescendo, he continued:

> *Where is Nimrod (Namrūd) son of Canaan?*[14] *Where is Korah (Qārūn)? Where is Pharaoh (Firʿawn)? Where is Hāmān? Where is Ubayy b. Khalaf (d. 3/625)?*[15] *Where are Abū Jahl (d. 2/624)*[16] *and Abū Lahab (d. 2/624)?*[17] *Where is Ḥajjāj al-Thaqafī (d. 95/714)?*[18] *Where is [King] Farouk (d. 1384/1965) and where are his father and grandfather?*[19] *Where is Abdel Nasser (d. 1390/1970)? Where is Sadat (d. 1401/1981)? Where is Mubarak? All of them have gone!* Nothing remains but God. *Everyone will come to an end. 'Everything is destined to perish except He! (Q. 28:88)' 'Everyone on earth will perish!* Only the Person of your Lord, full of majesty and splendor, will endure' (Q. 55:26).[20]

Zakī then proceeded to relate the story of the infamous prison director under Gamal Abdel Nasser, Ḥamza al-Basyūnī (d. 1391/1971), who he alleges to have exclaimed to his Islamist prisoners in the 1950s and 1960s: 'If your Lord descended from the heavens, I would imprison him in cell nineteen.' In response to this blasphemous utterance, Zakī asked: 'Where has Ḥamza al-Basyūnī gone? *How did he die?*' He then related the story of his death, for the benefit of those unfamiliar from the younger generation. He was driving his car to Alexandria when he was struck by a lorry carrying steel reinforcing bars used in construction. According to Zakī, the bars struck him in the neck and dragged him out of his car cutting him to pieces. Zakī concluded: 'He did not imprison our Lord, but rather God imprisoned him in steel in this world,' adding quietly, 'and prison awaits him in the next life.'[21]

The shaykh noted that these words were intended as a means of compassionate exhortation and sincere advice (*naṣīḥa*) so that he could stand before God having fulfilled his obligations. He next addressed the coup regime's rulers directly with the words: 'Fear God (*ittaqū-Llāh*). *Before you is Ḥamza al-Basyūnī*—the closest person to you, your teacher, your educator.' He repeated his exhortation:

> Fear your Lord. The world is worthless. Political power is worthless. Were you to strip yourself of all of your medals and ranks, and then meet with your Lord *on the day you die, your hands cleansed of innocent blood,* nothing will harm you. You will have succeeded in attaining the best of this world and the next. But if you [...] are resurrected before God *while your hands are stained with blood, the burning of mosques, and the murder of people praying,* then no one will be able to help you, by God besides whom there is no god! The world is short. *Its value is paltry.* Turn back to God![22]

Zakī's exhortations continued in an unrelenting fashion as he expressed his anger at the regime's crimes. He pointed out how even God did not respond to disbelief by annihilating people, but rather gave them the choice to believe or disbelieve (Q. 18:29). Raising his voice once again, he cried: 'This is our Lord! This is our Lord! *It is not General Sisi or Muhammad Ibrahim. It is God! He says: 'Whoever wishes may believe'—he is free to do that—'and whoever wishes can disbelieve'—he is free to do that! (Q. 18:29).*' Even God, Zakī noted, gives people the option, and they would face the consequences of their choices in the next life. He asked rhetorically, slipping into the casual intonations of the Egyptian dialect as he once again built a gradual crescendo of anger: 'My brother, are you better than our Lord? Are you more generous than our Lord? *Are you more powerful than our Lord? Are you more high and mighty than God?!*' He concluded with a soft reply: 'Never. Never.'[23]

At this point, the shaykh had been speaking for a little over twenty minutes. He was about to come to the final section of the first part of his roughly half-an-hour-long sermon. Now he started building up to a final and particularly powerful crescendo by addressing his congregation directly. He told them that Egypt had entered a very difficult period that would harm a lot of people indiscriminately. He noted in a solemn drawn-out tone: 'On the day that they stand before God, He will ask us about the blood [that was spilt], about the children [who were killed or orphaned], about the women who [were murdered or widowed].' Finally, his exhortation increased in tempo and volume as it moved towards its crescendo:

> *I had been standing with the protestors in Rabaa square everyday, and I swear by God—and God will ask me about this oath of mine—that what was said in the statement of [Minister of Interior] Muhammad Ibrahim is all lies, fabrications, and slander! God will most certainly silence his tongue! And we will witness in him the wonders of God's power [in punishing him], if not in this world, then in the next life! On the day the Hour arrives!* And everyone who approved of it, consented to it, and participated in it, 'you will remember what I now say. I entrust my cause to God. *God is most watchful over His servants' (Q. 40:44). And I remind you of my words once again:* 'I entrust my cause to God. *God is most watchful over His servants.*' And [I remind you] of the words of the Prophet, peace and blessings of God be upon him: *'Piety does not wear away, sin is not forgotten, and the [Divine] Judge shall not perish!'*[24] *Do whatever you like! As you treat others, thus shall you be repaid. As you treat others O Muhammad Ibrahim, thus shall you be repaid! As you treat others O Sisi, thus shall you be repaid! As you treat others, O liars (*kadhaba*), O deceivers (*ghashasha*), O tyrants (*ẓalama*), O evil ones (*fajara*),* thus shall you be repaid.[25]

With this peroration, the shaykh completed the longer first part of his sermon and sat for the customary silent prayer. Over the microphone, despite its elevation from the ground level, the anguished crying of the worshippers could be heard for the next 16 seconds before the preacher began the shorter second half of the sermon.[26] In it, he asked the congregants of his large mosque that if anyone had any means of conveying his message to the coup leadership, that they should do so. Beseeching God, he cried:

> *My Lord, my Lord, my Lord,* let my voice reach one of these people—perhaps he will fear God, even if the time for that has passed, and matters have boiled over, but it is still possible to do something. The world will not help you. High public offices will not help you. High rank will not help you. Political power will not help you. The human being will die, and be shrouded in a shroud without any openings, he will be without any wealth, and he will enter the grave alone.[27]

Breaking into Egyptian dialect, he added, 'You won't be taking your guards with you, my friend. You won't be taking your artillery, or your machine guns, or your automatic weapons.' Resuming a more formal register, he repeated: '*You will enter the grave alone. And you will be resurrected on the Day of Judgement as vile (*dhalīl*), vile, vile, standing alone with your head hanging in humiliation!* Organize a reckoning for this day. *Make your preparations for it.*' Zakī finally declared that God was his witness in conveying this message. He stated that God knew that there was nothing in this for him. He simply wanted to please God by putting an end to the bloodshed. With complete composure, he added, 'We are prepared to face what we must afterwards, whatever the sacrifice.'

In his closing remarks, he mentioned 'even the shaykh al-Azhar, who participated, participated, participated!' In a rising crescendo, he added:

> *He has a large share in this [crime] like any of the soldiers from these people because he approved it. He is not excused by saying:* 'I did not know about the dispersing of the sit-in until [I saw it on] the television.' *What a wretched excuse O shaykh al-Azhar*; or I should say, you used to be the shaykh al-Azhar in our eyes, but now you are no shaykh to us.[28]

Continuing to address the coup leadership and soldiers, he added 'Be warned against taking the words of the shaykh al-Azhar or [Pope] Tawadros as justification for killing people.' Having mentioned the Coptic pope, he noted:

> And on this point, I am against, and Islam is against burning churches and attacking Christians. We have no problem with the Christian community. They are a people living life just like us. Between us is equity, kindness, and justice,

> so long as they treat us with equity and justice, and do not support waging war against us. *As for Tawadros as an individual*, his matter is with God. He will take care of his requital and taking revenge *against him* and his like in both this world and the next. As for the Christian community, they are an Egyptian community, citizens with the same rights and obligations as we have.[29]

In a final remark before the closing prayers, he warned people against taking fatwas from 'mercenary scholars' (*al-mashāyikh al-ma'jūrīn*), loudly repeating the word '*mercenary*' for emphasis. In his closing prayer, he called on God's support against the people of falsehood (*bāṭil*), and 'evil, murderous, and deceitful tyrants.' He also condemned the media that promoted the killing of people, and the burning and subsequent closing of mosques. Finally, he mentioned the desecration and mutilation of Muslim corpses, noting that the Prophet prohibited Muslims from mutilating corpses, even if they are non-Muslims in the battlefield.

Rajab Zakī's sermon is illustrative of a respected Azhar graduate, a popular preacher, and a noted reciter of the Qur'an with no formal affiliation with the MB, but one who likely spoke for many Azhar scholars on that day while smaller post-Rabaa massacres were still ongoing. The original Arabic sermon gives a sense of the intensity of passion that animated Cairo in those days among the coup's opponents. Perhaps no one was quite as eloquent in their denunciations of the Rabaa massacre as this relatively young scholar. I have tried to convey some of his eloquence and passion in the foregoing. As he had expected, Zakī was relieved of his duties as a preacher, although somewhat remarkably, he appears to have been spared any more serious consequences, perhaps in part because he left the country soon thereafter. Within ten days of giving his sermon, he was being interviewed in the London-based studios of al-Ḥiwār channel discussing the leaked videos of Islamic scholars, the most senior being Ali Gomaa, who had spoken privately to the military in support of the coup.[30] In the next sections, I will consider the responses of some of the other scholars we have met to the leaked videos of Gomaa.

Qaradawi on Gomaa's first leaked video

The release of Gomaa's private video lecture to the security forces prior to the Rabaa massacre resulted in recriminations from three of the scholars mentioned above on Yusuf al-Qaradawi's regular Al Jazeera show. As it would turn out, this also ended up being the final episode of Qaradawi's show ever to be broadcast. Pressure from other Gulf states hostile to Qatar giving Qaradawi the freedom to promote the Arab revolutions would ultimately force Qaradawi off the air, as he would diplomatically allude to in an interview years later.[31] Thus on 25 August 2013, he took to his show on Al Jazeera for what would turn out to be the last time, for his only *al-Sharīʿa wa-l-Ḥayāh* episode after the Rabaa massacre and after some of the leaks about Gomaa legitimating violence against protestors had surfaced. Qaradawi would, among other things, use the show to respond to Gomaa's assertions that the participants in these anti-coup protests were rebels (Khawārij), and thus justifiably massacred. Accordingly, the episode was entitled 'Rebels: Between Religion, History, and Politics' (*al-Khawārij bayn al-Dīn wa-l-Tārīkh wa-l Siyāsa*).[32]

In many respects, this episode of *al-Sharīʿa wa-l-Ḥayāh* was concerned with refuting Gomaa's arguments, and in order to do so, ʿImāra and Raysūnī were given some airtime towards the end of the show to make comments about Gomaa's problematic statements. The show began with the presenter citing the Qur'an (Q. 16:116) which warns against making false claims regarding what is lawful and unlawful in the eyes of God. This was followed by Qaradawi noting that modern Muslims were today confronted by people who gave fatwas that there was no Islamic justification for. These fatwas permitted the impermissible, prohibited the permissible, did away with obligations that had been set down by God, and set down obligations that God had not legitimated. He added that the major problem (*mushkila kubrā*) was that true ulama (*ʿulamāʾ ḥaqīqiyyūn*) were absent, and those who had emerged in their place were false scholars (*ʿulamāʾ muftaʿalūn*) who had been manufactured by the authorities so that they may appear before people to give them fatwas without themselves being qualified for this task. This necessitated that Muslims be on guard and learn to recognize what constituted a true alim, and not be taken in by outward appearances.

Qaradawi next addressed the more specific legal questions at issue. Some of these are familiar by now. He pointed out that the Khawārij, in a legal sense, were those who rebelled against a legitimate ruler whose legitimacy was grounded in the community giving the ruler their allegiance. In modern times, he argued that this was to be realized through a process of elections in accordance with a constitution, which, he highlighted, was the present norm in all democratic nations. The appropriate norms for governance in modern times, Qaradawi maintained, were realized through constitutions that had been voted on and supported by the majority of the population. These were constitutions that, in Qaradawi's words 'govern the people' (*taḥkum al-nās*).

The people would choose to be governed by a constitution that had been legitimated by a majority of the populace such that it became binding upon them. The constitution would then become a point of reference, and people would live in accord with it.

Qaradawi argued that the populace (*sha'b*) should have a say in matters pertaining to their own governance. He further asserted that the popular will could be recognized through the voting process. He maintained that on a given question, whether it be electing a leader or voting on a law, a society would be able to recognize what the majority of people wanted when put to the vote. In a sense, he appeared to be arguing for elements of both direct and representative democracy, although his discourse on democracy is not well-systematized as might be expected in a Middle Eastern context that does not, for the most part, enjoy democratic freedoms due to the persistence of repressive states. This notwithstanding, Qaradawi's remarks illustrated his aspiration towards realizing greater freedom and democracy and his assertion that such norms were the appropriate ones for modern Muslim societies. As for the legitimacy of constitutions, he noted that they were akin to contractual stipulations (*shurūṭ*), and that the Prophet stated that 'Muslims are obligated by their contractual stipulations' (*al-Muslimūn 'inda shurūṭihim*). Such contracts had to be adhered to so long as they did not prohibit the Islamically permissible or permit the Islamically impermissible. Qaradawi concluded by pointing out that not only were constitutions permissible but that people were required to abide by them (*al-dasātīr yajib an ya'mal bi-hā al-nās*).[33] A corollary of this was his opposition to the coup's annulment of Egypt's post-revolutionary constitution.

In response to a question about scholars who issued fatwas supporting the coup (accusing those who opposed it of being rebels and calling on people to fight and even kill the coup's opponents), Qaradawi said that such statements could not come from respectable scholars. The only scholars who are worthy of the name, he averred, were those who referred to the Qur'an, the Sunna, their commentators, and to the legal scholars of the various schools of law, and who had an understanding of modern realities. As for a scholar (alim) who followed his whims (*yatba' hawāh*) or the whims of the ruler, he was not in fact a scholar. The Sharia brought humans from a condition in which they were following their whims to a state of following God's law. So long as an individual followed their whims, he was not a true scholar. A true scholar, Qaradawi stated, is also not selective in reading the scriptural sources, disregarding certain texts or hadiths while taking others into consideration.

By contrast, Qaradawi claimed that the true scholars had declared Morsi to be the legitimate ruler, asserting that this is a matter of 'consensus' (*ijmāʿ*). In this instance, he was clearly using this word in a non-technical sense. What he appears to have meant by it was that there was agreement in modern democracies that all citizens had to abide by a social contract, usually embodied in a constitution and in statutes that were laid down by the people's representatives in a parliament. It is obvious that not every citizen in a modern democracy gives their explicit assent to national constitutions. Indeed, the older a constitution, the less likely that any citizens will have voted to support its introduction, as is the case in the United States, for example. However, there is a general consensus that it must be followed, just as modern democracies recognize that laws must still be upheld even if one's preferred candidate does not ultimately succeed in gaining office. While this does not correspond with juristic consensus in classical Islamic law, this seems to be the sense in which Qaradawi is speaking here.

In this *novel* technical sense, then, we can understand how Qaradawi claimed there was a consensus based on Morsi's election to the presidency, which Egyptian society accepted at the time after Morsi had succeeded in gaining office against all other contenders. And although Morsi's popularity undoubtedly waned in the course of the following year, Qaradawi's concern, like that of Shāfiʿī and ʿImāra, regarding Morsi's removal in a coup that did not follow any constitutionally recognized procedure was that it undermined the democratic process altogether, ushering in a new autocratic period in Egyptian history. Consequently, in a manner similar to his anti-coup fatwa, he defiantly reiterated his insistence that Morsi remained the legitimate president of Egypt, citing scripture to underline this.

A natural consequence of Qaradawi's arguments for Morsi's democratic legitimacy was that he considered those who had participated in the coup to be rebels (*khawārij*). To this, he added that Sisi had violated his oath of office that entailed following orders from the president under whom he was sworn in, namely Morsi. Qaradawi's forceful denunciation culminated in his citation of the hadith quoted earlier by Ali Gomaa regarding those who rebel. This canonical hadith reports from the Prophet the following statement: 'Whoever comes to you, while you are unified around a single leader, and wishes to sow dissension in your ranks and create rifts between you, then kill him whoever he may be.' While Gomaa used the hadith to justify to Egyptian security forces killing the protesters against the coup, Qaradawi would invert this, pointing out that the hadith actually applied to those who rebelled against Morsi.[34]

While he would go on to clarify that he was not advocating the perpetration of violence against the coup regime, he stressed that if Gomaa was a genuine scholar, he would have cited these hadiths to the coup leaders not to goad on the security forces to set upon protestors but to dissuade them from carrying out the great crime of rebellion against a legitimate ruler as well as the mass murder that the coup regime would ultimately perpetrate. With this now coming to pass, he insisted that the coup regime had to be resisted and was not to be accepted. Quite how this was to be done was not clear, and it was this lack of any remaining path to effective resistance that ultimately rendered such opposition ineffectual against the Egyptian coup regime of Abdel Fattah al-Sisi. In his Al Jazeera show, Qaradawi was only willing to countenance peaceful resistance against the regime. He asserted with pride that all of the resistance against the coup had been peaceful (*muqāwama silmiyya*), citing the statement of the General Guide of the MB, Muḥammad Badīʿ (b. 1362/1943), who declared early on in the protests at Rabaa: 'Our revolution is a peaceful one, and will remain peaceful, and our peacefulness is more powerful than bullets.'[35]

Qaradawi also took direct aim at Gomaa, who he asserted could not be taken as an authority on Islamic matters. He characterized Gomaa as 'a slave of those in power' (*ʿabd al-sulṭa*) and scholars like him as 'scholars serving those in power and agents of the security apparatus' (*ʿulamāʾ al-sulṭa wa-ʿumalāʾ al-shurṭa*).[36] 'Whatever those in power wanted him to say he would say.' Thus, Qaradawi declared that such 'scholars' could not be seen as religious authorities, adding: 'these people are not free, we cannot [depend on] slaves' to lead the umma. He portrayed Gomaa as having 'permitted the killing of peaceful protestors.' Qaradawi asserted that Gomaa's position had no supporters among the ulama, adding that one could not possibly obtain a sound Islamic ruling from such an individual.

Comments from Raysūnī and ʿImāra

Two colleagues of Qaradawi's would call in to the show that day to convey a similar message regarding Gomaa. The first was the notable Moroccan scholar, Aḥmad al-Raysūnī, then a junior colleague of Qaradawi at the IUMS. Raysūnī began by noting that he had been following Gomaa's statements closely for some years, particularly since the 25 January revolutions of 2011, and that it was clear that Gomaa, who he described as 'unfortunately an old friend' had displayed considerable inconsistency in his fatwas. His fickleness and the contradictions of his statements had, in Raysūnī's view, vitiated his scholarship, character, and legal standing (*asqaṭat ʿilmahū wa-khuluqahū wa-ʿadālatah*). This was why, Raysūnī argued, the regime had secretly been taking him to address the army, who are generally ignorant of Islamic law, and they used him to give supposedly Islamic justifications to violently quell the protestors against the coup. They also took him to various television channels which were presenting tendentious arguments in favor of the coup with the support of Gomaa.[37]

In opposition to Gomaa's stances, Raysūnī emphasized the right, if not the obligation, of the protestors to demonstrate in Egypt in those days. The role of the scholars, he added, was to guide such protestors as leaders and participants in the protests. To say otherwise, and to justify the killing of protestors is not fiqh (Islamic law), he declared, but the 'sale of legal judgements' (*tijāra fiqhiyya*). Raysūnī concluded by saying that a scholar had to exercise the utmost caution against giving a free rein to those bearing arms, such as armies and security forces, for if such groups are given fatwas permitting them to shoot and kill protestors, they would take them as an open license to perpetrate massacres. Armies and those state forces bearing arms would likely pay little heed to any conditions that were placed on them when it came to opening fire on protestors, given the prevailing atmosphere in Egypt at the time. He was obviously saying so with the benefit of hindsight. As we shall see shortly, when further leaks of Gomaa's post-Rabaa speech to the armed forces emerged, Raysūnī declared Gomaa a 'participant' in the mass slaughter in Egypt's streets after the coup.

After Raysūnī's comments, the presenter introduced a second caller from Egypt, Muḥammad ʿImāra, to hear his comments on the Egyptian predicament. ʿImāra began by pointing out that the problem Egypt was experiencing was a political disagreement and a political struggle, and not one that was a matter of religious belief or pertained to the foundational tenets of faith. Given this, ʿImāra argued that the appropriate measure for assessing these disagreements were those of benefit (*nafʿ*) and harm (*ḍarar*) or right (*ṣawāb*) and wrong (*khaṭaʾ*) but not belief (*īmān*) and disbelief (*kufr*). In other words, ʿImāra argued that such disagreements could not result in accusations of disbelief which would raise the stakes of a disagreement considerably.[38]

ʿImāra next implied that Gomaa, his colleague on the CSS, served as a mouthpiece for the Egyptian police state. While he did not say so with the forthrightness of Qaradawi, he made the suggestion with a historical anecdote about the questionable standing of scholars who associated with the security services. He pointed out that Egypt had been suffering for a long time at the hands of a 'military and police state,' and in particular, this had given rise to numerous religious figures who had served as mouthpieces for the security forces. He further pointed out that the Islamic umma had historically questioned the standing of those ulama who sought to consort with rulers, and asked rhetorically, 'so what can be said of those ulama who have sought to consort with the security forces, and considered themselves mouthpieces for the security forces?'

'Imāra also reiterated some of Qaradawi's earlier points, which are reflected in his own post-coup public statements considered earlier, that the only way to ascertain a leader's legitimacy in modern states was through the electoral process, and in this respect, he added, Mohamed Morsi won the support of the majority of those who voted in Egypt's elections. He highlighted that these elections were supervised by the army, the judiciary, and international observers. Thus, he concluded, Morsi had effectively been given a pledge of allegiance (*bay'a*) by the populace, in accordance with the constitution. He again characterized the constitution as a social, political, legal, and Sharia contract (*'aqd ijtimā'ī siyāsī qānūnī Shar'ī*) between those who govern and the governed. The pledge was valid for four years according to the constitution. 'Imāra also reiterated his earlier arguments that rebellion (*khurūj*) was defined in Islamic law as armed rebellion (*khurūj musallaḥ*). Thus, in the case of the coup in which the army and security forces had descended upon the streets with arms, tanks and armored vehicles, *they* were the ones to be considered rebels against Morsi.

A final point that 'Imāra highlighted was that the reason for the coup regime seeking such fatwas from Ali Gomaa was because of the magnitude of the crimes committed against the peaceful protestors. Given the scale of the mass murder perpetrated in the streets of Egypt with potentially thousands of dead and many more injured, it was necessary to enlist a scholar who would provide cover for what were ultimately outrageous crimes. While he did not say so explicitly, the obvious implication was that Ali Gomaa was such a scholar.[39]

Reactions to Gomaa's post-Rabaa video

The last episode of Qaradawi's Al Jazeera show was broadcast on 25 August and addressed only Gomaa's first post-Rabaa private lecture to the military alongside his public statements in support of the coup. Gomaa's more shocking post-Rabaa lecture was not released for another six weeks, on 10 October, eliciting a further written response from Yusuf al-Qaradawi and Aḥmad al-Raysūnī, now that televised avenues appeared to be considerably limited. The following day, and with characteristic alacrity, the eighty-seven-year-old Qaradawi published a 2,000-word refutation of the video on his website.[40] Entitled 'Refuting the Army's Mufti,' it is a derisive critique of 'Shaykh or General Ali Gomaa.' In the course of this piece, Qaradawi asked why Gomaa had said what he had to the army 'in secret.' He answered that this was because none of Egypt's scholars or scholarly institutions would ever have accepted the use of such language as 'shoot to kill.' Citing the Qur'an (Q. 47:4), he noted that even with respect to unbelievers in wartime, the Qur'an did not exhort such rapaciousness. But Gomaa had no qualms in 'supporting the people in power (*ahl al-quwwa*) over the people in the right (*ahl al-ḥaqq*)' with his 'poisonous fatwas' (*al-fatāwa al-sāmma*).

Qaradawi cited the words with which Gomaa was willing to attack his fellow Muslim Egyptians who he considered 'the Khawārij from whom we must purify Egypt ... blessed are those who kill them and are killed by them ... trash ... putrid people ... dogs of Hell ... who do not deserve our Egyptian identity, whom we are disgraced by our association with.' He addressed some of these remarks in turn. Responding to Gomaa's accusation that the protestors were Khawārij, he repeated his point from earlier statements that such a label applied only to those who came out in 'open armed rebellion against the legitimate ruler.' Qaradawi insisted that the absence of weapons in these protests, or perhaps more accurately the apparently miniscule presence of such weapons, refuted Gomaa's accusation. He reiterated his more plausible counter-claim describing the coup leadership as Khawārij. Similarly, he expressed his revulsion at Gomaa describing the protestors, many of whom were talented middle-class contributors to society, as 'trash.' He also expressed astonishment at Gomaa citing dreams in support of the massacres. 'Who among the ulama has said: "these dreams legitimate the spilling of sacrosanct blood, imprisoning noble people, and dragging chaste women to concentration camps overseen by soldiers who do not fear God or have any sense of shame"?' Qaradawi had much more to say in the piece of which the foregoing gives the general tenor. He concluded with a prayer asking God to humiliate those who would play with His religion in such a manner.

Two days later, Qaradawi's younger Moroccan colleague would express his shock at Gomaa's leaked video in a written Al Jazeera interview in less animated, though no less severe, terms than his more senior colleague.[41] In Raysūnī's opinion, Gomaa was a 'participant' in mass murder. Raysūnī, who was roughly the same age as Gomaa, said in the interview that he had long considered the former grand mufti 'one of his friends,' someone for whom he harbored love and respect which was why his recent statements were 'very painful' for him personally. Speaking in his 2013 interview, Raysūnī put it thus:

> The reality is that Dr Ali Gomaa lost his balance since Hosni Mubarak appointed him to the post of Mufti of the Republic ten years ago. Since that time, his confused and anomalous fatwas began to emerge in quick succession. Those who know him noticed the radical transformation (*inqilāb*) that took hold in his thought, his stances, and his temperament. The way this is understood by people who know the man is that he began intensely to aspire to and covet the post of the shaykh al-Azhar, particularly after seeing a dream which he narrated (one of his students told me this directly) which indicates—according to his interpretation—that he would become the Mufti of Egypt, and then the shaykh al-Azhar. But if he had lost his balance since that time for the sake of official posts, now he has lost his senses. For in the address he gave in a closed hall to the top brass of the army and police, and which people later saw in a leaked recording, the shaykh and mufti speaks with uncontrolled emotion and agitation that manifests in his movement and tone even before his words.[42]

Like Qaradawi and ʻImāra before him, Raysūnī reiterated that as the protestors were not engaged in an 'armed rebellion' against a 'legitimate ruler,' the term Khawārij could not logically be applied to them, although it 'applied perfectly' to the perpetrators of the coup. Being a highly regarded jurist, he was also asked whether Gomaa's words could constitute 'incitement to murder' according to Islamic law. Raysūnī's response was unequivocal:

> All of [Gomaa's] speech is explicit incitement to murder and making an example of the opposition. In fact, he went further and called to purifying Egypt of them, meaning extirpating them. He is therefore a participant in the murder of every person killed and every outrage perpetrated under the influence of his speech and fatwas.

Interestingly, among the many other trenchant criticisms leveled by both Qaradawi and Raysūnī at Gomaa, neither responds to Gomaa's inexplicit excommunication of Qaradawi. It is possible that the scholars did not make the connection, given that Qaradawi's name was not explicitly mentioned. Quite conceivably, they did not wish to dignify the slur with a response.

Conclusion

The foregoing provides what I hope is a representative snapshot of the innumerable hostile scholarly responses to the Egyptian coup and the massacres that took place in the weeks that followed. It was clear by this time, however, that these juridico-ethical exhortations would have little impact on the political realities in the region. By October 2013, it was apparent that outside of Egypt, and arguably even within it, Gomaa and his pro-coup colleagues had largely lost the moral argument. This was most strikingly illustrated by the absence of any defenders of Gomaa's post-Rabaa private lecture aside from Gomaa himself. While he could not avoid confronting such arguments as they occasionally cropped up in his public classes, all the other pro-autocracy scholars we have seen over the course of the present work said nothing to defend Gomaa's pronouncements that the security forces could 'shoot to kill' protestors. Yet their silence may have indicated something else. In the new authoritarian context, Islamic legal and moral arguments meant little before the brute force of the state. No matter what Qaradawi, Shāfiʿī, or any of the other learned and eloquent critics of the murderous new regime had to say, the renewed Egyptian state and its autocratic rulers were only interested in their own perpetuation, no matter the cost. No amount of moralizing could change that. The autocrat's existence was its own self-justifying moral ideal, and all other legal and ethical norms were subordinated to it.

As we saw in Chapter 4, Abdallah bin Bayyah had actually developed an exceptional Islamic legal argument to rationalize this state of affairs. As I have discussed elsewhere in greater detail, Bin Bayyah has never publicly commented on the Egyptian coup and its aftermath,[43] but his more developed arguments, which I will briefly explore towards the end of the next chapter, would seem to legitimize such behavior on the part of the state if its rulers considered it appropriate. Aside from remaining studiously silent on Egypt during this period, Bin Bayyah was additionally noteworthy for resigning his post as Qaradawi's vice president at the IUMS, doing so on 7 September 2013, three weeks after the Rabaa massacre.[44] The reason for this would become clearer with the passage of time.

A few months after leaving Qaradawi's organization, Bin Bayyah would set up a counter-revolutionary counter-organization to the IUMS in Abu Dhabi, where he would become the founding president. Its patron, emblazoned as such on its website, was the UAE foreign minister, Abdullah bin Zayed.[45] The same country had of course lobbied for and funded the Egyptian counter-revolutions. As David Kirkpatrick documents, the then US ambassador to Egypt, Anne Patterson, warned Morsi's team in March 2013 that Muhammad bin Zayed, Abdullah's older brother and the de facto ruler of the UAE, was 'spearheading a campaign to lobby for a military takeover to remove Morsi.'[46] Then, ten or so days before the Rabaa massacre in August, Kirkpatrick notes that Abdullah bin Zayed flew to Egypt and 'goaded the Egyptian generals to do whatever it took to break the Islamists, with as much force as needed. We have your back in Washington, he assured them.'[47] Less than a week earlier, he and his ruling siblings had been hosting Abdallah bin Bayyah in the Emirates, a scholar who within a few short years would become the country's most senior religious official as its grand mufti.[48] In the latter part of the next chapter, we will explore Bin Bayyah's activities in the UAE in greater detail. First however, I will more thoroughly engage the growing secondary scholarship exploring the possible historico-theological explanations behind the support for the Egyptian coup on the part of Gomaa, Ṭayyib, and Jifri. It is to an intervention in this particular debate that I shall now turn.

9

UNDERSTANDING COUNTER-REVOLUTIONARY FATWAS AND THEIR RAMIFICATIONS BEYOND EGYPT

The preceding chapters have focused on the events and religious arguments relating to the early Arab revolutionary period. We have in the main considered how various ulama viewed and responded to these events, with either enthusiasm or hostility for the most part. While I have often referred to discussions in the secondary scholarship over the course of these pages, particularly in the endnotes, the present chapter will engage that literature more directly in addressing a number of questions that academics have already begun to grapple with.[1] In doing so, I will seek to account for the dramatically contrasting fatwas we have seen over the preceding pages. This will help us understand why these scholars, who in many cases were Azharīs trained in broadly the same tradition of scholarship and shared much in their outlook on how Islam should respond to modernity, arrived at diametrically opposed perspectives on the Egyptian revolution. In particular, I hope to explore debates in the secondary scholarship as to why Ali Gomaa, who remains an important religious figure in Egyptian public life today, legitimated and subsequently praised the killing of overwhelmingly unarmed protestors in the streets of Cairo in the summer of 2013.

A number of academics have argued that we can understand the setback faced by the Egyptian revolution in the coup of 2013 with reference to classical Sunnism. In particular, they contend that the behavior of Ṭayyib and Gomaa in support of the military is best explained by the pragmatic realism of premodern Sunni political thought. These academics include Ebrahim Moosa, Amr Osman, Mohammad Fadel and Muhamed Muzakkir. To a certain extent, this viewpoint appears to be supported by the fact that 2011 inaugurated a highly productive period in Islamic jurisprudence in articulating a new field of study, namely the Fiqh of Revolution (*fiqh al-thawra*) as has been explored by Aria Nakissa.[2] The fact that fatwas had to be written and books authored, and indeed, a sub-field of Islamic law created, suggests prima facie that pro-revolutionary fatwas represent a break from the Sunni heritage.

The present chapter has two parts. The larger first part seeks to problematize the aforementioned reading of the Arab revolutions and their aftermath. It begins by presenting the views of the scholars just cited and follows this with the alternative reading of David Warren and Youssef Belal who argue that modern considerations played a significant role in the development of both revolutionary and of counter-revolutionary fatwas. Additionally, I draw on the wider secondary literature to argue that the notion of 'quietism' is itself highly problematic and does not explain premodern Sunni political thought nor the behavior of modern Sunni ulama. Accordingly, I contend that the so-called premodern quietist precedents do not help us account for fatwas supportive of the Egyptian coup, contrary to much of the secondary scholarship just mentioned. I also seek to show that appeals to the ideas of the influential Persian polymath Abū Ḥāmid al-Ghazzālī (d. 505/1111) do not explain Gomaa's fatwas and that they are better explained in light of Gomaa's espousal of what I am tentatively calling 'autocratic Islam.' The shorter second part of this chapter considers how the Egyptian coup and the Rabaa massacre marked a turning point for religious discourse in the region and has resulted, not coincidentally, in the twin rise of the violent nihilism of groups like ISIS and a formalized transnational counter-revolutionary religious infrastructure under the leadership of Abdallah bin Bayyah in the service of the UAE's geopolitical aims.

Locating authoritarianism in premodern Islam

In a 2015 essay, Ebrahim Moosa argues that there is 'a distinct Muslim political theology that lends itself to an authoritarianism' which was upheld by scholars like Ṭayyib and Gomaa in legitimating the coup.[3] Elaborating further, he argues that al-Azhar appeared to have 'adopted the age-old political-theological pragmatism' according to which it is safer to side with whoever wields 'overwhelming authority (*shawka*).'[4] This reversion to medieval tradition, as Moosa suggests, caused the scholars affiliated with the Azhar to cast aside the modern concern for constitutional government and democracy in favor of the 'long-established, pro-status quo, pragmatist Muslim political theology.'[5] Islam's inherited political theology, he insists, has 'built-in presumptions of autocracy.'[6] More specifically in explaining Gomaa's choice to support the Rabaa massacre despite having expressed support for liberal democracy less than three years earlier, Moosa again suggests that premodern political theology may provide an explanation. According to such norms, Morsi had lost his legitimacy as president through forceful deposition, and ultimately, the 'Islamic pragmatist norms of early political theology' took precedence over democratic norms. For Moosa, these norms even explain the reluctance the Azhar leadership showed in 2011 to the popular revolutionary demand that Mubarak be removed.[7]

Moosa is hardly alone in believing that the political theology of premodern Sunnism may ultimately be to blame for the failure of the ulama to stand up for democracy in Egypt since, to cite Amr Osman, this political theology 'privileged stability over any other values.'[8] In an article published the same year as Moosa's piece, Osman argues that the fatwas prohibiting protests against Mubarak as well as those legitimating the Egyptian coup of 2013 were grounded in Sunni Islam's 'aversion to any kind of unrest,' especially the kind that arises as a consequence of 'rebellion against one's rulers.'[9] While Moosa does not make this as explicit, Osman argues that a desire for stability was the overriding concern of premodern political theology. In the latter's view, confronted by the internecine warfare in the early generations of Muslims after the Prophet's passing, 'Sunni scholars came to detest any act of rebellion against rulers and the violence and civil disorder that usually accompany it' in order to preserve the 'integrity of the community.'[10] The extreme aversion to social unrest led, in Osman's assessment, to Sunni scholars' ultimate legitimation of 'the usurpation of authority' so as to preserve communal unity.[11]

Notably, however, Osman appears to disregard important distinctions that pro-revolutionary ulama have posited between the peaceful revolution that they advocate and armed rebellion. Instead, he avers that the modern Arabic word for revolution (*thawra*) is equivalent to the premodern usage of terms like *khurūj* and fitna. This would appear to beg the question in favor of counter-revolutionary jurists rather than seriously engage with the modern distinction posited by pro-revolutionary ulama. In fact, this appears to be a distinctly modern problem, for revolutionaries are encouraged to proceed peacefully by ulama who support them, but they both also want, in most cases, to force the current ruler to abdicate. Pro-revolutionary scholars argue that the peaceful nature of this demand legitimates this form of protest; counter-revolutionary ulama could argue that attempting to remove a ruler even by peaceful means constitutes a form of sedition prohibited in hadiths.

Mohammad Fadel's intervention in this debate delineates two distinct perspectives that exist in opposition to each other in modern Islamic political thought.[12] On the one hand, one finds a 'republican' outlook that is democratic in orientation and wishes to create constitutional checks on the executive and the public accountability of the political elite. He locates this in a tradition of Islamic modernism inspired by early modern Muslim scholars' engagements with the West, most notably Rifāʿa al-Ṭaḥṭāwī (d. 1290/1873) and Khayr al-Dīn al-Tūnisī (d. 1307/1890).[13] In the Egyptian revolutionary context, the inheritor of this tradition in Fadel's estimation is Yusuf al-Qaradawi.[14] This contrasts with a 'traditionalist' outlook that, as its name suggests, finds its inspiration in the premodern Islamic tradition and is grounded in conceptions of social and religious hierarchy and paternalism which Fadel attributes to the writings of Ghazzālī. Fadel draws extensively on Ghazzālī's writings to argue that the influential jurist, philosopher, theologian, and Sufi conceived of 'the ideal ruler [...] as the ideal autocrat: rational, pious, and strong.'[15] Al-Ghazzālī's Sufism, metaphysics, and consequently his politics were, in Fadel's estimation, profoundly hierarchical and this could be seen as inspiring a Sufi jurist and theologian like Ali Gomaa.

As Fadel puts it:

> While it would be speculative to claim that the politics of ʿAlī Jumuʿa and other traditionalist scholars who support authoritarian orders in the Muslim world is a direct result of their adherence to the political philosophy articulated by medieval theologians such as al-Ghazālī, these scholars share a certain political aesthetic with al-Ghazālī that assumes that a hierarchical order that unifies symbolic (religious) authority and coercive power is necessary for the maintenance of social and religious unity.[16]

Dismissing the charge that we saw some scholars level against Gomaa in the last chapter, namely that his pro-autocracy position was 'simply that of a sycophant or a hypocrite ready to exploit religious doctrine to support his political master,'[17] Fadel further argues that Gomaa was particularly exercised by the rise of heterodox religious ideas in the context of democratic pluralism: 'In light of establishment theologians' fears of religious pluralism as a source of political instability and religious disorder, it is unsurprising that they demanded that the state put an end to the perceived crisis in religion stemming from the pluralism of the post-Mubarak period.'[18] For Gomaa, he avers, preserving religious orthodoxy takes priority over 'establishing a representative government,' a view that Fadel places squarely in the 'well-established line of reasoning in Islamic political thought' of which Ghazzālī is in his view a notable exponent.[19]

The most recent effort to methodically grapple with the fatwas produced in the context of the Egyptian revolution comes from Muhamad Muzakkir in an article dedicated to understanding Gomaa's support for the military coup of 2013.[20] While early in his article Muzakkir is careful to note that the Islamic tradition is not 'monolithic' in its approach to the question of rebellion, his language often suggests that acquiescing to power for fear of fitna was a general Sunni norm.[21] Certainly, with respect to the three influential premodern jurists on whose writings he bases his argument, namely al-Māwardī (d. 450/1058), al-Ghazzālī, and Ibn Jamāʿa (d. 733/1333), he argues that their views aligned with those of Gomaa on the question of the legitimacy of a usurper's political authority.

However, Muzakkir does add that in practice Gomaa departed from the norms laid down by his medieval juristic forebears in a number of respects. While Gomaa drew on premodern notions of legitimating those who gain power by force (*taghallub*), Muzakkir also asserts that Gomaa's appeals to tradition were frequently 'dishonest,' giving the impression that the tradition was weaponized to facilitate the consolidation of the military coup.[22] Indeed, alluding to Rabaa, he states plainly that Gomaa 'legalized killing people for political reasons.'[23] I share Muzakkir's assessment in this regard, although he is on a less firm footing in his other contentions regarding Gomaa's intellectual inspiration. His assertion that Gomaa shared the political worldview of the aforementioned medieval jurists is too general a claim to be meaningful.[24] The relevant medieval jurists worked in a political context that was radically different from the modern nation state system within which Gomaa operates. Similarly, the contention that a 'complete absence of any notion of accountability from those in power and of checks and balances against rulers' is a shared feature of the discourse of Gomaa and the premodern jurists would seem to be contradicted by Muzakkir's later remark that premodern jurists placed 'several moral obligations' on usurpers to which the latter were bound.[25] As several academics have argued, the jurists, as a body, would often act as a check on the executive in premodern Islam, despite the executive having come to power by force, which was arguably often an inescapable reality of large premodern polities.[26]

Aria Nakissa might be added to the foregoing authors, though with an important caveat. Nakissa does not explicitly argue that the premodern Islamic tradition is more amenable to autocratic rather than republican interpretations in the contemporary context, but he does present the development of the 'Fiqh of Revolution' (*fiqh al-thawra*) as an innovation both as a subfield within Islamic law, and more importantly for our purposes, in terms of the form of religious reasoning that is employed in its generation and justification. That is to say, according to Nakissa the scholars who wished to support the Arab revolutions needed to innovate, while those opposed to it relied on more conventional legal approaches. Once again, while this does not state explicitly that premodern Islam is more readily understood as requiring obedience to even tyrannical rulers, Nakissa's mode of argumentation suggests that this may be the case. In this regard, he draws on Wael Hallaq's conception of premodern Islamic law as being characterized by formal legal methods at odds with the highly subjective and utilitarian calculus of modern reformist legal reasoning like that of Qaradawi and his colleagues.[27] However, recent work by Ahmed Fekry Ibrahim calls into question this generalization about the character of the premodern tradition and, in my estimation, demonstrates that the forms of argument put forward by modern reformists find their parallels and antecedents in the late premodern tradition if not earlier.[28]

Alternative readings

Against the foregoing scholars as I have presented them, one finds two authors who offer interesting counterpoints in this debate, namely David H. Warren and Youssef Belal. In a 2014 article, Warren followed Nakissa in assessing Qaradawi's fatwas in support of the 2011 revolutions as entailing 'novel and utilitarian reasoning,' though Warren considered Qaradawi's subsequent insistence on the ousted Morsi's legitimacy in 2013 to reflect a reversion to traditional Sunni quietism.[29] This might suggest that he belongs to the same category as the scholars seen in the previous section. However, in his 2014 article, Warren does not evaluate Gomaa's fatwas in support of the coup. This he does in a 2017 essay in which he pushes back against arguments that these fatwas were grounded in premodern doctrines of political quietism and provides an alternative and novel reading of Gomaa's behavior. In particular, arguing contra Fadel, he proposes that Gomaa's support for authoritarianism may also be located within the traditions of Islamic modernism which Fadel presents as republican in orientation.[30] More specifically, Warren argues that Rifāʿa al-Ṭahṭāwī's conception of political rule may be understood as legitimating authoritarianism, and that Gomaa's interventions fit squarely within such a reading of Ṭahṭāwī. Most innovatively perhaps, Warren argues that rather than the premodern Islamic tradition, the main inspiration for Gomaa's support for the coup and his advocacy for the killing of largely unarmed protestors by the military was a concern for the preservation of the Egyptian nation state. In Warren's telling, 'the concepts of nationhood and the nation state are highly significant for understanding Jumʿa's Islamic legal arguments in favor of the coup and the subsequent crushing of anti-coup demonstrations.'[31] Contrasting with the previous authors we have seen, Warren states: 'appeals to national progress also make possible all kinds of horrors including, I suggest, the liquidation of recalcitrant citizens at Rabiʿa al-ʿAdawiyya.'[32]

While Gomaa did draw on the language of the premodern Islamic tradition through the use of terms like *taghallub* and by casting protestors against the coup as Khawārij, Warren identifies 'several novelties' in Gomaa's deployment of such concepts. These include connecting the notion of *taghallub* in the context of the coup to 'the modern concept of Egyptian national will' and 'the sovereignty (*siyāda*) of the people.'[33] Rather than finding their origins in the premodern tradition, such ideas are more plausibly understood as an inheritance of Islamic modernism in Warren's opinion. The transformation of the notion of Khawārij from a theological notion to one indicating exclusion from 'membership in the Egyptian nation' is similar in his view. Indeed, Warren points out that Qaradawi's arguments are, like those of Gomaa, also legible through the paradigms of nationalism and that both are indebted to the intellectual legacy of Ṭahṭāwī.[34] In this regard, Warren suggests that the disagreement between Gomaa and Qaradawi was ultimately about contending visions of the Egyptian nation rather than fundamentally contrasting visions of political theology grounded in premodern Islam.

Another recent effort to understand the contrasting fatwas vis-à-vis the Egyptian revolution (but not the coup) may be found in the analysis of Youssef Belal. Belal notes that while the two scholars' fatwas 'formulated distinct and potentially contradictory prescriptions,' they still shared certain fundamental assumptions that set them apart from Salafi scholars. Unlike the latter, neither Gomaa nor Qaradawi ground their posture towards protests in a hermeneutic that required explicit authorization of a particular political act in Prophetic precedent. Instead, Belal argues, both scholars 'share similar scholarly assumptions about Islamic jurisprudence,' and they both present themselves as advocates of Islamic moderation (*wasaṭiyya*).[35] Rather than seeing the difference between Qaradawi and Gomaa (and one could also include their respective colleagues in this comparison) as appealing to premodern as opposed to modernist precedents, Belal argues that the operative difference between the two approaches lies in their divergent attitudes towards justice and order. Qaradawi's fatwas exemplified a privileging of justice to which considerations of preserving order and obeying one's rulers were subordinated. For Gomaa, on Belal's account, the priority was the preservation of order in the interest of communal peace.[36] This is, of course, also how the premodern juristic acquiescence to usurpers is often interpreted, but I am contrasting Belal with the scholars of the last section due to Belal locating such concerns for justice or stability among contemporary jurists rather than in premodern discourses that are thought to influence modern scholars in a quietist direction.

When considering the contrasting fatwas of Gomaa and Qaradawi, Belal thus concludes:

> it appears that the labor of Islamic jurisprudence is less to formulate universal and immutable rules than to allow scholars to rely on their judgment on a case-by-case basis while using the same sources of evidence offered by the Quran and the Sunna and the procedures delineated in the discipline of *usul al-fiqh*. That is the reason why several Islamic scholars may formulate different rules in response to the same case, or why the same Islamic scholar may formulate different rules in response to similar cases over time and space.[37]

In some respects, Belal may be viewed as stressing the flexibility of the Sharia in juristic practice, a fact that helps us recognize that a range of possible interpretations reside within the Sharia's conceptual universe, some of which may be highly contentious, as with the case of Gomaa's pronouncements regarding Rabaa. Gomaa's fatwas pertaining to Rabaa in particular seem to test the limits of what can legitimately be attributed to Islamic jurisprudence.

Both Warren's and Belal's views appear to be helpful correctives to the portrayal of Gomaa's fatwas as falling unproblematically within the paradigms of a supposed Sunni quietism. Warren's argument is a reminder of the inescapability of modernity's impact, even among those like Ali Gomaa who take great pride in self-reflexively drawing inspiration from tradition.[38] It also reminds us of the close relationship between violence and the nation state in modernity. Belal's intervention is different. While he is only addressing Gomaa and Qaradawi's fatwas from 2011, rather than placing the motivations for the fatwas of these scholars within tradition or in a break from tradition, he suggests that they are both engaged in a modern exercise in case-by-case interpretation in light of modern conditions but with reference to authoritative texts from the past. In Belal's assessment, these texts do not necessarily prescribe a particular outcome on the modern mufti, and this results in interpretive diversity in contemporary fatwas. While Belal is concerned with contemporary anthropology, his reflections on the causes of interpretive diversity are also true for premodern jurisprudence as scholars have long recognized. This diversity of perspectives also impinges on the question of how premodern Sunnism responded to tyrannical rulers, an aspect of the post-Arab revolutionary scholarly debate to which I shall now briefly turn.[39]

Is Sunnism 'quietist'?

Scholars have for some years illustrated the nuances of Sunnism's attitudes towards the question of rebellion that render the label 'quietist' decidedly problematic as a broad generalization about Sunnism. Yet, as we have seen, whether describing Sunni political theology as 'quietist' or 'pragmatic,' there appears to be a persistent belief that premodern Sunnism legitimates modern state repression of the kind we have witnessed repeatedly after the Arab revolutions. Several of the scholars we have considered above, namely Moosa, Osman, Fadel, and Muzakkir, all to a greater or lesser extent take for granted that the premodern Sunni tradition's dominant tendency towards quietism explains the support provided by Aḥmad al-Ṭayyib and Ali Gomaa for Sisi's coup and Gomaa's support for the subsequent massacres.

Yet quietism is seldom clearly defined by these scholars. This may well be because of the nebulousness of the concept and the quietism-activism binary of which it is a part.[40] The problems of appealing to the concept of quietism to explain premodern Sunni political thought had, however, already been incisively expressed by Khaled Abou El Fadl two decades ago in a form that deserves to be reproduced in full:

> The accepted view maintains that Muslim jurists had become quietist because they had accepted the legitimacy of the usurper and forbade rebelling against anyone coming to power, regardless of the means by which they acquired power. But if one argues that power could legitimately be obtained by usurpation, the necessary implication is that usurpers could be legitimate. In other words, if the act of usurpation could create political legitimacy, then the attempt to achieve this legitimacy is not necessarily reprehensible. Or, to put it differently, if those who are in power are perceived, in an ideal sense, to have an absolute moral claim to power, then those who rebel cannot be perceived to have any legitimacy. But if those who are in power are perceived to have a functional claim to power, that cannot preempt the moral claim of those who rebel against them. If, for example, a jurist claims that a usurper must, of necessity, be obeyed, the jurist is conceding a functional or practical legitimacy to the usurper. But this means that the usurper's claim to power is relative because it arises out of simple necessity. The necessary implication is that a challenger to the usurper's power may also have a relative claim to legitimacy. In other words, as a matter of logic, if one recognizes the legitimacy of usurpation, one also implicitly recognizes the functional legitimacy of rebellion. This point demonstrates the extent to which the language of quietism versus activism is unhelpful. Pursuant to the logic above, recognizing the legitimacy of a usurper could be an activist stance.[41]

The above passage would seem to undermine claims that Sunnism was in fact opposed to rebellion tout court, since the affirmation of usurpers implicitly legitimates successful rebellions. Rather, as alluded to in Chapter 1, Sunnism opposed unsuccessful rebellion after the fact for reasons that will be discussed further below. But the success or otherwise of an act of rebellion is not something that can usually be adjudged with certainty until an attempt at rebellion has come to its conclusion. Indeed, this would appear to qualify somewhat the characterization of the premodern Islamic tradition by Michael Cook as recognizing that 'in the face of the delinquency of the ruler, there is a clear mainstream position: rebuke is endorsed while rebellion is rejected.'[42] Instead, it would appear that what was rejected was unsuccessful rebellion that caused greater disruption than the ruler it sought to unseat. Given that it is in the nature of most rebellions to be unsuccessful, most jurists appear to have simply expressed a general opposition to rebellion, perhaps as a means of discouraging them.

But while the general rule may have been one of prohibition, there was understandably no consensus on prohibiting rebellion. This can be gathered from Crone's observation that the prominent Ashʿarī theologian al-Bāqillānī (d. 403/1013) 'knew of many people (*kathīr min al-nās*) who believed that a wrongdoing and oppressive caliph should be deposed.'[43] Even in the mature Sunni tradition within which Ibn Khaldūn (d. 808/1406) writes, he complains of the fact that 'many of the *ʿāmma* (laity) and the *fuqahāʾ* (jurists) advocate or become involved in rebellions,' suggesting that the notion of Sunni 'quietism' may frequently have been a custom more honored in the breach than the observance.[44] As Michael Cook points out, the condemnation by Ibn Khaldūn of ineffectual rebels was owing to 'their foolishness in acting when they lack the power (*qudra*) without which there is no obligation—not because what they are doing is intrinsically sinful.'[45]

Sunnism, usurpers, the modern state, and rebels

As Noah Feldman has convincingly argued, there was a good reason for Māwardī's famous 'legitimation' of usurpers in his *al-Aḥkām al-Sulṭāniyya*, namely that such normalization allowed society to continue with minimal disruption, and returned rule of law back to the hands of the ulama.[46] In Feldman's assessment, this was not 'a scholarly concession to power, but [...] a brilliant maneuver that successfully preserved the law and the scholars in their constitutional position even after the caliphate had failed in its assigned task of preserving orderly government.' Feldman continues:

> If Buwayhids or Seljuks [i.e. the dynasties that had usurped power] had assumed power without acknowledging the primacy of the shariʿa, then all might have been lost. From Mawardi's standpoint, the shariʿa was everything; the prerogatives of caliphate (almost) nothing. This [normalization] was, then, a victory for the shariʿa and the scholars who guarded it. To lament the decline of the caliphate or to excoriate Mawardi for permitting usurpation would be to miss the point, which was the preservation of the shariʿa. Arguably, it was Mawardi's intellectual foundation that preserved the balance of powers in the classical Islamic constitution for another seven hundred years.

So long as the Sharia, which was historically under the ulama's control and authority, was preserved as the basis of the social contract and rule of law, it made perfect sense for the ulama to generally not oppose successful usurpers. But to read this as an explanation for modern ulama legitimating the acquisition of political power by force without qualification does not sufficiently account for the radically changed circumstances within which they find themselves. This may be further illustrated by juxtaposing Crone's remarks about premodern Sunni political norms and Qaradawi's remarks about how the modern state presents unprecedented challenges to the social and legal authority of the ulama. Crone notes that medieval Sunnis recognized that as a general rule '[a]rmed revolt led to civil war, a source of worse disorder, bloodshed and immorality than anything a ruler could inflict, and was forbidden. A quasi-caliph did not matter enough at the level of either everyday life or future salvation for such sacrifices to be worth it.'[47] This is an important reality about the premodern period regarding which a scholar like Yusuf al-Qaradawi is keenly aware.

In a 2007 work on religion and politics, Qaradawi argues that the modern state represents a radical break with states from the medieval era. The modern state, he insists, impinges on every aspect of an individual's life, regulating education, law, culture, the media, the economy, and society.[48] While this is certainly true of the authoritarian states of the Middle East, given the nature of the modern bureaucratic state in general, one could argue that it is true for all modern states to some degree. In stark contrast with the modern state, Qaradawi points out that in premodern Islam the state was a decidedly provincial affair influencing only the imperial capital and perhaps major cities. Otherwise, he asserts, social life was largely managed by the ulama who were the educated elite of Muslim societies and who administered the rule of law as encapsulated by the Sharia. They attended to people's education, guidance, and the administration of justice largely independently of the state. Similarly, their sources of income were to be found in religious endowments that were legally independent of the ruler's control. Thus, while Qaradawi essentially shares the view with Crone that the medieval Islamic state 'did not matter enough at the level of [...] everyday life' to be a major concern of the ulama of the day, he argues that modern transformations of the state require another approach.[49] Despite and perhaps because of the dramatically changed context in which modern states are not only deeply influential in the everyday lives of Muslims but also possess institutions of violence to impose their will on the populace, Qaradawi does not call for initiating armed insurrection against the rulers of modern states, as we have seen.[50]

In this regard, Qaradawi and his colleagues' approach might even be recognized as a deeper level of engagement with the premodern tradition than that of counter-revolutionary scholars like Gomaa and Ṭayyib. But there is another respect in which scholars like Gomaa, Ṭayyib, Yusuf and Bin Bayyah break with the premodern tradition. As Crone points out, the premodern Sunni approach towards a tyrannical ruler would be to recognize the need to 'admonish him, preach Hell-fire to him and refuse to obey him whenever he ordered something in disobedience to God.'[51] As she highlights, medieval Sunnis were not simply 'spineless supporters of the powers-that-be.' She adds that as part of a long community-centered tradition that read the Quran in an 'anti-authoritarian vein,' Sunni ulama 'refused to equate God and His Messenger with the state; as communitarians, they took God and His Messenger to stand for Muslim society.'[52]

By contrast, the counter-revolutionary scholars seen in the preceding pages place the state, to a greater or lesser degree, as the paramount source of authority, subordinating Islam to the status of a servant to the state in a way that would likely have shocked their premodern forebears. This may be seen in theory in the thought of Abdallah bin Bayyah, as explored in Chapter 4, and is a framework whose practical implications we will consider later in this chapter. It may be seen in practice in the actions of Ali Gomaa in support of the Rabaa massacre. Gomaa's discourse may also be viewed as state-centric if we grant that he identifies the state with the Egyptian army. As we have seen in past chapters, Gomaa places ultimate authority in the army's hands, viewing it in some sense as both inviolable and infallible. The quasi-divinization of the Egyptian army and/or the ruler in the discourse of scholars like Gomaa and Bin Bayyah also helps us to understand the radical break with Sunnism's traditionally soft approach towards rebels. As noted by Crone, premodern Sunnis viewed rebels against the state not as 'enemies of God' but rather as fellow believers who had lost their way and had to be reintegrated into the community 'as soon and as gently as possible.'[53]

This is striking in how it contrasts with the approach of a figure like Gomaa and his modern-state-centric rereading of the Islamic tradition. Rebels, as we have seen in earlier discussions, are by definition armed in the juristic understanding, including in the understanding of Gomaa himself. In Rabaa square in the summer of 2013, the protestors were overwhelmingly unarmed. Yet, with the blessing of Ali Gomaa, the state sought to liquidate potentially thousands of unarmed protestors, something premodern Sunnism does not even countenance in the face of an armed insurrection. Gomaa's justification for such actions thus represents a radical departure from premodern Sunni doctrine.

On Ghazzālī, Sufism, and tyranny

Another respect in which Gomaa breaks with his forebears may be found in how his choices stand at odds with the prescriptions of the influential Persian polymath Abū Ḥāmid al-Ghazzālī. As noted above, Fadel contends that al-Ghazzālī and Gomaa shared a certain 'political aesthetic' in their common interest in supporting autocrats and in their Sufi outlook. But Fadel's reading is at odds with a number of other academics. Ghazzālī's considerable and complex oeuvre is admittedly amenable to a variety of readings, but I would argue that Fadel's is less than compelling for several reasons.

Firstly, as Michael Cook has illustrated at considerable length, Ghazzālī's influential and relatively radical articulation of the duty to command right and forbid wrong does not shy away from confronting the state in harsh oppositional terms.[54] While it is true that Ghazzālī conceived of society in de jure hierarchical terms that are at odds with the de facto forms of hierarchy that pervade today's globalized neoliberal order, it does not seem to follow from this that he legitimated absolutism in the way that Gomaa does. This can be seen in the fact that with respect to the duty of commanding right and forbidding wrong Ghazzālī notes that it is equally the duty of men and women, slaves and free persons, the righteous and sinners.[55] In general, he requires no permission to be granted by the ruler to perform the duty, and hierarchy has, in principle, no bearing on the obligation.[56] The ruler and officers of the state may be the target of the duty, including through the use of harsh language, but rebellion is naturally not countenanced.[57] This is in striking contrast with a statement Fadel attributes to Ghazzālī, namely that 'the ruler is chosen by God, and for this reason the people are under an obligation to love him, obey him, and not resist him.'[58] However, this quotation is drawn from the second part of Ghazzālī's *Naṣīḥat al-Mulūk*, a part that is generally seen as pseudepigraphical.[59] Indeed, David Decosimo has recently argued that the first (authentic) part of the *Naṣīḥa* exemplifies a republican outlook that reflects Ghazzālī's deep-seated hostility towards authoritarianism.[60]

Additionally, Crone's treatment of Ghazzālī's political writings provides further corroboration for his hostility towards the political classes more generally, a point on which he had been critiqued by an older generation of scholars in the secondary literature.[61] As Crone puts it, Ghazzālī speaks 'in cynical tones' about the military dynasties that had usurped the state in his times, adding:

> The reason why he does so, however, is not that he is sacrificing his scruples in order to accommodate it, but on the contrary that he is putting it in its place: *shawka* is mere muscle power, mere brute force, and there is nothing exalted or elevated about it, though one cannot do without it. Far from selling out to secular power he is going out of his way to belittle its moral significance.

> [...] Unlike the caliph, the king was not the leader of the community founded by Muḥammad, or his representative, just a crude soldier given to self-indulgence, abuse of power, misuse of funds and other violations of the law. One did not gain virtue by frequenting the courts of kings or working for their cause. On the contrary, one should avoid the company of rulers (*ṣuḥbat al-sulṭān*), as so many ascetics and *aṣḥāb al-ḥadīth* had said. But though secular government was ugly, oppressive, and immoral, there was no question of managing without it. Oppressive rulers had to be left in place *if they were too powerful to be removed* without civil war; and one had to be grateful to God for raising up the brutes who took it upon themselves to provide some minimal order in allegiance to the caliph. But the power they exercised had no positive moral meaning in itself. *It was only as a sword wielded on behalf of Islam that it acquired value.* The only legitimacy the secular ruler could hope for was instrumental, *as a mere tool of the religious institution.*[62]

It bears repeating that a figure like Ghazzālī would likely have been horrified by the association of his name with the sorts of scholars who consort with rulers and use religion in their service rather than using rulers to serve religion.

Finally, much of what has just been cited is drawn from Ghazzālī's magnum opus, *Iḥyā' 'Ulūm al-Dīn*, possibly the most important Sufi work ever written.[63] His Sufism was clearly amenable to cynicism and severity towards the politically powerful. While it is true that a number of the counter-revolutionary scholars considered in the present work are of a Sufi orientation—some would argue that Neo-traditionalism is a synonym for Sufism—and that some scholars have argued that Sufi esotericism can lend itself to authoritarianism, I would argue that there is no necessary connection between the two.[64] As Fait Muedini has argued, drawing on the work of Carl Ernst, Sufis have with great frequency played an oppositional role vis-à-vis oppressive political power in recent centuries.[65] A similar message is conveyed by Meir Hatina's study of the ulama of Egypt in the early modern period.[66]

Rereading Gomaa and autocratic Islam

In contrast with Fadel, then, rather than viewing Gomaa as reflecting a Ghazzālīan acceptance of the pious usurper who would uphold religious orthodoxy and maintain a decidedly hierarchical view of society, I would propose viewing Gomaa as engaged in an exercise of legitimating the modern Egyptian state under military control with any religious arguments he can muster. This is not to say that Gomaa is unprincipled in general. His guiding principle, I would submit, is his commitment to the Egyptian army. This is legitimated in Islamic terms on the basis of hadiths we have discussed in earlier chapters, and so from Gomaa's perspective, it need not necessarily be the case that he is contradicting his Islamic values. But it does mean that in his anomalous conception of Islam, all other religious considerations must be subordinated to the interests of the Egyptian army.

In a previous attempt at understanding Gomaa's fatwas, I argued that we can understand Gomaa's advocacy of the Rabaa massacre as reflecting his desire to protect what he saw as 'true Islam' that was threatened with corruption by the rise of the MB and a democratic Egypt.[67] In that piece, I did not define what constituted true Islam. Here, I would tentatively suggest that for Gomaa and his fellow travelers true Islam refers to the forms that establishment Islam takes in authoritarian modern states. A major pillar of this conception of Islam is an absolute fealty to such a state. With Bin Bayyah, who upholds this conception, we saw that this was justified with reference to the notion of *taḥqīq al-manāṭ* through which he granted carte blanche to the ruler on all affairs that concern the all-encompassing modern state. With Ṭayyib, while his support had its limits, we saw his commitment to autocratic Islam in his legitimation of the military coup—an armed rebellion against a Muslim ruler that he and Gomaa actively legitimated rather than simply acquiesced to, as might be expected in premodern Sunnism.

In the dominant premodern Sunni conception, the actions of the peaceful protests that Qaradawi was encouraging in January 2011 would probably not have qualified as a rebellion. As Gomaa noted after the Rabaa massacre, as we have seen in an earlier chapter, to qualify as a rebellion in Islamic law it had to be armed. But as the pro-revolutionary scholars insisted at the time, a rebellion was in fact what took place in the summer of 2013 when the Egyptian armed forces ousted Morsi with support from Ṭayyib and Gomaa. That this was a case of usurpation was frankly expressed by Gomaa in his post-Rabaa interview in which he said, 'we have become the victors/usurpers' (*asbaḥnā al-mutaghallibīn*).[68]

Strikingly at odds with premodern norms in 2013, Ṭayyib and Gomaa neither opposed an unsuccessful rebellion, nor quietly acquiesced to a successful one against a ruler of questionable legitimacy. Rather they actively participated in a rebellion against a ruler whose rule many if not most scholars held to be legitimately constituted. In this regard, they broke with the more general premodern Sunni norm of opposing rebellion against a legitimate ruler. It is also unclear just how successful the rebellion they participated in has been. Gomaa and Ṭayyib presented the coup as an effort to restore stability to Egypt which had been experiencing considerable instability in the final months of the Morsi presidency, in part because of opposition to Morsi within the Egyptian state institutions that formed the so-called deep state. But the coup led to significant protests in opposition to the end of Egypt's democratic experiment as well as a renewed insurgency in the Sinai. The Egyptian army's heavy-handed response to both peaceful protests and violent insurgents has resulted in vastly more deaths and cases of incarceration in Egypt than took place during the period of instability that was used by these scholars to justify the coup. As we shall see in the next section, authoritarian Islam comes with significant costs to which scholars who support it have undoubtedly contributed.

The failure of democracy and the rise of ISIS

Inasmuch as the Rabaa massacre exemplified the failure of democratic powers worldwide to support democracy in the Middle East, it had other significant ramifications. Most notable among these, I would argue, was the meteoric rise of ISIS throughout the Middle East region. While President Obama attempted to place at least some of the blame of ISIS on his predecessor by stating that the group was a 'direct outgrowth of al-Qaeda in Iraq that grew out of our invasion,' his own administration's remarkable continuation of virtually unconditional support for Sisi in the wake of the coup and its massacres—which he personally refused to call a coup so as to continue supporting the Egyptian military—undoubtedly shares in the blame for the failure of Egyptian democracy and the concomitant rise of ISIS.[69]

Naturally, these are complex phenomena, but two things can be said about US support for Sisi and its connection with ISIS. Firstly, as David Kirkpatrick masterfully documents, despite the US enjoying a great deal of leverage over the Middle Eastern actors who were lobbying for and/or orchestrating the coup and its bloody aftermath, Obama and most of his team simply chose to support the military whatever the consequences rather than displease US allies in the Middle East who harbored extreme hostility towards the MB. In no small measure, this was also a consequence of an Islamophobic fear of the MB, a fear that was actively promoted by its Persian Gulf allies in Washington without effective rebuttal but which also found willing ears in the US President's secretary of defense, Chuck Hagel, as well as his secretary of state, John Kerry.[70] Kirkpatrick is worth citing at length here. As he relates:

> When I met him in early 2016, [former Secretary of Defense] Hagel recalled that he had been besieged by complaints about Morsi [around the time of the coup] from the defense ministers in Israel, Saudi Arabia, and the United Arab Emirates—especially from Mohammed bin Zayed (MBZ), the crown prince of Abu Dhabi and the de facto ruler and military chief of the UAE.
>
> 'MBZ and other leaders in the Middle East were warning me then that the Muslim Brotherhood is the most dangerous element afoot in the Middle East today,' Hagel said, and he had always agreed. 'I said, yes, it is dangerous. We recognize that. I am not contesting that. You are right.'
>
> 'I said the same thing I said to Sisi. "We have got to deal with this in a smart way, in a wise way,"' Hagel said. 'The Gulf States were focused on "Let's just hammer them and extinguish them now. Let's just get rid of them now and if anybody gets in the way, well, you don't understand how ruthless these people are. They will destroy us. It is not in your interests. Why can't you Americans understand that?" And they would go back to their old refrain, 'You let Mubarak go down.'
>
> The Israelis made clear that they were backing Sisi, too. 'Sisi and the generals have a very close relationship with the Israelis. The Israelis were letting us know very clearly that Sisi was the only guy protecting everything here, and they were concerned.'
>
> Hagel agreed with them. 'We get that,' Hagel said he told Israeli Defense Minister Moshe 'Bogie' Ya'alon and Prime Minister Benjamin Netanyahu. 'The security arrangement is in our interest, too.'[71]

Kirkpatrick similarly documents Kerry's long-standing fear of the MB, noting that Kerry was 'partly relieved' in early 2013 by the prospect of a military takeover led by Sisi.[72]

But beyond crucial US political support for the machinations of regional allies, one can secondly point to the symbolic victory for ISIS vis-à-vis the emerging voices of Islamic democracy in the region. As alluded to earlier, Western support for the Egyptian coup served as a major recruiting tool in their propaganda. It was difficult to refute because it was such an obvious display of Western double standards regarding democracy promotion when it came to Muslims, even with the blood of thousands of pro-democracy activists flowing in the streets. For ISIS, this simply underlined their core message—the only way out was violence. As one Rabaa protestor, Mohamed Soltan, recalls from his subsequent time in the coup regime's prisons with ISIS members:

> They would make very simple arguments telling [other prisoners] that the world doesn't care about values and only understands violence [...]. Because of the gravity of the situation [we] were all in, by the time the ISIS guys were finished speaking, everyone, the liberals, the Brotherhood people, would be left completely speechless. When you're in that type of situation and don't have many options left, for some people these kinds of ideas start to make sense.[73]

This risk was always obvious to thoughtful Western observers. In the wake of the 27 July Cairo massacre, which killed around a hundred protestors, *The Economist* spoke of this double standard in a trenchant piece appropriately entitled 'Democracy and Hypocrisy' noting that:

> The Muslim Brothers—and other Muslims across the Middle East—will conclude from all this that the West applies one standard when secularists are under attack and another when Islamists are. Democracy, they will gather, is not a universal system of government, but a trick for bringing secularists to power. [...] [B]y so conspicuously holding back criticism first of the coup and now of the shooting of unarmed civilians, the West has confirmed the view of enemies of democracy everywhere: that its preaching is riddled with hypocrisy.[74]

Keen observers like David Kirkpatrick and Jean-Pierre Filiu have made similar cases in their books on the region's revolutions, arguing that it was the closing of the democratic opening that contributed to the rise of groups like ISIS.[75] The Egyptian coup may not have created ISIS, but it certainly gave it a shot in the arm.

The transnational network of counter-revolutionary scholars

But despite the important role of the US, the serious work was arguably being led by its Persian Gulf allies. Returning to the role of scholarly actors, the UAE in particular led the charge in cultivating counter-revolutionary and anti-democratic voices among the scholarly classes through new transnational institutions and initiatives that doubtless also contributed to the rise of ISIS. Yet, these same scholars also made a great show of leading the charge in criticizing ISIS.[76] In September 2014, an open letter to the then head of ISIS, Abu Bakr al-Baghdadi (d. 1441/2019), was published bearing the signatures of over a hundred Islamic scholars. The top four scholars listed on the website's slide show will be mostly familiar to us by now. In order of appearance, they were: Abdallah bin Bayyah, Shawqī 'Allām, Ali Gomaa and Hamza Yusuf.[77] The unnamed coordinators of the anti-ISIS campaign clearly felt that a scholar like Gomaa, who by this time had been shown to have called for mass murder against unarmed pro-democracy activists in the streets of Egypt, sufficiently exemplified Islam's moral authority to confront the murderous behavior of ISIS. In fact, the difference between Baghdadi and Gomaa should have been obvious to observers by this point. While Baghdadi was clearly an advocate of celebrating blood-thirsty violence in front of the global media, Gomaa was only willing to do so behind closed doors. For both, the ends of power justified any means.

By 2014, Abdallah bin Bayyah and Hamza Yusuf had also fully entered the orbit of the UAE's scholarly armory. In 2014, Bin Bayyah, working closely with Shaykh al-Azhar Aḥmad al-Ṭayyib, established the UAE-based Forum for Promoting Peace in Muslim Societies (FPPMS), an institution whose name, it would soon become clear, was worthy of George Orwell's Newspeak. Bin Bayyah served as its president, and Yusuf would soon become his vice president, with the organization leading the charge against democracy in the Middle East in the name of Islam. The Forum's website would feel no hesitation in pointing out that its official patron was UAE Foreign Minister Abdullah bin Zayed. As noted earlier, Bin Zayed had incited Egypt's generals just before the Rabaa massacre to crush the anti-coup protestors while reassuring them that he had their back in Washington.[78] He and his brother Crown Prince Muhammad, the de facto ruler of the UAE, would often appear in the company of Bin Bayyah in the coming years, possibly in their effort to appear generous to a man recognized as an Islamic scholar of global standing. Muhammad bin Zayed, who was described by *The New York Times* in 2019 as the most powerful ruler in the Arab world, had been leading the counter-revolutionary charge soon after the Arab revolutions began in 2011. He may well be the region's single most powerful force against democracy.

Bin Bayyah, for his part, remained on message in his keynote address at the Forum's inaugural annual meeting in March 2014, less than seven months after the Rabaa massacre. In the Middle East, where societies were 'not ready' for democracy, he argued, calling for accountable government was 'essentially a call for war.'[79] Separately, he had also argued as a point of religious principle that rulers were above the oversight of religious scholars and jurists in their public acts.[80] In effect, by 2014 he had theorized a form of autocratic Islam that put rulers above the law. At the same Forum, Yusuf took to the podium and reminded his listeners of the Islamic obligation to obey one's rulers whom he characterized as 'God's shadow.'[81] The context indicated that he was referring to the current rulers rather than those they had deposed in a recent coup. Later that year, the UAE successfully lobbied for the Forum and Bin Bayyah to be mentioned as an excellent example of 'a voice of moderate Islam' by then President Obama in his UN General Assembly speech.[82]

By 2017, however, after another crown prince had emerged on the Middle Eastern scene, the Forum's fealty would extend to him too. In June of that year, Saudi King Salman's favorite son, Muhammad bin Salman, effected a 'soft coup' against his cousin and former crown prince, Muhammad bin Nayef, after reportedly subjecting him to humiliating torture.[83] It was a sign of things to come. Already, a couple of weeks earlier, Bin Salman had, in partnership with the UAE and Egypt, instigated a completely unexpected blockade against Qatar primarily for its support for the Arab revolutions in recent years. The octogenarian jurist, Bin Bayyah, found himself called upon by his new sponsor to support a boycott against his previous one. Possibly without his permission, the state-owned newswire would issue a fierce condemnation of Qatar in the name of the presidency of the FPPMS, that is, Bin Bayyah's office.[84] Some hours later, a copy of the statement would appear on the Forum's Twitter feed.[85] Bin Bayyah's personal website and social media accounts remained silent, possibly indicating that his UAE government sponsors had issued it without his consent. Yet, he never publicly expressed any objections to the move, even after the blockading countries named Yusuf al-Qaradawi, whom he considered a teacher, on a list of terrorists they demanded be handed over to them.[86]

Only four years earlier, Bin Bayyah had served as a vice president under Qaradawi when he was the President of the IUMS, a position Bin Bayyah had held since the founding of the IUMS in 2004 until shortly after the Rabaa massacre in 2013.[87] Bin Bayyah's respect for Qaradawi went back many years. He wrote a particularly adulatory panegyric to Qaradawi in 1996, on the occasion of his seventieth birthday, which is reproduced in the appendices of the present work.[88] In another article published by a UAE newspaper in late 2000 which reported the country bestowing a major honor on Qaradawi, Bin Bayyah is quoted as referring to the scholar as 'the conscience of the umma.'[89] This was all before Bin Bayyah had even joined the IUMS in 2004. Indeed, as late as October 2011, after Qaradawi's support for the Arab revolutions had caused him obvious misgivings, Bin Bayyah still referred to him in the CBC interview we examined in Chapter 4, as his 'teacher' (*shaykhunā*), and an eminently learned scholar (*'allāma*).[90]

Even Bin Bayyah's resignation letter to the IUMS in September 2013 expressed his esteem for the scholar.[91] But all of these endorsements fell to the wayside now. Qaradawi was a 'terrorist,' because the rulers decreed it, and true to his newly enunciated principles, for Bin Bayyah, the ruler's opinion was gospel. It is not clear how he reconciled this with the fact that other rulers, namely those of Qatar, rejected the appellation.[92] These theoretical kinks in his system had not been worked out yet. Nor was Qaradawi the only victim of the counter-revolutionaries to whom Bin Bayyah had switched his allegiances, just the most high profile one. Four other scholars are worth mentioning in this connection, all of whom were students and admirers of the Saudi-based Bin Bayyah, but whose Islamist leanings led to their imprisonment in the new Saudi crown prince's crackdown against prominent religious scholars. In September 2017, Salmān al-ʿAwda (b. 1376/1956), ʿAwaḍ al-Qarnī (b. 1376/1957), ʿAlī al-ʿUmarī (b. 1393/1973), and ʿĀdil Bānāʿma (b. 1393/1974) were among dozens of scholars summarily rounded up and incarcerated by the Saudi authorities.[93] Reports of their torture and incarceration in inhumane conditions have surfaced since then, and some of the scholars have been charged by the authorities with prosecutors seeking the death penalty against them.[94] Not only are all of these scholars either direct students or associates of Bin Bayyah, they had also written essays and, in one case, a poem in praise of the older scholar which adorned a section of the latter's personal website dedicated to scholarly endorsements of Bin Bayyah.[95] As of 2021, nearly four years after the arbitrary incarceration of these scholars by the same Saudi authorities that granted Bin Bayyah an audience with the Saudi king in 2019, Bin Bayyah has neither commented on their incarceration, nor intriguingly has he taken down their endorsements of his scholarly standing from his website.[96]

Bin Bayyah's deputy, the American Hamza Yusuf, has exhibited similar political transformations. As we have seen above, he reportedly defended Ali Gomaa's reputation despite the latter's lethal post-coup fatwas. Yusuf's enthusiasm for the counter-revolutionary cause would repeatedly land him in hot water as he imbibed the global vision of his sponsors in the UAE. As we considered in Chapter 4, matters would come to a head in late 2016 at the Reviving the Islamic Spirit (RIS) Convention, a major North American Muslim gathering, where Yusuf made a number of controversial remarks about the African American community in the United States alongside comments critical of the MB and Salafism. The comments on race have briefly been addressed above, but his other remarks are more relevant to the present discussion. These comments were initially made on a short blog post that Yusuf had published in July of that year in which he had argued that groups like ISIS were the product of a marriage between 'an exclusivist *takfiri*' sect from the Arabian Peninsula and 'the political Islamist ideology that has permeated much of the Arab and South Asian world for the last several decades.'[97] In his RIS remarks, he made clear that these were references to Salafism and the MB.

Yusuf's somewhat reductive genealogy was beginning to reflect the harder edge of counter-revolutionary discourse as represented by the likes of the Libyan scholar and politician Aref Nayed and UAE officialdom.[98] By assimilating the MB to groups like ISIS, states like the UAE tried to cast them as 'terrorists,' a term so powerful in global politics that it allows states to violate their usual laws and norms in confronting menaces they merely perceive. Even though Yusuf does not personally appear to have gone so far as calling the MB a terrorist group, it was arguably only a matter of time before he could be understood as holding such a view. By 2018, alongside being vice president of the FPPMS, he had become a member of the newly established Emirates Fatwa Council. Both institutions were official UAE bodies headed up by Yusuf's shaykh, Abdallah bin Bayyah. Already in 2014, the UAE had designated the MB as terrorists.[99] By 2020, Bin Bayyah had fully aligned himself with this viewpoint, and issued a statement in the name of the Emirates Fatwa Council declaring the MB a terrorist organization.[100] The ensuing controversy led to Bin Bayyah being removed from the speakers' lineup of the 2020 RIS Convention at which he had hitherto been a consistent fixture for well over a decade.[101] For his part, Yusuf did not publicly distance himself from the position taken by the Emirates Fatwa Council of which he was a member. He also would skip that year's RIS convention, though it was similarly unclear whether he had withdrawn or was disinvited. A few months earlier, Bin Bayyah and Yusuf had been criticized for the Emirates Fatwa Council's support of the UAE–Israel peace deal which was viewed as deeply damaging to the prospects of Palestinians living under Israeli occupation.[102]

Yusuf and his teacher's many engagements with the UAE would have repercussions among their Western audiences over the years, considerably accentuating the sense of crisis in Neo-traditionalist religious authority. In 2018, HRW criticized Yusuf for calling the UAE 'a tolerant country,' given its well-known record for arbitrary arrests and forced disappearances. As Kristian Ulrichsen has noted, the country has 'one of the highest rates of political prisoners per capita in the world.'[103] Then in 2019, Yusuf would cause an outcry in Western Muslim communities for agreeing to work as part of a commission advising the Trump administration.[104] That year, a recording surfaced from 2016 which some viewed as a case of Yusuf mocking Syrian refugees fleeing their country's civil war.[105] They had wrongfully rebelled against their ruler, Bashar al-Assad, and were thus being humiliated by God, he seemed to say. Outrage at his 2016 remarks led Yusuf to issue an apology, albeit one that did not satisfy some of the offended.[106] Many Muslims in the West clearly could not abide his work with autocrats and his promotion of a counter-revolutionary narrative.

The fortunes of Neo-traditionalism post-Rabaa have thus been decidedly mixed. While its scholars have been generously rewarded by autocratic states who have given them positions of great public prestige with seemingly endless funding and photo opportunities in the company of the global political and economic elite, their full-throated support for counter-revolutionary state repression on an epic scale has also cost their reputations dearly. As Masooda Bano has suggested, for some years now, but most acutely since 2013, Neo-traditionalism in the Middle East has been undergoing a very serious crisis of moral authority that hinges primarily upon its relationship with the autocratic state.[107] The crisis has arguably deepened the closer this relationship has become, and in the wake of the Arab revolutions, the autocratic state in many Middle Eastern nations has sought to increasingly police the Islamic scholarly sphere. This has meant the silencing of dissident scholarly voices through imprisonment or other forms of repression, as we have seen.

In fact, it is not only the scholars who are imprisoned in inhumane conditions. In 2017, shortly after the Qatar blockade had been announced, one of the blockading states, Egypt, arrested the 55-year-old daughter of Yusuf al-Qaradawi, herself a grandmother, and her husband.[108] The two US residents have since been held without charge in solitary confinement and denied access to basic needs, such as adequate access to food, medicine, and bedding. Their story is hardly exceptional—Egypt has reportedly imprisoned as many as 60,000 in counter-revolutionary crackdowns.[109] However, the relatively high profile and US residency status of Qaradawi's daughter and her husband have lent them greater visibility. But that visibility proves cold comfort when the international community looks the other way, often because of ongoing crises in the domestic politics of the powerful nations that might otherwise have been inclined to stand up for human rights in a place like Egypt. Indeed, in 2019 the first president elected in a free and fair election in Egypt's history died in custody due to extreme and quite possibly calculated medical neglect.[110] Western leaders passed over the news in silence reinforcing a sense of impunity when democracy and the rule of law are flagrantly undermined on the global stage.[111] In fact, the following year, France would bestow on Sisi the country's highest state award, the Legion of Honor, just weeks after he had cracked down on a major human rights organization.[112]

As we have seen, in order to paper over such rampant and systemic abuses, counter-revolutionary regimes have carefully cultivated a class of what we can refer to, adapting Qaradawi's usage, as *'ulamā' al-sulṭān*—scholars at the service of state authority. I would argue that such a label would apply to all of the counter-revolutionary scholars we have seen thus far, especially to those who appear to legitimize arbitrary power in principle.

Conclusion

In this chapter, I have sought to explain the religious basis for the fatwas issued in support of both the Egyptian coup and the subsequent Rabaa massacre. In contrast with several scholars who explain these fatwas with reference to premodern Sunni quietism, I have argued that these fatwas are better understood as reflecting a relatively radical break with premodern norms. I have done this by drawing on the secondary literature on premodern Islamic political thought which illustrates that: (1) the notion of 'quietism' when used as a general characterization of the premodern Sunni tradition lacks coherence; (2) the premodern legitimation of usurpers was a means of privileging the Sharia over the state; and (3) modern counter-revolutionary ulama have inverted this historical rationale for legitimating usurpers by subordinating the Sharia to the needs of the modern authoritarian state. As a consequence, I argue against scholars like Moosa, Osman, Fadel, and Muzakkir inasmuch as they locate counter-revolutionary fatwas in the premodern tradition. I also offer a counterpoint to the view put forward by Mohammad Fadel that counter-revolutionary ulama 'share a certain political aesthetic' with Ghazzālī. By contrast I suggest, similarly to Warren and Belal, that the explanation for Gomaa's fatwas is best sought in the modern context in which he operates. I have also argued that a causal connection may be discerned between the crushing of Egypt's democratic experiment in a military coup and the emergence of the twin institutions of ISIS and the FPPMS. What I am suggesting in connecting the two is that far from representing antithetical visions of the modern Middle East, these two institutions may be seen as legitimating and entailing each other as essential features of what I am calling 'autocratic Islam'.

CONCLUSION

In the Introduction, I set out to answer certain questions in an effort to understand why the ulama diverged in their responses to the Arab revolutions of 2011. These questions guided the inquiry over the course of this study and hopefully they would have been largely answered in the analysis offered up to this point. Presupposed in these questions was a divide between scholars who supported the revolutions and those that supported the pre-revolutionary order. Of the former scholars, we considered Yusuf al-Qaradawi, Ḥasan al-Shāfiʿī, Muḥammad ʿImāra, Aḥmad al-Raysūnī, and Rajab Zakī. Scholars who favored the pre-revolutionary order were Ali Gomaa, Aḥmad al-Ṭayyib, Ali al-Jifri, Abdallah bin Bayyah and Hamza Yusuf. The two sets of scholars engaged Islamic sacred texts and the Islamic scholarly tradition in very different ways to each other, and ultimately their often unstated hermeneutic assumptions would be the deciding factor as to whether they supported the revolutions or the counter-revolutions.

Institutional membership

A number of features of these scholars and their arguments are worth highlighting in these concluding reflections. Firstly, very few of these scholars were actual members of the MB or their offshoots, although those who were sided with the revolutionary camp. Specifically, Yusuf al-Qaradawi and Aḥmad al-Raysūnī were members of the MB or an affiliate, although in the case of Qaradawi, he was no longer a part of the organization's institutional structure. Neither was it the case that affiliation with the Azhar, even in a relatively senior formal capacity, necessitated siding with the anti-revolutionary, pro-coup camp. Of the scholars considered in this work, more Azharīs supported the revolutions than opposed them. Specifically, while Ṭayyib and Gomaa opposed the revolutions and supported the coup, Qaradawi, Shāfiʿī, ʿImāra, Zakī, and even ʿAlī al-Qaradāghī, the Kurdish Azharī who was cited on a couple of occasions co-signing IUMS statements with Qaradawi, all opposed the coup.

In terms of members of the Azhar's highest decision-making body, the CSS, more members of it appear to have been vocal supporters of the revolutions than vocal opponents of it until Qaradawi's resignation from it in December 2013. At that point, Shāfiʿī and ʿImāra remained as the scholars who had been vocally supportive of the revolutions, while Gomaa and Ṭayyib were the ones who had been vocally supportive of the coup. This does not appear to be entirely a consequence of selection bias; as noted earlier, Nathan Brown recognized that the Azharīs he met appeared roughly evenly divided between supporters and opponents of the Egyptian coup. But the most senior Egyptian state officials, those who were originally political appointees and afforded the greatest state recognition of their offices, namely Ṭayyib and Gomaa, opposed the revolutions and supported the coup, albeit to differing degrees. Indeed, in subsequent years, Ṭayyib's resistance to entirely assimilate the kind of statism that Gomaa would exemplify created rifts between himself and Sisi.

Values

Appeals to particular political values also appear to have differed between the scholars we are concerned with in ways that, perhaps unsurprisingly, aligned with their attitudes towards the revolution. Those supportive of the revolutions highlighted values like freedom and democracy, while those opposed to them warned against social breakdown (fitna) and emphasized the legitimacy of the incumbent in the case of Hosni Mubarak. However, the dividing line is not entirely clear, since Ṭayyib did not explicitly question Morsi's legitimacy while Gomaa explicitly impugned it in both of his private lectures to the security forces as can be seen in the transcripts appended below. With regard to the question of fitna, this concept appeared to be poorly defined for counter-revolutionary scholars—opposing Mubarak constituted fitna but opposing Morsi and his supporters to the point of killing hundreds of them in the streets did not. Notable in Ṭayyib's demurrals regarding the Rabaa massacre was the absence of references to fitna.

Hamza Yusuf's response, although it changed significantly over time, was notable for its consistent opposition to democracy. Even when he enthusiastically supported the ouster of Mubarak and appeared to ground a ruler's legitimacy in their popularity, he still made explicit his view that Egypt did not need the potential 'destabilizing factor' of democracy. It just needed a government that 'respected' and 'served' its people. For Bin Bayyah, as we have seen, calls for democracy in the region were tantamount to a 'call for war.' Yet, even for Islamists like Qaradawi, their calls for democracy were by no means calls for liberalism, an issue I alluded to with reference to Andrew March's observation that the Islamic democracy called for by Islamists presupposes levels of consensus regarding metaphysical and ethical truths that are unlikely to be obtained without 'the kinds of coercion and limitation on freedoms of conscience and speech that Islamic democrats claim to reject.'

This question cannot be dealt with in this short conclusion in a way that would assuage the anxieties expressed by liberals like March, a fact which itself suggests the urgent need for ongoing reflection on such issues. But it may still be useful to consider the following. Firstly, liberalism is currently struggling with the question of how to deal with the Islamic other in ways that I would argue bear more than a passing resemblance with the kinds of religious intolerance that characterized pre- and early modern Europe. The rise of so-called 'muscular liberalism' in Europe brings into question whether liberalism can similarly cope with the lack of 'consensus regarding metaphysical and ethical truths' held by those who would have identified as liberals in the recent past. It would seem that liberalism may also struggle to preserve itself without resorting to forms of coercion that it would, in principle, reject. The securitization of Muslims that has characterized the post-9/11 era has shown what liberalism can become, in spite of itself, when it feels threatened.

This suggests to me that Islamic democracy, like liberal democracy, would probably face some challenges as it tries to realize the promotion of Islamic values in ostensibly Islamic societies, just as liberalism is facing challenges in promoting liberal values in ostensibly liberal democracies. Current Islamist discourse, and in the Tunisian case current practice, suggests that responses to this state of affairs will likely be more restrained than the liberal securitization of Islam and Muslims in the West. But these anxieties have been testing liberalism to its limits, resulting in illiberal politicians like Trump being elected (albeit for one term), illiberal policies like Brexit succeeding in Britain, and illiberal laws being instituted in France and Austria against Muslims, to take just four prominent recent examples. As Shadi Hamid notes, politics is not a morality play, and so Islamists need to recognize the coercive contexts in which they operate.[1]

The flipside of calls for democracy were warnings against fitna. As we have seen, democracy could itself result in fitna, according to counter-revolutionary scholars, a perspective that the UAE and Saudi Arabia expended enormous resources to make a reality. In practice then, Bin Bayyah's viewpoint could be expressed thus: calls for democracy in the region would result in authoritarian states aggressively seeking to destabilize (i.e. foment fitna against) such aspiring democracies. While Bin Bayyah was doubtless aware of the role of the UAE, one of the region's most aggressive counter-revolutionary states, in destabilizing democracies in the region, it was in keeping with his principles that the ruler was not to be questioned on matters of state policy. Yet, Qaradawi also warned against fitna. Fitna was thus a contested concept among these scholars. Everyone was against fitna, but they differed over what constituted fitna.

Qaradawi argued that resorting to violence against a tyrant was to be avoided in most cases because it led to fitna, but peaceful protests were acceptable if not actively encouraged. This was then a different notion of fitna to that of Bin Bayyah. Gomaa, on the other hand, had yet another conception of fitna. Gomaa warned against fitna when protesters demanded the removal of Mubarak but did not consider protests calling for the removal of Morsi to constitute fitna. The protests against Mubarak were, for him, the source of fitna, but while protests against Morsi's rule were not fitna, those seeking the reinstatement of Morsi were unequivocally deemed to be causing fitna. For Gomaa, fitna was not a principle for explaining what kind of political action was prohibited. Rather, it was a concept to be deployed against threats to authoritarianism.

Qur'an and hadith

Naturally, both parties appealed to Qur'an and Sunna, but the texts they emphasized were different. As Youssef Belal suggests, the flexibility of the Sharia unmoored in modernity allows for the generation of interpretive diversity, including, I would add, the citation of pro- or counter-revolutionary texts depending on the political proclivities of the interpreters. For Gomaa, Bin Bayyah, and Ṭayyib, authoritarian readings of the Sharia were not just possible but essential. For scholars like Qaradawi, Shāfiʿī, and ʿImāra, democratic readings were far more convincing. In my own assessment, although this is not systematically investigated in the foregoing pages, the substantive detail and cogency of Qaradawi's arguments appear considerably more persuasive than the relatively mercenary style of Ali Gomaa or the ad hominem attacks deployed by Jifri, for example. Bin Bayyah's arguments, however, have not been as systematically elaborated in this work as those of Qaradawi—something I look forward to doing in future—and although I have offered a critical appraisal of his state-centric reading in the foregoing pages, a more detailed treatment is necessary to demonstrate that his state-centrism is less cogent than Qaradawi's democratic discourse.

Nonetheless, the arguments of counter-revolutionary scholars as a whole are notably thin in their citations from the Qur'an and hadith when compared with the arguments of Qaradawi that were mentioned in the first two chapters. Rather than citing the Qur'an and hadith, these scholars tended to invoke values like fitna and legitimacy, or in the case of Gomaa, made appeals to esoteric authority, as with references to dreams of the righteous as vindicating the massacres perpetrated by the security forces. Another feature, as alluded to above, is the very different approach to hadith citation between pro- and counter-revolutionary scholars, although for the former, I am referring mainly to Qaradawi. Based on this admittedly limited sample, it would appear that the citation of weak hadiths is far more a feature of counter-revolutionary scholars than pro-revolutionary ones. Certainly, Gomaa appears to entirely disregard concerns for authenticity or, indeed, interpretive plausibility in his citation of alleged hadiths regarding the modern Egyptian army or hadiths that exhort people to stay home in general. However, as noted in the conclusion of Chapter 1, premodern Sunnism appears to have been fairly relaxed about citing weak hadiths, a tendency that has been considerably attenuated in the modern period, arguably for good reason. At the same time, the rise of the Madkhalī trend, which as a branch of Salafism would presumably place a premium on hadith authenticity, would suggest that it is still perfectly possible to support absolutism while relying on authentic hadiths. Ultimately, it is a question of how such hadiths are interpreted (or interpreted away) to allow for the legitimation or otherwise of a given position.

None of the scholars were quietist

As noted in the final chapter, the political quietism versus activism binary is not a useful analytical framework for understanding the behavior of the scholars considered in this work. Rather, to adapt David Warren's argument beyond Ali Gomaa, the most significant factor in explaining whether a scholar was pro-revolutionary or anti-revolutionary, pro-coup or anti-coup was their commitment or opposition to the autocratic nation state. Those who recognized the state's absolute right to authority, usually located in the head of state, were anti-revolutionary and pro-coup, and the converse was true for those who rejected such absolutism. As noted earlier, Bin Bayyah's line of thought actually offers a systematic Islamic justification for such absolutism. This meant that these scholars were quietist vis-à-vis absolutist rulers, but activists vis-à-vis the opponents of such absolutist rulers. Thus, Gomaa was a quietist with respect to Sisi, but was not with respect to Morsi. Conversely, Qaradawi was a quietist with respect to Morsi (although this did not mean that he considered Morsi not open to criticism in keeping with his anti-absolutism), and he was not quietist vis-à-vis Mubarak. Yet, even in his opposition to Mubarak, Qaradawi was a quietist of sorts, because he vocally opposed armed rebellion against Mubarak, and indeed, even against Sisi after the Rabaa massacre. Rather, he insisted exclusively on peaceful protest. All of this simply illustrates that the distinction between quietism and activism is unhelpful in trying to understand these scholars' choices.

Qaradawi, Bahrain, and violent rebellion

While a scholar like Gomaa has shown a consistent commitment to authoritarianism, Qaradawi's commitment to democracy arguably wavered in relation to the abortive Bahraini revolution. It would seem that his stance can be explained in light of widespread fear of Iranian influence in the region that appeared to have little to do with the actual reality of the democratic uprisings of the island state as David Warren has argued. Although it strikes me as highly unlikely that Qaradawi was directed by the Qatari state on this, it is quite conceivable that, given Qaradawi's influence in the region in this period, they would have nudged him in that direction owing to the commitments of GCC states at the time to come to each other's aid if their security was threatened, even if that threat, as turned out to be the case, came from a state's own people. Warren argues that this move damaged Qaradawi's reputation for independence at the time, and this seems quite understandable.

On the other hand, some may question Qaradawi's commitment to non-violence given his support for those who violently rebelled in Libya and Syria. This, however, misunderstands his argument for peaceful protest. As we have seen in Chapter 1, Uriya Shavit points out that Qaradawi was not a pacifist who would oppose violence in a context of fully fledged civil war.

To resort to violence in such a case was, for Qaradawi, to engage in self-defense against an aggressor. As a general rule, he held peaceful protest to be legitimate and violent protest to be illegitimate. Yet, if a state engaged in a sustained all-out war against peaceful protestors such that this led to circumstances resembling civil war, then this had a different ruling. Individual massacres like those of Rabaa did not in and of themselves constitute civil war for Qaradawi. In Syria and Libya, by contrast, where civil war obtained, violence in the interest of self-preservation was an obligation. As we have seen in Chapter 4, this was also more or less the view of Bin Bayyah.

Surrendering to the autocratic state

The philosophy underlying the discourse of counter-revolutionary ulama was fundamentally about obedience to one's rulers. Whoever ruled the state was the ultimate sovereign, and their word was placed over and above everyone else's, including those who traditionally spoke in God's name, that is, the ulama. Gomaa's approach differed subtly from Bin Bayyah, although so far the results have been similar—the placement of supreme authority in the hands of the ruler. Gomaa offered the security forces the service of justifying in religious terms all the actions of the Egyptian deep state, apparently without question. Bin Bayyah took a different tack. In keeping with his jurisprudential proclivities, he developed a juristic justification for placing the ruler's authority in public affairs and state law-making over and above the ulama on the grounds that the ruler, by virtue of having access to all the relevant information, knew better what laws were best. In effect, he articulated an unprecedented legal argument for an Islamic jurist, one which placed state law beyond the reach of the Sharia, thereby subordinating the latter to the former.

While this may be seen as Bin Bayyah effectively surrendering his own authority as a jurist entirely to the state, he has been lavishly rewarded for such a move. Having joined the UAE's political class, he now rubs shoulders with the global elite and enjoys a platform, resources and recognition that few Islamic jurists can aspire to. Rendering oneself a servant of autocracy doubtless offers immense personal rewards. Bin Bayyah and Gomaa's approaches may be contrasted with that of Qaradawi. While Qaradawi had also been promoted aggressively by the Qatari nation state, he managed to maintain a degree of independence that Bin Bayyah and Gomaa have both seen fit to forgo. Qatar had effectively ceded a degree of authority to Qaradawi after a fashion that resembles a limited degree of political freedom. Gomaa and Bin Bayyah do not enjoy the same degree of freedom to criticize their patrons.

For now, authoritarian scholars have the political upper hand while democratic scholars have the discursive upper hand. So long as authoritarians are able to cling to power, their scholars will enjoy prominence and dominate the airwaves of state media. But their condition appears precarious. The Arab revolutions of 2011 broke the fabled barrier of fear. The large-scale massacres of 2013 and the persistence of civil war has helped rebuild much of that barrier. Yet something has changed. The aggressive promotion of authoritarian Islamic discourses is perhaps a reflection of deeper changes in attitudes. The buildup of Islamic democratic discourses in the region over the past three decades, mainly at the initiative of Islamist scholars and writers, followed by the short-lived experience of democratic openings seems to have given at least some people in the region a sense of democratic possibility.

The barrier of fear has been rebuilt by states that now exhibit unprecedented levels of repression, surveillance, and a willingness to pursue enemies beyond their borders. Yet, such measures appear to have been driven in part by the genuine threat democracy now poses to autocracy in the region. It is not possible to prognosticate on such matters, but one hopes that the barrier of fear has been permanently weakened. Doubtless there will continue to be severe repression in the region with powerful states like the UAE and Saudi Arabia leaning more heavily in an authoritarian direction. But the democratic possibilities unleashed by the revolutions continue to inspire protest a decade on. This fact alone should inspire fear in the region's autocrats and hope in the region's democrats.

EPILOGUE

The future of Neo-traditionalism

As noted in the introduction, I am myself trained as an alim.[1] During my undergraduate years at the University of Oxford, I had the good fortune to attend the Al-Salam Institute established and run by a scholar of Indian origin, Dr Mohammad Akram Nadwi, then a research fellow at the Oxford Centre for Islamic Studies. Shaykh Akram, as his students referred to him, taught a modified *Dars-i Niẓāmī* syllabus, in keeping with the curriculum of most Indian institutions of Islamic higher learning. Seminary training in the modern world is perhaps by default Neo-traditionalist in orientation, and that is the context in which I developed my own intellectual lens as a Muslim seminarian. Unlike my academic course in Arabic and Islamic studies at the University, my studies at the Institute were meant to shape my religious sensibilities and my identity, all while highlighting a direct connection, through a long chain of authorities, to the Prophet himself.

Shaykh Akram was himself a graduate of Dār al-ʿUlūm Nadwat al-ʿUlamāʾ in Lucknow in India, hence his adopted last name.[2] He was a student of, among many other scholars, the former rector of the Nadwa, Abū al-Ḥasan ʿAlī Nadwī (d. 1420/1999), described by Muhammad Qasim Zaman as 'the most influential Indian religious scholar of his generation.'[3] The older Nadwi came from a scholarly family whose lineage went back to the Prophet. Given his scholarly pedigree, we were told that the lineage was actually traceable through the history books, unlike many modern claimants to this noble lineage. He was also the rector of one of the world's most reputable centers of Islamic higher learning, a jurist in the Ḥanafī school (the dominant legal school found among Indian Muslims), and a Sufi shaykh with his own *murīd*s (novices) and a *khanqāh* (Sufi lodge) close to the Nadwa— all unimpeachable trappings of an eminent Neo-traditionalist. But he also associated with scholars of a range of other denominations. For a short period of his life, he worked closely with Abū al-Aʿlā Mawdūdī (d. 1399/1979) as a senior member of the latter's political party, Jamāʿat-i Islāmī. He also maintained ties with major Salafi figures, like the Saudi Grand Mufti, ʿAbd al-ʿAzīz b. Bāz (d. 1420/1999). Indeed, while he was a student at the Nadwa, he studied for a period with the notable Moroccan Salafi, Muḥammad Taqī al-Dīn al-Hilālī (d. 1407/1987). Clearly, for the older Nadwi, Neo-traditionalism was not an exclusivist denomination that prevented intra-Sunni cooperation.

His student, my teacher, embodied much the same perspective. While he proudly saw himself as a Ḥanafī mufti and personally abjured the label Salafi, his conception of the Islamic tradition allowed for considerable variation, albeit all within a Sunni framework. It is a perspective that has undoubtedly influenced my own. Once again, his perspective is not unique. Another such example would be the Mauritanian Islamist, Muḥammad al-Ḥasan al-Dadaw (b. 1383/1963), a Mālikī jurist who is theologically Salafi and harbors great respect for much of the Sufi tradition. Such scholars actively encourage their students to seek out other teachers to avoid developing an unhealthy sense of partisan affiliation (*taʿaṣṣub*) towards a single teacher or outlook. In adhering to such advice, I have personally been fortunate enough to study with ulama of a Salafi and an Islamist orientation alongside my studies with Neo-traditionalists. Thus, while I have repeatedly used phrases like Neo-traditionalism, Islamism, and Salafism throughout these pages, as I hope to have suggested already, these analytic distinctions, while useful, also have their limits. Rather than conceiving of them as mutually exclusive claims to Sunni orthodoxy, they may also be viewed as manifesting some of the more notable discursive possibilities that the historical Sunni tradition has bequeathed to modern Muslims. They need not be viewed as limiting the possibilities of the Sunni, or indeed, the Islamic tradition. Yet, such a perspective is by no means universally shared.

There is a tendency within Neo-traditionalism, as illustrated by scholars like H.A. Hellyer and Abdal Hakim Murad, to define the denomination in contradistinction to 'ideological' forms of Sunnism, most notably Islamism and Salafism.[4] Similar exclusivist claims are made by some Salafis and Islamists. Accordingly, it is claimed that the distinctions between what I have called different denominations of Sunnism are relatively clear-cut, at least where it matters. Similarly, it is suggested that these groupings are internally fairly cohesive. But these claims seem quite suspect to me, or at the very least, contestable, and the three denominations appear to me to be fairly imbricated and not themselves as internally unified as some ulama would seem to suggest.

To take one controversial example, in a 2004 article, Abdal Hakim Murad condemned 'suicide bombing' as a perversion of Islamic teachings promoted by Islamists and Salafis.[5] Yet, some of its most prominent scholarly proponents happen to be Neo-traditionalist graduates of the Azhar, including Gomaa, Būṭī, and the last four shaykhs of al-Azhar, including its current incumbent at the time of writing, Ṭayyib.[6] Elsewhere, I have critiqued Hellyer's portrayal in *The Financial Times* of Neo-traditionalism as having a monopoly over the preservation of tradition through chains of scholarly authorities (*asānīd*) and licenses to teach (*ijāzāt*).[7] Hellyer appeared to suggest that a major reason for the early Wahhabi movements deviating from the path of Neo-traditional Islam was a disregard for these forms of passing on scholarship. Yet, their tradition remains preserved today using the same apparatus of *asānīd* and *ijāzāt*.[8] I pointed out that Anwar al-Awlaki (d. 1432/2011), killed by the US as an al-Qaeda operative, had advertised the considerable extent of his *asānīd* and *ijāzāt* on his now defunct website.[9] The fact that consecutive shaykhs of the Azhar have championed suicide bombings or, as they refer to them, martyrdom operations, against Israel as a legitimate form of resisting occupation would seem to suggest that these trappings of traditional learning are no sure-fire way to indicate that their bearers would always reject forms of violence that are condemned as terrorism in the West.

More directly relevant to the question of revolutions, in the wake of the Arab Spring, Hamza Yusuf has portrayed the Islamic tradition as virtually unified in its opposition to rebelling against one's rulers no matter how bad they are.[10] As a major Western proponent of Neo-traditionalism, his assertion may be understood as a Neo-traditionalist claim to Islamic orthodoxy. Yet, as Thomas Pierret has ably illustrated, large numbers of Syrian Neo-traditionalist ulama actively sanctioned the anti-Assad rebellion in Syria that began in 2011.[11] The conception of Neo-traditionalism promoted by the likes of Yusuf and Hellyer should thus be understood as a reductive one that ignores the denomination's internal flexibility and potential capaciousness. One might even describe Yusuf's particular understanding as an ideologically statist variant of Neo-traditionalism. Such a label likely also applies to Bin Bayyah's conception of Islam. It is this narrow ideologization that results in a figure like Qaradawi routinely being cast outside the realm of Neo-traditionalism with the use of the epithet Islamist, usually as a term of disapprobation. Yet

Qaradawi is as much of an Azharī scholar as one might find anywhere today, and wears his Azharī identity, in the form of the distinctive Azharī habit, as a badge of honor.[12]

After memorizing the Qur'an at the age of nine in his village, his entire formal education took place within the Azhar system, all the way to his doctorate. Indeed, in his final exams at what would be the equivalent of both undergraduate and postgraduate levels, he graduated at the top of his class. This was reportedly across all three colleges of the Azhar, where he came first out of 500 students.[13] His scholarly pedigree is certainly not in question. He was trained at the Azhar in the Ḥanafī school, although he does not make a point of affiliating with a single school while accepting that Muslims are at liberty to do so.[14] As Ahmed Fekry Ibrahim has shown, however, such switching between schools has a long pedigree in the late Sunni tradition, which is why he describes Qaradawi as one of the Azhar's 'towering figures' alongside prominent shaykhs of al-Azhar in the past, such as Muṣṭafā al-Marāghī (d. 1364/1945) and Maḥmūd Shaltūt (d. 1383/1963).[15] Qaradawi also defends the Ash'arī school of theology as the main school representing Sunnism and is deeply influenced by the Sufism of Abū Ḥāmid al-Ghazzālī (d. 505/1111).[16] While he warns against 'excesses' in Sufism, he still considers aspects of it essential to a sound understanding of Islam. In this regard, Qaradawi is arguably not significantly different in his conception of Sufism to someone like Jifri, although Jifri would likely sanction certain practices that Qaradawi would discourage.[17]

For those scholars who wish to serve as global spokespeople for Islam, whether as the political appointees of states like Bin Bayyah and Yusuf or from less state-centric perspectives, there undoubtedly is a need for less ideologically intolerant readings of Sunni Islam to be promoted. It would seem to be a small but essential step to reducing the conflict caused because of a desire to preserve 'true Islam.' Of course, the same would apply to the way in which a figure like Qaradawi has taken to speaking about Shi'ism since the late 2000s. More specifically, in the case of state-sponsored scholars like Yusuf and Bin Bayyah, they need to reflect on the symbolic significance of investing their spiritual capital in legitimizing states like the UAE with an extensive public record of championing murderous regimes and perpetrating vicious wars throughout the Middle East. For Hamza Yusuf in particular, the damage this does to the credibility of the US institution he leads, the like of which are so crucial to the development of modern ulama in the West, should be a great cause for concern.

Indeed, the events outlined in the preceding pages illustrate modern Muslims' desperate need for moral leadership that also exemplifies practical wisdom. There can be little doubt that the post-coup massacres, most notably Rabaa, have been a serious indictment of the failure of Neo-traditionalism's moral leadership. If the leading lights of Neo-traditionalism's most globally hallowed institution can legitimate anti-democratic coups, as Shaykh al-Azhar al-Ṭayyib did, and then celebrate the murder of hundreds if not thousands of unarmed pro-democracy activists in the streets of Egypt in full view of the global media, as Ali Gomaa did, what moral authority can Neo-traditionalism claim if its other leading figures are not willing to loudly condemn these so-called leaders of the movement? This should be an existential concern for the entire denomination. It cannot look away and pretend one of its most globally celebrated teachers did not actively sanction mass murder and go on preaching its supposed message of moderation to future generations without being accused of the most craven moral cowardice.

A religion whose senior scholars advocate mass murder and autocracy possesses precious little moral authority. The reality is, of course, that large numbers of senior scholars condemned the likes of Gomaa, as we have seen from a small but representative sample. Even within the ranks of Azharīs who are Neo-traditionalist by default, we saw the fiery sermon of Rajab Zakī. Other critics have been far more muted. Abdal Hakim Murad has obliquely critiqued scholars like Bin Bayyah and Yusuf without mentioning their names. In May 2014, 2 months after the inaugural 'Forum for Promoting Peace' in the UAE, he wrote the following words in an essay on a very different subject:

> So many of our scholars attend jamboree conferences arranged by various regimes, which end with platitudinal resolutions about 'peace and moderation.' I think we should stop doing that now. How useful it would be if our scholars could attend a different event, to learn of our situation, hear the different viewpoints, and explain how our response ought to be, as a cool Shari'a judgement, far from panic and fearfulness.[18]

For most of his readers who would have been unaware of the Forum's activities, it would seem to be a tangential comment. Four years later in November 2018, he would speak thoughtfully about 'curricular heteronomy,' a phrase referring to attempts by modern political authorities in much of the Muslim world to control the content of religious teachings and curtail scholars' freedom of speech. He approvingly cited the poem of the great Senegalese Sufi, Amadou Bamba (d. 1346/1927) in which the latter expressed 'his confidence in God's support for independent and unbowed scholars who could speak truth to power and who thought that God's religion ought to side with the helpless.'[19] In this context, he also criticized the pliant Saudi 'Caesaropapist clericy' for providing Islamic justifications for the 2017 Saudi boycott of Qatar. Arguably, the Salafi establishment was an easy target for him. He could also admonish his colleague, Hamza Yusuf, the vice president of the FPPMS at the time, for doing the same.

Still, Murad's comments appear to be more than many other Neo-traditionalists have been willing to say on the matter. This silence, papering over Neo-traditionalism's complicity in naked abuses on the part of states like the UAE and Egypt, continues to cast a shadow over the Sunni denomination. It would seem that moral opprobrium will continue to be attached to Neo-traditionalism so long as a loud and vocal rejection of the hard-statist direction of the denomination's leading lights fails to materialize. As a young alim of largely Neo-traditionalist seminary training, I hope that this epilogue lends at least a modest voice to what should be an unequivocal chorus of condemnations. In this regard, I follow in the footsteps of Jonathan A.C. Brown, a onetime student of Gomaa and Jifri and a scholar whom I consider a friend and a teacher.[20] A concomitant of the stance I am advocating is that Western Muslims in particular should not promote as exemplars scholars who have either advocated murderous behavior such as Ali Gomaa or publicly justified such acts as was done by his student, Ali al-Jifri.[21] As alluded to in Chapter 7, Jifri has visited the UK on multiple occasions since showing strong support for Gomaa's advocacy of violence against protestors in Egypt. He has also been a regular guest of the Egyptian military, serving to provide them with religious legitimacy as noted above.

Lessons for Islamist ulama

It is arguably both more difficult and easier for Islamist ulama to learn from the experiences of the past few years. It is difficult because so many of the actors they supported, and indeed, so many of the ulama themselves, have been assassinated, incarcerated, exiled, or otherwise persecuted. Learning from an ordeal ideally requires some time to regroup and recuperate in dialogue between activists and ulama, but such luxuries do not appear to be available to Islamists. Rather, those who live in relative freedom today, usually in exile from their countries of origin in places like Turkey or further West, are more often than not engaged in campaigning and human rights advocacy in support of their incarcerated and disappeared fellows in their countries of origin. Reflection must take place in challenging circumstances, often in the absence of major leaders of the movements' political wings.

Yet it is also easier. The discussion doubtless needs to confront serious failings of a practical and strategic nature for the activists, but the moral failings of Islamist ulama, at least in the Egyptian case, seem far tamer than those of Neo-traditionalists. Yet, no one can claim to escape unscathed from the calamities that have afflicted Egypt from 2013 onwards. While blame for mass killings falls ultimately on the security forces and those who supported them, there also has to be soul-searching among Islamist ulama as to how they arrived at the summer of 2013 and what they could have done to avoid such a tragedy for Egypt and themselves. From an Islamic perspective, dying for a righteous cause as a martyr may be redeeming for the dead, but it is certainly not meant to be an option for most of the living, nor does it provide answers for those who survive into the aftermath of a massacre.

As this book focuses primarily on scholarly actors, I will restrict my comments to them. It is clear that Islamist ulama like Qaradawi and 'Imāra, among many others not explored in this work, had developed a basic discursive framework for contesting tyrannical government in the modern world, proposing, as an alternative, to borrow modern Western norms of democratically accountable government. But it is clear that they had little by way of effective spiritual advice for the long game after the fall of Mubarak. Like their activist counterparts, they had underestimated the extent to which they were at the mercy of deep-state actors and foreign interference with seemingly limitless resources. Islamists in particular suffer from a serious image problem, associated as they routinely are with terrorists of the ISIS and al-Qaeda variety. This is not, in my view, because they are more likely to engage in sectarian discourse than, say, Neo-traditionalists. The events of 2013 should have definitively disabused observers of this fact. Ironically for the most democratically oriented Islamic denomination in the Middle East, Islamists seem among the most likely to be associated with terrorism and security threats in the minds of influential Western observers. As we saw earlier, both Obama's Republican secretary of defense, Chuck Hagel, and his Democratic secretary of state, John Kerry, harbored deep misgivings about the dangers of the MB. The same was true for most of the Obama team, was true a fortiori for the Trump administration, and will likely remain true in future administrations.

A number of experts have argued that the evidence from Morsi's single year in office shows that he was hardly the autocrat he was made out to be.[22] But what is probably a combination of a long history of Orientalist presuppositions and their modern equivalent, Islamophobic prejudice regarding the MB, have meant that the odds are stacked against such movements. As explained in the Introduction, I use the term Islamist to designate a democratically oriented group of Arab activists and scholars who themselves use the Arabic designation *Islāmiyyūn*. Islamist is the most literal translation of this word. However, in English, the word is often overlaid with decidedly pejorative implications suggestive of violence and terrorism, something that is systematically reinforced and exploited by Arab autocracies.[23] Any project championing political liberation and democratic accountability in the region needs to grapple head on with this serious problem of perception and what underlies it.

The problem of accountability

The Arab revolutions appeared in their heady early days to finally offer the promise of accountable government that had been sought for so long by the people of the region. With this work's focus on the ulama, another kind of accountability is demonstrated as desperately wanting in the region, namely the accountability of the ulama. Unfortunately, in autocratic states, holding the ulama who support autocracy to account is currently wishful thinking. But in light of the rise of counter-revolutionary ulama, we can recognize the importance of aspiring to accountability in all aspects of the public sphere in the Middle East, especially with respect to scholars operating in an official or quasi-official capacity. Ultimately, a call for accountability of public officials is a recognition of the imperative of political liberty in the region. Without political liberty, there cannot be accountability in the public sphere at large, and without accountability in the public sphere at large, there cannot be accountability in the religious sphere. This is why, as noted in Chapter 1, even an Islamist alim like Qaradawi argues that political liberty is a greater priority than the state's 'implementation of the Sharia.'

Of course, autocracy in the political sphere breeds autocracy in the religious sphere, and there is also the possibility for this to be true in the reverse. Autocracy in the political and religious spheres will stunt the healthy development of those spheres, both in theoretical and practical terms. Autocracy would thus necessarily hamper the development of religious ideas in response to the needs of a society. Rather it could only respond to the needs of those who control public discourse and in directions that those controllers permit or desire. It is hardly conceivable that regimes such as post-coup Egypt will be able to address the needs of their own people, let alone contribute anything meaningful to confront the kinds of challenges faced by wider humanity.

David Decosimo discerns a long tradition of liberty within the Islamic scholarly tradition that he describes as aligning remarkably well with the modern republican tradition of liberty that is concerned, in contrast with liberalism, with liberty understood as freedom from the arbitrary domination of others. As he argues, the premodern polymath Ghazzālī and the modern Islamist thinker Abū al-Aʿlā Mawdūdī share a comparable conception of republican liberty that may be viewed as an indigenously Islamic tradition of political freedom.[24] As noted earlier, Mohammad Fadel maintains that in the context of the Arab revolutions, Yusuf al-Qaradawi promoted a republican conception of political subjectivity while Ali Gomaa advocated an authoritarian conception of the same. If the counter-revolutions have demonstrated anything, they have shown the urgency of articulating such indigenously Islamic conceptions of republican freedom with even greater force.

In their focus on liberty, Islamists have not necessarily been wrong. In terms of strategy against an unrelenting foe, they doubtless have been. This does not mean they need to rethink the focus on republican liberty as an Islamic ideal, although they clearly need to more effectively bring about its enactment in society. This work has not been focused on Islamist activists, however. Its focus has self-consciously been on the ulama who also have an important role to play in public discourse in Islamic societies. In closing, I would like to suggest that it is the role of the ulama to translate a scriptural tradition and religious heritage whose republican strands are of crucial importance today so that they can win the argument against all the forces arrayed for the purpose of making Islam autocratic. They could regain a sense of purpose in the modern world by shaping its ethical sensibilities and restraining the excesses of the 'impossible state' as they appear to have done with much success vis-à-vis Islamic governance in the premodern world. Whether they will be able and willing to take on this challenge today, we will have to wait and see.

والْحَمْدُ للهِ أَوَّلًا وآخِرًا

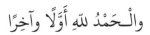

APPENDIX 1

YUSUF AL-QARADAWI: ONE OF THE IMAMS OF THE MUSLIMS

By Abdallah bin Bayyah[1]

All praise is due to God, and prayers and peace be upon our Master Muhammad, the Messenger of God, upon his Family, and his Companions.

To proceed:

> Indeed the supremely erudite Shaykh Dr Yusuf al-Qaradawi needs no praise or panegyric, for he is as al-Khansāʾ[2] (d. 24/645) said:
>
> > Indeed *Yusuf* is one whom guides take as their guide,
> > *Because* he is a mountain upon whose peak there is *light*[3]

The changes in the verse are intended for the occasion, for Imam Yusuf is an oceanic scholar, a moving preacher (*dāʿīya*), and a pedagogue (*murabbī*) for generations, and a great reformer by means of both his spiritual state (*ḥāl*) and his statements—he spreads knowledge and wisdom as a teacher and a muftī. His methodology is that of Islamic moderation (*wasaṭiyya*) with which al-Shāṭibī (d. 790/1388)[4] characterizes the Islamic Sharia, saying that:

> it follows, for [those] observing its obligations, the most moderate (*al-awsaṭ*) and most balanced (*al-aʿdal*) way, taking from both sides with justice, without any inclination [towards either extreme], falling within the ability of [God's] servant, placing upon him neither undue hardship nor complete lack of restriction. Rather it consists of responsibilities placed in accordance with a balancing of considerations requiring, with respect to all legally competent individuals, the utmost moderation (*ghāyat al-iʿtidāl*).[5]

He inclines towards making things easy for people in his fatwas, but he himself is characterized by vigor that is nearer rigor in the foundational issues, and those aspects [of Islam] that are not subject to change. [He does this by] marrying the texts with the higher aims [of the Sharia] in a dialectic in whose trackless desert none are guided, nor can anyone undertake its balancing, except the ones who are deeply rooted in knowledge (*al-rāsikhūn fī al-ʿilm*), and whom Shaykh Yusuf has described, and it is as though he is describing himself, when he says in his book, *al-Marjiʿiyya al-ʿUlyā fī al-Islām li-l-Qurʾān wa-l-Sunna* [*The Highest Authority in Islam Belongs to the Book and the Sunna*], as follows:

> The task of those who are deeply rooted in knowledge is to search for the higher aims of the Sharia through the texts, having roamed their horizons, and immersed oneself in their depths, and tied their particulars (*juzʾiyyāt*) with their universals (*kulliyyāt*), and brought their branches (*furūʿ*) back to their roots (*uṣūl*), and bound their rulings to each other such that the jewels are composed and ordered in its necklace, with the conviction that the illustrious Sharia does not make legal distinctions between identical [cases], nor render distinct [cases] identical.[6]

This is the finest description that can be presented to describe the person we are writing about. Add to this that the shaykh is not of those jurists who suffice with the theoretical treatment of the socioeconomic issues of the umma, but rather he is a man of the field, who takes to the field of knowledge and its application, and participates in the establishment of research centers, universities, and charitable organizations.

In summary, the erudite Shaykh Yusuf al-Qaradawi is indeed one of the imams of the Muslims in this age, and a shaykh al-Islām[7] in this time. You may agree with him and be convinced of his argument and his proof, or you may differ with him but respect his opinion because it is the opinion of a God-fearing scholar that does not arise from ignorance, nor from arbitrary whims—and these two are conditions that are indispensable if a fatwa is to have its sanctity, and a word, its value. These two conditions have been combined, in my judgement, by this imam.

He has been rendered worthy of all these characteristics due to his abundant knowledge that is multifaceted and wide-ranging, for he has indeed joined between the revealed (*manqūl*) and the rational (*maʿqūl*) disciplines, in the Book and the Sunna, in their branches (*furūʿ*) and their roots (*uṣūl*), in language and literature, in addition to an extensive and reliable [understanding of] contemporary culture. For this reason his proofs are clear, his clarifications are compelling, alongside dignified personal characteristics, including a noble soul, humility, moderation in speech, and deliverance from envy. Indeed we admire his book on one of his scholarly contemporaries—Shaykh Muḥammad al-Ghazālī (d. 1416/1996), may God show him mercy—written during his lifetime, in which he praised and defended him. It is indeed a rare example among the scholars, particularly in this time of ours.

We ask God to reward him and give him strength, and benefit us and the Muslims through him and his knowledge.

APPENDIX 2

TRANSLATION OF ALI GOMAA'S PRE-RABAA LECTURE TO THE EGYPTIAN SECURITY FORCES[1]

[On screen heading:]

Talk by Dr Ali Gomaa: Member of the Council of Senior Scholars (*Hay'at Kibār al-'Ulamā'*) of the Honorable Azhar

[Ali Gomaa's lecture:]

In the name of God the compassionate, the merciful. All praise is due to God, and peace and blessings be upon our master, the Messenger of God, upon his Family, his Companions, and those who support him. O God, open our hearts, forgive our sins, conceal our flaws, and ease all our affairs, O most merciful One.

[Praise for the protests of 30 June]

In these days and moments, Egypt is going through many changes. Among them is what happened on 30 June in the year 2013 after the honorable birth of our master Christ. This [was an] outpouring (*khurūj*), the like of which we have never ever seen, not in our lifetimes, nor around the world. The Egyptian people came out in protest (*kharaja*). They came out in protest, and all the people have seen this; and the strange thing is that some of us, our own people (*min banī jildatinā*) who speak our language (*bi-lughatinā*), as the Messenger of God, peace and blessings of God be upon him reported,[2] deny this outpouring. All of the aerial observations, and international observers, state that [the crowds] were more than thirty million. But these [deniers] say that they were not even 30,000!

Ibn Ḥazm (d. 456/1064), may God be pleased with him, says: 'Whoever denies the palpable reality, which people have testified to, cannot be engaged in discussion.' We do not wish to stop talking with anyone; and we hope for guidance for everyone, and we feel the same way that the Messenger of God, peace and blessings of God be upon him, would feel such that God would comfort him by saying: 'You do not guide whomever you love, but rather God guides whomever He wills.' (Q. 28:56) O God, guide our people, for indeed they do not understand. Guide our youth, O Lord of the worlds, for indeed they have been confused and duped. The matter is grave; and giving sincere advice (*naṣīḥa*) is the religion itself. The Prophet, peace and blessings of God be upon him, said 'The religion is sincerity/sincere advice.' [His Companions] asked: 'To whom, O Messenger of God.' He replied: 'to God, His Messenger, the leaders of the Muslims, and the lay Muslims.'

On this day, on 30 June, the people (*sha'b*) came out in an astonishing way, after they had had enough of the anarchy of [their] lives, the country, and the people. They had had enough after these crises that had affected their daily lives—[crises affecting the supply] of electricity, gas, and petrol. Prices had become inflated, security was compromised, and on top of that the interests of the country were adversely affected nationally and internationally.[3]

The people came out expressing themselves in a way we have not previously witnessed—neither in [the revolution of] 25 January [2011], nor before it, nor after it. And it was peaceful. They did not bear arms. They did not kill anyone. They did not aggress against people's honor (*'irḍ*). They did not steal money. Rather it was peaceful. Thus their coming out [in protest] was a form of commanding the right (*amr bi-l-ma'rūf*), forbidding the wrong (*nahy 'an al-munkar*), and giving sincere religiously mandated advice. [The second Caliph] 'Umar used to say, 'If I make a mistake, then correct me, even if it be by your swords.'[4] So what about a situation in which we wish to correct [our leaders], so we correct them through those who have the right to correct them, that is, the people (*al-sha'b*). The populace is the primary [authority], and everyone else is secondary.

[Praise for Egyptian armed forces]

The Egyptian armed forces—that great army that the Prophet, peace and blessings be upon him, praised and used to refer to as the western army (*al-jund al-gharbī*)—western army because they are west of Madina. The Companions [also] used to refer to them as the western army, as has been narrated from 'Amr b. al-Ḥamiq al-Khuzā'ī.[5] He relates: 'I heard the Messenger of God (peace and blessings be upon him) say, "there will be civil strife (fitna), the safest people in it will be the western army," and this is why I have come to you in Egypt.' 'Amr b. al-Ḥamiq came to Egypt because of this hadith after he heard it from the Messenger of God.[6]

[Another Companion,] Tubay' b. 'Āmir al-Kalā'ī narrates:[7] 'I came from a summer expedition to Abū Mūsā al-Ash'arī and he asked: "Where are you from?" I replied, "From the people of Egypt." He asked, "From the western army?" I replied, "Yes." He asked, "From the weak army?" I replied, "Is it weak?"' He was surprised that Abū Mūsā referred to the Egyptian army as the weak army, and that is because it is small in number, and despite its small numbers, it is supported by God. So Abū Mūsā said to him, 'Yes, no one can conspire against them except that God will seize them, and give victory to [the Egyptian army] over them.'[8]

There is no strength or power except in God! Our master the Messenger of God said this to Abū Mūsā! Abū Mūsa [then] said to [al-Kalā'ī], 'Go to Mu'ādh b. Jabal and he will narrate to you,' so Tubay' went to Mu'ādh b. Jabal. [Mu'ādh] asked him, 'What did the elder (Abū Mūsā) say to you?' So he told him, and [Mu'ādh] replied: 'Is there anything better than this ḥadīth with which you can return to your country?'

The Messenger of God spoke the truth; his noble Companions spoke the truth; and the pious Successors spoke the truth, informing us of the revelation from the Messenger of God, peace and blessings of God be upon him, that the Egyptian army will be safe from strife (*fitan*), that it supports the truth, that it eliminates oppression, that it prevents aggression, and that it punishes rebels. The Prophet, peace and blessings of God be upon him, says of these people who kill Muslims—the Khawārij—he says about them in authentically transmitted reports: 'the Khawārij are the dogs of the Hellfire.'[9] He also said: 'you will despise your prayers when you compare it with theirs, and your fasting when you compare it with theirs; [yet] blessed are those who kill them and are killed by them.' Those who kill them are more worthy of God than they are, because they raised weapons against the Muslims, and because they kill Muslims, and the Prophet, peace and blessings of God be upon him, was severe in his warning that we do not descend into such civil strife.

Whoever approaches the Egyptian army, whom God, Most High, has granted assistance, he is destroying his own life. The reason for this is that the Egyptian army is assisted by God, Most High. Thus this coming out in protest (*khurūj*), and this situation in which the army has taken a stand with the people, has not occurred as was desired by people with vested interests, whims, and desires, nationally and internationally; and those who do not wish for Egypt to rise, due to their own economic interests, their own social interests, and their own dogmatic interests.

This is the mutual harmony between the Egyptian army, which is supported by God, and the Egyptian people regarding whom the Messenger of God (peace and blessings be upon him) said that the people of the West (*ahl al-gharb*)—that is, Egypt—will continue to be with the truth until the Day of Judgment.[10] He also said, 'there will always be a group of my umma clearly with the truth, unharmed by those who disagree with them, until the Day of Judgment.' Ibn Fadl Allāḥ al-'Umarī (d. 749/1349) said, 'they are the western army,' i.e. they are the people of Egypt and the army of Egypt.

[Removing Morsi was not a coup]

This was not a coup. In a coup, the coup regime usurps authority for itself, and this has not happened. And it occurs because of a desire for this authority, and this has not happened. Rather, when anarchy took hold, and people protested, gave sincere advice, and came out in the millions; the Egyptian army had to answer this call. Is it permitted to depose a President? In Islamic law (fiqh) it is permitted to depose a President. It is permitted to depose a President if he goes insane. It is even permitted to depose a President if he is imprisoned by the enemy. It is permitted to depose a President if he loses his senses. It is permitted to depose a President if there is anarchy in the land and among the people, and rights are no longer protected. It is permitted to depose a President if he commits high treason. And it is permitted to depose a President if he becomes a disbeliever (*kafara*). Thus, it is permitted to depose a President.

An example of this is what took place in the Kingdom of Saudi Arabia, when Muḥammad b. Ibrāhīm (d. 1389/1969), the Mufti of those lands at that time, deposed King Saud, because there was anarchy [in society]. [The King] had borrowed money from business people, and bankrupted the treasury; so he deposed him, and replaced him with his brother Faisal. Did Muḥammad b. Ibrāhīm orchestrate a coup? Did Muḥammad b. Ibrāhīm contravene the sacred law? Did Muḥammad b. Ibrāhīm, the Mufti of Saudi lands, upon whom they relied for [their religious] knowledge, contravene the religion?! Of course not. This did not occur. Therefore, it is permitted to depose a President.

[The Egyptian army always sides with the truth]

This is legitimate when it is in the interests of the populace and the people, the possessors of [the right to] command and prohibit; the possessors (*ṣāḥib*) of what they refer to in modern writings as rule (*al-siyāda*). They are the true possessors (*al-ṣāḥib al-aṣīl*) of such things. The true possessor is not a written constitution; nor is the true possessor a group of people; nor is the true possessor the president of a place. Of course not. The true possessor [of power] is the people (*sha'b*). Thus,

> if these people wish to live,
> then fate (*qadar*) must respond accordingly.[11]

This wise saying that the philosophers have said applies to the present situation, according to both secular and Islamic law. The stance of the armed forces has always, and throughout the centuries, been siding with the truth. Siding with the people (*sha'b*). Siding with the weak. Siding with those who have been aggressed against. Why did we participate in the war of 1948? Why did we go to Mexico in the days of Muḥammad Ali [Pasha]? Why did we go so far as to enter Vienna? Why did we do all that? Because we wanted to defend those who were weak; and defend the truth. The history of the Egyptian army is an untarnished one because it never acted in self-interest. It never went to the marketplace to beat people or steal their wealth. On the contrary, it builds rather than destroys. We have seen it pave roads and the infrastructure of the country. It is concerned with universal human development. It is concerned with increasing the wealth of the country. Thus, these armed forces, as the Messenger of God reported, are supported by God, and rely on God. Pay attention, and listen to the speech of the Messenger of God, peace and blessings of God be upon him, and do not listen to anyone else. Do not listen to rumors. Do not listen to deception and duplicity. The Messenger of God, peace and blessings of God be upon him, said 'it is enough of a lie for a man to relay everything he has heard.'[12] The Devil (Iblīs) brings one truth and mixes it with several lies, then he spreads it among the people. So people become confused and muddled because they hear a partial truth.

[The deadly lies of the Khawārij]

This is what [the second caliph,] ʿAlī, may God be pleased with him, used to say regarding the Khawārij. He would say: '[They utter] a word of truth, intending falsehood.' They would say, "There is no god but God,' means 'there is no ruler (*ḥākim*) but God." ʿAlī would say: 'This is true, there is no ruler but God, but do you want there to be no one ruling over the people?' This would cause a great deal of corruption.

There are those who incite (*yuḥarriḍ*), and this incitement (*taḥrīḍ*), in reality, is a fitna; and the Prophet, peace and blessings of God be upon him and his Family, says regarding fitna, 'The statement of the tongue in such cases is like the striking of the sword.'[13] Incitement against the Muslims, incitement against the Egyptian people, incitement against the security of society, incitement against the social peace: all of these things are like the strike of a sword. [The individual] is using his tongue, but God will judge him for it as though he used a weapon. He is figuratively killing people, but God will judge him for it as though he has killed a human being.

[The sanctity of blood]

Consider the Prophet, peace and blessings of God be upon him, when he says to the Kaaba, 'How great is your sanctity before God, but the blood of a Muslim has greater sanctity before God than you have.'[14] He also used to say, 'For the Kaaba to be destroyed, and taken apart stone by stone, is less grave to God than killing a believer.'[15] And he said: 'the human is the edifice of the Lord. Accursed are those who destroy the edifice of the Lord.'[16] Listen to the Messenger of God, and do not listen to impassioned emotional rhetoric that is deceptive. Rhetoric that incites against the Muslims. Rhetoric that uses words that they do not believe in to start with, like the word 'legitimacy' (*al-sharʿiyya*) and democracy (*al-dīmuqrāṭiyya*), and the like. And they do not even believe in them! Then you will realize who is deceiving and who is deceived. The Egyptian armed forces have always been against this incitement, which has come to the use of weapons, as we have seen in Sinai—people who have lost their minds.[17]

Abū Mūsā al-Ashʿarī states in a long hadith that, a neighbor will kill his neighbor, and will not even know what he killed him for; and a brother will kill his brother, and will not even know what he killed him for. The Messenger of God, peace and blessings of God be upon him, says in another hadith that the killer will not know why he killed, nor the one killed, why he was killed. So [the Companions] asked the Messenger of God, 'Will they be in possession of their mental faculties on that day?' He replied, 'On that day, God will take away their mental faculties.'[18] There is no sound thinking. There is no logical thinking. We hear talk, and find that it is all empty [of meaning]. Some of us may be given [an attractive] style of speech, and such a person is the most dangerous for the people, because he commands to the wrong, because he forbids the right, because he inverts the truth, because he changes the reality, but he does not wish to acknowledge [what he is doing]—an astounding state of affairs.

Incitement is forbidden by Islam because it is the essence of civil strife. The Prophet, peace and blessings of God be upon him, said about civil strife that: the one sitting in the midst of it is better than the one standing; and the one standing is better than one who is walking, and the one walking is better than one who is running.[19] Beware of participating in this civil strife because of some call, for indeed the Prophet, peace and blessings of God be upon him, the truthful one and the one who is to be believed, informed us in detail about this. On civil strife, [it is transmitted] from Nuʿaym b. Ḥammād through Yazīd b. Abī Ḥabīb that the Prophet, peace and blessings of God be upon him, said: 'There will be civil strife that encompasses everyone, except the western army.'[20] It will encompass everyone. Look around us, to our west, to our east, to our south, to our north—everywhere there is civil strife. Everywhere, blood is being spilt. But God, Most High, saves the western army, the Egyptian army, from this civil strife.

The religion is against everyone who incites and everyone who instigates or participates in the creating of civil strife. For as long as there is civil strife (fitna), there is Hellfire (*nār*). So be cautious against any of them taking you to the Hellfire. For that is what we have fled from, and it is for the sake of that fleeing that we live. Thus you must avoid civil strife just as you stay away from the Hellfire.

['Kill' those who sow dissent]

There are those who wish to split the ranks, and the Prophet (peace and blessings be upon him) says: 'If you are all unified around a single man'—*all* (*jamīʿan*) of you, not a single party (*jamāʿa*)—all unified around a single man. And this is what happened in the revolution (*thawra*) of 30 June—the [Egyptian] people came out (*kharaja*); and this is why the army stood with them. Thus we are *all* unified around a single man. 'And there comes someone who wishes to divide you, kill him whoever he may be.' Despite the sanctity and seriousness of [shedding] blood, the Prophet permits us to kill this rebel (*khārijī*). The rebel who wishes to create civil strife (fitna) in the land: splitting the ranks, trying to shake [the convictions of] those who are listening [to their superiors]. No! Yield to your [commanding] brethren. [The Prophet] taught us to follow in prayers so that we may learn the first lesson in military training: [recognizing] the leader; [rendering] obedience; unified movement; the unified ranks seeing which pleases God, Most High. For God (Most High) is pleased when even in fighting we fight in unified ranks.

[Islamic legal justification for killing aggressors]

There is, in Islamic law, what is referred to as repelling the aggressor (*dafʿ al-ṣāʾil*); and *ṣāʾil* refers to someone who is attacking you. [In such a case,] one must respond by gradually escalating the degree to which one threatens/frightens [the aggressor]. If he has nothing in his hands, then push him with your hands, push him with a stick. If he has a knife he wishes to stab you with, then you should strike his hand with a stick from a distance. If he is strong and trained, then shoot him—there is no other option. Repelling the aggressor in Islamic law has its rulings and evidence in the Sunna. This is why, when a qadi judges a case, he considers: Who is this? 'This is a burglar who is committing an act of aggression in my house.' Where was he killed? 'He was killed in my house.' Or in his house? Or on the road? Or in the mosque? 'No, he was in my house.' Then this falls under repelling the aggressor. [...] this burglar, this aggressor; what is his punishment with God? The Hellfire—a terrible end—because he attempted to kill me; and I defended myself, I repelled him.

The army and police are revered, and trained to stop aggression, and remove oppression; trained to be noble in character. The noble knight cannot be aggressed against and their reverence cannot be diminished. [Our] religion commands us not to approach such actions; that we do not aggress against him. Firstly because they protect us; secondly, because they are supported by God; and thirdly, because they have power with which they defend us. This is why we must not aggress against them (*naʿtadī ʿalayhim*).

If someone comes in jest brandishing a knife before his brother, and the knife ends up in [the aggressor], there is no compensation due to him. Rather this [person] has died in vain, and this is a type of suicide. God, Most High, says: 'Do not cast yourselves towards annihilation' (Q. 2:195). What happens when I go and play with a gun, and birdshot from it hits my face, and I claim that the other person killed me? Who killed who? The killer is the one who was playing around, and the Messenger of God has prohibited us from jesting in this manner. The killer is the one who aggressed. The killer is he who came to where I was, when I did not go to him.

There is a major difference between permitted peaceful protests: those who express themselves however they wish, by way of giving advice, by way of freedom of expression, by way of commanding to right and forbidding wrong in accord with one's opinion. [This contrasts with] one who goes to army barracks, and these barracks are secure, and know only that they are always in a state of preparedness against those who aggress against them.[21] They cannot but receive these aggressors as conquerors would.

These [aggressive actions] that terrify the mother bereaved of her child; cause the pregnant to miscarry, cause hair to go white (with fear); are rejected by religion; are rejected by the world, all the laws of the world; and are rejected by the Islamic Sharia, as it rejects all folly.

Where are you standing? Why have you done this? Why are you aggressing against a strong army? [Such a person] is under the delusion that he will succeed against this army. How misguided! For indeed whoever conspires against them will be humiliated and destroyed by God, who will give [the army] victory over them. This is what the Prophet (peace and blessings be upon him) said. We believe the Prophet, and we do not believe much of what people say. These things that [people] say indicate their own weakness. There are also [...] those among the police forces and the army who ask: what should we do with respect to those who aggress against us. I respond: repel the aggressor, as is noted in the book.

[Rules of engagement: when to kill]

What is the book? The police forces and the army have guides (*adilla*) that they have been trained in accordance with. These guides direct them in their actions. These guides are universal—we have ensured in them the protection of human rights, the Sharia, the law, and justice. The police deal with the troublemakers (*mushāghibīn*) among the protestors—the troublemakers who wish to destroy private or public property, who wish to destroy people's reputations (*aʿrāḍ*), who wish to assault people, who close the roads and paths with claims of prayer. This is a disaster! This is no longer peaceful. [It would be peaceful] on the condition that it does not harm anyone. No one should cause harm. Do not harm yourself, and do not put others in harm's way.

[The security forces] have a system, and that is to repel the aggressor through gradual escalation. There are eleven stages that they go through. Among them is [using] water. We spray them with water when they assemble in a manner that is illegal, in a manner that is no longer peaceful. But in the end, it comes to killing. When [the protestors] begin to use weapons and Molotov cocktails, when the fighter is causing mischief and is going to kill me, I am no longer defending myself and defending the religion. I am defending life and safety. I am defending life, and [the aggressor] wishes to obliterate life. We have seen and heard the soldiers, while they are fasting, being aggressed against by these vile enemies, and they massacre and kill them while they are fasting. Those who survived among them say, as they killed us they were calling us disbelievers (*kafara*).

['Blessed are those who kill them']

They are Khawārij, and the Khawārij are the dogs of the Hellfire. They are Khawārij, blessed are those who kill them! We ask God, Most High, to grant success to the Egyptian army in completely obliterating those who spread lies to create agitation in the land. These are the people who spread false rumors (*ahl al-irjāf*), which we refer to today in modern language as terrorism (*irhāb*). As for the one who spreads lies (*murjif*), his punishment is death. God has permitted us to kill him so that we may end his evil. He is like the wretched boy who [...] is never silent. We have no choice with respect to this person who spreads lies but to strike his hands and kill him. He is the one who asked for this, not us. He is the one who wishes to commit suicide. This is why you see them commit suicide, and put explosives on themselves and blow up people.

The Prophet (peace and blessings be upon him) says: whoever rebels against my community (umma) not making a distinction between its pious and impious, I will be their adversary on the Day of Judgment. So the Prophet will oppose these people on the Day of Judgment. [This is the case] even if they appear claiming to be representing the religion of Islam—and it has not penetrated the depths of their hearts—this [is] corruption—'and God does not love corruption' (Q. 2:205).

'Among people is he whose speech in this world impresses you; and God bears witness to what is in his heart'—he deludes himself to this degree of ignorance and stupidity—'and God bears witness to what is in his heart, that he is the most obstinate antagonist' (Q. 2:204). What are his signs? 'When he goes away, he strives throughout the land to cause corruption and destroy crops and animals; and God does not love corruption' (Q. 2:205). Look to this situation [...], and its sign is that he destroys crops and animals. This is why [he earns] God's wrath, to the point that God permits us to extirpate him and thereby earn great rewards with God, Most High. We have stated that despite the sanctity and seriousness of [shedding] blood before God, this person is to be killed in order that he may not kill others at random. This person is to be killed because God has commanded it; because our Messenger warned us against him; and because he causes corruption in the land.

[A Qur'anic license to kill]

God says: 'If the hypocrites, those in whose hearts is disease, and those who spread lies in Madina do not desist, we will incite you against them. Then they will not remain your neighbors except for a short time. They are accursed; wherever they are found, they are to be seized and completely massacred' (Q. 33:60). The explicit text of the Qur'an with respect to those who spread lies states that God has permitted for his Prophet to kill them. The Prophet was patient, and did not kill the hypocrites, saying 'let them not say, 'Muḥammad kills his Companions." But God, Most High, knows what will happen in His umma, so He reveals these two verses in Sūrat al-Aḥzāb and grants us this dispensation for the sake of preventing civil strife (fitna); preventing [the shedding of] blood; and preventing the corruption which God, Most High, hates.

What is taking place in the Sinai Peninsula is a disgrace. We do not want it to reach us [in Cairo], we will do away with this disgrace. It is a disgrace that we must be patient with. The sanctity of Egyptian blood is great indeed, and this is why we will oppose with full force those who deem licit [the shedding of] this blood. With full force against those who do not love this homeland (*waṭan*). We will oppose with full force those who wish to show contempt to this country, and the people (*sha'b*) of this homeland. This is our homeland. We are in [...] our country, and for us it is the most beloved of the countries of God's [creation].

[The great sin of desertion]

Mecca, the birthplace of the Messenger of God, peace and blessings be upon him, was the most beloved land to him, peace and blessings be upon him. The sanctity of Egyptian blood does not need any more explanation, but it is necessary for us to understand, and for God to enlighten us in order for us to understand and realize the truth: who is in the right, and who is the one that speaks incessantly and tries to go against the will of God, Most High. There are those who try to lose hope, saying 'I am a soldier and I wish to leave,' or 'I do not wish to take part in the army.' This person has the status of a deserter (*wallā al-adbār*). He who deserts commits a grave enormity, God knows best if he will be forgiven for it or not. [It is] one of the enormities! [...] One of the deadly sins (*mūbiqāt*)! Beware of this, O soldier. [...]

Beware of learning anywhere but the school of the Egyptian army. Beware of heeding the excessive speech of this or that person. For the Prophet (peace and blessings be upon him) said: 'God has disliked for you [to engage in] rumors, and asking too many questions [...].' The people of God used to say four things will help you reach God: speaking little, eating little, sleeping little, and spending little time with people. All of these things occur in Ramadan. Eating little occurs in fasting. Sleeping little occurs in [night] prayer. Talking little occurs through silence—and the Prophet, peace and blessings be upon him said, 'If you see a man given to silence, he is granted wisdom.'[22]

[Prayer and conclusion]

Our Lord says, 'He grants wisdom to whomever He wills; and whomever is granted wisdom, has been granted much good' (Q. 2:269). [Finally], spending little time with people occurs in devotional seclusion (*iʿtikāf*). All of them occur in Ramadan. [They are] the path to God. Beware, O soldier, of following your whims, and beware of following others, and beware of committing one of the enormities that only God knows if you will be forgiven for it or not—that is, deserting on the day of battle (*tawallī yawm al-zaḥf*).

We ask God, Most High, to enlighten our hearts, to enlighten our insights, to forgive our sins, to conceal our faults, [...] to establish our authority in the earth, to aid us in the establishment of prayer and giving of zakat, and commanding right and forbidding wrong, to make faith beloved to us, and illuminate our hearts, to make disbelief, sin, and transgression hateful to us. O God, make us rightly guided, God-fearing, and with the people of truth, O most merciful One. Raise us under the standard of Your Prophet on the Day of Judgment; let us drink from his sacred hand a sip after which we shall never feel thirst. And enter us into Paradise without any reckoning, punishment or castigation. Amen.

May God send blessings and peace upon our master Muhammad, upon his Family, and his Companions.

APPENDIX 3

TRANSLATION OF ALI GOMAA'S POST-RABAA LECTURE TO THE EGYPTIAN SECURITY FORCES[1]

[On screen writing:]

The Ministry of Defense
The Department of Moral Affairs presents:
The lecture of Dr Ali Gomaa in the meeting of the Commander-in-Chief [al-Sīsī] with the army and police in the Central Military Region on 18 August 2013

[Speaker at podium inviting Gomaa:]

On [the topic of] Islam's Tolerance, we will be addressed by the esteemed professor Dr Ali Gomaa, the former grand mufti of Egypt.

[Audience applause. Gomaa's speech begins:]

In the name of God the Compassionate, the Merciful.

All praise is due to God, and peace and blessings be upon our master, the Messenger of God, upon his Family, his Companions, and those who support him. I greet you with the greeting of Islam, and the greeting of Islam is peace (*al-salām*), so peace be upon you, and the mercy of God, and His Blessings, His Salutations, His Contentment, in perpetuity.

[Your] Excellency, the General, Abdel Fattah al-Sisi; the Esteemed Minister, Muhammad Ibrahim; respected attendants. May God be pleased with you, and may He please you. May He move you from the circle of His wrath to the circle of His contentment. May He support you. May He put your hearts at peace. May He make you firm in your stance. May He guide your gunfire. And may He prepare [your affairs] for you in this world and the next. [I ask you to] thank God, Most High, that He has placed you where He has placed you; and pray that he grants you success in doing what He loves and finds pleasing. Indeed, he has given you a gift in tribulation. Stand firm; be patient collectively and individually, for God, Most High, is your Supporter. 'The [enemy] shall be vanquished, and they shall turn their backs [in retreat].'[2] And all praise is due to God, the Lord of the worlds.

[The Egyptian situation]

In these days, Egypt is going through what the Messenger of God, peace and blessings of God be upon him and his family, has informed us of. The more we read his words, the more we are amazed by him, for he is supported by his Lord. He was not one who knows the unseen, but God, Most High, informed him, and taught him. The more we read what he said and what he warned, the more we increase in faith, amazement, and love for him, peace and blessings of God be upon him and his family.

This is with respect to the exoteric meaning of the Sharia, and praise be to God, we have exoteric proofs that need no interpretation, from the Qur'an, from the Sunna, from the reports of the Messenger of God, peace and blessing of God be upon him, and from his actions, his behavior, and his stances. Know that you are in the right (*ḥaqq*). Let no one detract from the clarity of your vision. Let no one detract from your path, for you are traveling on the path of God. God is the destination of all of you.

O heroic knights! This is with respect to the exoteric meaning of the Sharia. As for the glad tidings (*bushrā*), when the Prophet, peace and blessings of God be upon him, informed the Companions that God, Most High, had sealed through him prophecy, rendering him the Messenger of God and the Seal of the Prophets; this was difficult for them to bear. They asked, 'How will we know the news of the Heavens after you have passed, O Messenger of God? And how will we distinguish between what angers God and what pleases Him?' He said, 'there will remain glad tidings—a righteous dream (*al-ru'yā al-ṣāliḥa*) which a righteous servant [of God] sees, or is shown.'

[In praise of the Egyptian army]

Countless dreams have been reported in support of you from the Messenger of God, from the Friends (*awliyā'*) of God, and from members of the Prophet's Household (*Ahl al-Bayt*) who fled to Egypt to seek refuge therein. This is because the Prophet, peace and blessings of God be upon him, used to say [according to a weak narration]:[3] 'The safest people from civil strife (fitna) are the western soldiers (*al-jund al-gharbī*),' and 'the western soldiers' refers to the people of Egypt and the soldiers of Egypt, including the police and the army.

'Amr b. al-Ḥamiq[4] al-Khuzā'ī came to Egypt. Tubay' b. 'Āmir al-Kalā'ī came to Egypt.[5] Because they knew that the Prophet, peace and blessings of God be upon him, commended the western soldiers. Yes, you are the western soldiers, because we are west of the Illuminated City (Madina). The Prophet, peace and blessings of God be upon him, spoke of the fitna that would come from the east. We do not have time now to go into it or its details, even if it is related to what we are going through now—clearly related. However, he commended the western soldiers.

For this reason 'Amr, may God be pleased with him, and may He please him ... who is this 'Amr? This 'Amr once came in a ship; and the Prophet, peace and blessings of God be upon him, said, 'people of the ship will come out to you—its commander is of the people of Paradise;' and 'Amr b. al-Ḥamiq al-Khuzā'ī came out. He is someone the Messenger of God, peace and blessings of God be upon him, gave glad tidings of Paradise to. He used to say, the Messenger of God, peace and blessings of God be upon him, said [according to a weak narration] 'the western soldiers are the safest people,' or 'the best people in civil strife (fitna).' Thus there is fitna, but there is also superiority [of certain people in the fitna].

[Today's Khawārij]

There is what we have seen on Wednesday [the day of the Rabaa massacre], Thursday, Friday, Saturday, and Sunday [the day of this speech]. And these despicable people are saying, 'We will show you,' just as the Khawārij used to. The Prophet, peace and blessings of God be upon him, said regarding the Khawārij: 'you will despise your prayers when you compare it with theirs, and your fasting when you compare it with theirs.' They will quote the speech of the Best of Creation (i.e. the Prophet), but their faith does not go beyond their collar bones [to their hearts]. 'Blessed are those who kill them and are killed by them! Those who kill them are more worthy of God than they are.'

He, peace and blessings of God be upon him, states that 'the Khawārij are the dogs of the Hellfire.' Why? Because they raise the banner of religion, and thereby deceive the world. People say, these people are right because they quote scripture (lit. they say 'God says...' and 'His Messenger says...'); but in fact they are misguided. And the Prophet, peace and blessings of God be upon him, speaks of generalized fitna—which seems to be a reference to the colonial period. Then of the fitna of expansion (*basṭ*)—which seems to be a reference to ease that occurs after it. Then of the fitna of calamity (*dahmā'*)—which it seems we have not yet entered, but we are on its edges. Then of the fitna of the Antichrist (*Dajjāl*). [Gomaa correcting himself:] Before the fitna of the Antichrist is the fitna of persistence (*aḥlās*). After it comes the fitna of calamity (*dahmā'*) that encompasses the lands, and after it the fitna of the Antichrist (*Dajjāl*).[6] What is the Antichrist? He will have 'Paradise' with him. Look at this deception! It is [in fact] Hellfire. And he will have 'Hellfire' with him, while it is Paradise.

In the hadith of Abū Mūsā al-Ashʿarī, may God be pleased with him, and may He please him, [we learn] that the Prophet, peace and blessings of God be upon him, spoke of those among whom there is much *harj*. They asked: 'What is *harj*, O Messenger of God?' He replied: '*harj* is lying and killing.' This is what we witness, with our own eyes, they lie and they kill. They know nothing else but that. This is nothing new with [these people]. I heard this with my own ears, more than forty years ago, over and over again. They say, we will attain power, and as soon as we attain power, we will put an end to democracy. Over and over again, and in many places around the world. What is this? They said this is a tactic. [Rather,] this is a lie! [They] are deceiving people, and the Prophet was not one who deceived people.

This is why our Lord says, 'And among the people is he whose speech pleases you in worldly life, and he declares God as his witness as to what is in his heart, yet he is the fiercest of opponents. (Q. 2:204)' [God then] gives us a clear sign: 'And when he goes away, he strives throughout the land to cause corruption therein and destroy crops and animals. And God does not like corruption. And when it is said to him, 'Fear God', pride in sin takes hold of him. Sufficient for him is the Hellfire, an evil resting place. And among the people is he who sells his soul for the pleasure of God. And Allah is kind to [His] servants' (Q. 2:205f).

[Killing versus fighting]

It is clear. The sign is causing corruption in the land, and killing. Who is the one who has deemed killing licit? There is a major difference between killing (*qatl*) and fighting (*qitāl*). Fighting is the activity of knights! As for killing, it is the activity of trash (*awbāsh*). There is a difference between killing and fighting. You are the knights of the country and the people. You are the fighters. They are the killers. Fighting (*qitāl*) is four letters [in Arabic]. Killing (*qatl*) is three letters. The highest rank is yours with God, with the people, and with history. Stand firm!

In some of our hearts may be repeated: 'What is all this blood?' We are not the reason for it. Indeed repelling [more deaths] through [pre-emptive] killing renders [this pre-emptive] act of killing more pure. Killing more effectively prevents [further] killing. I will kill 100 in order not to kill 1,000. The Prophet, in the hadith of Abū Mūsā, states that there will be much *harj*. They asked: 'What is *harj*?' He replied: 'lying and killing.' They asked, 'O Messenger of God, more than we kill now?!' The number killed in all the battles of the Muslims, of Muslims and non-Muslims, is 1,006. [This] in twenty-three years—ten years in Madina—1,006. That is, less than [the casualties of] car accidents in Paris in a year.

They said, 'more than what we do now?' He said, 'you kill polytheists'—1,006 of which 700 are polytheists, and 300 are Muslims. They said, 'O Messenger of God, more than we kill now?!' He replied, 'You fight and kill polytheists, but in that time, a man will kill his brother, and he will kill his uncle, and he will kill his neighbor. Neither the killer will know why he is killing, nor the killed why he was killed.' Who is the cause of this fitna? The dogs of the Hellfire. Those of whom our master 'Abdullāh b. 'Umar said: 'They will take verses that God revealed regarding the polytheists, and use them against the Muslims.'

[Killing today's Khawārij]

These people are the Khawārij. They were 6,000 in the days of 'Alī b. Abī Ṭālib. The Prophet said, 'The truth is with 'Alī wherever he may be;' and he said to 'Ammār b. Yāsir, 'You will be killed by the rebellious party;' and he was [subsequently] killed by the Khawārij. These Khawārij were 6,000, so 'Alī b. Abī Ṭālib sent to them Ibn 'Abbās, who debated with them, and brought 2,000 of them back [into the Islamic mainstream], while there remained 4,000 in their misguided state, false beliefs, and their corrupting the land. The Prophet, peace and blessings of God be upon him, when [his Companions] asked him in the same hadith, 'will they have their senses that day?!' He replied: 'On that day, God will strip them of their senses. One of them will think that he is [rightly guided], and they will be completely lost.' The Messenger of God supports you, in the exoteric (*ẓāhir*) and the esoteric realms (*bāṭin*). The Messenger of God, peace and blessings of God be upon him, called our attention to silver-tongued people.

[Excommunicating Qaradawi]

This person [Yusuf al-Qaradawi] who came out yesterday claiming that the army of the Jews is better than the Egyptian Army;[7] he is a disbeliever (*kāfir*)! He is a disbeliever in God's bounty. In fact he is a disbeliever in God's intent. In fact, I do not wish to say we should not pay attention to him, rather we wish to purify our city and our Egypt of this trash. They do not deserve our Egyptian identity. We are disgraced by our association with them. And just as we defend our land, our people, our creed, our religion, our history, and our civilization, we must wash our hands of these people, just as the wolf was free of the blood of the son of Jacob (Ya'qūb). The wolf did not eat Joseph (Yūsuf). This is why we do not recognize these people, nor do we listen to them, for God has blinded their hearts.

On one occasion [on 15 August 2009], Hamas attacked a mosque that had been occupied by an [armed al-Qaeda] group called Ahl al-Nuṣra [Jund Anṣār Allāh] of the Khawārij.[8] [Here,] Khawārij are striking Khawārij. [Qaradawi] gave a fatwā then, saying they were in the right. But when the aggressors attacked the mosque of God, Most High, in Rābi'a al-'Adawiyya (Rabaa Square), and yesterday in [the mosque of] Fatḥ, he gave a fatwā saying that [the security forces] had set fire to the mosque—lying outrageously. We say to him: 'O compulsive liar (*kadhdhāb*)! Know your place! For indeed God, Most High, has disgraced you in front of the worlds.' However, many deluded people are influenced by him. This influence will surely pass, for indeed the truth is more rightfully followed. For the truth is clear. Therefore do not pay any attention to these lies (*turrahāt*), or any of this [dog's] barking (*nubāḥ*).[9]

Be with God. Remember God abundantly (Q. 33:41). Remember Me and I will remember you; be thankful to Me and do not reject Me (Q. 2:152). God, Most High, illuminates your hearts, forgives your sins, and gives you a stupendous reward. O God, our Lord, make this group such that the world is in their hands, and is not in their hearts.[10] Do not become happy at what you have; nor be sad at what you have lost. Rely on God! None of us dies, except at their appointed time. We pray for mercy upon the martyrs, but our souls are in the palms of our hands for the sake of God, first and foremost; then, for these poor people, this impoverished hardworking people; then for the sake of this country whose sky has given us shade, whose earth has borne us, and which has given us more than we have given it, even if we give our very souls for it. The martyr lives a glorious life, and dies a commendable death. Yes, the time of death (*ajal*) neither comes before nor after its appointed time; and the time at which you would be martyred is the same time that you would have died in your bed. However, [in battle] you die without there being anything between you and Paradise except death; and you become an intercessor [with God] on behalf of seventy people from your household. You would reach Paradise before other people. O God, make us of the martyred ones, O Most Merciful One.

[Security before faith]

It is an established precept according to us, the scholars of the Muslims—[a precept] which the Khawārij are ignorant of—that security (*amn*) comes before faith (*īmān*). This statement is one that we stated, spread through the land, and highlighted when the fitna occurred in Algeria. And the Khawārij were completely astonished at it: 'Is there something that comes before faith!?' We say to them: yes—all the evidence from the Book and the Sunna, indicate that security comes before faith. Because if security is lacking, then there is no [possibility of] faith. Faith is lost with the loss of security.

[The Companion] Khabbāb b. al-Aratt, may God be pleased with him, came to the Prophet, peace and blessings of God be upon him, and said: 'O Prophet, let us massacre [the people in] the valley.' Let us go down and we'll drench it in blood. At the time, there were two hundred people in Mecca engaged in revolt [...]. two hundred people in Mecca ... or 2,000.[11] [The Prophet's] facial expression then changed to one of anger—it turned red with anger—and he said:

> I am indeed the Messenger of God, and God will grant me victory, to the point that a female traveler will go from Mecca to Hira (an ancient city in Iraq), fearing nothing but God, and the wolves that may attack her sheep. Indeed those who were before you would bring a man [believing in God], and place a saw on the

middle of his head and saw him [in two]; and this would not stop him from believing in God.

The Prophet was angered that this kind of misunderstanding could arise, and he commanded that security comes before faith. Because this misunderstanding would lead to killing, not fighting. Thus when he went to Madina, and money started to come in, and the state was formed, he did not proceed to aggress against anyone. Rather they came to him at Badr, then at Uḥud, then at Khandaq, then at Muraysīʿ, and so on. They are the ones who came [aggressing against the Prophet], and he was always in a posture of defense, until he established the principle of pre-emptive war to prevent bloodshed. Yes, we know that blood is sacred. But what are we to do when these putrid things [i.e. protestors] have assembled around us. Putrid! Putrid people. Their odor is disgusting—outwardly and inwardly (*fī al-ẓāhir wa-l-bāṭin*). The Prophet, peace and blessings of God be upon him, warned us against this.

[Morsi has no legitimacy]

They claim legitimacy (*sharʿiyya*) [for Morsi's rule]. What legitimacy? Do they not speak bombastically about Islam? The jurists of Islam talk about the 'legally restricted head of state' (*al-imām al-maḥjūr*). There is a head of state (*imām*) to whom we have pledged our allegiance. But the land and its people fall into disarray. So his fellows—this is how they write in Islamic law (fiqh)—arrest him, and place him in a legally restricted state. They say to him sit here, and they lock him away. [In such a case,] the legitimacy of his rule is gone. He no longer has legitimacy. Because the head of state (*imām*) is someone who speaks and acts, and he can no longer act, so that is it, the legitimacy of his rule is finished.

What legitimacy of rule is this, through which they make a mockery of themselves and of the people. The legally restricted head of state, in Islamic Law, has no legitimacy of rule. So on what basis do they struggle and defend. It is merely corruption. The legally restricted head of state—memorize this phrase—this head of state is legally restricted, meaning he has been arrested. The calamity is that his matter was taken to the courts [who ruled against him], and so his legitimacy of rule was voided if there was any specious remnant of legitimacy to his rule—and he never even had a specious remnant of legitimacy to his rule. [...]. The matter is decided.

['Shoot to kill']

What legitimacy of rule is this? You [i.e. Morsi's supporters] go out to kill the people,[12] and to spill blood, when the Prophet [once] looked at the Kaaba and said: 'How great is your sanctity before God, but the blood of a Muslim—in another narration, believer—is more sacred to God than you. [Elsewhere,] he said, even if the [Kaaba] were to be destroyed stone by stone, it would be less grave with God than the killing of a believer.[13] And he said: 'the believer—the human is the edifice of the Lord. Accursed is he who destroys the edifice of the Lord.'[14] So what should we do? We fight (*nuqātil*), we are not killing (*naqtul*). [The protestor] is the one who exposes himself to that. Therefore, if a single shot is fired from these rebels (*bughāh*), Khawārij—whether it is from them, or from those who have joined them, but are not of them; or from their direction—if a single bullet is fired, then shoot to kill (*iḍrab fi-l-malyān*).[15] Beware of sacrificing your members and soldiers because of these Khawārij.

What caused them to come out? What has made them cause this misfortune? The jurists have stated explicitly that we should strike them. Except that—and we follow this, God be praised—we do not chase their injured. We shoot one of them in their legs. He falls. That's all. We take him to the hospital, and then we arrest him. [...] We do not chase them to slaughter them. Look at this chivalry. And you know the laws pertaining to prisoners of war. Even with prisoners, we treat them in this [chivalrous] way.[16] But this is our situation. Do not be afraid of these claims of religion. For the religion is on your side; God is on your side; His Messenger is on your side; the believers are on your side; thereafter the people are your supporters; and the angels are supporting you from the Heavens. Stand firm! Let no one among you ever hesitate to do this for the sake of God. Stand before God on the Day of Resurrection and say, 'O my Lord, I prevented the evil of evil people and the corruption of the corrupt from reaching people.'

[Hadiths about the western army]

Our master, Abū Mūsā al-Ashʿarī (d. c. 44/664), in a hadith, called you the weak army (*al-jund al-ḍaʿīf*). In the hadith of Tubayʿ b. ʿĀmir, [Abū Mūsā] asked [Tubayʿ], 'Where are you from?' He replied, 'From the people of Egypt.' [Abū Mūsā] asked: 'From the western army?' He replied, 'Yes.' He asked: 'From the weak army?' So [Tubayʿ] expressed surprise and said, 'Are they weak?' This is the best army in the world; how can it be weak? The scholars say that it is because they believe that strength and power is God's and comes from God. That is, they rely on God. They do not see in their power—however great—or in their prestige—however established—other than the fact that God is the One who acts in this world. Even if they are limited in number and military preparedness, God will give them victory. Abū Mūsā [added]: 'No one conspires against them, except that God will seize them.'[17] This is the meaning of their weakness. That is, I do not rely on my strength or my power. I only rely on God. Let your hearts be attached to God.

[The siege of the mosque of Fatḥ]

'And who are more oppressive than those who prevent the name of Allah from being mentioned in His mosques and strive towards their destruction. It is not for them to enter them except in a state of fear. For them in this world is disgrace, and they will have in the Hereafter a great punishment' (Q. 2:114). It was as though I was reading this verse for the first time when I saw the images of the mosque of Fatḥ yesterday. The garbage (*zibāla*), filth (*najāsa*), and terror in which they were. It was as though God had revealed [the verse talking] about them. It is as though, by making a display of their religion, they [really] want something else which God and His Messenger scorn. They remind me of the verse of [Sura] al-Tawba, where God, Most High, says, while speaking of the Mosque of Harm (*masjid al-ḍirār*); regarding those who built a mosque 'for causing harm and disbelief and division among the believers and as a station for whoever had warred against Allah and His Messenger before (Q. 9:107).' All of this in a mosque! However, 'the building which they built will never cease to be a misgiving in their hearts until their hearts are cut to pieces (Q. 9:110).'[18]

[Khārijī blindness]

Determination and obstinacy! A *mosque* that the Messenger of God set fire to. Why? Because he does not desire this deception, nor this scheming, nor this outward sin, and inward corruption. For this reason, he called the Khawārij the dogs of the Hellfire, despite their praying, fasting, reciting the Qur'an, and so on. Even, [despite] their apparent Godliness. A Khārijī was on his way to kill 'Alī, and he was eating a date. His brother said to him, 'Do you know where this is from?' He replied, 'No.' So he induced himself to vomit. He is so God-fearing that he is unwilling to swallow a date whose origin he does not know, even though it is not something he has picked up from the ground, which is legally permissible to eat in any case. He is on his way to kill the Prophet's cousin!

One of them [once] swatted a mosquito on his hand, and its blood came out—the blood of the mosquito. So he asked: 'Is this impure? Have my ablutions (*wuḍū'*) been nullified? Should I make ablutions again?' And they consider licit the blood of our master 'Alī, regarding whom the Messenger of God said: 'I am the city of knowledge, and 'Alī is its gate. The truth is with 'Alī wherever he may be. Your station is like that of Aaron with respect to Moses.' And he closed all the doors leaving the mosque except the door of 'Alī, because it is the door of his daughter, Fāṭima, and he is the father of the entire Ahl al-Bayt: Ḥasan and Ḥusayn. Imagine him asking about a mosquito while he is on his way to kill [...]. This is the very thinking that we have here! Don't be surprised. How can this be, when they [who oppose the coup] claim to be following the religion; when we have good relations with them; and they desire to [please] God and His Messenger? They are lying. Had God given them [spiritual] success, he would have illuminated their sight [with the truth]. But when God blinded them in this way, we came to realize that they have been forsaken by God.

[Conclusion and prayer]

Thank you. This is Islam's tolerance. This is the power of Islam. This is the sweetness of Islam. Thank you for this meeting. Thank you for undertaking the defense of the realm. Thank you for the fact that God has made you stand firm, making you the heroes of this world, and knights of the Hereafter. Thank you for this meeting which is encompassed by the angels. Trust in God, and place Him before you, 'regardless of [our limited righteous] actions.' We are all different. Some of us are strong, and some of us are weak. 'Regardless of actions.' Faith is in God. Thereafter, God is forgiving and merciful. 'Regardless of actions.' Stand firm; and convey these sentiments to your families, your neighbors, your people, and your soldiers. Convey them, spread them. We are on the truth. 'The group shall be vanquished, and they shall turn their backs [in retreat].'[19]

I am sorry for taking long. We pray to God saying: O God, place the world in our hands, but not in our hearts. Illuminate our hearts, forgive our sins, conceal our faults, ease our concealed [difficulties], bring our hearts together, unify us, direct our gunfire, make firm our stance and put our hearts at rest [regarding it], and gather us under the banner of our Prophet on the Day of Resurrection. Give us to drink, from his noble hand, a sip after which we shall never thirst again. Then enter us into Paradise without reckoning, nor with prior punishment or reprimand. Be with us, and be not against us. Show mercy to our living, our dead, our present, and our absent. Make this gathering one that is shown mercy, and make our parting ways a protected parting. Do not leave among us anyone who is distressed or in deprivation.

O Most Merciful of the merciful ones, show mercy. O the succor of those who seek assistance, grant us succor. O God, O our Lord, we call upon You to witness that: we love You, we love Your Messenger, we love those who love You. Therefore, O God, protect us from the evil of all evil people; keep evil away from us in whatever way You wish. O Most Merciful of the merciful ones, show us mercy. O God, O Lord of the worlds, help us towards Your remembrance, Your thanks, and Your goodly worship. Make the Noble Qur'an the life of our hearts, the easing of our distress and sorrow, the light of our eyes and our hearts, and make it a proof for us, not against us. Teach us what is beneficial from it, and benefit us from what You have taught us. O God, we ask you through Your most beautiful Names, and your most sublime Attributes, to give us victory over those who show us enmity. O God, O Lord of the worlds, destroy them. O God, destroy them. O God, destroy them. O God, destroy them. O God, destroy them. O God, destroy them. O God, destroy them. And may the peace and blessings of God be upon our master, Muhammad, upon his Family, his Companions. Peace be upon you, and the mercy of God, and His Blessings.

[Applause]

ABBREVIATIONS

CPI — Corruption Perceptions Index is a global ranking of countries according to 'perceived levels of public sector corruption, as determined by expert assessments and opinion surveys' published annually by Transparency International since 1995.

CSS — Council of Senior Scholars of the Azhar, the most senior scholarly body of the Egyptian Azhar, reconstituted in 2012.

DMA — Department of Moral Affairs—the propaganda arm of the Egyptian armed forces.

FPPMS — Forum for Promoting Peace in Muslim Societies—an institution established by Abdallah bin Bayyah under the patronage of the UAE as a counter-revolutionary counterweight to the IUMS.

GCC — The Gulf Cooperation Council—a union of Arab petroleum-producing states composed of the following six member states: Bahrain, Kuwait, Oman, Qatar, Saudi Arabia, and the UAE.

HRW — Human Rights Watch—a New York-based international organization defending human rights.

ISIS — Islamic State of Iraq and Syria—a terrorist organization that gained global recognition in 2014 not long after the Egyptian coup.

IUMS — The International Union of Muslim Scholars—a transnational institution established in 2004 that seeks to represent the views of ulama from around the world and to defend Islamic causes. It strongly supported the Arab revolutions under the leadership of Yusuf al-Qaradawi who retired in 2018. Its current president is Aḥmad al-Raysūnī.

MB	The Muslim Brotherhood—the world's oldest and most important Islamist organization.
NDP	The National Democratic Party—the ruling political party of Egypt until 2011. It was headed by Hosni Mubarak and counted Aḥmad al-Ṭayyib as a loyal member until he was obliged to resign in order to become the shaykh al-Azhar.
RIS	Reviving the Islamic Spirit, an annual convention usually held in Toronto Canada that brings thousands of Muslims together to attend lectures by globally recognized Islamic scholars and public figures.
SCAF	The Supreme Council of the Armed Forces—the committee of generals who oversee the Egyptian armed forces, headed by the Egyptian defense minister who theoretically answers to the Egyptian president.
UAE	The United Arab Emirates.

TIMELINE

This timeline only covers the key events discussed in this book, and so may appear somewhat disjointed.

2010

17 December: Tunisian street vendor, Mohamed Bouazizi, sets himself on fire leading to his death on 4 January 2011, sparking the Tunisian revolution and the subsequent Arab Spring.

2011

14 January: Tunisian dictator Zine al-Abidine Ben Ali was ousted after protests, sparked by Bouazizi's self-immolation.
16 January: Yusuf al-Qaradawi, president of the IUMS, celebrates the success of the Tunisian revolution on his weekly Al Jazeera show *al-Sharīʿa wa-l-Ḥayāh*.
23 January: Qaradawi excoriạtes regional autocracies on his weekly Al Jazeera show.
24 January: Qaradawi gives a lecture at the Azhar in Cairo, as a guest of the Shaykh al-Azhar Aḥmad al-Ṭayyib.
25 January: Anti-Mubarak protesters begin demonstrations in Egypt.
27 January: Still in Cairo, Qaradawi gives an interview to the *Shurūq* newspaper in support of the revolutions. He would continue to make statements supportive of the revolutions in the weeks and months that follow.
2 February: Government thugs attack protestors on camel and horseback in what would come to be known as the 'Battle of the Camel.'
7 February: American scholar Hamza Yusuf writes enthusiastically in support of the Egyptian revolution while arguing against the need for democracy in Egypt.
11 February: Mubarak announces his resignation, leaving the generals of the army in power.
13 February: Qaradawi celebrates the success of the Egyptian revolution on his weekly Al Jazeera show.

18 February: Qaradawi returns to Cairo to give a sermon and lead an open-air Friday prayer service in Tahrir Square.

21 February: Qaradawi gives an on-air fatwa on Al Jazeera legitimating Gaddafi's assassination.

18 March: Qaradawi expresses his opposition to the 'sectarian' Bahraini revolution.

September: Hamza Yusuf argues against democracy in favor of monarchy in an interview with the UAE-based Al Arabiya channel.

October: Abdallah bin Bayyah, a vice president to Qaradawi at the IUMS, expresses for the first time his considerable misgivings concerning the Arab revolutions on an Egyptian satellite channel.

2012

8 June: Ali Gomaa encourages voters to support the military's preferred candidate in opposition to the Muslim Brother, Mohamed Morsi, in the upcoming presidential elections.

30 June: Mohamed Morsi wins presidential elections.

12 August: General Abdel Fattah al-Sisi appointed defense minister by President Morsi.

2013

18–20 February: Bin Bayyah presents a juristic argument for empowering absolute rulers at a conference in Kuwait which he subsequently publishes in written form.

23 February: UAE Foreign Minister Abdullah bin Zayed visits Bin Bayyah at his home and then praises him in a Twitter post.

21 March: The most important Syrian scholarly supporter of the Assad regime, Muḥammad Saʿīd Ramaḍān al-Būṭī, is killed in a bomb blast during a mosque class.

19 June: Ṭayyib issues a fatwa in support of 'peaceful protest' in the lead up to anti-Morsi mass protests orchestrated by the military, planned for 30 June.

25 June: IUMS issues a statement warning against destabilizing Egypt and calls to preserve democracy.

30 June: Massive anti-Morsi protests are held on the anniversary of Morsi's election as president.

3 July: A military coup, led by General Sisi, removes President Morsi and suspends the constitution in a televised event supported by Aḥmad al-Ṭayyib among others.

6 July: Qaradawi issues a fatwa stating that opposing the coup and supporting Morsi was a religious obligation.

8 July: Over fifty anti-coup protestors are killed by security forces at the Republican Guard headquarters. Condemnations follow from the IUMS and senior Azhar scholar, Ḥasan al-Shāfiʿī, who also condemns the coup.

9 July: UAE and Saudi Arabia pledge to give $8 billion to the coup regime. Over the coming years, the regular support they would receive from Gulf states would amount to tens of billions of dollars.

13 July: Another senior Azhar scholar, Muḥammad ʿImāra, condemns the coup and massacres in a 'Statement to the People.'

24 July: General Sisi calls for a protest on 26 July to give him a 'mandate' to confront 'terrorism' so that he can crackdown on opponents of the coup. IUMS and Ḥasan al-Shāfiʿī prohibit joining these protests.

27 July: Massacre of nearly 100 protestors by security forces shortly after military-backed protests were seen by the regime as giving a mandate to kill protestors. The IUMS, Ḥasan al-Shāfiʿī and Muḥammad ʿImāra condemn the massacre.

27 July: Bin Bayyah is invited to a public event by the UAE rulers and praises them profusely. In attendance are Crown Prince Muhammad bin Zayed and his brother, Foreign Minister Abdullah bin Zayed.

July – early August: Ali Gomaa gives multiple public and private lectures in support of the Egyptian security forces' violent actions. His private lecture to the security forces is more explicit in justifying violence against protestors.

Early August: UAE Foreign Minister Abdullah bin Zayed visits Egypt's generals and goads them on to violently crush the tens of thousands of anti-coup protestors gathered at the Rabaa Square sit-in.

14 August: Rabaa massacre takes place. Egyptian security forces violently clear tens of thousands of anti-coup protestors from a sit-in at Cairo's Rabaa Square, leaving over a thousand dead. The IUMS, Ḥasan al-Shāfiʿī and Muḥammad ʿImāra loudly condemn the massacre. Aḥmad al-Ṭayyib disavows having prior knowledge of the massacre.

16 August: Azharī imam, Rajab Zakī, gives a sermon powerfully condemning the coup and Rabaa massacre.

18 August: Ali Gomaa gives a private lecture to the Egyptian security forces celebrating their actions in recent days and encouraging them to 'shoot to kill' those who oppose the Egyptian army. He also appears to indirectly excommunicate Yusuf al-Qaradawi, calling him a disbeliever (*kāfir*). This recording is leaked in October.

21 August: Ali al-Jifri publicly defends Ali Gomaa, denying that he gave a fatwa legitimating the killing of protestors.

22 August: IUMS condemns massacres and attacks on mosques and churches.

23 August: Gomaa publicly defends his pre-Rabaa private lecture to the Egyptian security forces on an Egyptian satellite television show, reasserting the right of the military to use deadly force against protestors whom he characterizes as armed rebels.

25 August: Qaradawi dedicates what would end up being his Al Jazeera show's last episode to criticizing the religious justifications of Ali Gomaa for the coup and Rabaa massacre. ʿImāra and Raysūnī join the show by phone.

26 August: Ali al-Jifri publicly defends Ali Gomaa more forcefully after the full video of Gomaa's pre-Rabaa private lecture to the military is leaked. He tries to argue that Gomaa only permitted the killing of armed rebels.

3 September: Qaradawi publishes a detailed critique of shaykh al-Azhar's stance toward the coup.

7 September: Abdallah bin Bayyah resigns from IUMS, publishing his resignation letter online shortly thereafter while continuing his silence regarding events in Egypt.

8 October: Gomaa's private lecture to the security forces is leaked. It was originally given on 18 August. In it, Gomaa celebrates the Rabaa massacre and encourages the security forces to 'shoot to kill' their opponents.

11 October: Qaradawi publishes a detailed refutation of Gomaa's religious arguments from this leaked private lecture.

13 October: Qaradawi's colleague, Aḥmad al-Raysūnī, declares Gomaa a 'participant in murder.'

19 October: Gomaa uploads a response to the accusation that he permitted the killing of protestors. He denies ever doing so.

2014

9 March: Bin Bayyah holds the inaugural conference of the counter-revolutionary FPPMS as its founding president. The Forum's patron is the UAE's foreign minister. Hamza Yusuf would become the Forum's vice president.

19 July: Bin Bayyah and Shaykh al-Azhar Aḥmad al-Ṭayyib found the Muslim Council of Elders in the UAE.

19 September: An open letter condemning ISIS is signed by over a hundred scholars. The website prominently features Abdallah bin Bayyah, Hamza Yusuf, and Ali Gomaa.

24 September: Obama praises Bin Bayyah and the FPPMS in UN General Assembly speech.

November: UAE officially designates the MB a terrorist organization.

2015

4 March: Gomaa publishes a fifty-two-minute video taken from one of his mosque classes denying that he ever permitted the killing of protestors at Rabaa.

2016

5 August: Gomaa survives an assassination attempt. He blames the MB, although there is no evidence to suggest they are responsible.

24 December: Hamza Yusuf causes controversy with comments on race and religious extremism at the RIS convention in Canada.

2017

5 June: Saudi Arabia, the UAE, Egypt, and Bahrain initiate a blockade of Qatar precipitating a major diplomatic crisis in the region that would not end until January 2021.

7 June: The UAE newswire publishes a condemnation of Qatar in Bin Bayyah's name. Some days later, Yusuf al-Qaradawi, a former close associate and 'teacher' of Bin Bayyah, is added to a list of 'terrorists' by the blockading states.

21 June: Muhammad bin Salman is appointed crown prince of Saudi Arabia after he successfully displaces his much older cousin from the position.

30 June: Qaradawi's daughter and son-in-law, themselves grandparents and US residents, are arrested while on holiday in Egypt and incarcerated in solitary confinement.

7 September: Popular reformist Saudi scholar and student of both Qaradawi and Bin Bayyah, Salman al-'Awda, is arrested in Muhammad bin Salman's crackdown. Other prominent students of the Saudi-based Bin Bayyah are also arrested. Bin Bayyah makes no comment.

2018

24 June: Bin Bayyah is appointed chairman of the Emirates Fatwa Council, formally becoming the country's highest-ranking Islamic juristic authority.

2 October: Saudi journalist Jamal Khashoggi killed in Saudi Consulate in Turkey. A global outcry ensues after it emerges that the killing was likely ordered by Muhammad bin Salman. UAE stands by Muhammad bin Salman.

7 December: Hamza Yusuf criticized by rights groups for calling the UAE a tolerant country.

2019

19 May: Bin Bayyah visits King Salman of Saudi Arabia as head of the Emirates Fatwa Council.

17 June: Mohamed Morsi, Egypt's first and only democratically elected president, dies in Sisi's prisons at the age of sixty-seven after suffering severe medical neglect over many years.

8 July: Hamza Yusuf announced as member of a 'Commission on Unalienable Rights' set up by the Trump administration to advise it on human rights and public policy.

10 September: The publication of a clip of a lecture by Hamza Yusuf given in 2016 causes controversy after it appears to suggest that Syrians who rose against the Assad regime were being humiliated by God for their rebellion against their ruler.

2020

14 August: The Emirates Fatwa Council issues a statement in the name of its scholars, including Bin Bayyah and Hamza Yusuf, praising the UAE's crown prince for normalizing relations with Israel.

23 November: Bin Bayyah denounces MB as a terrorist organization in a statement of the Emirates Fatwa Council. Hamza Yusuf, also a member of the Emirates Fatwa Council, makes no comment. Bin Bayyah and Yusuf removed from a major North American Islamic conference apparently as a consequence of the anti-MB statement.

10 December: France awards Sisi its highest honor shortly after he cracked down on a human rights organization in Egypt.

NOTES

INTRODUCTION

1. While I do not theorize revolution in this work, I follow a number of scholars who refer to the events of 2011 onwards in the Arab world as 'revolutions,' both early on and many years later. Among these, two scholars who justify their choice of the term explicitly include: Jean-Pierre Filiu, *The Arab Revolution: Ten Lessons from the Democratic Uprising* (New York: Oxford University Press, 2011), 146; Jean-Pierre Filiu, *From Deep State to Islamic State: The Arab Counter-Revolution and Its Jihadi Legacy* (Oxford: Oxford University Press, 2015), 150; Saïd Amir Arjomand, *Revolution: Structure and Meaning in World History* (Chicago: University of Chicago Press, 2019), 330f.
2. The original Arabic word, *'ulamā'* is the plural form of *'ālim*, meaning 'one who possesses knowledge (*'ilm*)'. This word has now entered the English language in a spelling closer to its conventional Arabic transliteration than the more conventional 'ulema,' doubtless assisted by the writings of important Western scholars like Malika Zeghal and Muhammad Qasim Zaman. See Malika Zeghal, *Gardiens de l'Islam: Les ulama d'al-Azhar dans l'Egypte contemporaine* (Paris: Presses de la fondation nationale des sciences politiques, 1995); and Muhammad Qasim Zaman, *The Ulama in Contemporary Islam: Custodians of Change* (Princeton: Princeton University Press, 2002). For a recent study of the emergence of the ulama as a scholarly class in early Islam, see Jonathan Brockopp, *Muhammad's Heirs: The Rise of Muslim Scholarly Communities, 622–950* (Cambridge: Cambridge University Press, 2017).
3. For more on Qaradawi's life and thought, see Gudrun Krämer, 'Drawing Boundaries: Yūsuf al-Qaraḍāwī on Apostasy' in Gudrun Krämer and Sabine Schmidtke (eds), *Speaking for Islam: Religious Authorities in Muslim Societies* (Leiden, Holland: Brill, 2006), 184–200; Bettina Gräf and Jakob Skovgaard-Petersen (eds), *The Global Mufti: The Phenomenon of Yusuf al-Qaradawi* (London: Hurst Publishers, 2009); Mu'tazz al-Khaṭīb, *Yūsuf al-Qaraḍāwī: Faqīh al-Ṣahwa al-Islāmiyya: Sīra Fikriyya Taḥlīliyya* (Beirut: Markaz al-Ḥaḍāra li-Tanmiyat al-Fikr al-Islāmī, 2009); Roxanne Euben and Muhammad Qasim Zaman (eds), *Princeton Readings in Islamist Thought: Texts and Contexts from al-Bannā to Bin Laden* (Princeton: Princeton University Press, 2009),

224–9; Deina Ali Abdelkader, *Islamic Activists: The Anti-Enlightenment Democrats* (New York: Pluto Press, 2011), 43–65; Muhammad Qasim Zaman, *Modern Islamic Thought in a Radical Age: Religious Authority and Internal Criticism* (Cambridge: Cambridge University Press, 2012), 18–24; David H. Warren, 'The *'Ulamā'* and the Arab Uprisings 2011-13: Considering Yusuf al-Qaradawi, the 'Global Mufti', between the Muslim Brotherhood, the Islamic Legal Tradition, and Qatari Foreign Policy,' *New Middle Eastern Studies*, 4 (2014), 4–10; Ron Shaham, *Rethinking Islamic Legal Modernism: The Teaching of Yusuf al-Qaradawi* (Leiden: Brill, 2018).

4. See Jakob Skovgaard-Petersen, 'Yūsuf al-Qaraḍāwī and al-Azhar,' in Skovgaard-Petersen and Gräf (eds), *Global Mufti*.
5. For a concise biography of Bannā, see: Gudrun Krämer, *Ḥasan al-Bannā* (Oxford: Oneworld Publications, 2010). For the classic study of the early history of the Muslim Brotherhood, see Richard P. Mitchell, *The Society of the Muslim Brothers* (Oxford: Oxford University Press, 1969).
6. See Warren, 'The *'Ulamā'* and the Arab Uprisings,' 8. See also: Yūsuf al-Qaraḍāwī, *Kayfa Nata'āmal ma'a al-Turāth wa-l-Tamadhhub wa-l-Ikhtilāf?*, 3rd edn. (Cairo: Maktabat al-Wahba, 2011), 5–9. Here, he suggests that while he writes this and other works of his as commentaries on Bannā's ideas, the ideas they contain are relevant to any Islamic activist, and not exclusive to any group.
7. See note 3 above.
8. There is little secondary scholarship on Ṭayyib. See: Jonathan Brown, 'Salafis and Sufis in Egypt,' *The Carnegie Papers*, Dec 2011, http://carnegieendowment.org/files/salafis_sufis.pdf; Usaama al-Azami, 'Neo-traditionalist Sufis and Arab Politics: A Preliminary Mapping of the Transnational Networks of Counter-revolutionary Scholars after the Arab Revolutions' in Mark Sedgwick and Francesco Piraino (eds), *Global Sufism: Boundaries, Structures, and Politics* (London: Hurst Publishers, 2019). This chapter also contains a short biography of Ali Gomaa. More specifically on the latter see: Heba Raouf Ezzat, 'Gumaa, Ali' in John L Esposito (ed.), *The Oxford Encyclopedia of the Islamic World* (New York: Oxford University Press, 2009); Zareena Grewal, *Islam is a Foreign Country: American Muslims and the Global Crisis of Authority* (New York: New York University Press, 2013), especially 191–4; Mary Beinecke Elston, 'Reviving Turāth: Islamic Education in Modern Egypt,' PhD dissertation (Harvard University, 2020), passim. For a translation of his fatwas, see: Sheikh Ali Gomaa, *Responding from the Tradition: One Hundred Contemporary Fatwas by the Grand Mufti of Egypt* (Louisville, KY: Fons Vitae, 2012).
9. For Jifrī's biography, see: Besnik Sinani, 'In the Path of the Ancestors: The Bā 'Alawī Sufi Order and the Struggle for Shaping the Future of Islam' in Sedgwick and Piraino (eds), *Global Sufism*. More biographical material is found below.
10. For further information on Yusuf, see: Sadek Hamid, *Sufis, Salafis and Islamists: The Contested Ground of British Islamic Activism* (London: IB Tauris, 2016), 78ff; Grewal, *Islam is a Foreign Country*, 159–69; Scott Korb, *Light Without Fire: The Making of America's First Muslim College* (Boston, MA: Beacon Press, 2013), passim; and al-Azami, 'Neo-traditionalist Sufis.'
11. For more on Abdallah bin Bayyah in the secondary literature, see: Usaama al-Azami, 'Abdullāh bin Bayyah and the Arab Revolutions: Counter-revolutionary Neo-

traditionalism's Ideological Struggle against Islamism,' *The Muslim World*, 109:3 (2019), 343–61; Christopher Pooya Razavian's chapters in Masooda Bano (ed.), *Modern Islamic Authority and Social Change, Volume 1: Evolving Debates in Muslim Majority Countries* (Edinburgh: Edinburgh University Press, 2018), 102–23 and 172–91. For Bin Bayyah's influence in the West, see the first chapter by Razavian and Nathan Spannaus in Masooda Bano (ed.), *Modern Islamic Authority and Social Change, Volume 2: Evolving Debates in the West* (Edinburgh: Edinburgh University Press, 2018), 56–71.

12. 'Peripheral ulama' is a phrase coined by Malika Zeghal to refer to Egyptian scholars whose prominence was a result of their cultivation of a popular grassroots following rather than being appointed to positions of seniority within the Azhar establishment, something such ulama appeared to deliberately avoid. See: Malika Zeghal, 'Religion and Politics in Egypt: The Ulema of al-Azhar, Radical Islam, and the State (1952-94),' *International Journal of Middle East Studies*, 31:3 (1999), 371–99.
13. For a brief discussion of Ḥasan al-Shāfiʿī, see: Elston, 'Reviving Turāth,' 230f., 300f. I am not aware of any other treatment of him and his thought in the secondary literature. For a discussion of some of ʿImāra's ideas, see: Mona Abaza, 'Two Intellectuals: The Malaysian S. N. Al-Attas and the Egyptian Mohammed 'Immara [*sic*], and the Islamization of Knowledge Debate,' *Asian Journal of Social Science* 30:2 (2002), 354–83. In the epilogue, I will argue that these denominations should be understood as overlapping with each other rather than having clear dividing lines.
14. I hope to engage in a more systematic study of this somewhat problematic term in future.
15. See Roxanne Euben and M. Qasim Zaman (eds), *Princeton Readings in Islamist Thought: Texts and Contexts from al-Bannā to Bin Laden* (Princeton: Princeton University Press, 2009), 10.
16. Peter Mandaville, *Islam and Politics*, 2nd edn. (London: Routledge, 2014), 12f. On how this perpetuates Eurocentrism in scholarship, see: Usaama al-Azami, 'Locating *Ḥākimiyya* in Global History: Premodern Islamic Conceptions of Sovereignty and their Islamist Reception after Mawdūdī and Quṭb,' in *Journal of the Royal Asiatic Society* (forthcoming).
17. I briefly discuss the problems entailed in blurring these lines in: Usaama al-Azami, 'Why Words Matter: The Problem with the Term Islamist,' *Sadeq Institute*, 23 Nov 2020, https://www.sadeqinstitute.org/short-reads/why-words-matter-the-problem-with-the-term-islamist.
18. See, for example, Daniel Lav, *Radical Islam and the Revival of Medieval Theology* (Cambridge: Cambridge University Press, 2012), 179.
19. For example, the notable Moroccan Islamist alim we will meet in Chapter 6, Aḥmad al-Raysūnī, asserts that the term 'Islamist' had been imposed upon Islamic activists by the media and was not of their own choosing. See: https://youtu.be/xY2UY0Qp3Uo?t=314 (https://www.youtube.com/watch?v=xY2UY0Qp3Uo). For the claim that it is an indigenous term to Islamic activists, see: Tariq Ramadan, *Islam and the Arab Awakening* (Oxford: Oxford University Press, 2012), 71f.
20. My usage of Neo-traditionalist bears more than a passing resemblance to Ahmed El Shamsy's use of the term 'postclassical.' See: Ahmed El Shamsy, *Rediscovering the*

Islamic Classics: How Editors and Print Culture Transformed an Intellectual Tradition (Princeton: Princeton University Press, 2020).

21. For more detailed definitions of Neo-traditionalism, see: al-Azami, 'Neo-traditionalist Sufis' and Kasper Mathiesen, 'Anglo-American 'Traditional Islam' and Its Discourse of Orthodoxy,' *Journal of Arabic and Islamic Studies* 13 (2013), 191–219. Matheisen uses 'Traditional Islam' to refer to the same denomination. Some adherents of Neo-traditionalism use this term in recognition of the transformed modern context in which this denomination seeks to adhere to its particular conception of traditional Islam. See Abdullah Ali, ''Neo-Traditionalism' vs 'Traditionalism',' *Lamppost Education Initiative*, 22 January 2012, available at: https://lamppostedu.org/neo-traditionalism-vs-traditionalism-shaykh-abdullah-bin-hamid-ali/.
22. I use the term Salafi to refer to those whom Henri Lauzière refers to as 'purist' as opposed to 'modernist' Salafis. The latter are a twentieth-century trend that may be viewed as antecedents to today's Islamist ulama. See: Henri Lauzière, *The Making of Salafism: Islamic Reform in the Twentieth Century* (New York: Columbia University Press, 2015). For an edited volume which constitutes an important and extensive survey of Salafi studies with contributions from leading scholars of Salafism published shortly before the Arab revolutions, see: Roel Meijer (ed.), *Global Salafism: Islam's New Religious Movement* (London: Hurst Publishers, 2009). The broader literature of Salafism is fairly extensive. Some important recent works that do not address the Arab revolutions but which provide valuable background information, include: Stèphane Lacroix, *Awakening Islam: The Politics of Religious Dissent in Contemporary Saudi Arabia*, trans. G. Holoch (Cambridge, MA: Harvard University Press, 2011); Joas Wagemakers, *A Quietist Jihadi: The Ideology and Influence of Abu Muhammad al-Maqdisi* (Cambridge: Cambridge University Press, 2012).
23. See Bernard Haykel, 'On the Nature of Salafi thought and Action,' in Roel Meijer (ed.), *Global Salafism*; Lauzière, *The Making of Salafism*.
24. An excellent post-Arab revolutionary edited volume on Salafism is: Francesco Cavatorta and Fabio Merone (eds), *Salafism After the Arab Awakening: Contending with People's Power* (London: Hurst Publishers, 2016). This collection of essays provides an important overview of the diverse ways in which Salafis responded to the Arab revolutions in different countries throughout the Middle East. For other post-Arab revolutionary assessments, see: Aria Nakissa, 'The Fiqh of Revolution and the Arab Spring: Secondary Segmentation as a Trend in Islamic Legal Doctrine,' *The Muslim World* 105:3 (2015): 398–421; Ovamir Anjum, 'Salafis and Democracy: Doctrine and Context,' *The Muslim World* 106 (2016), 448–73; Adnan Zulfiqar, 'Revolutionary Islamic Jurisprudence: A Restatement of the Arab Spring,' *New York University Journal of International Law and Politics* 49 (2017), 443–97. Another excellent, if tantalizingly brief treatment of Salafism in the context of the Egyptian revolution may be found in David D. Kirkpatrick, *Into the Hands of the Soldiers: Freedom and Chaos in Egypt and the Middle East* (London: Bloomsbury, 2018).
25. I make an initial effort in this direction by studying two Salafi ulama in: 'Legitimizing Political Dissent: Islamist Salafi Discourses on Obedience and Rebellion after the

Arab Revolutions,' in Masooda Bano (ed.), *Salafi Social and Political Movements: National and Transnational Contexts* (Edinburgh: Edinburgh University Press, 2021).

26. Helpful early overviews include: Filiu, *The Arab Revolution*; Marc Lynch, *The Arab Uprising: The Unfinished Revolutions of the New Middle East* (New York: Public Affairs, 2012). Important edited volumes include: Fawaz Gerges (ed.), *The New Middle East: Protest and Revolution in the Arab World* (Cambridge: Cambridge University Press, 2013); Larbi Sadiki (ed.), *Routledge Handbook of the Arab Spring* (London: Routledge, 2014); Marc Lynch (ed.), *The Arab Uprisings Explained: New Contentious Politics in the Middle East* (New York: Columbia University Press, 2014); Mehran Kamrava (ed.), *Beyond the Arab Spring: The Evolving Ruling Bargain in the Middle East* (Oxford: Oxford University Press, 2014); Bernard Rougier and Stéphane Lacroix (eds), *Egypt's Revolutions: Politics, Religion, and Social Movements* (New York: Palgrave Macmillan, 2016); Bessma Momani and Eid Mohamed (eds), *Egypt beyond Tahrir Square* (Indiana University Press, 2016); Stéphane Lacroix and Jean-Pierre Filiu (eds), *Revisiting the Arab Uprisings: The Politics of a Revolutionary Moment* (Oxford: Oxford University Press, 2018); Eid Mohamed and Dalia Fahmy (eds), *Arab Spring: Modernity, Identity and Change* (New York: Palgrave Macmillan, 2020).
27. Neil Ketchley, *Egypt in a Time of Revolution: Contentious Politics and the Arab Spring* (Cambridge: Cambridge University Press, 2017).
28. Hazem Kandil, *Soldiers, Spies and Statesmen: Egypt's Road to Revolt* (London: Verso, 2012); Steven Brooke and Elizabeth R. Nugent, 'Exclusion and Violence After the Egyptian Coup,' *Middle East Law and Governance* 12:1 (2020), 61–85.
29. Genevieve Barrons, "Suleiman: Mubarak Decided to Step Down #egypt #jan25 OH MY GOD': Examining the Use of Social Media in the 2011 Revolution,' *Contemporary Arab Affairs* 5:1 (2012), 54–67; Axel Bruns, Tim Highfield, and Jean Burgess, 'The Arab Spring and Social Media Audiences,' *American Behavioral Scientist* 57:7 (2013), 871–98; Saba Bebawi and Diana Bossio, *Social Media and the Politics of Reportage: The 'Arab Spring'* (New York: Palgrave Macmillan, 2014); David Faris, 'Dissent and Revolution in a Digital Age: Social Media, Blogging, and Activism in Egypt,' *European Journal of Communication* 29:3 (2014), 392; Reza Jamali, *Online Arab Spring: Social Media and Fundamental Change* (Waltham: Chandos Publishing, 2015); Courtney C. Radsch, *Cyberactivism and Citizen Journalism in Egypt: Digital Dissidence and Political Change* (New York: Palgrave Macmillan, 2016).
30. Samuli Schielke, 'There will be Blood: Expectation and Ethics of Violence during Egypt's Stormy Season,' *Middle East Critique* 26 (2017): 205–20; Hiba Ghanem, 'The 2011 Egyptian Revolution Chants: A Romantic-Muʿtazilī Moral Order,' *British Journal of Middle Eastern Studies* 45:3 (2017), 430–42; Walter Armbrust, *Martyrs and Tricksters: An Ethnography of the Egyptian Revolution* (Princeton: Princeton University Press, 2019).
31. Gilbert Achcar, *The People Want: A Radical Exploration of the Arab Uprising*, Trans. G. M. Goshgarian (Berkeley: University of California Press, 2013); idem., *Morbid Symptoms: Relapse in the Arab Uprising* (Stanford University Press, 2016);

Asef Bayat, *Revolution without Revolutionaries: Making Sense of the Arab Spring* (Stanford University Press, 2017); Dalia Fahmy and Daanish Faruqi (eds), *Egypt and the Contradictions of Liberalism: Illiberal Intelligentsia and the Future of Egyptian Democracy* (Oxford: Oneworld, 2017); Shadi Hamid, *Islamic Exceptionalism: How the Struggle Over Islam Is Reshaping the World* (New York: St. Martin's Press, 2016).

32. Khalil al-Anani, *Inside the Muslim Brotherhood: Religion, Identity, and Politics* (New York: Oxford University Press, 2016); Cavatorta and Merone (eds), *Salafism*; Hazem Kandil, *Inside the Brotherhood* (Cambridge: Polity Press, 2015); Shadi Hamid, *Temptations of Power: Islamists and Illiberal Democracy in a New Middle East* (New York: Oxford University Press, 2014); Rachel M. Scott, 'What Might the Muslim Brotherhood Do with Al-Azhar? Religious Authority in Egypt,' *Die Welt Des Islams* 52:2 (2012), 131–65; Nathan J. Brown, 'Post-Revolutionary Al-Azhar,' *Carnegie Endowment for International Peace* (2011).
33. Geneive Abdo, *The New Sectarianism: The Arab Uprisings and the Rebirth of the Shi'a-Sunni Divide* (New York: Oxford University Press, 2017); Filiu, *From Deep State to Islamic State*; Nader Hashemi and Danny Postel (eds), *Sectarianization: Mapping the New Politics of the Middle East* (London: Hurst Publishers, 2017); Toby Matthiesen, *Sectarian Gulf: Bahrain, Saudi Arabia, and the Arab Spring That Wasn't* (Stanford: Stanford University Press, 2013).
34. Several works on this theme have been published by Masooda Bano and colleagues. See: Masooda Bano (ed.), *Modern Islamic Authority and Social Change, Volume 1*; Masooda Bano and Keiko Sakurai (eds), *Shaping Global Islamic Discourses: The Role of Al-Azhar, Transnational Contexts* (Edinburgh: Edinburgh University Press, 2021; Masooda Bano, 'At the Tipping Point? Al-Azhar's Growing Crisis of Moral Authority,' *International Journal of Middle East Studies* 50:4 (2018), 715–34; Masooda Bano and Hanane Benadi, 'Official Al-Azhar versus al-Azhar Imagined: The Arab Spring and the Revival of Religious Imagination,' *Die Welt Des Islams* 59:1 (2019), 7–32; Nathan Brown, *Arguing Islam after the Revival of Arab Politics* (Oxford: Oxford University Press, 2016).
35. In wider post-2011 ulama studies, David H. Warren's valuable recent work, *Rivals in the Gulf*, came out too late for me to engage it in the present work.
36. Malika Zeghal, *Gardiens de l'Islam: Les ulama d'al-Azhar dans l'Egypte contemporaine* (Paris: Presses de la fondation nationale des sciences politiques, 1995); idem., 'Religion and Politics in Egypt: The Ulema of al-Azhar, Radical Islam, and the State (1952-94),' *International Journal of Middle East Studies* 31:3 (1999), 371–99.
37. Muhammad Qasim Zaman, *The Ulama in Contemporary Islam: Custodians of Change* (Princeton: Princeton University Press, 2002); idem., *Modern Islamic Thought in a Radical Age: Religious Authority and Internal Criticism* (Cambridge: Cambridge University Press, 2012).
38. Henri Lauzière, *The Making of Salafism: Islamic Reform in the Twentieth Century* (New York: Columbia University Press, 2015).
39. Stèphane Lacroix, *Awakening Islam: The Politics of Religious Dissent in Contemporary Saudi Arabia*, Trans. G. Holoch (Cambridge, MA: Harvard University Press, 2011).
40. Nabil Mouline, *The Clerics of Islam: Religious Authority and Political Power in Saudi Arabia*, Trans. Ethan Rundell (New Haven: Yale University Press, 2014).

41. Madawi Al-Rasheed, *Muted Modernists: The Struggle over Divine Politics in Saudi Arabia* (Oxford: Oxford University Press, 2015).
42. Meir Hatina, *'Ulama,' Politics, and the Public Sphere: An Egyptian Perspective* (Salt Lake City: University of Utah Press, 2010). Hatina is also the editor of and a contributor to a volume that seeks to clarify how the ulama fit into the competitive marketplace of contemporary religious authority. See: Meir Hatina (ed.), *Guardians of Faith in Modern Times: 'Ulama' in the Middle East* (Boston: Brill, 2009).
43. Thomas Pierret, *Religion and State in Syria: The Sunni Ulama from Coup to Revolution* (Cambridge: Cambridge University Press, 2013). Pierret's final chapter considers the political interventions of the ulama in the Syrian uprising of 2011.
44. Youssef Belal, 'The Life of *Shari'a*,' PhD Dissertation (University of California, Berkeley, 2017); Walaa Quisay, 'Neo-Traditionalism in the West: Navigating Modernity, Tradition and Politics,' DPhil dissertation (University of Oxford, 2019); Mary Beinecke Elston, 'Reviving Turāth: Islamic Education in Modern Egypt,' PhD dissertation (Harvard University, 2020).
45. See: Ebrahim Moosa, 'Political Theology in the Aftermath of the Arab Spring: Returning to the Ethical,' in Charles Villa-Vicencio, Erik Doxtader, Ebrahim Moosa (eds), *The African Renaissance and the Afro-Arab Spring: A Season of Rebirth?* (Georgetown: Georgetown University Press, 2015); Amr Osman, 'Past Contradictions, Contemporary Dilemmas: Egypt's 2013 Coup and Early Islamic History,' *Digest of Middle East Studies*, 24:2 (2015); Mohammad Fadel, 'Islamic Law and Constitution-Making: The Authoritarian Temptation and the Arab Spring,' *Osgoode Hall Law Journal* 53:2 (2016); David H. Warren, 'Cleansing the Nation of the 'Dogs of Hell': 'Ali Jum'a's Nationalist Legal Reasoning in Support of the 2013 Egyptian Coup and its Bloody Aftermath,' *International Journal of Middle East Studies*, 49:3 (2017); Youssef Belal, 'Islamic Law, Truth, Ethics,' *Comparative Studies of South Asia, Africa and the Middle East* 38:1 (2018); Muhamad Rofiq Muzakkir, 'Understanding the Discourse of 'Alī Jum'ah on the Military Coup During the Arab Spring in Egypt,' *Ilahiyat Studies* 10:2 (2019). I have also commented briefly on this debate in Usaama al-Azami, 'Neo-traditionalist Sufis and Arab Politics: A Preliminary Mapping of the Transnational Networks of Counter-revolutionary Scholars after the Arab Revolutions,' in Mark Sedgwick and Francesco Piraino (eds), *Global Sufism: Boundaries, Structures, and Politics* (London: Hurst Publishers, 2019).
46. See, for example: Nakissa, 'Fiqh of Revolution;' Zulfiqar, 'Revolutionary Islamic Jurisprudence.'
47. Brown, *Arguing Islam*, 66. While Brown speaks of 'imams,' most Egyptian imams would likely also be trained ulama.
48. Ebrahim Moosa, 'Political Theology in the Aftermath of the Arab Spring: Returning to the Ethical,' in Charles Villa-Vicencio, Erik Doxtader, Ebrahim Moosa (eds), *The African Renaissance and the Afro-Arab Spring: A Season of Rebirth?* (Georgetown: Georgetown University Press, 2015), 115.

1 YUSUF AL-QARADAWI: EARLY SUPPORTER OF THE ARAB REVOLUTIONS

1. On his play, see Husam Tammam, 'Yūsuf al-Qaraḍawi and the Muslim Brothers: The Nature of a Special Relationship,' in Bettina Gräf and Jakob Skovgaard-Petersen (eds), *The Global Mufti: The Phenomenon of Yusuf al-Qaradawi* (London: Hurst Publishers, 2009), 64; David H. Warren, 'The *'Ulamā'* and the Arab Uprisings 2011-13: Considering Yusuf al-Qaradawi, the 'Global Mufti', between the Muslim Brotherhood, the Islamic Legal Tradition, and Qatari Foreign Policy,' *New Middle Eastern Studies*, 4 (2014), 11. Qaradawi's advocacy for Islamic democracy in a fatwa published in the 1990s particularly highlights his Islamic opposition to despotism. It is translated in Roxanne Euben and M. Qasim Zaman (eds), *Princeton Readings in Islamist Thought: Texts and Contexts from al-Bannā to Bin Laden* (Princeton: Princeton University Press, 2009), 230–45. For his more recent work on jihad, see: Yūsuf al-Qaraḍāwī, *Fiqh al-Jihād: Dirāsa Muqārana li-Aḥkāmihi wa-Falsafatihi fī Ḍaw' al-Qur'ān wa-l-Sunna*, 3rd edn. (Cairo: Maktabat Wahba, 2010).
2. See: https://youtu.be/PGpRu2nE2hA (https://www.youtube.com/watch?v=PGpRu2nE2hA). For a full transcript of the show, see: https://www.aljazeera.net/programs/religionandlife/2011/1/19/جهاد-الظلم-ووسائله.
3. This aspect of the show was reportedly an innovation of Qaradawi's. See Skovgaard-Petersen and Gräf (eds), *Global Mufti*, 151.
4. Marc Lynch, 'Qaradawi's Revisions,' *Foreign Policy*, 9 July 2009, https://foreignpolicy.com/2009/07/09/qaradawis-revisions/.
5. https://youtu.be/PGpRu2nE2hA?t=84.
6. See Hans Wehr, *Arabic–English Dictionary* (ed.), J Milton Cowan (Ithaca, NY: Spoken Language Services, 1994), 656; Edward William Lane, *Arabic-English Lexicon* (London: Williams & Norgate, 1863), 1857.
7. https://youtu.be/PGpRu2nE2hA?t=208. Of course, in the West, the word jihad is associated with terrorism. This is not usually the case in the Muslim world.
8. https://youtu.be/PGpRu2nE2hA?t=367.
9. See Yūsuf al-Qaraḍāwī, *Bayyināt al-Ḥall al-Islāmī wa-Shubuhāt al-'Almaniyyīn wa-l-Mutagharribīn*, 2nd edn. (Cairo: Maktabat Wahba, 1993), 179f. The first edition of the work was published in 1987 according to Mu'tazz al-Khaṭīb. See his *Yūsuf al-Qaraḍāwī*, 228. Qaradawi is hardly exceptional among leading Islamists in seeking to limit the application of the *ḥudūd* on the basis of Islamic legal principles. Perhaps the most important South Asian Islamist of the twentieth century, Abū al-A'lā Mawdūdī, held a similar opinion. See: Seyyed Vali Reza Nasr, *Mawdudi and the Making of Islamic Revivalism* (New York: Oxford University Press, 1996), 98. For a detailed treatment of how Muslim jurists have historically tried to avoid implementing the *ḥudūd* through appeals to doubt, see: Intisar Rabb, *Doubt in Islamic Law: A History of Legal Maxims, Interpretation, and Islamic Criminal Law* (Cambridge: Cambridge University Press, 2014).
10. https://youtu.be/PGpRu2nE2hA?t=477.
11. https://youtu.be/PGpRu2nE2hA?t=570.
12. Ahmad Najib Burhani has also examined Qaradawi's response, which he portrays as influential in the public debate at the time. See: Ahmad Najib Burhani,

'Fatwās on Mohamed Bouazizi's Self-Immolation: Religious Authority, Media, and Secularization,' in Thomas Daniels (ed.), *Sharia Dynamics: Contemporary Anthropology of Religion* (Cham: Palgrave Macmillan, 2017).

13. See: https://youtu.be/PGpRu2nE2hA?t=730.
14. See https://www.ahlalhdeeth.com/vb/showthread.php?t=236167. The discussion paraphrases Ibn Ḥazm, even though it uses quotes. Ibn Ḥazm discusses this in his *Muḥallā*, at the end of the section on zakat when addressing a legal question (*mas'ala*) entitled '*'alā al-aghniyā' min ahl kull balad an yaqūmū bi-fuqarā'ihim.*' See: Ibn Ḥazm, *al-Muḥallā bi-l-Āthār* (Beirut: Dār al-Kutub al-'Ilmiyya, 2003), 4:281–4.
15. For a detailed *takhrīj* and evaluation of the authenticity of the hadith, see Aḥmad b. Ḥanbal, *Musnad al-Imām Aḥmad b. Ḥanbal* (Beirut: Mu'assasat al-Risāla, 1999), 17:228ff., n. 3, esp. 230. For another discussion on its authenticity, see: https://www.ahlalhdeeth.com/vb/showthread.php?t=179208.
16. This tradition is narrated in *Ṣaḥīḥ Muslim* whose hadiths are generally deemed authentic by Sunnis. See: Muslim b. al-Ḥajjāj, *Ṣaḥīḥ Muslim bi-Sharḥ al-Nawawī* (Cairo: al-Maṭba'a al-Miṣriyya bi-l-Azhar, 1929), 16:131f.
17. These are found in the following Qur'anic verses: 2:258; 3:86; 5:51; 6:144; 9:19; 9:109; 28:50; 46:10; 61:7; 62:5.
18. https://youtu.be/PGpRu2nE2hA?t=1196.
19. This interpretation, i.e. understanding *rukūn* as *mayl*, is affirmed by the authoritative early Sunni exegete al-Ṭabarī. See: al-Ṭabarī, *Jāmi' al-Bayān fī Tafsīr Āy al-Qur'ān*, ed. 'Abd al-Muḥsin al-Turkī et al. (Giza: Dār Hajar, 2001), 12:599.
20. See: https://youtu.be/PGpRu2nE2hA?t=1366. There appears to be some debate as to the authenticity of this hadith. Some scholars, such as Dhahabī and the modern Albānī, regard it as authentic, while others such as Ibn Ḥajar al-'Asqalānī regard it as weak. For a brief discussion, see: https://www.ahlalhdeeth.com/vb/showthread.php?t=263032.
21. The reliability of this hadith also appears to be a matter of disagreement, with some deeming it authentic, while others considering it weak. For a brief discussion, see: https://majles.alukah.net/t89176/.
22. See: https://youtu.be/PGpRu2nE2hA?t=1412. Qaradawi complains about this kind of Sufism in a book he published the previous year. See Yūsuf al-Qaraḍāwī, *Fiqh al-Wasaṭiyya al-Islāmiyya wa-l-Tajdīd* (Cairo: Dār al-Shurūq, 2010), 206. It is worth highlighting that in the post-Arab Spring context, such quietist statements are not only the preserve of Sufis. For an example from a prominent Madkhalī Salafi, see: https://twitter.com/dr_alqarnee/status/894588895987466241.
23. This hadith is found in a number of collections and is deemed authentic (*ṣaḥīḥ*). See al-Tirmidhī, *al-Jāmi' al-Kabīr (Sunan al-Tirmidhī)*, ed. Shu'ayb al-Arna'ūṭ et al. (Beirut: Dār al-Risāla al-'Ālamiyya, 2009), 4:242f.; and Ibn Ḥanbal, *Musnad*, 1:177f.
24. https://youtu.be/PGpRu2nE2hA?t=1465.
25. Michael Cook, *Commanding Right and Forbidding Wrong in Islamic Thought* (Cambridge: Cambridge University Press, 2000), 3–12.
26. Other Qur'anic verses that mention this duty are: 3:110, 3:114, 7:157, 9:71, 9:112, 22:41, 31:17. For a discussion of how these verses have been understood by premodern Qur'anic exegetes, see: ibid., 13–31.

27. Cook also refers to this iteration of the command. See: ibid., 35f.
28. See: ibid., 32.
29. Ibn Rajab al-Ḥanbalī, *Jāmiʿ al-ʿUlūm wa-l-Ḥikam*, ed. Māhir Yāsīn al-Faḥl (Damascus: Dār Ibn Kathīr, 2008), 698. The hadith in question is no. 34 in al-Nawawī's collection on which Ibn Rajab's work forms a commentary.
30. On privacy in relation to the duty, see: Cook, *Commanding*, 479–86. For a useful summary of Sunni attitudes towards rebellion, see: Patricia Crone, *Medieval Islamic Political Thought* (Edinburgh: Edinburgh University Press, 2004), 228–32.
31. See, for example: Cook, *Commanding*, 98, 434f.
32. See: ibid., 431–3 (in favor of admonishing rulers), and 101f. (against). Notable dissent comes from Aḥmad b. Ḥanbal for whom the concern for social stability overrode such traditions that would suggest verbal confrontation with tyrannical rulers. Given he is the eponym of the school of law dominant in the modern Saudi state, this may account for the Saudi ulama establishment's general quiescence vis-à-vis the state. See: Saud al-Sarhan, "Patience in Our Situation is Better than Sedition': The Shift to Political Quietism in the Sunnī Tradition,' in Saud al-Sarhan (ed.), *Political Quietism in Islam: Sunni and Shiʿi Practice and Thought* (London: I. B. Tauris, 2019), 81–97.
33. See: Cook, *Commanding*, 479.
34. Ibid., 476.
35. Ibid., 523.
36. On his relationship with Bannā, see Tammam, 'Yūsuf al-Qaraḍawi,' 55–83.
37. See: Uriya Shavit, 'The Muslim Brothers' Conception of Armed Insurrection against an Unjust Regime,' *Middle Eastern Studies* 51 (2015), 600–17.
38. Ibid., 602.
39. By using the term 'mainstream,' I am setting aside violent offshoots, such as the Quṭbist wing that emerged in the context of the 'ordeal' (*miḥna*) of the Abdel Nasser years, and whose ideas were rejected by the organization's mainstream under the leadership of Ḥasan al-Huḍaybī (d. 1393/1973). For a discussion of how Huḍaybī responded to Quṭbism, see: Barbara Zollner, *The Muslim Brotherhood: Hasan al-Hudaybi and Ideology* (London: Routledge, 2009).
40. Shavit, 'The Muslim Brothers' Conception of Armed Insurrection,' 614.
41. Yūsuf al-Qaraḍāwī, *Min Hady al-Islām: Fatāwā Muʿāṣira* (Kuwait: Dār al-Qalam, 2009), 2:688–90. My dating is an estimate. The volume's preface is dated 1412/1991, but Qaradawi notes that most of the text was ready for publication years earlier and needed only modest editing. (pp. 9, 13). Qaradawi reproduces this discussion in later writings in slightly expanded form. See: idem., *Min Fiqh al-Dawla fī al-Islām*, 3rd edn. (Cairo: Dār al-Shurūq, 2001), 125f.; idem., *Fiqh al-Jihād*, 2:1151–54.
42. Qaraḍāwī, *Min Hady al-Islām*, 689.
43. Ibid., 690.
44. https://youtu.be/PGpRu2nE2hA?t=1514.
45. For more on Qaradawi's conception of this central idea in his worldview, see Bettina Gräf, 'The Concept of *Wasaṭiyya* in the work of Yūsuf al-Qaraḍāwī,' in Gräf and Skovgaard-Petersen (eds), *Global Mufti*. For his comprehensive articulation of the idea in Arabic, see: al-Qaraḍāwī, *Fiqh al-Wasaṭiyya*.

46. This is reported in the canonical collections of Bukhārī and Muslim. For a *takhrīj*, see: Ibn Ḥanbal, *Musnad*, 30:602, n. 2.
47. https://youtu.be/PGpRu2nE2hA?t=1563.
48. Muslim, *Ṣaḥīḥ*, 2:27.
49. Muslim, *Ṣaḥīḥ*, 2:22–5. This hadith is better known, as it is found in Nawawī's popular forty hadith collection.
50. https://youtu.be/PGpRu2nE2hA?t=1855.
51. https://youtu.be/PGpRu2nE2hA?t=2355.
52. Qaradawi paraphrased the narration that is found in certain historical works, although the closing phrase is as found in these narrations. The historicity of the overall story may be unverifiable. The earliest citation of the story I have found is in *Manāqib al-Imām Aḥmad* of the prolific Baghdadi scholar Ibn al-Jawzī (d. 597/1201), but the latter narrates the story without a chain hundreds of years after its claimed occurrence. For a discussion of the provenance of the story and the hadith it appears to be referring to, see: https://majles.alukah.net/t163120/ and https://www.ahlalhdeeth.com/vb/showthread.php?t=380014. Qaradawi may have been aware of the problems of the report's historicity, and thus used language that does not explicitly adjudicate the issue by saying 'they narrate from Imam Aḥmad [...].'
53. This is a reference to a phrase found in the Islamic scholarly tradition in the writings of several scholars: 'Whoever remains silent about what is right is a silent devil' (*man sakata ʿan al-haqq fa-huwa shayṭān akhras*). For a discussion of the possible provenance of this phrase, see: https://www.islamweb.net/ar/fatwa/58360/-مصدر-عبارة-الساكت-عن-الحق-شيطان-أخرس/.
54. https://youtu.be/PGpRu2nE2hA?t=2093. Qaradawi cites only part of the hadith.
55. For a detailed *takhrīj*, see Ibn Ḥanbal, *Musnad*, 11:59.
56. For the view of the important early exegete, Abū Jaʿfar al-Ṭabarī (d. 310/923), see: al-Ṭabarī, *Tafsīr al-Ṭabarī: Jāmiʿ al-Bayān ʿan Taʾwīl Āy al-Qurʾān*, ed. ʿAbd al-Muḥsin al-Turkī (Cairo: Dār Hajar, 2001), 19:120ff.
57. This was also the view of *The New York Times* from this period, see: Robert F. Worth and David D. Kirkpatrick, 'Seizing a Moment, Al Jazeera Galvinizes Arab Frustration,' *The New York Times*, 28 January 2011, https://www.nytimes.com/2011/01/28/world/middleeast/28jazeera.html. Subsequent scholarship has also highlighted this. See: Ezzeddine Abdelmoula, 'Al Jazeera and Televised Revolution,' in *Routledge Handbook of the Arab Spring* (ed.) Larbi Sadiki (Abingdon: Routledge, 2014). The channel's selective support for the revolutions, apparently in line with Qatari foreign policy, most notably in the form of its silence in the face of the GCC suppression of the revolution in Bahrain, has been commented on by several scholars. See, for example, Marc Lynch, *The Arab Uprising: The Unfinished Revolutions of the New Middle East* (New York: Public Affairs, 2012).
58. https://youtu.be/PGpRu2nE2hA?t=2317.
59. See: Kristian Coates Ulrichsen, *Qatar and the Arab Spring* (New York: Oxford University Press, 2014), 50. Ulrichsen argues that Al Jazeera's reputation for independence has been adversely impacted by the Arab revolutions, in part due to the sudden departure of its former director general, Wadah Khanfar, in September 2011 and his replacement with a member of the Qatari royal family. See also:

Courtney Freer, *Rentier Islamism: The Influence of the Muslim Brotherhood in Gulf Monarchies* (Oxford: Oxford University Press, 2018), 126–8.

60. Ulrichsen, *Qatar and the Arab Spring*, 104.
61. See David H. Warren, 'Qatari Support for the Muslim Brotherhood is More Than Just Realpolitik, it has a Long, Personal History,' *Maydan*, 12 July 2017, https://themaydan.com/2017/07/qatari-support-muslim-brotherhood-just-realpolitik-long-personal-history/.
62. Qatar has repeatedly delayed even relatively modest internal democratic reforms in recent years. On this, see: Ulrichsen, *Qatar and the Arab Spring*; Freer, *Rentier Islamism*.
63. 'Arab media code 'risk to freedom',' *Al Jazeera English*, 15 Feb 2008, https://www.aljazeera.com/news/middleeast/2008/02/200852514291444 7849.html.
64. 'Ben Ali gets refuge in Saudi Arabia,' *Al Jazeera English*, 16 Jan 2011, https://www.aljazeera.com/news/middleeast/2011/01/201111652129710582.html.
65. https://youtu.be/PGpRu2nE2hA?t=2608.
66. This is drawn from the final couplet of a poem describing Paradise composed by the prolific Damascene polymath, Ibn Qayyim al-Jawziyya (d. 751/1351). See: Ibn Qayyim al-Jawziyya, *Ḥādī al-Arwāḥ ilā Bilād al-Afrāḥ*, ed. Zā'id al-Nushayrī (Jeddah: Dār 'Ālam al-Fawā'id, 1428 [2007]), 15.
67. https://youtu.be/PGpRu2nE2hA?t=2712. A version of this report from 'Umar may be found in: Abū Bakr al-Bayhaqī, *al-Sunan al-Kubrā* (ed.) Muḥammad 'Aṭā (Beirut: Dār al-Kutub al-'Ilmiyya, 2003), 6:581. I have found no discussion as to its authenticity.
68. Musa Furber, 'Elements of a Fatwa and Their Contribution to Confidence in Its Validity,' *Tabah Analytic Brief*, no. 14 Abū (2013).
69. Jonathan Brown, 'Even If It's Not True It's True: Using Unreliable Hadīths in Sunni Islam,' *Islamic Law and Society* 18 (2011), 1–52.
70. Ibid., 44.

2 QARADAWI AND THE EGYPTIAN REVOLUTION

1. See the mid-January 2011 announcement here: https://www.facebook.com/elshaheeed.co.uk/photos/a.134576649914661/176594399046219/?type=3.
2. https://youtu.be/Fcgfthka4FI?t=460 (https://www.youtube.com/watch?v=Fcgfthka4FI). The transcript may be found on Al Jazeera's website: https://www.aljazeera.net/programs/religionandlife/2011/1/25/فرعون-وإرث-للطغاة.
3. Qaradawi glossed the Qur'anic usage of *'uluww* (exorbitant pride) with respect to Pharaoh as referring to his *ṭughyān* (tyranny) against his subjects. Cf. Edward William Lane, *Arabic-English Lexicon* (London: Williams & Norgate, 1863), 2143.
4. https://youtu.be/Fcgfthka4FI?t=693.
5. https://youtu.be/Fcgfthka4FI?t=1015.
6. I follow the translation of M. A. S. Abdul Haleem here, as it fits well with Qaradawi's understanding.
7. This story is not preserved in reliable sources. Early Muslim scholars did not generally concern themselves with the historicity of narrations that did not bear any

legal import. A version of the story is found in the writings of Wāqidī (d. 207/823). For a somewhat contentious discussion on its historic merit, see: http://www.ahlalhdeeth.com/vb/showthread.php?t=152596.

8. https://youtu.be/Fcgfthka4FI?t=1331.
9. 'A Tunisian Revolution that's More Bloody than Jasmine,' *Human Rights Watch*, 24 January 2011, https://www.hrw.org/news/2011/01/24/tunisian-revolution-thats-more-bloody-jasmine.
10. See David H. Warren, 'The *'Ulamā'* and the Arab Uprisings 2011-13: Considering Yusuf al-Qaradawi, the 'Global Mufti', between the Muslim Brotherhood, the Islamic Legal Tradition, and Qatari Foreign Policy,' *New Middle Eastern Studies*, 4 (2014), 17. Warren cites a sermon of Qaradawi's from March 2011: https://youtu.be/3tGJvhR0hYg (https://www.youtube.com/watch?v=3tGJvhR0hYg). For the role that anti-Shia sectarianism played in the crushing of the Bahraini revolution, see Toby Matthiesen, *Sectarian Gulf: Bahrain, Saudi Arabia, and the Arab Spring That Wasn't* (Stanford: Stanford University Press, 2013). Sectarianism has become a deeply embedded component of Middle Eastern politics in recent years. For an important recent collection of essays that explores this transformation, see: Nader Hashemi and Danny Postel (eds), *Sectarianization: Mapping the New Politics of the Middle East* (Oxford: Oxford University Press, 2017).
11. https://youtu.be/Fcgfthka4FI?t=1515.
12. https://youtu.be/Fcgfthka4FI?t=1593.
13. For a brief discussion of the statement's weak attribution to the Prophet, see: http://www.islamweb.net/ar/fatwa/18065.
14. https://youtu.be/Fcgfthka4FI?t=1734.
15. Ibid.
16. This is reported in the text *Nahj al-Balāgha*, which Sunnis do not generally view as a reliable source of reports from 'Alī b. Abī Ṭālib.
17. See: al-Bukhārī, *Ṣaḥīḥ al-Bukhārī*, ed. Muṣṭafā Dīb al-Bughā (Beirut: Dar Ibn Kathīr, 1987), 2:863. For a detailed *takhrīj*, see Aḥmad b. Ḥanbal, *Musnad al-Imām Aḥmad b. Ḥanbal* (Beirut: Mu'assasat al-Risāla, 1999), 19:14–16, n. 3.
18. For a brief consideration of Qaradawi's democratic ideas including a translation of his fatwa in support of democracy, see Roxanne Euben and M. Qasim Zaman (eds), *Princeton Readings in Islamist Thought: Texts and Contexts from al-Bannā to Bin Laden* (Princeton: Princeton University Press, 2009), 224ff.
19. See: al-Bukhārī, *Ṣaḥīḥ*, 4:1726.
20. For his comments made on Al Jazeera on 23 January 2011, see: https://youtu.be/Fcgfthka4FI?t=128. For his comments on the following day while sitting next to Shaykh al-Azhar Aḥmad al-Ṭayyib, see: https://youtu.be/OHqM0iPieN8 https://www.youtube.com/watch?v=OHqM0iPieN8.
21. https://youtu.be/0-zuqEwVFFk (https://www.youtube.com/watch?v=0-zuqEwVFFk).
22. 'al-Qaraḍāwī yuftī li-'anāṣir al-amn al-Miṣrī bi-taḥrīm al-i'tidā' 'alā al-mutaẓāhirīn,' *al-Shurūq*, 28 January 2011, https://www.echoroukonline.com/القرضاوي-يفتي-لعناصر-الأمن-المصري-بتح/.
23. https://youtu.be/0-zuqEwVFFk.

24. 'al-Qaraḍāwī yuftī li-'anāṣir al-amn al-Miṣrī bi-taḥrīm al-i'tidā' 'alā al-mutaẓāhirīn,' *al-Shurūq*, 28 January 2011, https://www.echoroukonline.com/القرضاوي-يفتي-لعناصر-الأمن-المصري-بتح/.
25. Ibid.
26. The photos may be viewed at this link: https://akukau-dia.blogspot.com/2011/01/blog-post.html.
27. The MB leadership's caution was hardly surprising. For decades they had operated within the restrictive legal framework of the Mubarak regime, and as an enormous organization that operated in the open, they had much to lose by engaging in openly subversive behavior. For a brief discussion of why they did not officially join the protests from the beginning, although many of the MB youth activists did, see David D. Kirkpatrick, *Into the Hands of the Soldiers: Freedom and Chaos in Egypt and the Middle East* (London: Bloomsbury, 2018), 30f, 346. For the post-coup consequences of operating in the open, see Steven Brooke, 'Egypt,' in Shadi Hamid and William McCants (eds), *Rethinking Political Islam* (Oxford: Oxford University Press, 2017).
28. https://youtu.be/336tK8gxjIk?t=83 (https://www.youtube.com/watch?v=336tK8gxjIk).
29. https://youtu.be/336tK8gxjIk?t=527.
30. 'Al-jaysh al-Miṣrī: lan nalja' li-istikhdām al-quwwa ḍidd al-sha'b al-Miṣrī,' *Reuters Arabic*, 31 January 2011, http://ara.reuters.com:80/article/idARACAE70U1B520110131. For a video from *Euro News Arabic*, see: https://youtu.be/hWbqmQQvs-A (https://www.youtube.com/watch?v=hWbqmQQvs-A).
31. See, for example, Kirkpatrick, *Into the Hands of the Soldiers*, 6f.
32. https://youtu.be/336tK8gxjIk?t=527.
33. https://youtu.be/336tK8gxjIk?t=769. This term and the way it has been deployed in modern Egypt in the twentieth century has been studied at length by Jeffrey T. Kenney. See his *Muslim Rebels: Kharijites and the Politics of Extremism in Egypt* (Oxford: Oxford University Press, 2006).
34. For a discussion of the diachronic transformations of the Sunni tradition in this regard, see Khaled Abou El Fadl, *Rebellion and Violence in Islamic Law* (Cambridge: Cambridge University Press, 2001).
35. See: Kenney, *Muslim Rebels*, 90.
36. Two hadiths which later Muslims would take as referring to the Khawārij are relevant here. One points out that they are devout but also akin to apostates. This hadith is found in the canonical collections of Bukhārī and Muslim. For a detailed *takhrīj*, see: Aḥmad b. Ḥanbal, *Musnad al-Imām Aḥmad b. Ḥanbal* (Beirut: Mu'assasat al-Risāla, 1999), 17:46–9. Another weaker version of the report points out that it is praiseworthy to kill them and be killed by them. See ibid., 2:430f.
37. For a discussion of this position, see Muhammad al-Yaqoubi, *Refuting ISIS*, 2nd edn. (London: Sacred Knowledge, 2017). The author also holds this position.
38. https://youtu.be/336tK8gxjIk?t=769.
39. https://youtu.be/336tK8gxjIk?t=902.
40. See: Kirkpatrick, *Into the Hands of the Soldiers*, 34.
41. https://youtu.be/336tK8gxjIk?t=924.

42. See Yūsuf al-Qaraḍāwī, *Min Hady al-Islām: Fatāwā Muʿāṣira* (Kuwait: Dār al-Qalam, 2009), 4:819ff. Qaradawi reproduces this fatwa in a 2012 publication on the Egyptian revolution. See: Yūsuf al-Qaraḍāwī, *25 Yanāyir Sanat 2011: Thawrat al-Shaʿb* (Cairo: Maktabat Wahba, n.d.), 15–25.
43. See Michael Cook, *Ancient Religions, Modern Politics: The Islamic Case in Comparative Perspective* (Princeton: Princeton University Press, 2014), 252. As Cook notes in a footnote, the hadith is found in *Ṣaḥīḥ Muslim*, which would usually make it authoritative for Sunnis.
44. This hadith is cited in his published fatwa from 2009. See: al-Qaraḍāwī, *Min Hady al-Islām*, 4:830. As he notes in a footnote, the source of the hadith is the non-canonical collection of Abū Nuʿaym al-Aṣbahānī (d. 430/1038). For a discussion of the weakness of this report, see: https://majles.alukah.net/t86731/.
45. https://youtu.be/wIhdO9XyEsc (https://www.youtube.com/watch?v=wIhdO9XyEsc).
46. https://youtu.be/336tK8gxjIk?t=1052.
47. This hadith is deemed authentic by Sunni hadith experts. See Ch. 1, n. 15.
48. This hadith is deemed authentic by some Sunni hadith experts. See Ch. 1, n. 20.
49. This hadith is deemed authentic by Sunni hadith experts. See Ch. 1, n. 23.
50. This hadith is of disputed authenticity. See Ch. 1, n. 21.
51. This hadith is deemed authentic by Sunni hadith experts. See Ch. 1, n. 48.
52. This hadith is deemed authentic by Sunni hadith experts. See Ch. 1, n. 29.
53. https://youtu.be/336tK8gxjIk?t=1131.
54. For a discussion of this tension within the Sunni hadith canon, see Jonathan A. C. Brown, *Hadith: Muhammad's Legacy in the Medieval and Modern World*, 2nd edn. (Oxford: Oneworld, 2017), 216–22.
55. In a later episode of the show in 2011, Qaradawi notes that he does not encourage military coups, as armies have a tendency to create new dictatorships as was the case with the Egyptian revolution of 1952. https://youtu.be/JPcwee-Y6lc?t=2462 (https://www.youtube.com/watch?v=JPcwee-Y6lc).
56. https://youtu.be/336tK8gxjIk?t=1391.
57. As we will see in Chapter 5, Gomaa will argue for the Islamic legitimacy of popular sovereignty when it serves the interests of the military coup in 2013.
58. https://youtu.be/336tK8gxjIk?t=1531.
59. For other scholars' arguments concerning the authenticity and meaning of this report, see Usaama al-Azami, 'Legitimizing Political Dissent: Islamist Salafi Discourses on Obedience and Rebellion after the Arab Revolutions,' in Masooda Bano (ed.), *Salafi Social and Political Movements: National and Transnational Contexts* (Edinburgh: Edinburgh University Press, 2021).
60. For a detailed study of the concept of martyrdom in the Islamic tradition, past and present, see: David Cook, *Martyrdom in Islam* (Cambridge: Cambridge University Press, 2007).
61. According to an official estimate, 846 people lost their lives in the course of the Egyptian revolution of early 2011. See: 'Government Fact-finding Mission Shows 846 Killed in Egypt Uprising,' *Haaretz*, 20 April 2011, https://www.haaretz.com/1.5001913.

62. This report is of disputed authenticity. See: al-Tirmidhī, *al-Jāmiʿ al-Kabīr (Sunan al-Tirmidhī)*, ed. Shuʿayb al-Arnaʾūṭ et al. (Beirut: Dār al-Risāla al-ʿĀlamiyya, 2009), 3:228, n. 1.
63. For two variants of this hadith, see Ibn Ḥanbal, *Musnad*, 2:56f., 128.
64. https://youtu.be/336tK8gxjIk?t=2361.
65. See Yūsuf al-Qaraḍāwī, *Ẓāhirat al-Ghuluww fī al-Takfīr*, 3rd edn. (Cairo: Maktabat Wahba, 1990). For an extensive treatment of the issue of *takfīr*, see: Camilla Adang, Hassan Ansari, Maribel Fierro, and Sabine Schmidtke (eds), *Accusations of Unbelief in Islam: A Diachronic Perspective on Takfīr* (Leiden: Brill, 2015).
66. See: Shadi Hamid, *Islamic Exceptionalism: How the Struggle Over Islam Is Reshaping the World* (New York: St. Martin's Press, 2016); Andrew F. March, *The Caliphate of Man: Popular Sovereignty in Modern Islamic Thought* (Cambridge: Harvard University Press, 2019).
67. March, *Caliphate*, 223.
68. See: Hamid, *Islamic Exceptionalism*, 257.
69. For more on this, see: Kirkpatrick, *Into the Hands of the Soldiers*; Dalia Fahmy and Daanish Faruqi (eds), *Egypt and the Contradictions of Liberalism: Illiberal Intelligentsia and the Future of Egyptian Democracy* (Oxford: Oneworld, 2017).
70. Uday Singh Mehta, *Liberalism and Empire: A Study in Nineteenth-Century British Liberal Thought* (Chicago: University of Chicago Press, 1999).
71. In a 2016 interview, Qaradawi diplomatically refers to this pressure and says that he chose to move away from his weekly show in order to preserve good relations between GCC states. See: https://youtu.be/7dMSK7YaNZg?t=406 (https://www.youtube.com/watch?v=7dMSK7YaNZg). He may not have actually had a choice in the matter.
72. See: Simeon Kerr, 'UAE clashes with Qatar over Brotherhood leader,' *Financial Times*, 2 Feb 2014, https://www.ft.com/content/551dd73e-8c2e-11e3-bcf2-00144feab7de.
73. For a study of his and other Islamists' democratic discourse, see Bruce Rutherford, *Egypt After Mubarak: Liberalism, Islam, and Democracy in the Arab World* (Princeton: Princeton University Press, 2008), 77–130.
74. This view was advocated in the early months of the Arab revolutions by a scholarly supporter of al-Qaraḍawi. See: Waṣfī ʿĀshūr Abū Zayd, *al-Qaraḍāwī: al-Imām al-Thāʾir: Dirāsa Taḥlīliyya Uṣūliyya fī Maʿālim Ijtihādihī li-l-Thawra al-Miṣriyya*, 2nd edn. (Cairo: Dār al-Maqāṣid, 2017).

3 ALI GOMAA, AḤMAD AL-ṬAYYIB, AND ALI AL-JIFRI: THE EARLY OPPOSITION TO THE EGYPTIAN REVOLUTION

1. 'Al-jaysh al-Miṣrī: lan nalja' li-istikhdām al-quwwa ḍidd al-shaʿb al-Miṣrī,' *Reuters Arabic*, 31 January 2011, http://ara.reuters.com:80/article/idARACAE70U1B520110131.
2. See: 'Shaykh al-Azhar: al-Maṭālib al-ʿĀdila lā Tubarrir al-Fawḍā,' *Islam al-Yawm*, 31 January 2011, http://islamtoday.net/albasheer/artshow-12-145381.htm. For a more hostile article, see: 'Shaykh al-Azhar Yadʿam al-Istibdād wa-Yuʿlin

Walā'ahu li-Mubārak,' *Djazairess*, 31 January 2011, https://www.djazairess.com/akhbarelyoum/18852. The difficulty of locating an original version of the statement suggests that the Azhar may have issued a press release that resembled the first article cited above, rather than simply being a statement articulating its position.

3. 'ElBaradei: No reverse in Egypt,' *Al Jazeera English*, 31 January 2011, https://www.aljazeera.com/news/middleeast/2011/01/2011130165636218719.html.
4. 'Death toll in Egypt's protests tops 100—sources,' *Reuters*, 29 January 2011, https://www.reuters.com/article/egypt-dead-idAFLDE70S0LX20110129.
5. 'Government Fact-finding Mission Shows 846 Killed in Egypt Uprising,' *Haaretz*, 20 April 2011, https://www.haaretz.com/1.5001913.
6. 'Shaykh al-Azhar: al-Maṭālib al-'Ādila lā Tubarrir al-Fawḍā,' *Islām al-Yawm*, 31 January 2011, http://islamtoday.net/albasheer/artshow-12-145381.htm.
7. Nadia Abou el Magd, 'Mubarak appoints a new chief of Al Azhar,' *The National*, 21 March 2010, http://www.thenational.ae/news/world/africa/mubarak-appoints-a-new-chief-of-al-azhar.
8. Diana Maher Ghali Katharina Natter, 'Mubarak accepts Azhar Sheikh's resignation from NDP,' *Masress*, 12 April 2010, https://www.masress.com/en/dailynews/64496.
9. See: Martin Asser, 'Egyptian media: State misinformation amid the protests?,' *BBC News*, 4 February 2011, https://www.bbc.co.uk/news/world-middle-east-12369422; 'Egyptian 'Battle of the Camels' officials acquitted,' *BBC News*, 10 October 2012, http://www.bbc.co.uk:80/news/world-middle-east-19905435. It seems entirely incidental that this is the name of a significant battle in early Islamic history in the year 36/656.
10. 'Five dead as shots fired during Cairo clashes,' *Radio New Zealand*, 3 February 2011, https://www.rnz.co.nz/news/world/67633/five-dead-as-shots-fired-during-cairo-clashes.
11. For the statement as preserved on a chat forum online, see: https://oyon.ahladalil.com/t2591-topic.
12. Ibid.
13. https://youtu.be/VcbQfHkK5ac (https://www.youtube.com/watch?v=VcbQfHkK5ac).
14. The earliest references to this statement are from 4 February, but most news organizations reported the story on 6 or 7 February. See: 'Shaykh al-Azhar Yuḥadhdhir min al-La'ib bi-'Awāṭif al-Jamāhīr 'abra al-Fatāwā al-Dīniyya,' *Mawqi' Baldat Barjā*, 4 February 2011, https://www.ebarja.com/?p=1697; 'al-Azhar yudīn al-Siyāsāt al-Īrāniyya wa-l-Taṣrīḥāt al-Ūrubbiyya wa-l-Amrīkiyya allatī Tatadakhkhal fī al-Sha'n al-miṣrī, *Masress*, 6 February 2011, https://www.masress.com/ahram/61602; 'al-Azhar Yudīn al-Siyāsāt al-Īrāniyya: Khurūj Sāfir 'alā al-Qur'ān wa-l-Sunna,' *al-Ittiḥād*, 6 February 2011, https://www.alittihad.ae/article/13141/2011/الأزهر-يدين-السياسات-الإيرانية-خروج-سافر-على-القرآن-والسنة; 'al-Azhar yantaqid fatāwā tad'am al-iḥtijājāt,' *Al Jazeera Arabic*, 7 February 2011, https://www.aljazeera.net/news/arabic/2011/2/7/الأزهر-ينتقد-فتاوى-تدعم-الاحتجاجات.
15. The roughly four-minute continuous clip is available here, uploaded by a third party: https://youtu.be/3V0p9AqrlM4 (https://www.youtube.com/watch?v=3V0p9AqrlM4). Although it is undated and was uploaded in June of 2013,

Ṭayyib's remarks make clear that he made his statement on 11th February, the day after Mubarak had transferred his powers to his deputy, Omar Suleiman. Ṭayyib's recorded statement was aired live from 1:18 to 1:22 pm local time according to the on-screen clock. Mubarak's resignation occurred at 6 pm.

16. For the crowd's response, see Marc Lynch, *The Arab Uprising: The Unfinished Revolutions of the New Middle East* (New York: Public Affairs, 2012), 1; Anthony Shadid and David D. Kirkpatrick, 'Mubarak Refuses to Step Down, Stoking Revolt's Fury and Resolve,' *New York Times*, 10 February 2011, https://www.nytimes.com/2011/02/11/world/middleeast/11egypt.html.
17. Ṭayyib further claims in this statement that he was perhaps the first to say that the youths who had died were martyrs (*shuhadā'*). This seems unlikely given that Qaradawi referred to protestors who had been killed as martyrs in an interview he gave on 27 January as noted in the last chapter.
18. An apparent reference to his earlier pronouncements to the same effect, as noted above.
19. https://youtu.be/-bFg3MfyPuI (https://www.youtube.com/watch?v=-bFg3MfyPuI).
20. To see a detailed *takhrīj* of the canonical hadith to which Ṭayyib is referring, and which is deemed authentic by Sunni scholars, see: Aḥmad b. Ḥanbal, *Musnad al-Imām Aḥmad b. Ḥanbal* (Beirut: Mu'assasat al-Risāla, 1999), 38:316–9.
21. For a hadith to this effect, which is deemed authentic by Sunni scholars, see: Ibn Ḥanbal, *Musnad*, 30:303–5.
22. Qaradawi has long critiqued the expression 'political Islam' as a secularizing tautology. See, for example, Yūsuf al-Qaraḍāwī, *Min Fiqh al-Dawla fī al-Islām*, 3rd edn. (Cairo: Dār al-Shurūq, 2001), 88–100.
23. For Qaradawi's influence on Islam in Qatar over the decades, see: David H. Warren, 'Qatari Support for the Muslim Brotherhood is More Than Just Realpolitik, it has a Long, Personal History,' *Maydan*, 12 July 2017, https://themaydan.com/2017/07/qatari-support-muslim-brotherhood-just-realpolitik-long-personal-history/.
24. See: Robert F. Worth and David D. Kirkpatrick, 'Seizing a Moment, Al Jazeera Galvinizes Arab Frustration,' *The New York Times*, 28 January 2011, https://www.nytimes.com/2011/01/28/world/middleeast/28jazeera.html.
25. For the generally scant coverage of the Bahraini revolution, see: Andrew Hammond, 'Gulf media find their red line in uprisings: Bahrain,' *Reuters*, 14 April 2011, https://www.reuters.com/article/oukwd-uk-mideast-protests-media-idAFTRE73D1HB20110414. On its English documentary and coverage of the Bahraini revolution, see: 'Al Jazeera English named channel of the year,' *Al Jazeera English Website*, 23 February 2012, https://www.aljazeera.com/news/europe/2012/02/201222335857553595.html.
26. For the relevant clip uploaded by a third party, see: https://youtu.be/BThSZ-MC-vE (https://www.youtube.com/watch?v=BThSZ-MC-vE). For the full program, see: 'Barnāmaj fī al-Ṣamīm ma'a al-Shaykh al-Qaraḍāwī,' YouTube.com (originally aired by BBC Arabic in February 2009), available at: https://youtu.be/sNfgV55olrE (https://www.youtube.com/watch?v=sNfgV55olrE). See Ch. 3, n. 72 below for references to other examples.

27. For a critical interview of the then Qatari Foreign Minister by Al Jazeera's Mehdi Hasan in 2015, see: https://youtu.be/x9vDs3PVeCE (https://www.youtube.com/watch?v=x9vDs3PVeCE). For another example, see: 'Al-Jazeera TV in Rare Criticism of Qatar: Our Freedom of Expression Is in Fact Freedom to Normalize Relations with Israel,' *MEMRI TV*, 26 October 2018, https://www.memri.org/tv/jazeera-rare-criticism-of-qatar-freedom-to-normalize-relations-with-israel.
28. Of course, Herman and Chomsky have argued that corporate media institutions that dominate Western democracies face constraints of their own that inveigh against notions of a genuinely free press. See Edward S. Herman and Noam Chomsky, *Manufacturing Consent: The Political Economy of the Mass Media* (New York: Pantheon Books, 1988).
29. ONtv, an Egyptian channel with a regime-loyalist stance, published part of this statement on its YouTube channel on 16 February 2011. See: 'Baladunā: al-Azhar: al-Sharʿ yarḍā ʿan al-ḥukm alladhī yarḍāhū al-nās,' https://youtu.be/t9xRQad4Wuc (https://www.youtube.com/watch?v=t9xRQad4Wuc). Assuming it was published on the same day as the clip was broadcast, the statement is from the same day, as noted by the presenter. For a news article on the press conference, which also does not give a date for the event but is published on 16 February, see: Lu'ayy ʿAlī, 'Shaykh al-Azhar fī Mu'tamar Ṣaḥafī: Mawqiʿunā min Thawrat 25 Yanāyir Wāḍiḥlā Labsa fīh wa-Narfuḍal-Muzāyada ʿalayhi wa-lam wa-lan Natamallaq ayy Niẓ ām Ḥākim wa-Nuṭālib bi-Qawānīn Ṣārima Tujarrim al-Taʿdhīb,' *al-Yawm al-Sābiʿ*, 16 February 2011, https://www.youm7.com/story/2011/2/16/شيخ-الأزهر-فى-مؤتمر-صحفى-موقفنا-من-ثورة-52-يناير/248253. A full video recording of this statement has been uploaded by a third party here: https://youtu.be/VcbQfHkK5ac (https://www.youtube.com/watch?v=VcbQfHkK5ac).
30. https://youtu.be/VcbQfHkK5ac.
31. https://youtu.be/VcbQfHkK5ac?t=119.
32. https://youtu.be/VcbQfHkK5ac?t=168.
33. https://youtu.be/VcbQfHkK5ac?t=284.
34. https://youtu.be/VcbQfHkK5ac?t=407.
35. See https://youtu.be/7leQws-tEB0. As the video speaks of Mubarak's concessions from his 1 February speech that was made at 11 pm local time, this video, which is time stamped 8:39 pm, and was uploaded to YouTube on 2 February, can only have been broadcast on the same day it was uploaded. The live blog on Al Jazeera English refers to it at 4:36 pm on 2 February, and so the YouTube clip represents a replay of it on the same day.
36. The hadith is deemed extremely weak in its attribution to the Prophet by Sunni hadith experts. For a discussion, see: https://www.ahlalhdeeth.com/vb/showthread.php?t=19297.
37. This hadith is also deemed weakly attributed to the Prophet by Sunni hadith experts, though this does not necessitate that its meaning is contrary to Islamic teachings. For a brief discussion, see the conclusion of this fatwa: https://www.islamweb.net/ar/fatwa/331309. For a brief commentary on the hadith, see: Shams al-Ḥaqq al-ʿAẓīmābādī, *ʿAwn al-Maʿbūd Sharḥ Sunan Abī Dāwūd*, ed. ʿAbd al-Raḥmān M. ʿUthmān (Medina: Muḥammad ʿAbd al-Muḥsin, 1969), 11:346. For a *takhrīj*, see

Abū Dāwūd, *Sunan Abī Dāwūd*, ed. Shuʿayb al-Arnaʾūṭ et al. (Beirut: Dār al-Risāla al-ʿĀlamiyya, 2009), 6:321–3.

38. See https://youtu.be/7leQws-tEB0 (https://www.youtube.com/watch?v=7leQws-tEB0&gl=US&hl=en).
39. See: https://youtu.be/OZZE7PlWYyI (https://www.youtube.com/watch?v=OZZE7PlWYyI). A version of this video was uploaded on 3 February 2011, and refers to Qaradawi's statement, apparently published in numerous newspapers in Egypt and elsewhere on 2 February 2011, calling on the Egyptian people to come out in their millions in support of the revolution. This long statement can be found in Yūsuf al-Qaraḍāwī, *25 Yanāyir Sanat 2011: Thawrat al-Shaʿb* (Cairo: Maktabat Wahba, n.d.), 43–8. The pagination is according to the version of the text found on Qaradawi's website. For Qaradawi's call for millions of Egyptians to march in peaceful protest on Friday 4 February 2011, see p. 46.
40. As noted earlier, some observers considered the creation of a security vacuum to be a deliberate tactic used by the Mubarak regime. For a BBC Arabic report on this from the period, see: https://youtu.be/SMdYKY2KHSg (https://www.youtube.com/watch?v=SMdYKY2KHSg).
41. Armbrust, *Martyrs and Tricksters*, 184; Kirkpatrick, *Into the Hands*, 263–5, 290f., 316f. and passim.
42. A BBC Arabic report from this period describes the protests at Tahrir Square as containing hundreds of thousands of protestors, while crowds in Mustafa Mahmud Square as comprising roughly 2,000 people. See: https://www.bbc.com/arabic/middleeast/2011/02/110204_tahrir_moreprotest.shtml. Similarly, *The New York Times* described protests at Muṣṭafā Maḥmūd Square as a 'small gathering' contrasting it with the 'large demonstrations in Tahrir Square.' See Robert Mackey, 'Updates on Day 11 of Egypt Protests,' *The New York Times*, 4 February 2011, https://thelede.blogs.nytimes.com/2011/02/04/latest-updates-on-day-11-of-egypt-protests/.
43. https://youtu.be/OZZE7PlWYyI?t=162.
44. https://youtu.be/ylJcq2lYKsY?t=641 (https://www.youtube.com/watch?v=ylJcq2lYKsY).
45. Ibid.
46. https://youtu.be/ylJcq2lYKsY?t=560.
47. David D. Kirkpatrick and Kareem Fahim, 'Mubarak Allies and Foes Clash in Egypt,' *The New York Times*, 3 February 2011, https://www.nytimes.com/2011/02/03/world/middleeast/03egypt.html.
48. Kirkpatrick, *Into the Hands*, 49.
49. https://youtu.be/OZZE7PlWYyI.
50. It was uploaded by a hostile third party on 21 October 2011 and does not appear to have been modified from the original: https://youtu.be/HiCG2Ra_b4Y (https://www.youtube.com/watch?v=HiCG2Ra_b4Y).
51. This is clear from the discussion that follows Gomaa's comments: http://youtu.be/HiCG2Ra_b4Y?t=6m7s.
52. A BBC Arabic report from the early hours of 5 February 2011 makes a reference to clashes in the locations of Shubrā and al-Muhandisīn in Cairo, and the recording

of Gomaa's interview appears to show live feeds from these two locations alongside Tahrir Square. This suggests that it is possible Gomaa was interviewed on 4 or 5 February.

53. A similarly worded hadith is found in Ibn Ḥanbal, *Musnad*, 28:569–71. The editors deem it sound (*ḥasan*).
54. Gomaa paraphrases the hadith which is considered to be sound (*ḥasan*) by contemporary Sunnis. A version of it is found in al-Tirmidhī, *al-Jāmiʿ al-Kabīr*, 4:371f.
55. https://youtu.be/HiCG2Ra_b4Y.
56. This was an oblique reference to a weak hadith he mentioned earlier. See Ch. 3, n. 37.
57. In addition to remarks made in later chapters, I briefly discuss what might make such a stance meaningful to pro-autocracy scholars in Usaama al-Azami, 'Neo-traditionalist Sufis and Arab Politics: A Preliminary Mapping of the Transnational Networks of Counter-revolutionary Scholars after the Arab Revolutions,' in Mark Sedgwick and Francesco Piraino (eds), *Global Sufism: Boundaries, Structures, and Politics* (London: Hurst Publishers, 2019).
58. For a study of Jifri's Sufi affiliation and preaching, see Besnik Sinani, 'In the Path of the Ancestors: The Bā ʿAlawī Sufi Order and the Struggle for Shaping the Future of Islam,' also in Sedgwick and Piraino (eds), *Global Sufism*.
59. See: https://www.tabahfoundation.org/en/about/senior-scholars-council/.
60. The five scholars who make up the council are, in the order that they are listed: Muḥammad Saʿīd Ramaḍān al-Būṭī, Abdallah bin Bayyah, Nūḥ ʿAlī al-Quḍāh (d. 1432/2010), Ali Gomaa, and ʿUmar b. al-Ḥafīẓ (b. 1383/1963). Despite the deaths of two of the five scholars, they continue to be listed on the website.
61. Despite his relative youth, in late 2017, Jifri had by far the largest following on Facebook (roughly 6.2 million followers) and Twitter (roughly 5.1 million followers) of the scholars we are considering.
62. See ʿAbd al-Raḥmān al-Jifrī (b. 1943) in Charles Schmitz and Robert D. Burrowes, *Historical Dictionary of Yemen*, 3rd edn. (Lanham, Maryland: Rowman & Littlefield, 2018), 268f.
63. See: https://youtu.be/Hg3x0A451tQ (https://www.youtube.com/watch?v=Hg3x0A451tQ). This is the full version of his phone call into the show of Khayrī Ramaḍān, *Miṣr al-Nahārda*. Jifri's phone call and concluding prayer took up the last fifteen minutes of the show, after which it promptly ended. These videos have been uploaded by multiple third parties on 10 February 2011, and by some thereafter. That it was aired on this day is strongly suggested by a message on an online discussion forum, posted on 10 February, in which the forum member states that it was aired on the day of posting. See: https://www.dawshagya.org/vb/dawshagya117622/. A slightly clearer version of the phone call, albeit a slightly shorter one, is available here: https://youtu.be/4-s1uiy_fYE (https://www.youtube.com/watch?v=4-s1uiy_fYE).
64. *Ghawghāʾī* could mean 'rabble-rousing,' but also 'consisting of rabble and riffraff.'
65. See: http://www.globalsecurity.org/military/facility/udeid.htm for the Al Udeid Base and https://www.globalsecurity.org/military/facility/camp-as-sayliyah.htm for the As Sayliyah Base.

66. On this, see: https://247wallst.com/special-report/2019/04/08/americas-largest-military-bases-around-the-world/. See also the US Department of Defense's 'Base Structure Report - Fiscal Year 2017 Baseline,' available here: https://www.acq.osd.mil/eie/Downloads/BSI/Base%20Structure%20Report%20FY17.pdf.
67. For a regional view of US bases, including the various bases in the UAE, see the map here: https://www.google.com/maps/d/u/0/viewer?mid=zQVqvB9UmUTc.kCl6RXZmRmIs&usp=sharing. See also: Ben Piven 'Map: US bases encircle Iran,' *Al Jazeera English*, 1 May 2012, https://www.aljazeera.com/indepth/interactive/2012/04/2012417131242767298.html.
68. I have translated *ba'ḍ al-shuyūkh* here as 'a certain scholar' rather than 'certain scholars,' following a more classical usage, since it is obvious from the context that he is referring to Qaradawi.
69. This was aired by BBC Arabic on 8 February 2010, almost exactly a year before Jifri made his comments, on the program *Fi al-Ṣamīm* (*Fiassameem*) with host Ḥasan Mu'awwaḍ (Muawad). A full version of the program has been uploaded by a third party here: https://youtu.be/ZQJeV0DYGQY (https://www.youtube.com/watch?v=ZQJeV0DYGQY). BBC Arabic's official page does not include this video in its uploads. The clip we are concerned with was uploaded to YouTube by a third-party on 15 February 2010, a week after the original aired, and is available here: https://youtu.be/BThSZ-MC-vE.
70. For information on Peres' visit, see Jim Krane, 'Israeli Deputy PM Visits Qatar,' *The Washington Post*, 29 January 2007, http://www.washingtonpost.com/wp-dyn/content/article/2007/01/29/AR2007012901473_pf.html.
71. This is based on a hadith that is found in many of the canonical collections and is deemed authentic by Sunnis. For a detailed *takhrīj*, see Ibn Ḥanbal, *Musnad*, 12:300f.
72. See Courtney Freer, *Rentier Islamism: The Influence of the Muslim Brotherhood in Gulf Monarchies* (Oxford University Press, 2018), 94. She is drawing on Bernard Haykel's assessment, who she cites as asserting that Qaradawi has 'never commented on domestic Qatari politics.' In addition to the foregoing example, one may also cite Qaradawi's criticism in a Friday sermon of the apparently widespread celebration of Christmas in Qatar by Muslims in December 2009. This may reasonably be construed as criticism of the Qatari government. For a report on the sermon, see: 'Iḥtifāl al-Muslimīn bi-A'yād Krīsmās Ḥarām,' *Sunni Online*, 12 December 2009, http://sunnionline.us/arabic/2009/12/467/. For a clip of the criticism, see: https://youtu.be/l7D3pCoCb9I (https://www.youtube.com/watch?v=l7D3pCoCb9I).
73. The IUMS' Arabic name, *al-Ittiḥād al-'Ālamī li-'Ulamā' al-Muslimīn*, is more accurately translated as 'The Global Union for the Scholars of the Muslims.' Qaradawi, as its leader until 2018, was in many respects operating as a spokesperson for the scholars of the umma. In his writings, Qaradawi has spoken of his seeking to guide the Muslim umma as a whole. See Motaz al-Khateeb, 'Yūsuf al-Qaraḍāwī as a Marji'iyya' in Bettina Gräf and Jakob Skovgaard-Petersen (eds), *The Global Mufti: The Phenomenon of Yusuf al-Qaradawi* (London: Hurst Publishers, 2009), esp. 92.
74. As Amnesty International notes of the 2011 uprisings, '[m]ost of the protests were peaceful, yet the authorities' response was not.' Their report from May 2011

'describes [...] the patterns of repression by security forces.' See: 'Egypt rises: Killings, detentions and torture in the '25 January Revolution'', *Amnesty International*, 19 May 2011, https://www.amnesty.org/en/documents/MDE12/027/2011/en/.

4 HAMZA YUSUF AND ABDALLAH BIN BAYYAH: FROM SUPPORT TO OPPOSITION

1. What I refer to as Neo-traditionalism is referred to by Yusuf as 'traditional Islam.'
2. Hamza Yusuf, 'Deferred Dreams, Self-Destruction, and Suicide Bombings,' *Sandala.org*, 29 January 2011, https://sandala.org/deferred-dreams-self-destruction-and-suicide-bombings/.
3. For one such example, see a discussion of his from 2016 where he refers to his family's active involvement in the civil rights movement: https://youtu.be/4oqlvuQqET8 (https://www.youtube.com/watch?v=4oqlvuQqET8). Cited by Azad Essa, 'Hamza Yusuf and the struggle for the soul of western Islam,' *Middle East Eye*, 8 August 2019, https://www.middleeasteye.net/big-story/hamza-yusuf-and-struggle-soul-western-islam.
4. Yusuf, 'Deferred Dreams.'
5. Yusuf, 'When the Social Contract is Breached.'
6. Ibid.
7. See, for example, Yūsuf al-Qaraḍāwī. *Min Fiqh al-Dawla fī al-Islām*, 3rd edn. (Cairo: Dār al-Shurūq, 2001), 132.
8. Yusuf, 'When the Social Contract is Breached' (emphasis added).
9. For an audio recording of this conversation, see: https://clyp.it/0kxuerpl. The discussion of racism begins around the fifteen minute mark. For a thoughtful reflection on the controversy that ensued from Yusuf's comments about the Black Lives Matter movement in December 2016, see Ubaydullah Evans and Junaid Rana, "Make a Way Out of No Way': An Interview with Ustadh Ubaydullah Evans on the Islamic Tradition and Social Justice Activism,' in Sohail Daulatzai and Junaid Rana (eds), *With Stones in Our Hands: Writings on Muslims, Racism, and Empire* (Minneapolis: University of Minnesota Press, 2018), 354–64.
10. For these remarks by the black Canadian poet, Boonaa Mohammed, see: https://www.facebook.com/BoonaaMohammed/videos/10154883756469583.
11. On the point of rebellion, for a broader Islamic historical perspective on Yusuf's claims see: Usaama al-Azami, 'Shaykh Hamza Yusuf and the Question of Rebellion in the Islamic Tradition,' *MuslimMatters*, 15 September 2019, https://muslimmatters.org/2019/09/15/shaykh-hamza-yusuf-and-the-question-of-rebellion-in-the-islamic-tradition/.
12. 'World Press Freedom Index 2011/2012,' *Reporters without Borders*, https://rsf.org/en/world-press-freedom-index-20112012; and specifically on Egypt: https://rsf.org/en/egypt.
13. Hamza Yusuf, 'On Libya,' 12 March 2011, *Sandala.org*, https://sandala.org/on-libya/.
14. Mark Mazzetti, 'Year Before Killing, Saudi Prince Told Aide He Would Use 'a Bullet' on Jamal Khashoggi,' *The New York Times*, 7 February 2019, https://www.nytimes.com/2019/02/07/us/politics/khashoggi-mohammed-bin-salman.html.

15. Julian E. Barnes, 'C.I.A. Concludes That Saudi Crown Prince Ordered Khashoggi Killed,' *The New York Times*, 16 November 2018, https://www.nytimes.com/2018/11/16/us/politics/cia-saudi-crown-prince-khashoggi.html. For Dakhīl's piece in defense of the Saudi crown prince, see: Turki Aldakhil, 'US sanctions on Riyadh would mean Washington is stabbing itself,' *Al Arabiya*, 14 October 2018, http://english.alarabiya.net/en/views/news/middle-east/2018/10/14/OPINION-US-sanctions-on-Riyadh-means-Washington-is-stabbing-itself.html.
16. David D. Kirkpatrick, 'The Most Powerful Arab Ruler Isn't M.B.S. It's M.B.Z.,' *The New York Times*, 2 June 2019, https://www.nytimes.com/2019/06/02/world/middleeast/crown-prince-mohammed-bin-zayed.html.
17. Habib Toumi, 'Al Dakheel appointed Saudi ambassador to UAE,' *Gulf News*, 10 February 2019, https://gulfnews.com/world/gulf/saudi/al-dakheel-appointed-saudi-ambassador-to-uae-1.61986944.
18. Peter Feuilherade 'Al-Jazeera competitor launches,' *BBC News*, 20 February 2003, http://news.bbc.co.uk/2/hi/middle_east/2780985.stm.
19. https://youtu.be/WhV791UyT0o?t=961 (https://www.youtube.com/watch?v=WhV791UyT0o).
20. https://youtu.be/WhV791UyT0o?t=1139.
21. This translation is taken, with only slight modifications, from Yahya Michot's translation of the sermon. For the original see: Yahya Michot, 'The Tahrir Square Sermon of Shaykh Yûsuf al-Qaradâwî,' 15 March 2011, http://www.islamophobiawatch.co.uk/wp-content/uploads/Qaradawi-Tahrir-Square.pdf. Michot has also translated Qaradawi's more controversial and quite exceptional fatwa stated live on air on 21 February 2011 in which he legitimated the killing of Gaddafi, which Michot defends the legitimacy of in the introduction to the translation. See: https://www.scribd.com/document/51219918/The-fatwa-of-Shaykh-Yusuf-al-Qaradawi-against-Gaddafi. For a discussion of the controversy around it, see: David H. Warren, 'The *'Ulamā'* and the Arab Uprisings 2011–13: Considering Yusuf al-Qaradawi, the 'Global Mufti', between the Muslim Brotherhood, the Islamic Legal Tradition, and Qatari Foreign Policy,' *New Middle Eastern Studies*, 4 (2014), esp. 15f.
22. Although I use a gender-neutral pronoun, it is worth bearing in mind that the rulers are almost always male in the context in which we speak.
23. I draw on the citation of this hadith by Ovamir Anjum on Facebook which I thank Omar Anchassi for directing my attention to.
24. Muḥammad b. Nāṣir al-Dar'ī, *The Prayer of the Oppressed*, ed. Hamza Yusuf (Sandala Productions, 2010), 3.
25. Al-Dar'ī, *Prayer of the Oppressed*, 3.
26. I am excluding constitutional monarchies in which the monarch is a ceremonial position, such as the UK or Denmark.
27. In fact, the Moroccan king's concessions were slight. See Michael Willis, 'Evolution not Revolution? Morocco and the Arab Spring,' in Larbi Sadiki (ed.), *Routledge Handbook of the Arab Spring: Rethinking Democratization* (London: Routledge, 2015).
28. Al-Dar'ī, *Prayer of the Oppressed*, 17.
29. Ibid., 24.

30. Ibid., 27.
31. Ibid., 29.
32. https://youtu.be/hXVpuEDqkzE (https://www.youtube.com/watch?v=hXVpuEDqkzE).
33. https://youtu.be/2nc-4BNSUJs (https://www.youtube.com/watch?v=2nc-4BNSUJs).
34. https://youtu.be/vUpP--Th44o (https://www.youtube.com/watch?v=vUpP--Th44o). For the other lectures, see: https://youtu.be/QwnJMxFXfFM (https://www.youtube.com/watch?v=QwnJMxFXfFM) and https://youtu.be/Bth_mJnIAtY (https://www.youtube.com/watch?v=Bth_mJnIAtY).
35. The clip containing Bin Bayyah's interview was uploaded to his personal YouTube page on 28 October 2011. See: https://youtu.be/9Mba1RLzaWU (https://www.youtube.com/watch?v=9Mba1RLzaWU). The full original ninety-minute show was uploaded to CBC's official YouTube channel six days earlier on 22 October 2011. See: https://youtu.be/RZ6HXXrRYVQ (https://www.youtube.com/watch?v=RZ6HXXrRYVQ).
36. https://youtu.be/9Mba1RLzaWU?t=534.
37. https://youtu.be/9Mba1RLzaWU?t=673.
38. On Gomaa's position, which he would actually articulate two years later in 2013, see Chapter 7.
39. https://youtu.be/9Mba1RLzaWU?t=730.
40. https://youtu.be/9Mba1RLzaWU?t=748.
41. https://youtu.be/9Mba1RLzaWU?t=877.
42. https://youtu.be/9Mba1RLzaWU?t=930.
43. https://youtu.be/9Mba1RLzaWU?t=1039.
44. https://youtu.be/vD3GRY72zrs?t=688 (https://www.youtube.com/watch?v=vD3GRY72zrs).
45. https://youtu.be/vD3GRY72zrs?t=932.
46. https://youtu.be/2C9mPoaik6g?t=2195 (https://www.youtube.com/watch?v=2C9mPoaik6g).
47. https://youtu.be/vD3GRY72zrs?t=815.
48. https://youtu.be/ZbgHsmer8S8?t=2539 (https://www.youtube.com/watch?v=ZbgHsmer8S8).
49. See, for example, Abdullāh b. Bayya, *al-Irhāb: Tashkhīṣ wa-Ḥulūl* (Riyadh: al-'Ubaykān, 2007), 62.
50. https://youtu.be/LXt7FzX7LLo?t=3621 (https://www.youtube.com/watch?v=LXt7FzX7LLo).
51. https://youtu.be/LXt7FzX7LLo?t=4342.
52. https://twitter.com/ABZayed/status/305368708728098816. On the concept of the *mujaddid*, see: Donzel, E. van, 'Mudjaddid', in: *Encyclopaedia of Islam, Second Edition* (eds) Peri Bearman et al. (Leiden: Brill, 1960–2007).
53. http://binbayyah.net/arabic/archives/1412. I have discussed Bin Bayyah's relationship with the UAE in greater detail in Usaama al-Azami, "Abdullāh bin Bayyah and the Arab Revolutions: Counter-revolutionary Neo-traditionalism's Ideological Struggle against Islamism,' *The Muslim World*, 109:3 (2019), 343–61.

54. This is widely recognized in the secondary scholarship. See, for example, Andrew March, *The Caliphate of Man: Popular Sovereignty in Modern Islamic Thought* (Cambridge, MA: Harvard University Press, 2019), esp. 18–22; Wael Hallaq, *The Impossible State: Islam, Politics, and Modernity's Moral Predicament* (New York: Columbia University Press, 2013), esp. 37–73. Noah Feldman, *The Fall and Rise of the Islamic State* (Princeton: Princeton University Press, 2008), 54f. Khaled Abou El Fadl, 'The Centrality of Sharīʿah to Government and Constitutionalism in Islam,' in Rainer Grote and Tilmann Röder (eds), *Constitutionalism in Islamic Countries: Between Upheaval and Continuity* (New York: Oxford University Press, 2012); Sherman Jackson, *Islamic Law and the State: The Constitutional Jurisprudence of Shihāb al-Dīn al-Qarāfī* (Leiden: Brill, 1996).
55. Abdallah bin Bayyah et al., *In Pursuit of Peace: Framework Speech for the Forum for Promoting Peace in Muslim Societies* (Abu Dhabi: FPPMS, 2014), 22.
56. In this connection, it is also worth highlighting that Bin Bayyah was systematizing and rationalizing a state of affairs that had been normative for many of the official jurists in the region for some time. As Malika Zeghal illustrates through a consideration of the contrasting responses of Qaradawi and the then Egyptian Grand Mufti Muḥammad Sayyid Ṭanṭāwī (d. 1431/2010) to the French headscarf controversy of 2003, the latter justified the state's legal prerogatives unconditionally, while Qaradawi sought to contest them using all legal means available. See: Malika Zeghal, 'The 'Recentering' of Religious Knowledge and Discourse: The Case of al-Azhar in Twentieth-Century Egypt,' in Robert W. Hefner and Muhammad Qasim Zaman, *Schooling Islam: The Culture and Politics of Modern Muslim Education* (Princeton: Princeton University Press, 2007), 107–30.

5 ALI GOMAA AND THE COUNTER-REVOLUTIONARY MASSACRES

1. Masooda Bano, 'At the Tipping Point? Al-Azhar's Growing Crisis of Moral Authority,' *International Journal of Middle East Studies* 50:4 (2018), 715; idem., 'Protector of the 'al-Wasatiyya' Islam: Cairo's al-Azhar University' in Masooda Bano and Keiko Sakurai (eds), *Shaping Global Islamic Discourses: The Role of Al-Azhar, Al-Madinah and Al-Mustafa* (Edinburgh: Edinburgh University Press, 2015), 87.
2. H. A. Hellyer, 'The Battle for al-Azhar,' *Foreign Policy*, 2 August 2012, https://foreignpolicy.com/2012/08/02/the-battle-for-al-azhar/.
3. Lu'ayy 'Alī, 'al-Mahdī yarudd ʿalā al-muftī: hādhā ijtihādunā wa-lā nalūmuka ʿalā ijtihādika li-Shafīq,' *al-Yawm al-Sābiʿ*, https://www.youm7.com/story/2012/6/8/208996/المهدى-يرد-على-المفتى-هذا-اجتهادنا-ولا-نلومك-على-اجتهادك.
4. https://youtu.be/Zb24X0TYmSo (https://www.youtube.com/watch?v=Zb24X0TYmSo). I have called this YouTube channel semi-official as it is not Gomaa's main YouTube channel, but rather is associated with an organization that publishes his books. It appears to have stopped uploading videos some years ago after Gomaa's official channel came of its own. The semi-official channel may be viewed here: https://www.youtube.com/user/sheikhaligomaa. Gomaa's official channel may be viewed here: https://www.youtube.com/user/DrAliGomaa.

5. https://youtu.be/w_Qhbt8Dg1I (https://www.youtube.com/watch?v=w_Qhbt8Dg1I), https://youtu.be/qZS20BztqXQ (https://www.youtube.com/watch?v=qZS20BztqXQ).
6. https://youtu.be/xB645BXoZI0 (https://www.youtube.com/watch?v=xB645BXoZI0).
7. For a brief look at the strong pro-coup bias in the Egyptian media under the coup regime, see Mona El-Naggar and Alyssa Kim, 'Military Dominates Airwaves in Egypt,' 20 August 2013, *The New York Times*, http://www.nytimes.com/video/world/middleeast/100000002397509/egypts-military-dominates-its-airwaves.html. This had been building up over many months.
8. For examples of private media channels working in coordination with the military and intelligence services to undermine democracy, see Walter Armbrust, *Martyrs and Tricksters: An Ethnography of the Egyptian Revolution* (Princeton: Princeton University Press, 2019), chapter 9, esp. 184; Kirkpatrick, *Into the Hands of the Soldiers*, passim. I am grateful to Dina El Odessy for helpful comments on this.
9. This description of the DMA is drawn from Kirkpatrick, *Into the Hands of the Soldiers.*
10. I do not consider this to be undermined by his remarks after the coup mentioned in Chapter 3 that suggested that channels of communication had been closed around early 2011. This appears to have been a temporary breakdown of communication that was fully restored by 2012.
11. https://youtu.be/Zb24X0TYmSo.
12. https://youtu.be/Zb24X0TYmSo?t=620.
13. Ibid. This hadith is narrated in *Ṣaḥīḥ Muslim*. See: Muslim b. al-Ḥajjāj, *Ṣaḥīḥ Muslim bi-Sharḥ al-Nawawī* (Cairo: al-Maṭbaʿa al-Miṣriyya bi-l-Azhar, 1929), 16:174.
14. https://youtu.be/Zb24X0TYmSo?t=918.
15. For more on al-Jamʿiyya al-Sharʿiyya, see: Aaron Rock-Singer, *Practicing Islam in Egypt: Print Media and Islamic Revival* (Cambridge: Cambridge University Press, 2019), passim.
16. Khalid Musa, 'al-Jamʿiyya al-Sharʿiyya tadʿam Mursī fī al-iʿāda wa-tuʾakkid: al-imtināʿ ʿan al-taṣwīt maʿṣiya,' 30 May 2012, *al-Shuruq*, https://www.shorouknews.com/news/view.aspx?cdate=30052012&id=5c9c9c30-5dc0-4aba-a4e8-842ae039ab76. The head of the Jamʿiyya, Shaykh Muḥammad Mukhtār al-Mahdī (d. 1437/2016), a member of the Azhar's CSS until his death, would express surprise at Gomaa's castigation of his institution, while politely disagreeing with his much younger colleague.
17. https://youtu.be/Zb24X0TYmSo?t=983.
18. In an earlier publication, I erroneously identified this person as Yāsir al-Burhāmī, the vice president of the party. See: Usaama al-Azami, 'Neo-traditionalist Sufis and Arab Politics: A Preliminary Mapping of the Transnational Networks of Counter-revolutionary Scholars after the Arab Revolutions,' in Mark Sedgwick and Francesco Piraino (eds), *Global Sufism: Boundaries, Structures, and Politics* (London: Hurst Publishers, 2019), 281, n. 29.
19. Aya Batrawy and Maggie Fick, 'Egypt's Copts choose new pope for uncertain times,' 4 November 2012, *San Diego Union Tribune*, https://www.sandiegouniontribune.

com/sdut-egypts-copts-choose-new-pope-for-uncertain-times-2012nov04-story.html.

20. https://youtu.be/dyolDqBaIeQ (https://www.youtube.com/watch?v=dyolDqBaIeQ).
21. https://youtu.be/9cDiv9-iESE (https://www.youtube.com/watch?v=9cDiv9-iESE).
22. https://youtu.be/sKEAxbZKLug (https://www.youtube.com/watch?v=sKEAxbZKLug).
23. This is discussed in detail by HRW in their comprehensive report on the massacre. See: Omar Shakir, *All According to Plan: The Rab'a Massacre and Mass Killings of Protesters in Egypt* (New York, NY: Human Rights Watch, 2014), available at https://www.hrw.org/report/2014/08/12/all-according-plan/raba-massacre-and-mass-killings-protesters-egypt. In particular, Sisi had called for a 'mandate' to confront 'terrorism' some weeks before the massacre, and in the days leading up to it HRW points out that 'two prominent newspapers cited security sources as indicating that the Interior Ministry's dispersal plan anticipated several thousand casualties.'
24. https://youtu.be/z4cyz7LR9og (https://www.youtube.com/watch?v=z4cyz7LR9og). For another version, see here: https://youtu.be/Z7eZxVVwxMg (https://www.youtube.com/watch?v=Z7eZxVVwxMg).
25. Serving as a preacher for the military was not without precedent for Gomaa. He did so shortly after the ouster of Mubarak with SCAF's head Field Marshal Muḥammad Ḥusayn al-Tanṭāwī in attendance sitting next to the Shaykh al-Azhar Aḥmad al-Ṭayyib in March 2012. See: https://youtu.be/Ew_6ATCDWnU (https://www.youtube.com/watch?v=Ew_6ATCDWnU). However, Gomaa effectively inciting violence against an overwhelmingly peaceful political opponent was new.
26. This video is available online in two parts. The first part may be viewed here: https://youtu.be/LCQqrryBy1E (https://www.youtube.com/watch?v=LCQqrryBy1E), and the second part here: https://youtu.be/fIGYRu6thyg (https://www.youtube.com/watch?v=fIGYRu6thyg).
27. For the beginning of Ramadan in Egypt that year, see 'al-Arbi'ā' awwal ayyām shahr Ramaḍān fī ghālibiyyat al-duwal al-'Arabiyya,' *Al Arabiya*, 8 July 2013, https://www.alarabiya.net/ar/arab-and-world/2013/07/08/أنباء-عن-تعذر-رؤية-هلال-رمضان-بمنطقة-سدير-بالسعودية. The first day of the following lunar month, corresponding with 8 August, is the day on which Gomaa gave an Eid sermon to the military which we will discuss briefly below.
28. https://youtu.be/LCQqrryBy1E.
29. https://youtu.be/52DMpHZBxE4?t=1869 (https://www.youtube.com/watch?v=52DMpHZBxE4).
30. Neil Ketchley, *Egypt in a Time of Revolution: Contentious Politics and the Arab Spring* (Cambridge, UK: Cambridge University Press, 2017). An earlier figure from a military source was 14 million, which Reuters characterized as 'implausibly high.' This is a bit of an understatement. See: Shaimaa Fayed and Yasmine Saleh 'Millions flood Egypt's streets to demand Mursi quit,' *Reuters*, 30 June 2013, https://www.reuters.com/article/us-egypt-protests/millions-flood-egypts-streets-to-demand-mursi-quit-idUSBRE95Q0NO20130630. Around the time, several commentators

also had suggested that the protests may have been in the hundreds of thousands rather than in the millions. Jack Brown, 'On Those Protest Numbers in Egypt,' *Counter Punch*, 18 July 2013, https://www.counterpunch.org/2013/07/18/on-those-protest-numbers-in-egypt/ and 'June 30 anti-Morsi crowd figures just don't add up,' *Middle East Monitor*, 5 May 2014, https://www.middleeastmonitor.com/20140505-june-30-anti-morsi-crowd-figures-just-don-t-add-up/.

31. See: Ketchley, *Egypt in a Time of Revolution*, 109. Cited in Kirkpatrick, *Into the Hands of the Soldiers*, 233.
32. Ketchley, *Egypt in a Time of Revolution*, 20.
33. https://youtu.be/LCQqrryBy1E?t=645.
34. See Yahya Michot, 'The Tahrir Square Sermon of Shaykh Yûsuf al-Qaradâwî,' 15 March 2011, http://www.scribd.com/doc/65022521/The-Tahrir-Square-Sermon-of-Shaykh-Yusuf-al-Qaradawi. See also Appendix 2, below.
35. The hadith that Gomaa mentions refers to 'the western army,' which Gomaa claims was a reference to the Egyptian army. For a brief discussion of these hadiths, see: Ṣalāh al-Dīn al-Idlibī, 'Mā ṣiḥḥat al-aḥādīth al-wārida fī jund Miṣr?,' *Rābiṭat 'Ulamā' al-Sūriyyīn*, 5 May 2013, https://islamsyria.com/site/show_consult/575. See also: Ṣalāh al-Dīn al-Idlibī, 'Satakūn fitna khayr al-nās fihā al-jund al-gharbī,' *Rābiṭ at 'Ulamā' al-Sūriyyīn*, 27 February 2017, https://islamsyria.com/site/show_consult/1010; http://www.islamweb.net/ar/fatwa/127084. All of these discussions consider the hadith about the western army to be extremely weak in its attribution to the Prophet.
36. For a scholar who reacted to Gomaa at the time by pointing out what he viewed as the patent absurdity of these hadiths from over a thousand years ago as somehow referring to modern Egypt, see: https://youtu.be/y95CcJHhZcI (https://www.youtube.com/watch?v=y95CcJHhZcI). Regarding the claims of invincibility, one might also consider the fact that the Egyptian army had been militarily defeated within living memory in two major engagements with the Israelis, once in 1967 and once in 1973. The defeat of 1973 was, however, not an unqualified defeat, with Egypt making important political gains after the rout of 1967. Thus, despite Israel's military victory, Egypt saw itself as regaining some of its military prestige as a consequence of the war.
37. For an example of such a hadith, see ibid., 36:518–20. These hadiths are less canonical, although in this particular instance, the modern editors deem it *Ṣaḥīḥ*.
38. See: al-Bukhārī, *Ṣaḥīḥ al-Bukhārī* (Beirut: Dār Ibn Kathīr, 1987), 3:1319f.
39. Kirkpatrick, *Into the Hands of the Soldiers*, 258, 276f.; Walter Armbrust, *Martyrs and Tricksters: An Ethnography of the Egyptian Revolution* (Princeton: Princeton University Press, 2019), 160–3.
40. Kirkpatrick, *Into the Hands of the Soldiers*, 258.
41. This is attributed to the Prophet in a weak (*ḍaʿīf*) narration. See Ch. 3, n. 37 above.
42. This statement is more accurately attributed to Ibn 'Umar according to modern experts, although given the nature of the report, it may be viewed as being something he learnt from the Prophet. See: Ibn Balbān al-Fārisī, *al-Iḥsān fī Taqrīb Ṣaḥīḥ Ibn Ḥibbān*, ed. Shuʿayb al-Arnaʾūṭ (Beirut: Muʾassasat al-Risāla, 1991), 13:75f. See also: https://www.ahlalhdeeth.com/vb/showthread.php?t=277993.

43. According to major premodern authorities, this statement is not preserved in any recognized source of hadiths, although a similar meaning is conveyed in sound hadiths. See: http://majles.alukah.net/t42086/ and https://www.islamweb.net/ar/fatwa/376867/درجة-حديث-لأن-تهدم-الكعبة-حجرًا-حجرًا،-أهون-عند-الله-من-أن-يراق-دم-امرئ-مسلم.
44. This 'hadith' does not appear in any hadith collection. Rather it is only cited, without a chain of authorities, in non-hadith works. For a brief discussion, see: https://www.ahlalhdeeth.com/vb/showthread.php?t=315472.
45. https://youtu.be/LCQqrryBy1E?t=844.
46. See: https://youtu.be/-cWUOHTdSAs (https://www.youtube.com/watch?v=-cWUOHTdSAs).
47. https://youtu.be/q-mDhr2Vees (https://www.youtube.com/watch?v=q-mDhr2Vees).
48. https://youtu.be/OMn0vEXMka0 (https://www.youtube.com/watch?v=OMn0vEXMka0).
49. See: https://youtu.be/M9jJUqFgwuo (https://www.youtube.com/watch?v=M9jJUqFgwuo); https://www.facebook.com/pg/masrelmahrousanews/about.
50. This version had been aired on the CBC satellite channel. See: https://youtu.be/BtWH9MMMozU (https://www.youtube.com/watch?v=BtWH9MMMozU). For the version aired on Channel 1, see: https://youtu.be/oVWOfNVzqY0 (https://www.youtube.com/watch?v=oVWOfNVzqY0). The same video was uploaded to Gomaa's official YouTube channel under the title: 'The hadith of the Messenger of God concerning the Egyptian army.' See: https://youtu.be/C8odslLsmrI (https://www.youtube.com/watch?v=C8odslLsmrI). I discuss the unreliability of the hadith above in n. 35.
51. https://youtu.be/y95CcJHhZcI.
52. The two parts may be viewed at the following two links: https://youtu.be/qD3d4k7EMFM (https://www.youtube.com/watch?v=qD3d4k7EMFM) and https://youtu.be/lVmgdSq8X9s (https://www.youtube.com/watch?v=lVmgdSq8X9s).
53. https://youtu.be/ARtNXcifcrs (https://www.youtube.com/watch?v=ARtNXcifcrs).
54. https://youtu.be/fIGYRu6thyg?t=246.
55. https://youtu.be/z2P1E7rxJSM (https://www.youtube.com/watch?v=z2P1E7rxJSM).
56. Muḥammad Mukhtār Jumʿa is not related to Ali Gomaa.
57. 'Egypt: Fresh Assault On Justice,' *Human Rights Watch*, 29 April 2014, https://www.hrw.org/news/2014/04/29/egypt-fresh-assault-justice; 'Egypt: prison sentence for Mohamed Morsi comes after sham trial,' *Amnesty International UK*, 21 April 2015, https://www.amnesty.org.uk/press-releases/egypt-prison-sentence-mohamed-morsi-comes-after-sham-trial; 'Mohammed Morsi death sentence upheld by Egypt court,' *BBC News*, 16 June 2015, https://www.bbc.co.uk/news/world-middle-east-33147206; 'Egypt's mufti endorsed Morsi death sentence, website says,' *Middle East Eye*, 6 June 2016, https://www.middleeasteye.net/news/egypts-mufti-endorsed-morsi-death-sentence-website-says. He has also avoided visiting Britain

since the coup for fear of arrest and prosecution: 'Egypt Grand Mufti cancels visit to Britain for fear of prosecution,' *Middle East Monitor*, 5 December 2014, https://www.middleeastmonitor.com/20141205-egypt-grand-mufti-cancels-visit-to-britain-for-fear-of-prosecution/.

58. https://youtu.be/z2P1E7rxJSM.
59. See: Shakir, *All According to Plan*.
60. David Kirkpatrick, *Into the Hands of the Soldiers: Freedom and Chaos in Egypt and the Middle East* (London: Bloomsbury, 2018), 276.
61. See: Shakir, *All According to Plan*, 80.
62. Shakir, *All According to Plan*, 31.
63. Kirkpatrick, *Into the Hands of the Soldiers*, 276.
64. See: Shakir, *All According to Plan*, 6.
65. Kirkpatrick, *Into the Hands of the Soldiers*, 270.
66. See: Shakir, *All According to Plan*, 126.
67. Ibid., 6.
68. 'Egypt's Brotherhood to hold 'march of anger,' *Al Jazeera English*, 16 August 2013,' https://www.aljazeera.com/news/middleeast/2013/08/ 201381522364486906.html.
69. Manar Mohsen, 'Health Ministry raises death toll of Wednesday's clashes to 638,' 16 August 2013, *Daily News Egypt*, https://wwww.dailynewssegypt.com/2013/08/16/health-ministry-raises-death-toll-of-wednesdays-clashes-to-638/.
70. See: Shakir, *All According to Plan*, 12, 102.
71. David Kirkpatrick, *Into the Hands of the Soldiers: Freedom and Chaos in Egypt and the Middle East* (London: Bloomsbury, 2018), 276f.
72. https://youtu.be/e3W2cP5Uxgc (https://www.youtube.com/watch?v=e3W2cP5Uxgc).

6 AZHARĪS OPPOSED TO THE COUP AND COUNTER REVOLUTIONS

1. 'Istiqālat al-Qaraḍāwī min Hay'at Kibār al-'Ulamā' bi-l-Azhar,' 3 December 2013, *Yusuf al-Qaradawi Website*, https://www.al-qaradawi.net/node/4760, 'al-Qaraḍāwī yastaqīl min Hay'at Kibār al-*'Ulamā'* bi-l-Azhar,' 3 December 2013,' *Al Jazeera Arabic*, http://www.aljazeera.net/news/arabic/2013/12/3/القرضاوي-يستقيل-من-هيئة-كبار-العلماء-بالأزهر. The shaykh al-Azhar heads the CSS.
2. David Kirkpatrick, *Into the Hands of the Soldiers: Freedom and Chaos in Egypt and the Middle East* (London: Bloomsbury, 2018), passim.
3. Anas Zakī, 'Shaykh al-Azhar: al-mu'āraḍa al-silmiyya jā'iza shar'an,' *Al Jazeera Arabic*, 19 June 2013, http://www.aljazeera.net/news/arabic/2013/6/19/شيخ-الأزهر-المعارضة-السلمية-جائزة-شرعا, 'Shaykh al-Azhar: al-taẓāhur ḍidd al-Ḥākim jā'iz,' *Sky News Arabia*, 19 June 2013, https://www.skynewsarabia.com/middle-east/297806-شيخ-الأزهر-التظاهر-ضد-مرسي-جائز, 'Top Egyptian cleric sanctions anti-Morsi protest,' *The Times of Israel*, 19 June 2013, http://www.timesofisrael.com/top-egyptian-cleric-sanctions-anti-morsi-protest/.
4. Yūsuf al-Qaraḍāwī and 'Alī al-Qaradāghī, 'al-Ittiḥād yuḥadhdhir min za'za'at al-istiqrār fī Miṣr wa-yuṭālib al-mu'āraḍa bi-ittibā' qawā'id al-dīmuqrāṭiyya,' *Yusuf al-Qaradawi Website*, 26 June 2013, https://www.al-qaradawi.net/node/4788.

5. https://youtu.be/N8-EXYEWczM (https://www.youtube.com/watch?v=N8-EXYEWczM), AJM official: https://youtu.be/N-YCdQtqg_c (https://www.youtube.com/watch?v=N-YCdQtqg_c), clearest version: https://youtu.be/n_15rESSUEg (https://www.youtube.com/watch?v=n_15rESSUEg).
6. Kirkpatrick, *Into the Hands of the Soldiers*, 267. The phrase 'a free-flowing spigot' was used by former US Secretary of State, John Kerry.
7. 'Al-Qaraḍāwī yuftī bi-wujūb ta'yīd Mursī,' *Al Jazeera Arabic*, 6 July 2013, https://www.aljazeera.net/news/arabic/2013/7/6/القرضاوي-يفتي-بوجوب-تأييد-مرسي. For the full fatwa, see: https://www.facebook.com/alqaradawy/posts/598404810199587.
8. Yūsuf al-Qaraḍāwī and 'Alī al-Qaradāghī, "*'Ulamā'* al-Muslimīn yunaddid bi-madhābiḥ al-inqilāb wa-intihākihi li-ḥurmat al-masājid wa-l-kanā'is,' *Yusuf al-Qaradawi Website*, 23 August 2013, https://www.al-qaradawi.net/node/4781.
9. https://youtu.be/lKSfzKPgWPM?t=1409 (https://www.youtube.com/watch?v=lKSfzKPgWPM).
10. Kirkpatrick, *Into the Hands of the Soldiers*, 254.
11. See: Omar Shakir, *All According to Plan: The Rab'a Massacre and Mass Killings of Protesters in Egypt* (New York, NY: Human Rights Watch, 2014), 112f. Available at https://www.hrw.org/report/2014/08/12/all-according-plan/raba-massacre-and-mass-killings-protesters-egypt.
12. Yūsuf al-Qaraḍāwī and 'Alī al-Qaradāghī, 'al-Ittiḥād yunaddid bi-majzara wa-yuḥadhdhir min khuṭūrat al-sukūt 'alā al-inqilāb,' *Yusuf al-Qaradawi Website*, 9 July 2013, https://www.al-qaradawi.net/node/4787.
13. https://youtu.be/oEG45y6I6rA (https://www.youtube.com/watch?v=oEG45y6I6rA). For a more complete version of the opening of the recording, see: https://youtu.be/gk7iTmszXA0 (https://www.youtube.com/watch?v=gk7iTmszXA0). The video was published online the following day. Because of it, Egyptian media targetted Shāfi'ī in a smear campaign a year later: https://youtu.be/bawXpH9qNsw (https://www.youtube.com/watch?v=bawXpH9qNsw).
14. Ashraf 'Īd al-'Antablī, 'D. Ḥasan al-Shāfi'ī: 'ālim rabbānī mala'a al-dunyāwa-asma'a al-nās,' *Ikhwan Wiki*, n.d., https://www.ikhwanwiki.com/index.php?title=حسن_الشافعي.
15. https://youtu.be/gk7iTmszXA0?t=1086.
16. https://youtu.be/gk7iTmszXA0?t=1149.
17. David Kirkpatrick makes the same point. See: Kirkpatrick, *Into the Hands*, 172.
18. See: Mohammad Fadel, 'Islamic Law and Constitution-Making: The Authoritarian Temptation and the Arab Spring,' *Osgoode Hall Law Journal* 53:2 (2016), 472–507.
19. A minor mistake in Shāfi'ī's reporting was to say that this took place at Rabaa Square rather than at the Republican Guard headquarters, where the shooting actually took place. Otherwise, his details are more or less in line with HRW's report. See the section on the Republican Guard Headquarters in: Shakir, *All According to Plan*, 112–20.
20. http://howiyapress.com/mohamed-3mara/. The original video appears to have been removed from YouTube. For a low-resolution copy of it, see: https://youtu.be/tIh9ryJ1PRA (https://www.youtube.com/watch?v=tIh9ryJ1PRA).
21. He appears to pronounce his surname 'Umāra in the recording. In communication with the scholar on 22 December 2019, he mentioned that although this is the

more accurate historical pronunciation of this name, he has no personal preference regarding how others pronounce it, as it is pronounced in various ways in modern Arabic. I have thus retained the more frequently used ʿImāra in the present work.

22. See Yūsuf al-Qaraḍāwī, *Ẓāhirat al-Ghuluww fī al-Takfīr*, 3rd edn. (Cairo: Maktabat Wahba, 1990), 22f., 75f.
23. See: Nader Hashemi, 'The ISIS Crisis and the Broken Politics of the Arab World: A Framework for Understanding Radical Islamism,' in Anthony Chase (ed.), *Routledge Handbook on Human Rights and the Middle East and North Africa* (London: Routledge, 2017), 91.
24. For a brief discussion of such encouragement in the case of Yemen, see: Elham Manea, 'Yemen's Arab Spring: Outsmarting the Cunning State?,' in *Routledge Handbook of the Arab Spring Rethinking Democratization*, ed. Larbi Sadiki (Abingdon: Routledge, 2014), 168. The case of Syria's Assad freeing jailed jihadists to radicalize the opposition to him is better known in this regard. See: Jean-Pierre Filiu, *From Deep State to Islamic State: The Arab Counter-Revolution and Its Jihadi Legacy* (Oxford: Oxford University Press, 2015), 201.
25. https://youtu.be/3pfJDMiIrlo (https://www.youtube.com/watch?v=3pfJDMiIrlo).
26. Anas Zakī, 'Shaykh al-Azhar: al-muʿāraḍa al-silmiyya jāʾiza sharʿan,' *Al Jazeera Arabic*, 19 June 2013, http://www.aljazeera.net/news/arabic/2013/6/19/شيخ-الأزهر-المعارضة-السلمية-جائزة-شرعا. Sky News Arabia, perhaps unsurprisingly, given it is based in Abu Dhabi, did not refer to this aspect of the fatwa in its report on it. See: 'Shaykh al-Azhar: al-taẓāhur ḍidd al-ḥākim jāʾiz,' *Sky News Arabia*, 19 June 2013, https://www.skynewsarabia.com/middle-east/297806-شيخ-الأزهر-التظاهر-ضد-مرسي-جائز.
27. https://youtu.be/3pfJDMiIrlo.
28. https://youtu.be/lKSfzKPgWPM.
29. https://youtu.be/lKSfzKPgWPM?t=2258.
30. Yūsuf al-Qaraḍāwī and ʿAlī al-Qaradāghī, 'al-Ittiḥād yuʾakkid ḥurmat al-istijāba li-ayy nidāʾ yuʾaddī li-ḥarb ahliyya,' *Yusuf al-Qaradawi Website*, 25 July 2013, https://www.al-qaradawi.net/node/4786.
31. https://youtu.be/PZAdK2Z_ztI (https://www.youtube.com/watch?v=PZAdK2Z_ztI); 'Yūsuf al-Qaraḍāwī yuḥarrim al-istijāba li-daʿwat al-Sīsī,' *Al Jazeera Arabic*, 25 July 2013, https://www.aljazeera.net/news/arabic/2013/7/27/القرضاوي-يحرم-الاستجابة-لدعوة-السيسي.
32. https://youtu.be/YWS7fEb-lRQ (https://www.youtube.com/watch?v=YWS7fEb-lRQ), alternative version: https://youtu.be/cQ3q9iQZGFc (https://www.youtube.com/watch?v=cQ3q9iQZGFc). For a report on Sisi's call, see: Kareem Fahim and Mayy El Sheikh, 'Egyptian General Calls for Mass Protests,' *The New York Times*, 24 July 2013, https://www.nytimes.com/2013/07/25/world/middleeast/egypt.html.
33. See: Shakir, *All According to Plan*, 121.
34. https://youtu.be/2y2t6iE3nz0 (https://www.youtube.com/watch?v=2y2t6iE3nz0). For the full version lasting thirty-one minutes, see: https://youtu.be/PUMBeFwiEfw (https://www.youtube.com/watch?v=PUMBeFwiEfw).

35. Yūsuf al-Qaraḍāwī and ʻAlī al-Qaradāghī, ʻal-Ittiḥād yunaddid bi-majāzir al-inqilāb fī Miṣr,' *Yusuf al-Qaradawi Website*, 27 July 2013, https://www.al-qaradawi.net/node/4785.
36. For the fullest version, see: https://youtu.be/EEH9B04Q8vs (https://www.youtube.com/watch?v=EEH9B04Q8vs). Al Jazeera Arabic (AJA) version: https://youtu.be/j4GvQ3WG4Mk; alternative third-party version from a day earlier than the AJA version was published on YouTube: https://youtu.be/xJQh0KPgA_Q.
37. This is not deemed a hadith by experts, though its meaning is in keeping with sound hadiths. See Ch. 5, n. 43.
38. A reference to unsubstantiated rumors that Sisi had memorized the whole Qur'an. For a discussion of Sīsī's public image as a devout Muslim, see: Edward Stourton, 'Egypt's General al-Sisi: The man behind the image,' *BBC News*, 27 August 2013, http://www.bbc.co.uk/news/world-middle-east-23809507.
39. https://youtu.be/FA1qLB3imd0 (https://www.youtube.com/watch?v=FA1qLB3imd0). Reports of the attack's casualty figures running at the bottom of the screen around the three-minute mark indicate that this recording took place on the same day it was uploaded, i.e. 27 July 2013.
40. https://youtu.be/FA1qLB3imd0.
41. See: Shakir, *All According to Plan*.
42. https://youtu.be/7t3KnazKGLY (https://www.youtube.com/watch?v=7t3KnazKGLY).

7 ALI GOMAA: CELEBRATING THE RABAA MASSACRE

1. See: Jean-Pierre Filiu, *From Deep State to Islamic State: The Arab Counter-Revolution and Its Jihadi Legacy* (Oxford: Oxford University Press, 2015), 179; 'Government Assessment of the Syrian Government's Use of Chemical Weapons on August 21, 2013,' *The White House*, 30 August 2013, https://obamawhitehouse.archives.gov/the-press-office/2013/08/30/government-assessment-syrian-government-s-use-chemical-weapons-august-21.
2. 'Muftī Miṣr al-sābiq yu'ayyid qatl al-mutaẓāhirīn,' 8 October 2013, *Al Jazeera Arabic*, http://www.aljazeera.net/news/arabic/2013/10/8/مفتي-مصر-السابق-يؤيد-قتل-المتظاهرين. For the full video, see the next note.
3. https://youtu.be/gxm8w-yVyH8 (https://www.youtube.com/watch?v=gxm8w-yVyH8).
4. The first part of the prayer is repeated in the Qur'an in several instances. See: Qur'an 5:119, 9:100, 58:22, and 98:8.
5. See: ʻAlī Jumʻa, ʻLimādhā nuṭliq ism al-Khawārij ʻalā jamāʻāt al-ʻunf ka-Dāʻish wa-l-Qāʻida wa-mā yumaththiluhā?,' *Ali Gomaa Website*, 5 December 2014, https://www.draligomaa.com/index.php/قضايا-شغلت-الإمام/قضايا-على-مستوى-الأمة/item/٤٤٨-لماذا-نطلق-اسم-الخوارج-على-جماعات-العنف-كداعش-والقاعدة-وما-. For another discussion of this mainstream Sunni attitude towards the Khawārij, see: https://islamqa.info/ar/answers/224823/حقيقة-الخوارج-وهل-يصبح-المسلم-خارجيا-بمجرد-وصفه-لفعل-ما-بانه-من-الشرك.
6. https://youtu.be/0dwVEQgCnRg (https://www.youtube.com/watch?v=0dwVEQg CnRg).

7. See Ch. 5, n. 35 above. He also repeatedly mispronounced names of narrators who reportedly transmitted the hadith, suggesting he had not actually taken the trouble to properly research the transmission of the hadiths. See the translations in the Appendices for examples.
8. See: https://youtu.be/sNbk2anfwXk (https://www.youtube.com/watch?v=sNbk2anfwXk).
9. See: Omar Shakir, *All According to Plan: The Rab'a Massacre and Mass Killings of Protesters in Egypt* (New York, NY: Human Rights Watch, 2014), 131. Available at https://www.hrw.org/report/2014/08/12/all-according-plan/raba-massacre-and-mass-killings-protesters-egypt.
10. Ibid.
11. Gomaa is paraphrasing a hadith viewed as applying to the Khawārij that may be found in Aḥmad b. Ḥanbal, *Musnad al-Imām Aḥmad b. Ḥanbal* (Beirut: Mu'assasat al-Risāla, 1999), 21:51f. The modern editors deem it authentic.
12. On the unconvincing nature of such assertions, see Bruce Rutherford, *Egypt After Mubarak: Liberalism, Islam, and Democracy in the Arab World* (Princeton: Princeton University Press, 2008), 77–130.
13. For the *takhrīj* of this hadith, see: ibid., 1:288f. The editors deem it reasonably strong in its attribution to the Prophet. See also: http://www.ahlalhdeeth.com/vb/showthread.php?t=116180.
14. The earliest recording I have found for this was uploaded on YouTube by a third party on 16 August, which strongly indicates that this was the date of its initial broadcast. See: https://youtu.be/myLM6BMT8k0 (https://www.youtube.com/watch?v=myLM6BMT8k0). Many of the other uploaded videos of this interview on YouTube are from a day or so after this date. These clips were being used by Egyptian media after the coup to attack Qaradawi, as can be seen in this version of the clip: https://youtu.be/UdTFx4Z-i8k (https://www.youtube.com/watch?v=UdTFx4Z-i8k). It is unclear what channel is broadcasting Qaradawi's comments. The clips appear to have been edited to remove their channel's insignia, likely because they probably belonged to Al Jazeera Mubasher Misr—the Qatari channel's Egypt-based sister channel—with whom Qaradawi had a long-standing relationship.
15. https://youtu.be/gxm8w-yVyH8?t=954.
16. For Qaradawi's remarks, see: https://youtu.be/8VSECTsDlaU (https://www.youtube.com/watch?v=8VSECTsDlaU).
17. https://youtu.be/gxm8w-yVyH8?t=1041.
18. On this, see: Jonathan A. C. Brown, *Misquoting Muhammad: The Challenge and Choices of Interpreting the Prophet's Legacy* (Oxford: Oneworld, 2014), 66f.
19. For a *takhrīj* of this canonical hadith that is deemed authentic by Sunnis, see: Ibn Ḥanbal, *Musnad*, 8:314.
20. For the phrase *iḍrab fi-l-malyān*, see El-Said Badawi and Martin Hinds, *A Dictionary of Egyptian Arabic* (Beirut: Librarie du Liban, 1986), 834.
21. https://youtu.be/dNprN6ddA8Y (https://www.youtube.com/watch?v=dNprN6ddA8Y). I discuss these remarks later in the chapter.
22. https://youtu.be/gxm8w-yVyH8?t=1378.
23. https://youtu.be/gxm8w-yVyH8?t=2009.

24. See Steven Brooke, 'Egypt,' in Shadi Hamid and William McCants (eds), *Rethinking Political Islam* (Oxford: Oxford University Press, 2017), 22.
25. For the original interview, see: https://youtu.be/DcAoD8FttnU (https://www.youtube.com/watch?v=DcAoD8FttnU).
26. https://youtu.be/u5OEFoyrif8 (https://www.youtube.com/watch?v=u5OEFoyrif8).
27. https://youtu.be/52DMpHZBxE4?t=326.
28. https://youtu.be/52DMpHZBxE4?t=486.
29. See: https://youtu.be/52DMpHZBxE4?t=1215. Gomaa actually uses the expression 'one of my sons,' but this is how he refers to his students. He appears to clarify immediately that it is not a biological son by noting that he actually has no sons.
30. https://youtu.be/52DMpHZBxE4?t=1315.
31. https://youtu.be/52DMpHZBxE4?t=1558.
32. Specifically, he referred to 'nine automatic weapons, one pistol, five homemade pistols.' See: Shakir, *All According to Plan*, 80.
33. https://youtu.be/52DMpHZBxE4?t=1705.
34. https://youtu.be/52DMpHZBxE4?t=1947.
35. https://youtu.be/52DMpHZBxE4?t=2916.
36. https://youtu.be/52DMpHZBxE4?t=1737.
37. https://youtu.be/52DMpHZBxE4?t=2173.
38. For a similar version of this story from the director of the Special Operations unit, see: https://youtu.be/YZ_fnucxgoQ (https://www.youtube.com/watch?v=YZ_fnucxgoQ). The number of police deaths Gomaa mentioned was also exaggerated.
39. https://youtu.be/52DMpHZBxE4?t=2491.
40. https://youtu.be/52DMpHZBxE4?t=3342.
41. In Arabic, this is '*Hay'at Kibār al-'Ulamā'*.' This body was originally established in 1911 but dissolved by Gamal Abdel Nasser in 1961 before being reconstituted in 2012. It is not clear to me how Qaradawi joined the reconstituted CSS.
42. https://youtu.be/52DMpHZBxE4?t=3436.
43. David Warren notes that Egyptian media had 'mistakenly' portrayed Qaradawi as calling for jihadists to come to Egypt to help the MB. See David H. Warren, 'The *'Ulamā'* and the Arab Uprisings 2011-13: Considering Yusuf al-Qaradawi, the 'Global Mufti', between the Muslim Brotherhood, the Islamic Legal Tradition, and Qatari Foreign Policy,' *New Middle Eastern Studies*, 4 (2014), 25. I would argue that this was a case of deliberate misrepresentation as part of a propaganda war rather than an accidental misconstrual. It is hard to imagine that the well-known and oft-cited Qur'anic verse on *wasaṭiyya* (Q. 2:143), which Qaradawi was effectively citing, could have been misunderstood by Egypt's chattering classes which included its ulama.
44. See, for example: Courtney Freer, *Rentier Islamism: The Influence of the Muslim Brotherhood in Gulf Monarchies* (Oxford University Press, 2018), 94. Freer cites the Egyptian state-owned *al-Ahrām* newspaper as evidence for Qaradawi calling for violence in Egypt after the coup. As I argue in the previous endnote, this was coup regime propaganda.

45. For Qaradawi's interview, see: https://youtu.be/TxtBDjmWE8I (https://www.youtube.com/watch?v=TxtBDjmWE8I). For Gomaa's interview, see: https://youtu.be/xATINp1yi-o (https://www.youtube.com/watch?v=xATINp1yi-o).
46. The original post is available at: https://www.facebook.com/alhabibali/posts/612826942090623.
47. The original post was cross-posted on Facebook and Twitter here: https://twitter.com/alhabibali/status/370330404513140736. The Facebook post appears to have been deleted. I retain a screenshot of it taken on 31 August 2013.
48. For the original post, which remains accessible as of early 2020, see: https://twitter.com/alhabibali/status/371927682465804288. I have deleted the last two lines from the above translation. They read: 'Composed on 19 Shawwal 1434, corresponding with 26 August 2013.'
49. https://www.facebook.com/alhabibali/posts/10201748454249548.
50. *Irjāf* is the verbal noun of *arjafa*, a form IV verb, derived from the root *r-j-f*. The phrase '*arjafa fī al-shay*'' is glossed as follows in Lane's *Lexicon*: 'They said what was false respecting the thing [...] or they told many evil tales and uttered many discordant lying sayings, respecting the thing, in order that the people might become in a state of commotion, agitation, convulsion, tumult, or disturbance, in consequence thereof.' See: Edward William Lane, *Arabic-English Lexicon* (London: Williams & Norgate, 1863), 1042.
51. See al-Ṭabarī, *Tafsīr al-Ṭabarī: Jāmiʿ al-Bayān ʿan Taʾwīl Āy al-Qurʾān*, ed. ʿAbd al-Muḥsin al-Turkī (Cairo: Dār Hajar, 2001), 19:185.
52. See Gomaa's remarks to this effect here: https://youtu.be/fIGYRu6thyg?t=9m32s.
53. David D. Kirkpatrick and Mayy El Sheikh, 'Egypt Military Enlists Religion to Quell Ranks,' *The New York Times*, 25 August 2013, http://www.nytimes.com/2013/08/26/world/middleeast/egypt.html. This scrupulously accurate portrayal of events in Egypt at the time also discusses other public religious figures including the notable televangelist, Amr Khaled.
54. https://www.facebook.com/permalink.php?story_fbid=620774577952837&id=347684525261845.
55. Ibid.
56. https://youtu.be/OAZU6MML2Jk (https://www.youtube.com/watch?v=OAZU6MML2Jk).
57. Walaa Quisay, 'Neo-Traditionalism in the West: Navigating Modernity, Tradition and Politics,' DPhil dissertation (University of Oxford, 2019).
58. Quisay, 'Neo-Traditionalism in the West,' 295f.
59. In correspondence with the attendee on 1 December 2015.
60. Ibid.
61. A number of videos and articles had emerged in 2013 in the weeks and months after Būṭī's assassination on 21 March 2013 alleging that Qaradawi had given a fatwa to kill Būṭī. This allegation was made on the basis of a clip from Qaradawi's Al Jazeera show which aired on 2 December 2012 in which he was asked whether it was permitted to 'target' ulama in Syria who were supportive of the Assad regime. Qaradawi responded that it is permitted to 'fight' anyone who is supporting the regime. To take this as a fatwa to permit the assassination of Būṭī in a mosque seems

far-fetched. For Qaradawi's statements in this regard, see: http://www.aljazeera.net/programs/religionandlife/2012/12/6/حلقة-خاصة-حول-الشأن-العام-للأمة-ج٢.
For the video of the question and Qaradawi's response, see: https://youtu.be/aJlFVlc4HfM?t=2271 (https://www.youtube.com/watch?v=aJlFVlc4HfM). It is somewhat ironic that Jifri's teacher Gomaa had spent a good deal of time elaborating the difference between 'fighting' and 'killing' in response to Egypt's post-coup massacres, a distinction Jifri now failed to recognize. After the killing of Būṭī, Qaradawi issued a condemnation of the murder of the scholar, a scholar he once considered a friend. While he still excoriated Būṭī for standing with the Syrian regime, he also now prayed for God to forgive him. See: https://youtu.be/pu25qZJ6CZM (https://www.youtube.com/watch?v=pu25qZJ6CZM).

62. 'Sheikh Ali Gomaa, former mufti of Egypt, cancels London visit for fear of prosecution,' 5 February 2014, *Middle East Monitor*, https://www.middleeastmonitor.com/20140205-sheikh-ali-gomaa-former-mufti-of-egypt-cancels-london-visit-for-fear-of-prosecution/.
63. https://youtu.be/MKYVM5G6N7g (https://www.youtube.com/watch?v=MKYVM5G6N7g).
64. David D. Kirkpatrick, 'Senior Egyptian Police Officer Is Killed in a Raid on Islamists Near Cairo,' 19 September 2013, *The New York Times*, http://www.nytimes.com/2013/09/20/world/middleeast/egyptian-forces-raid-islamist-stronghold.html.
65. The interview uploaded to Gomaa's official YouTube channel may be viewed here: https://youtu.be/7SFtrzdKM1g. The other six interviews may be viewed at the following links: https://youtu.be/E7rJxAETfAY (https://www.youtube.com/watch?v=E7rJxAETfAY), https://youtu.be/FEI2g9O1v14 (https://www.youtube.com/watch?v=FEI2g9O1v14), https://youtu.be/ad6TS5I5sAc (https://www.youtube.com/watch?v=ad6TS5I5sAc), https://youtu.be/mINAk_noqJo (https://www.youtube.com/watch?v=mINAk_noqJo), https://youtu.be/5hgjwMt2Mok (https://www.youtube.com/watch?v=5hgjwMt2Mok), https://youtu.be/1S_xeJpBVzc (https://www.youtube.com/watch?v=1S_xeJpBVzc).
66. For a brief look at how the military brought Egyptian media in line immediately after the 2013 coup, see: Mona El-Naggar and Alyssa Kim, 'Military Dominates Airwaves in Egypt,' 20 August 2013, *The New York Times*, http://www.nytimes.com/video/world/middleeast/100000002397509/egypts-military-dominates-its-airwaves.html. The continuation of this anti-MB posture in later years is illustrated by the fact that Gomaa could have a regular show in 2015, lasting nine months, and with forty-two episodes of roughly half an hour each, which was dedicated to presenting a highly tendentious history of the MB as a means of discrediting them. For the full series, which may be watched on YouTube, see: https://www.youtube.com/watch?v=J1_qA5o9_yw&list=PLxQnfwkf6kshxdsmAtDUvgVffQUygDPnc&index=1.
67. https://youtu.be/7SFtrzdKM1g (https://www.youtube.com/watch?v=7SFtrzdKM1g). Footage from the event suggests that the numbers were far higher: https://youtu.be/KHn5Vfv8hLk (https://www.youtube.com/watch?v=KHn5Vfv8hLk).
68. https://youtu.be/7SFtrzdKM1g.

69. 'Update: Suspects arrested in Kerdasa violence,' *Mada Masr*, 19 September 2013, https://madamasr.com/en/2013/09/19/news/u/update-suspects-arrested-in-kerdasa-violence/.
70. https://youtu.be/qmBu8oA9Lv4 (https://www.youtube.com/watch?v=qmBu8oA9Lv4).
71. Ibid.
72. Ibid. Italics added for emphasis.
73. Ibid.
74. https://youtu.be/7IU06CVJVqA (https://www.youtube.com/watch?v=7IU06CVJVqA).
75. https://youtu.be/x0UBWxSpBR4 (https://www.youtube.com/watch?v=x0UBWxSpBR4).
76. 'Egyptian soldier shot dead in Cairo bus attack,' *BBC News*, 14 March 2014, http://www.bbc.co.uk/news/world-middle-east-26559184.
77. https://youtu.be/ht_F1w_vXGQ (https://www.youtube.com/watch?v=ht_F1w_vXGQ).
78. https://youtu.be/vRlYAvHv1NU (https://www.youtube.com/watch?v=vRlYAvHv1NU).
79. See: Ibn Ḥanbal, *Musnad*, 4:370f.
80. https://youtu.be/dNprN6ddA8Y.
81. https://youtu.be/mrqdr-qNgq4 (https://www.youtube.com/watch?v=mrqdr-qNgq4).
82. CBC's clip which is provided with a translation is available here: https://youtu.be/mrqdr-qNgq4. A fuller version may be viewed here: https://youtu.be/gyEgSi1__v8 (https://www.youtube.com/watch?v=gyEgSi1__v8). The propaganda was effective enough to take in seasoned Western Egypt watchers like the British-Egyptian academic H. A. Hellyer. See H. A Hellyer, *A Revolution Undone: Egypt's Road Beyond Revolt* (New York: Oxford University Press, 2016), 162.
83. https://youtu.be/Vmhyq8BUZsU (https://www.youtube.com/watch?v=Vmhyq8BUZsU).
84. As Kirkpatrick notes, the militants in the Sinai actually celebrated the failure of democracy that Morsi's ouster symbolized. See Kirkpatrick, *Into the Hands*, 283f.
85. https://youtu.be/LmDI7sky31U (https://www.youtube.com/watch?v=LmDI7sky31U).
86. https://youtu.be/IMuqA9oydDA (https://www.youtube.com/watch?v=IMuqA9oydDA).
87. https://youtu.be/6beJGJy2d0U (https://www.youtube.com/watch?v=6beJGJy2d0U) and https://youtu.be/lmRPi9D0fGM (https://www.youtube.com/watch?v=lmRPi9D0fGM).
88. 'Egypt's former grand mufti survives shooting west of Cairo,' *The Washington Post*, 5 August 2016, https://www.washingtonpost.com/world/middle_east/egypts-former-grand-mufti-survices-shooting-west-of-cairo/2016/08/05/1a140b18-5b25-11e6-831d-0324760ca856_story.html.
89. Ola Salem and Hassan Hassan, 'Arab Regimes Are the World's Most Powerful Islamophobes,' 29 March 2019, *Foreign Policy*, https://foreignpolicy.com/2019/03/29/arab-regimes-are-the-worlds-most-powerful-islamophobes/.

90. https://youtu.be/zH0mRCN9Oas (https://www.youtube.com/watch?v=zH0mRCN9Oas).
91. https://youtu.be/zH0mRCN9Oas?t=1412. Aḥmad Manṣūr, 'Ṣudūr kitāb 'Mawqif al-Azhar wa-'Ulama'ihīmin al-Ikhwān' 'an Dār al-Muqaṭṭam,' 30 June 2016, *al-Yawm al-Sābi'*, https://www.youm7.com/story/2016/6/30/-صدور-كتاب-موقف-الأزهر-وعلمائه-من-الإخوان-عن-دار-المقطم/7202872.
92. See: Jeffrey T. Kenney, *Muslim Rebels: Kharijites and the Politics of Extremism in Egypt* (Oxford University Press, 2006), esp. 89–116.
93. See: Usaama al-Azami, 'Neo-traditionalist Sufis and Arab Politics: A Preliminary Mapping of the Transnational Networks of Counter-revolutionary Scholars after the Arab Revolutions,' in Mark Sedgwick and Francesco Piraino (eds), *Global Sufism: Boundaries, Structures, and Politics* (London: Hurst Publishers, 2019), 234.

8 THE REACTIONS OF ANTI-COUP ULAMA TO THE RABAA MASSACRE

1. https://youtu.be/oveLBwTFStE (https://www.youtube.com/watch?v=oveLBwTFStE), for an alternative version, see: https://youtu.be/ccrQJD5Swds (https://www.youtube.com/watch?v=ccrQJD5Swds).
2. For the fullest version, see: https://youtu.be/jZ2B7R35Viw (https://www.youtube.com/watch?v=jZ2B7R35Viw).
3. https://youtu.be/5gODgqmYY-8 (https://www.youtube.com/watch?v=5gODgqmYY-8).
4. For Rajab Zakī's date of birth, see: https://youtu.be/80ktJXE8cIM (https://www.youtube.com/watch?v=80ktJXE8cIM).
5. Kishk's oratory has been the subject of a scholarly study. See: Charles Hirschkind, *The Ethical Soundscape: Cassette Sermons and Islamic Counterpublics* (New York: Columbia University Press, 2006).
6. https://youtu.be/13yWI2nxoh4 (https://www.youtube.com/watch?v=13yWI2nxoh4); a year later, Zakī would state in an interview that he had called on senior Azharī scholars to publicly express their opposition to the coup in its immediate aftermath: https://youtu.be/K3UwPN6X9sY (https://www.youtube.com/watch?v=K3UwPN6X9sY).
7. The Arabic verb *'-b-d* can refer to both worshipping (*'abada*) and being a slave (*'abuda*). See Edward William Lane, *Arabic-English Lexicon* (London: Williams & Norgate, 1863), 1934. Zakī plays on this polysemy in this sentence.
8. https://youtu.be/13yWI2nxoh4.
9. https://youtu.be/13yWI2nxoh4?t=460. I have not verified the accuracy of this citation.
10. https://youtu.be/13yWI2nxoh4?t=675.
11. https://youtu.be/13yWI2nxoh4?t=783.
12. For a study of Egypt's liberals, including their support for the 2013 coup, see: Dalia Fahmy and Daanish Faruqi (eds), *Egypt and the Contradictions of Liberalism: Illiberal Intelligentsia and the Future of Egyptian Democracy* (Oxford: Oneworld, 2017).
13. https://youtu.be/13yWI2nxoh4?t=868.

14. This is a Biblical and Qur'anic figure who is viewed as a tyrant and rebel against God.
15. This was a Meccan contemporary and opponent of the Prophet Muhammad who was killed by the Prophet at the Battle of Uḥud.
16. This was a senior Meccan contemporary and opponent of the Prophet. He was killed at the Battle of Badr.
17. This was another senior Meccan contemporary and opponent of the Prophet.
18. Better known as al-Ḥajjāj b. Yūsuf, this was an Umayyad commander who was reputed in Islamic history for his tyranny and ruthlessness.
19. These are the monarchs of modern Egypt who had been overthrown by the Free Officers' revolution in 1952.
20. https://youtu.be/13yWI2nxoh4?t=929.
21. https://youtu.be/13yWI2nxoh4?t=991.
22. https://youtu.be/13yWI2nxoh4?t=1047.
23. https://youtu.be/13yWI2nxoh4?t=1167.
24. This hadith is weakly attributed to the Prophet with some scholars attributing it to a Companion rather than the Prophet himself. For a brief discussion, see: http://www.islamweb.net/ar/fatwa/115011.
25. https://youtu.be/13yWI2nxoh4?t=1239.
26. https://youtu.be/13yWI2nxoh4?t=1342.
27. https://youtu.be/13yWI2nxoh4?t=1390.
28. https://youtu.be/13yWI2nxoh4?t=1522.
29. https://youtu.be/13yWI2nxoh4?t=1567.
30. https://youtu.be/IMivD-mgPYU.
31. See Ch. 2, n. 71 above.
32. https://youtu.be/V12zCzozumQ (https://www.youtube.com/watch?v=V12zCzozumQ).
33. https://youtu.be/V12zCzozumQ?t=376.
34. https://youtu.be/V12zCzozumQ?t=1302.
35. https://youtu.be/V12zCzozumQ?t=1412. See also his closing remarks to the episode: https://youtu.be/V12zCzozumQ?t=2801.
36. Qaradawi uses this phrase in his pre-Arab revolutionary writings. See: Yūsuf al-Qaradawi, *Fiqh al-Jihād: Dirāsa Muqārana li-Aḥkāmihi wa-Falsafatihi fī Ḍaw' al-Qur'ān wa-l-Sunna*, 3rd ed. (Cairo: Maktabat Wahba, 2010), 1:205. Cited in David H. Warren, 'The *'Ulamā'* and the Arab Uprisings 2011-13: Considering Yusuf al-Qaradawi, the 'Global Mufti', between the Muslim Brotherhood, the Islamic Legal Tradition, and Qatari Foreign Policy,' *New Middle Eastern Studies*, 4 (2014), 11.
37. https://youtu.be/V12zCzozumQ?t=1932.
38. https://youtu.be/V12zCzozumQ?t=2303.
39. https://youtu.be/V12zCzozumQ?t=2573.
40. Yūsuf al-Qaraḍāwī, 'al-Radd 'alā Muftī al-'Askar 'Alī Jum'a,' *Yusuf al-Qaradawi Website*, 11 October 2013, https://www.al-qaradawi.net/node/2836.
41. 'al-Raysūnī: Muftī Miṣr al-sābiq sharīk fī al-qatl,' *Al Jazeera Arabic*, 13 October 2013, http://www.aljazeera.net/news/reportsandinterviews/2013/10/13/الريسوني-مفتي-مصر-السابق-شريك-في-القتل.

42. Ibid.
43. See: Usaama al-Azami, 'Abdullāh bin Bayyah and the Arab Revolutions: Counter-revolutionary Neo-traditionalism's Ideological Struggle against Islamism,' *The Muslim World*, 109:3 (2019), 347.
44. Ibid., 350.
45. https://peacems.com/about-us/sponsor-message/.
46. Kirkpatrick, *Into the Hands of the Soldiers*, 208.
47. Ibid., 267.
48. See: 'UAE Cabinet forms Emirates Fatwa Council,' *The National*, 24 June 2018, https://www.thenational.ae/uae/government/uae-cabinet-forms-emirates-fatwa-council-1.743799.

9 UNDERSTANDING COUNTER-REVOLUTIONARY FATWAS AND THEIR RAMIFICATIONS BEYOND EGYPT

1. For convenience in distinguishing between the two sets of scholars under discussion, I will generally refer to contributors to the secondary literature as academics while the participants in the events will be referred to as ulama. In principle, I do not make very sharp distinctions between these two traditions of scholarship.
2. See: Nakissa, 'Fiqh of Revolution.'
3. Ebrahim Moosa, 'Political Theology in the Aftermath of the Arab Spring: Returning to the Ethical,' in *The African Renaissance and the Afro-Arab Spring: A Season of Rebirth?* (eds) Charles Villa-Vicencio, Erik Doxtader, and Ebrahim Moosa (Washington, DC: Georgetown University Press, 2015), 101.
4. Ibid., 114f.
5. Ibid., 115
6. Ibid., 113.
7. Ibid., 115f.
8. Amr Osman, 'Past Contradictions, Contemporary Dilemmas: Egypt's 2013 Coup and Early Islamic History,' *Digest of Middle East Studies* 24:2 (2015), 318.
9. Ibid., 324, n. 38.
10. Ibid., 317. Osman is in part citing: Nazih Ayubi, *Political Islam: Religion and Politics in the Arab World* (New York, NY: Routledge, 1991), 16.
11. Osman, 'Past Contradictions,' 318. Osman is citing: Heather Keaney, *Medieval Islamic Historiography: Remembering Rebellion* (New York: Routledge, 2013), 54.
12. Mohammad Fadel, 'Islamic Law and Constitution-Making: The Authoritarian Temptation and the Arab Spring,' *Osgoode Hall Law Journal* 53.2 (2016): 472–507.
13. See: ibid., 489–93. For a more detailed treatment, see: Mohammed Fadel, 'Modernist Islamic Political Thought and the Egyptian and Tunisian Revolutions of 2011' *Middle East Law and Governance* 3, no. 1–2 (2011): 94–104.
14. Fadel, 'Islamic Law,' 494.
15. See: ibid., 486.
16. See: ibid., 498.
17. See: ibid.
18. See: ibid., 500.

19. See: ibid., 507.
20. Muhamad Rofiq Muzakkir, 'Understanding the Discourse of 'Alī Jum'ah on the Military Coup During the Arab Spring in Egypt,' *Ilahiyat Studies* 10:2 (2019).
21. This may be inadvertent. In another instance, the author misunderstands a point made by Khaled Abou El Fadl to mean the opposite of what Abou El Fadl intends, as the latter notes in the next paragraph. See: ibid., 244. Cf. Khaled Abou El Fadl, *Rebellion and Violence in Islamic Law* (Cambridge: Cambridge University Press, 2001), 12.
22. Muzakkir, 'Understanding,' 248, 251, 257f.
23. Ibid., 257f.
24. Ibid., 254.
25. Ibid., 254–6.
26. See, for example: Sherman A. Jackson, *Islamic Law and the State: The Constitutional Jurisprudence of Shihāb al-Dīn al-Qarāfī* (Leiden: Brill, 1996); Noah Feldman, *The Fall and Rise of the Islamic State* (Princeton, N.J.: Princeton University Press, 2008); Wael Hallaq, *The Impossible State: Islam, Politics, and Modernity's Moral Predicament* (New York: Columbia University Press, 2013). My suggestion that usurpers seem to have been an inescapable reality in premodern politics reflects Crone's remark: 'for what could be more common in history than the recognition of usurpers?' See, Patricia Crone, *Medieval Islamic Political Thought* (Edinburgh: Edinburgh University Press, 2004), 233.
27. See: Nakissa, 'Fiqh of Revolution.' David Warren draws on Nakissa's reading in: David H. Warren, 'The *'Ulamā'* and the Arab Uprisings 2011-13: Considering Yusuf al-Qaradawi, the 'Global Mufti', between the Muslim Brotherhood, the Islamic Legal Tradition, and Qatari Foreign Policy,' *New Middle Eastern Studies*, 4 (2014).
28. See: Ahmed Fekry Ibrahim, *Pragmatism in Islamic Law: A Social and Intellectual History* (Syracuse: Syracuse University Press, 2015).
29. Ibid., 12, 23. Although Nakissa's article was published the following year, he had shared a draft of the article with Warren.
30. David H. Warren, 'Cleansing the Nation of the 'Dogs of Hell': 'Ali Jum'a's Nationalist Legal Reasoning in Support of the 2013 Egyptian Coup and its Bloody Aftermath,' *International Journal of Middle East Studies,* 49:3 (2017).
31. See: ibid., 459.
32. See: ibid., 460.
33. See: ibid., 465f.
34. Ibid., 474, n. 20.
35. Youssef Belal, 'Islamic Law, Truth, Ethics,' *Comparative Studies of South Asia, Africa and the Middle East* 38:1 (2018), 115.
36. Ibid. Belal's presentation of Qaradawi's reasoning behind opposing Mubarak, namely that Mubarak was not truly one of the 'faithful' (*mu'minīn*) may be misunderstood as his suggesting that Qaradawi was excommunicating him (ibid., 112). In personal communication with Belal, he points out that it is not his intention to make such a suggestion. Qaradawi's fatwa clearly does not intend this either. For the original statement, see: Yūsuf al-Qaraḍāwī, *25 Yanāyir Sanat 2011: Thawrat al-Sha'b* (Cairo: Maktabat Wahba, n.d.), 126f.

37. Belal, 'Islamic Law, Truth, Ethics,' 116.
38. For Gomaa's self-reflexive engagement with tradition, see Mary Beinecke Elston, 'Reviving Turāth: Islamic Education in Modern Egypt,' PhD dissertation (Harvard University, 2020).
39. Elsewhere, I have discussed the diversity of the premodern Sunni juristic tradition in a little more detail than I do here. See: Usaama al-Azami, 'Shaykh Hamza Yusuf and the Question of Rebellion in the Islamic Tradition,' *MuslimMatters*, 15 September 2019, https://muslimmatters.org/2019/09/15/shaykh-hamza-yusuf-and-the-question-of-rebellion-in-the-islamic-tradition/.
40. For an exploration of the difficulties in conceptualizing 'quietism' in Islamic thought, see: Jan-Peter Hartung, 'Making Sense of 'Political Quietism' – An Analytical Intervention,' in Saud al-Sarhan (ed.), *Political Quietism in Islam: Sunni and Shi'i Practice and Thought* (London: I. B. Tauris, 2019).
41. Abou El Fadl, *Rebellion*, 19.
42. Michael Cook, *Commanding Right and Forbidding Wrong in Islamic Thought* (Cambridge: Cambridge University Press, 2000), 479.
43. Crone, *Medieval*, 230f.
44. Abou El Fadl, *Rebellion*, 237, n. 4.
45. Cook, *Commanding*, 478, n. 71 and 390, n. 256. He is drawing on Abou El Fadl's dissertation. For the brief discussion in the latter's monograph, see Abou El Fadl, *Rebellion*, 237, n. 4.
46. Noah Feldman, *The Fall and Rise of the Islamic State* (Princeton, N.J.: Princeton University Press, 2008), 39f.
47. Crone, *Medieval*, 229.
48. Yūsuf al-Qaraḍāwī, *al-Dīn wa-l-Siyāsa: Ta'ṣīl wa-Radd Shubuhāt* (Dublin: al-Majlis al-Ūrubbī li-l-Iftā' wa-l-Buḥūth, 2007), 61.
49. See: ibid., 60–2.
50. See: Uriya Shavit, 'The Muslim Brothers' Conception of Armed Insurrection against an Unjust Regime,' *Middle Eastern Studies* 51 (2015): 600–17.
51. See: Crone, *Medieval*, 229. Michael Cook speaks of this dimension of the Islamic duty at considerable length. See: Cook, *Commanding*, passim. For specific pages, see the index (p. 693) under 'ruler/state.'
52. See: Crone, *Medieval*, 229f.
53. See: ibid., 230. For a far more detailed treatment of how rebels are to be dealt with, see: Abou El Fadl, *Rebellion*.
54. For Cook's fairly extensive discussion of Ghazzālī's treatment of the duty, see: Cook, *Commanding*, 427–68.
55. Ibid., 429.
56. Ibid., 430–2.
57. Ibid., 431, 445f.
58. Fadel, 'Islamic Law,' 486.
59. For critiques of its attribution to Ghazzālī, see: Patricia Crone, 'Did al-Ghazālī Write a Mirror for Princes?' *Jerusalem Studies in Arabic and Islam* 10 (1987), 167–91; Carole Hillenbrand, 'Islamic Orthodoxy or Realpolitik? Al-Ghazālī's Views on Government,' *Iran* 26:1 (1988), 91f.; Kenneth Garden, *The First Islamic*

Reviver: Abū Ḥāmid al-Ghazālī and His Revival of the Religious Sciences (New York: Oxford University Press, 2014), 213–14 n. 88; David Decosimo, 'An *Umma* of Accountability: Al-Ghazālī against Domination,' *Soundings: An Interdisciplinary Journal* 98:3 (2015), 284, n. 3.

60. See: Decosimo, '*Umma*.'
61. For a more recent and original critique of Ghazzālī's political outlook, and one that also references earlier scholarship, see Ovamir Anjum, *Politics, Law, and Community in Islamic Thought: The Taymiyyan Moment* (Cambridge: Cambridge University Press, 2012), 125–8 and passim.
62. Crone, *Medieval*, 246f.
63. Mark Sedgwick calls the *Iḥyā'* 'perhaps the single most influential Sufi work ever written.' See: Mark Sedgwick, *Western Sufism: From the Abbasids to the New Age* (Oxford: Oxford University Press, 2017), 41.
64. For the view that Sufi esotericism lends itself to authoritarianism, see Ovamir Anjum, 'Mystical Authority and Governmentality in Medieval Islam,' in John Curry and Erik Ohlander (eds), *Sufism and Society: Arrangements of the Mystical in the Muslim World, 1200–1800* (London: Routledge, 2012); Ahmed El Shamsy, *Rediscovering the Islamic Classics: How Editors and Print Culture Transformed an Intellectual Tradition* (Princeton: Princeton University Press, 2020), 31–62 and esp. 161f.
65. Fait Muedini, *Sponsoring Sufism: How Governments Promote 'Mystical Islam' in Their Domestic and Foreign Policies* (New York: Palgrave Macmillan, 2015), esp. 32–41.
66. Meir Hatina, *'Ulama,' Politics, and the Public Sphere: An Egyptian Perspective* (Salt Lake City: University of Utah Press, 2010).
67. See: Usaama al-Azami, 'Neo-traditionalist Sufis and Arab Politics: A Preliminary Mapping of the Transnational Networks of Counter-revolutionary Scholars after the Arab Revolutions,' in Mark Sedgwick and Francesco Piraino (eds), *Global Sufism: Boundaries, Structures, and Politics* (London: Hurst Publishers, 2019), 231–4.
68. Warren, 'Cleansing,' 465f.
69. For an article about Obama's interview, see: Jason Leopold, 'The CIA Just Declassified the Document That Supposedly Justified the Iraq Invasion,' *Vice News*, 19 March 2015, https://www.vice.com/en_us/article/9kve3z/the-cia-just-declassified-the-document-that-supposedly-justified-the-iraq-invasion. For the video, see: https://video.vice.com/en_us/video/president-barack-obama-speaks-with-vice-news/5612d6713ae8bc5740641c17?playlist=58fa89ab9c35eb60aed97316.
70. Kirkpatrick, *Into the Hands of the Soldiers*, esp. Ch. 18.
71. Ibid., 234f.
72. Ibid., 221
73. See: https://www.humanrightsfirst.org/sites/default/files/Mohamed-Soltan.pdf. Partially cited in Nader Hashemi, 'The ISIS Crisis and the Broken Politics of the Arab World: A Framework for Understanding Radical Islamism,' in Anthony Chase (ed.), *Routledge Handbook on Human Rights and the Middle East and North Africa* (London: Routledge, 2017), 91.
74. 'The crackdown in Egypt: Democracy and hypocrisy,' *The Economist*, 3 August 2013, https://www.economist.com/leaders/2013/08/03/democracy-and-hypocrisy.

75. See: Kirkpatrick, *Into the Hands of the Soldiers*, esp. Ch. 27; and Jean-Pierre Filiu, *From Deep State to Islamic State: The Arab Counter-Revolution and Its Jihadi Legacy* (Oxford: Oxford University Press, 2015).
76. Usaama al-Azami, 'How Not to Disown 'Islamist' Terrorism,' *HuffPost*, 17 December 2015, https://www.huffpost.com/entry/how-not-to-disown-islamis_b_8823864.
77. http://www.lettertobaghdadi.com/.
78. https://peacems.com/about-us/sponsor-message/.
79. Abdallah bin Bayyah et al., *In Pursuit of Peace: Framework Speech for the Forum for Promoting Peace in Muslim Societies* (Abu Dhabi: FPPMS, 2014), 22.
80. See 'Abdullāh b. Bayya, *Tanbīh al-Marāji' 'alā Ta'ṣīl Fiqh al-Wāqi'* (Beirut: Markaz Namā', 2014), 82ff. The book has multiple later editions with varying pagination. In all cases, the relevant chapter is entitled '*Man Yuḥaqqiq al-Manāṭ*?' It has been studied by Christopher Razavian in Masooda Bano (ed.), *Modern Islamic Authority and Social Change, Volume 1: Evolving Debates in Muslim Majority Countries* (Edinburgh: Edinburgh University Press, 2018), 102–23. We saw an earlier form of this position articulated in Bin Bayyah's disagreement with Ḥusayn Ḥāmid Ḥassān in Chapter 4.
81. https://youtu.be/g7_isEsApX8?t=2079 (https://www.youtube.com/watch?v=g7_isEsApX8). The phrase is drawn from the premodern tradition.
82. 'Remarks As Prepared for Delivery by President Barack Obama, Address to the United Nations General Assembly,' *The White House: Office of the Press Secretary*, 24 September 2014, https://obamawhitehouse.archives.gov/the-press-office/2014/09/24/remarks-prepared-delivery-president-barack-obama-address-united-nations-; for the video, see: https://youtu.be/tJemr-HiYg4 (https://www.youtube.com/watch?v=tJemr-HiYg4).
83. Dexter Filkins 'A Saudi Prince's Quest to Remake the Middle East,' *The New Yorker*, 2 April 2018, https://www.newyorker.com/magazine/2018/04/09/a-saudi-princes-quest-to-remake-the-middle-east.
84. http://wam.ae:80/ar/details/1395302617984.
85. https://twitter.com/PPeacenews/status/872415235512172545 (https://twitter.com/PPeacenews/status/872415235512172545).
86. 'Hādhihī Maṭālib al-duwal al-muqāṭi'a li-Qaṭar wa-muhlat 'ashrat ayyām li-tanfīdhihā' *Al Arabiya*, 23 June 2017, https://www.alarabiya.net/ar/arab-and-world/gulf/2017/06/23/أ-ب-الدول-المقاطعة-لقطر-تطلب-من-الدوحة-قطع-العلاقات-مع-إيران.html; Sudarsan Raghavan and Joby Warrick, 'How a 91-year-old imam came to symbolize feud between Qatar and its neighbours,' *The Washington Post*, 27 June 2017, https://www.washingtonpost.com/world/middle_east/how-a-91-year-old-imam-came-to-symbolize-feud-between-qatar-and-its-neighbors/2017/06/26/601d41b4-5157-11e7-91eb-9611861a988f_story.html.
87. Al-Azami, "Abdullāh bin Bayyah,' 345.
88. See: 'Abd al-'Aẓīm Dīb (ed.), *Yūsuf al-Qaraḍāwī: Kalimāt fī Takrīmihī wa-Buḥūth fī Fikrihi wa-Fiqhihi Muhdāh ilayhi bi-Munāsabat Bulūghihi al-Sab'īn* (Cairo: Dār al-Salām, 2004), 87f. The eventual publication was released some years after their compilation.

89. ‘Al-Duktūr Yūsuf al-Qaraḍāwī: al-jā’iza da‘wa li-l-tasābuq ilā al-khayr’ *al-Bayān*, 16 December 2000, https://www.albayan.ae/across-the-uae/2000- 12-16-1.1235238.
90. Al-Azami, “Abdullāh bin Bayyah,’ 346f.
91. Al-Azami, “Abdullāh bin Bayyah,’ 350.
92. Sudarsan Raghavan and Joby Warrick, ‘How a 91-year-old imam came to symbolize feud between Qatar and its neighbours,’ *The Washington Post*, 27 June 2017, https://www.washingtonpost.com/world/middle_east/how-a-91-year-old-imam-came-to-symbolize-feud-between-qatar-and-its-neighbors/2017/06/26/601d41b4-5157-11e7-91eb-9611861a988f_story.html.
93. David Hearst, ‘Saudi Arabia to execute three prominent moderate scholars after Ramadan,’ *Middle East Eye*, 21 May 2019, https://www.middleeasteye.net/news/exclusive-saudi-arabia-execute-three-prominent-moderate-scholars-after-ramadan. The alleged threat of execution has yet to be carried out. On Bāna‘ma, see: ‘Dā‘iya Su‘ūdī Mu‘taqal mundhu 2017 Yaẓhar bi-fidiyū li-‘Muḥammad ‘Abduh’ fī al-Sijn,’ *Al-Khalīj Online*, 4 April 2019, https://alkhaleejonline.net/سياسة/داعية-سعودي-معتقل-منذ-7102-يظهر-بفيديو-لمحمد-عبده-في-السجن.
94. ‘Rights group: Cleric Ali Al-Omari brutally tortured in Saudi prison,’ *Middle East Monitor*, 11 January 2019, https://www.middleeastmonitor.com/20190111-rights-group-cleric-ali-al-omari-brutally-tortured-in-saudi-prison/.
95. For Salmān al-‘Awda’s praise of Bin Bayyah, see: http://binbayyah.net/arabic/archives/319; for ‘Awaḍ al-Qarnī’s, see: http://binbayyah.net/arabic/archives/333; For ‘Alī al-‘Umarī’s, see: http://binbayyah.net/arabic/archives/ 336; for ‘Ādil Bānā‘ma’s panegyric poem, see: http://binbayyah.net/arabic/archives/326.
96. For Bin Bayyah’s audience with the king, see: ‘Al-Malik Salmān Yastaqbil ‘Ra’īs al-Iftā’’ bi-l-Imārāt ‘Ibn Bayyah’,’ *Arabi21*, 20 May 2019, https://arabi21.com/story/1182213/الملك-سلمان-يستقبل-رئيس-الإفتاء-بالإمارات-ابن-بية-شاهد.
97. Hamza Yusuf, ‘The Plague Within,’ 5 July 2016, *Sandala.org*, https://sandala.org/the-plague-within/.
98. On Aref Nayed’s anti-Islamist discourse, see: al-Azami, ‘Neo-traditionalist Sufis,’ esp. 232–4.
99. ‘List of groups designated terrorist organisations by the UAE,’ *The National*, 16 November 2014, https://www.thenationalnews.com/uae/government/list-of-groups-designated-terrorist-organisations-by-the-uae-1.270037.
100. ‘UAE’s Fatwa Council denounces Muslim Brotherhood as a terrorist organisation,’ *Middle East Eye*, 25 November 2020, https://www.middleeasteye.net/news/uae-muslim-brotherhood-fatwa-council-terrorist-organisation. This time his personal Twitter account did retweet this statement from the Emirates Fatwa Council’s official handle. ‘Muslim Brotherhood terrorist organisation, affirms UAE Fatwa Council,’ *Emirates News Agency*, 23 November 2020, https://www.wam.ae/en/details/1395302889318. For the original tweet, see: https://twitter.com/fatwauae/status/1331302687527333893.
101. ‘UAE fatwa council head Abdallah bin Bayyah ‘removed’ from Islamic conference line-up after backlash,’ *The New Arab*, 2 December 2020, https://english.alaraby.co.uk/english/news/2020/12/2/uae-fatwa-council-head-chair-removed-from-islamic-conference.

102. 'Shaykh Hamza Yusuf supports UAE-Israel peace deal,' *5 Pillars*, 22 August 2020, https://5pillarsuk.com/2020/08/22/shaykh-hamza-yusuf-supports-uae-israel-peace-deal/; 'International treaties, relations rightful authority of sovereign ruler: Emirates Fatwa Council,' Emirates News Agency, 14 August 2020, https://wam.ae/en/details/1395302862343.
103. Areeb Ullah, 'Influential Muslim scholar criticised for calling the UAE a 'tolerant country',' *Middle East Eye*, 7 December 2018, https://www.middleeasteye.net/news/influential-muslim-scholar-criticised-calling-uae-tolerant-country; Kristian Coates Ulrichsen, *The United Arab Emirates: Power, Politics and Policy-Making* (London: Routledge, 2016). The comment from Ulrichsen's work is cited in the *Middle East Eye* article.
104. Azad Essa, 'Hamza Yusuf and the struggle for the soul of western Islam,' *Middle East Eye*, 8 August 2019, https://www.middleeasteye.net/big-story/hamza-yusuf-and-struggle-soul-western-islam.
105. https://youtu.be/2C9mPoaik6g?t=2970 (https://www.youtube.com/watch?v=2C9mPoaik6g).
106. 'Hamza Yusuf issues apology for 'hurting feelings' with Syria comments,' *Middle East Eye*, 13 September 2019, https://www.middleeasteye.net/news/hamza-yusuf-issues-apology-hurting-feelings-over-syria-comments.
107. Masooda Bano, 'At the Tipping Point? Al-Azhar's Growing Crisis of Moral Authority,' *International Journal of Middle East Studies* 50:4 (2018).
108. 'Egypt: Renewed Detention of Scholar's Daughter Unlawful,' *Human Rights Watch*, 8 July 2019, https://www.hrw.org/news/2019/07/08/egypt-renewed-detention-scholars-daughter-unlawful.
109. See Michele Dunne and Scott Williamson, 'Egypt's Unprecedented Instability by the Numbers,' *Carnegie Endowment for International Peace*, 24 March 2014, https://carnegieendowment.org/2014/03/24/egypt-s-unprecedented-instability-by-numbers-pub-55078; Maged Mandour, 'Repression in Egypt from Mubarak to Sisi,' *Carnegie Endowment for International Peace*, 11 August 2015, https://carnegieendowment.org/sada/?fa=60985.
110. 'Egypt: Independently Investigate Morsy's Death,' *Human Rights Watch*, 17 June 2019, https://www.hrw.org/news/2019/06/17/egypt-independently-investigate-morsys-death.
111. 'US, EU 'turn a blind eye' to Morsi's death,' *TRTWorld*, 18 June 2019, https://www.trtworld.com/middle-east/us-eu-turn-a-blind-eye-to-morsi-s-death-27576.
112. Chloé Benoist, 'Explained: Sisi, Macron and the dubious history of France's Legion of Honour,' *Middle East Eye*, 18 December 2020, https://www.middleeasteye.net/news/egypt-france-sisi-legion-honneur-explained-history; 'France: Macron to Receive Al-Sisi on Heels of Repression,' *Human Rights Watch*, 2 December 2020, https://www.hrw.org/news/2020/12/02/france-macron-receive-al-sisi-heels-repression.

CONCLUSION

1. See: Shadi Hamid, *Islamic Exceptionalism: How the Struggle Over Islam Is Reshaping the World* (New York: St. Martin's Press, 2016), 257.

EPILOGUE

1. I use the word alim only to indicate that I have been through an *'ālimiyya* program in keeping with the conventions of the Indian subcontinental tradition of such studies. It is by no means a claim to great scholarly mastery sometimes associated with the Arabic word.
2. For his memoir of his time as a student, see: Mohammad Akram Nadwi, *Madrasah Life: A Student's Day at Nadwat al-'Ulamā'* (London: Turath Publishing, 2007).
3. See: Muhammad Qasim Zaman, *The Ulama in Contemporary Islam: Custodians of Change* (Princeton: Princeton University Press, 2002), 52.
4. See: H.A. Hellyer, "Egypt Killed Islam in the West': Revolution, Counterrevolution and Western Muslims,' *The Islamic Monthly*, 18 December 2014, http://www.theislamicmonthly.com/egypt-killed-islam-in-the-west/; Abdal Hakim Murad, *Travelling Home: Essays on Islam in Europe* (Cambridge: Quilliam Press, 2020).
5. Abdal Hakim Murad, 'Bombing Without Moonlight: The Origins of Suicidal Terrorism,' *Encounters* 10 (2004), 85–118.
6. On Gomaa's support, see: 'Awaḍ al-Ghannām, 'Muftī Miṣr: Ta'addud al-Fatwā Ikhtilāf Tanawwu' wa-Raḥma li-l-Umma,' *Mawqi' al-Shaykh Salmān al-'Awda*, 26 April 2006, http://webcache.googleusercontent.com/search?q=cache:http://www.islamtoday.net/salman/artshow-78-7161.htm. For a more extreme articulation of it from Gomaa where he expresses a willingness to excommunicate anyone who persists in holding the view that suicide bombings are illegitimate, see: https://youtu.be/-cWUOHTdSAs (https://www.youtube.com/watch?v=-cWUOHTdSAs). For Būṭī's support, see: Nawwāf al-Takrūrī, *al-'Amaliyyāt al-Istishhādiyya fī al-Mīzān al-Fiqhī*, 2nd edn. (Damascus: Dār al-Fikr, 1997), 102f; see also: http://azahera.net/showthread.php?t=1716. For former Shaykh al-Azhar Jād al-Ḥaqq's support, see: 'Jād al-Ḥaqq: Shaykh al-Azhar al-Munāhiḍ li-l-Taṭbī',' Al Jazeera Arabic, https://www.aljazeera.net/encyclopedia/icons/2016/9/21/جاد-الحق-شيخ-الأزهر-المناهض-للتطبيع. For former Shaykh al-Azhar al-Ṭanṭāwī's view, see: 'Egyptian grand shaykh: Islamic law sees suicide-bombers as martyrs,' 3 November 2003, http://www.imra.org.il/story.php3?id=18722. For former Shaykh al-Azhar, Naṣr Farīd Wāṣil's support, see: 'Muftī Miṣr: al-'Amaliyyat al-Istishhādiyya Mashrū'a,' *al-Bayān*, 6 December 2001, https://www.albayan.ae/last-page/2001-12-06-1.1167682. Aḥmad Ṭayyib, the current shaykh al-Azhar at the time of writing, issued his fatwa in support of suicide bombings during his tenure as grand mufti. He has not, to my knowledge, recanted. See: 'Muftī Miṣr: al-Istishhād Silāḥ al-Falasṭīniyyīn al-Waḥīd,' *al-Yawm*, 16 August 2002, http://www.alyaum.com/article/1010320. https://www.islamweb.net/ar/article/17235/.
7. Usaama al-Azami, 'How Not to Disown 'Islamist' Terrorism,' *HuffPost*, 17 December 2015, https://www.huffpost.com/entry/how-not-to-disown-islamis_b_8823864.
8. See, for example, the discussion of *isnād*s of an important precursor to the modern Salafi movement, Muḥammad b. 'Abd al-Wahhāb (d. 1792/1206) in Muḥammad Ziyād b. 'Umar al-Tukla, *Fatḥ al-Jalīl*, 2nd edn. (Beirut: Dār al-Bashā'ir al-Islāmiyya, 2008), 317. The same preservation of *asānīd* and *ijāzāt* may be found in the case of prominent Islamist ulama like Qaradawi. See: Muḥammad Akram al-Nadwī, *Kifāyat al-Rāwī 'an al-'Allāma Yūsuf al-Qaraḍāwī* (Damascus: Dār al-Qalam, 2001).

9. Although al-Awlaki was undoubtedly a promoter of extremist ideas, HRW pointed out shortly after his killing that the US government never publicly substantiated the claim that he was an al-Qaeda operative. See: https://www.hrw.org/news/2011/12/19/q-us-targeted-killings-and-international-law.
10. Usaama al-Azami, 'Shaykh Hamza Yusuf and the Question of Rebellion in the Islamic Tradition,' *MuslimMatters*, 15 September 2019, https://muslimmatters.org/2019/09/15/shaykh-hamza-yusuf-and-the-question-of-rebellion-in-the-islamic-tradition/.
11. See Thomas Pierret, *Religion and State in Syria: The Sunni Ulama from Coup to Revolution* (Cambridge: Cambridge University Press, 2013), esp. Ch. 6.
12. Bettina Gräf and Jakob Skovgaard-Petersen (eds), *The Global Mufti: The Phenomenon of Yusuf al-Qaradawi* (London: Hurst Publishers, 2009), 27.
13. Ibid., 33; al-Nadwī, *Kifāyat al-Rāwī*, 13.
14. Yūsuf al-Qaraḍāwī, *Kayfa Nataʿāmal maʿa al-Turāth wa-l-Tamadhhub wa-l-Ikhtilāf?*, 3rd edn. (Cairo: Maktabat al-Wahba, 2011), 62ff.
15. Ahmed Fekry Ibrahim, *Pragmatism in Islamic Law: A Social and Intellectual History* (Syracuse: Syracuse University Press, 2015), 224. While he does describe them as 'towering figures of modernism,' his definition of the term 'modernism' places it firmly within mainstream Sunnism.
16. Yūsuf al-Qaraḍāwī, *al-Ḥayāt al-Rabbāniyya wa-l-ʿIlm* (Cairo: Maktabat al-Wahba, 1995), 8.
17. For some of Jifri's critical comments about certain types of Sufism, see: https://youtu.be/dSNQmSIYUoA (https://www.youtube.com/watch?v=dSNQmSIYUoA).
18. Abdal Hakim Murad, 'Clarification: On the boundaries of da'wa,' *Masud.co.uk*, May 2014, masud.co.uk/clarification-on-the-boundaries-of-dawa/.
19. https://youtu.be/cGNyFVXrBqs?t=1811 (https://www.youtube.com/watch?v=cGNyFVXrBqs).
20. Brown's Facebook profile picture has, since 2013, been an image of the four-finger Rabaa salute which may be seen at the bottom panel of the cover of the present work. Beneath it, where a Facebook user would usually concisely introduce themselves, he notes: 'What's this profile pic? See http://almadinainstitute.org/blog/the-greatest-crime/.' The link is to a short article in which Brown explores the massacre of Bosnians in the 1990s before concluding with a reflection on the Rabaa massacre. He explains that years later he deliberately retains the Rabaa salute as his profile picture: 'I keep it up because I do not want to lapse into forgetfulness. I do not want time, which is wont to wash away all memories, distraction or social pressure to make me forget how people can be driven mad with hatred and convinced that men like their fathers, women like their mothers, and children like their own sons and daughters are no more than meat for the sword.'

    For his Facebook page, see: https://www.facebook.com/jonathanacbrown. For an archived link to the article, see: https://almadinainstitute.org/blog/the-greatest-crime.
21. https://youtu.be/5_8gHRCIDzI (https://www.youtube.com/watch?v=5_8gHRCIDzI).

22. See: David Kirkpatrick, *Into the Hands of the Soldiers: Freedom and Chaos in Egypt and the Middle East* (London: Bloomsbury, 2018), 172f.; on the unexpected decline of sectarian attacks on Christians during Morsi's year in office, see: ibid., 199–201; Shadi Hamid and Meredith Wheeler, 'Was Mohamed Morsi Really an Autocrat? Egypt's receding democracy, by the numbers,' *The Atlantic*, 31 March 2014, https://www.theatlantic.com/international/archive/2014/03/was-mohamed-morsi-really-an-autocrat/359797/.
23. See: Usaama al-Azami, 'Why Words Matter: The Problem with the Term Islamist,' *Sadeq Institute*, 23 November 2020, https://www.sadeqinstitute.org/short-reads/why-words-matter-the-problem-with-the-term-islamist.
24. David Decosimo, 'An *Umma* of Accountability: Al-Ghazālī against Domination.' *Soundings: An Interdisciplinary Journal* 98:3 (2015), 260–88; idem., 'Political Freedom as an Islamic Value,' *Journal of the American Academy of Religion* 86:4 (2018), 912–52.

APPENDIX 1

1. For the original, see: 'Abd al-'Aẓīm Dīb (ed.), *Yūsuf al-Qaraḍāwī: Kalimāt fī Takrīmihī wa-Buḥūth fī Fikrihi wa-Fiqhihi Muhdāh ilayhi bi-Munāsabat Bulūghihi al-Sab'īn* [*Yusuf al-Qaradawi: Words of Praise and Studies of His Thought and Legal Scholarship, Presented to Him on the Occasion of His 70th Birthday*] (Cairo: Dār al-Salām, 2004), 87f. It comprises essays by seventy of his prominent scholarly contemporaries, including Muṣṭafā Zarqā' (d. 1420/1999), Abū al-Ḥasan 'Alī al-Nadwī (d. 1420/1999), 'Abd al-Fattāḥ Abū Ghudda (d. 1417/1997), and Muḥ ammad Taqī Uthmānī (b. 1362/1943). The essays would have been compiled around 1996, when Qaradawi reached his seventieth birthday. The original piece had no footnotes.
2. Al-Khansā' was a Companion of the Prophet and Bedouin Arab poet. She is famous for her eulogies of her brother, Ṣakhr, whom she lost in inter-tribal conflict before the spread of Islam.
3. This line of poetry has been modified by Bin Bayyah, with the changes in italics above, from the following: 'Indeed Ṣakhr is one whom guides take as their guide / As though he were a mountain upon whose peak there is fire.' For the original, see: al-Khansā', *Dīwān al-Khansā'*, ed. Ḥamdū Ṭammās (Beirut: Dār al-Ma'rifa, 2004), 46.
4. Abū Isḥāq al-Shāṭibī (d. 790/1388) was an influential Mālikī jurist from Andalusia.
5. See: al-Shāṭibī, *al-Muwāfaqāt*, ed. Mashhūr Āl Salmān (Khobar: Dār Ibn 'Affān, 1997), 2:279. This edition uses the word *al-wasaṭ* rather than *al-awsaṭ*.
6. Yūsuf al-Qaraḍāwī, *al-Marji'iyya al-'Ulyā fī al-Islām li-l-Qur'ān wa-l-Sunna*, 2nd edn. (Cairo: Maktabat Wahba, 2001), 230.
7. This is a title given to scholars of particular eminence in Islamic history. It is a title that is commonly bestowed upon the eminent Cairene scholar, Zakariyyā al-Anṣārī (d. 926/1520), as well as the notable Damascene Ibn Taymiyya (d. 728/1328) in more recent times.

APPENDIX 2

1. This video is available online in two parts. The first part may be viewed here: https://youtu.be/LCQqrryBy1E, and the second part here: https://youtu.be/fIGYRu6thyg. As noted in Chapter 5, this lecture was likely given in Ramadan 2013.
2. Gomaa is referring to a canonical hadith found in both the collections of Bukhārī and Muslim. See Ch. 5 n. 38 above.
3. As David Kirkpatrick suggests, these crises appear to have been deliberately orchestrated in the run up to the coup. See: David Kirkpatrick, *Into the Hands of the Soldiers: Freedom and Chaos in Egypt and the Middle East* (London: Bloomsbury, 2018), 251.
4. This is also cited in Yūsuf al-Qaraḍāwī, *Min Fiqh al-Dawla fī al-Islām*, 3rd ed. (Cairo: Dār al-Shurūq, 2001), 138. Qaradawi does not provide a source. It appears that this form of the report from ʿUmar is not reliably preserved anywhere, although analogous reports are preserved and deemed to be sound by some. See, for example, al-Bukhārī, *al-Tārīkh al-Kabīr* (Hyderabad: Dāʾirat al-Maʿārif al-ʿUthmāniyya, n.d.), 2:98f. The only instance of this report being evaluated that I am aware of is on an online discussion forum where it was adjudged to be authentic, despite the authenticator's obvious discomfort with the report. See: http://www.tasfiatarbia.org/vb/showthread.php?t=11030.
5. Gomaa mispronounces this name as 'al-Ḥamqī'. For the basis of the correct vocalization used in the present translation, see: Ibn Nāṣir al-Dīn, *Tawḍīḥ al-Mushtabih*, ed. Muḥammad Naʿīm al-ʿAraqsūsī (Beirut: Muʾassasat al-Risāla, 1993), 2:426f. According to biographers, ʿAmr was a Companion of the Prophet, and later joined the faction of ʿAlī during the First Fitna (35/656–40/661). See Shams al-Dīn al-Dhahabī, *Tārīkh al-Islām wa-Wafayāt al-Mashāhīr wa-l-Aʿlām*, ed. Bashshār ʿAwwād Maʿrūf (Beirut: Dār al-Gharb al-Islāmī, 2003), 2:424.
6. These reports are considered dubious in their attribution to the Prophet. See Ch. 5, n. 35 and 36.
7. Gomaa also mispronounces this name as Tabīʿ b. ʿĀmir al-Kulāʿī. See: Ibn Ḥajar al-ʿAsqalānī, *Taqrīb al-Tahdhīb*, ed. ʿĀdil Murshid (Beirut: Muʾassasat al-Risāla, 1999), 69. His mispronunciations and frequent invocation of dubious hadiths are illustrative of his lack of concern for the strictures of rigorous hadith studies.
8. This narrative is of dubious attribution to the Prophet. See Ch. 5, n. 35 above.
9. This is found in sound hadiths. See: Ch. 5, n. 37.
10. See: Muslim b. al-Ḥajjāj, *Ṣaḥīḥ Muslim bi-Sharḥ al-Nawawī* (Cairo: al-Maṭbaʿa al-Miṣriyya bi-l-Azhar, 1929), 13:68. As Nawawī reports, the early hadith master, ʿAlī b. al-Madīnī (d. 234/849) considered the *ahl al-gharb* to refer to the Arabs more generally. It is not clear on what basis Gomaa says it refers to Egypt.
11. This is adapted from a line of poetry by the Tunisian revolutionary poet Abū al-Qāsim al-Shābbī which was invoked by Yusuf al-Qaradawi during his Taḥrīr Square sermon a week after Mubarak's ouster. See Ch. 5, n. 34 above.
12. This is deemed an authentic report by Sunnis. See: Muslim, *Ṣaḥīḥ Muslim*, 1:72.
13. This statement is weak in its attribution to the Prophet. See Ch. 3, n. 37 above.
14. See Ch. 5, n. 42 above for a discussion of the soundness of this report.

15. See Ch. 5, n. 43 above for a discussion of the soundness of this report.
16. See Ch. 5, n. 44 above for a discussion of this report.
17. This is a reference to the Sinai insurgency that was invigorated by the ouster of Morsi. See: David Kirkpatrick, *Into the Hands of the Soldiers: Freedom and Chaos in Egypt and the Middle East* (London: Bloomsbury, 2018), 283–5.
18. This is a soundly transmitted hadith. See: Aḥmad b. Ḥanbal, *Musnad al-Imām Aḥmad b. Ḥanbal* (Beirut: Mu'assasat al-Risāla, 1999), 32:241–3.
19. This is a canonical hadith recorded by both Bukhārī and Muslim. For a *takhrīj*, see: Ibn Ḥanbal, *Musnad*, 13:207f.
20. This report is of dubious authenticity. See Ch. 5, n. 35 above.
21. Gomaa is likely referring to the protests outside the Republican Guard on 8 July 2013.
22. This hadith is deemed weak. See: Ibn Mājah, *Sunan Ibn Mājah*, ed. Shu'ayb al-Arna'ūṭ et al. (Beirut: Dār al-Risāla al-'Ālamiyya, 2009), 5:224.

APPENDIX 3

1. This speech was given on 18 August 2013. For the original, see: https://youtu.be/gxm8w-yVyH8 (https://www.youtube.com/watch?v=gxm8w-yVyH8).
2. A reference to the Qur'anic verse 54:45 in which the disbelievers of Quraysh are addressed, and threatened with these words, referring to them in the third person.
3. This report is deemed a fabrication by a number of scholars. See Ch. 5, n. 35 above.
4. Gomaa mispronounces this name. See Appendix 2, n. 5 above.
5. Gomaa mispronounces this name. See Appendix 2, n. 7 above.
6. For a discussion of hadiths pertaining to these eschatological beliefs, some of which are of disputed reliability, see: http://www.ahlalhdeeth.com/vb/showthread.php?t=319052.
7. For my reasons for thinking Gomaa is referring to Qaradawi here, see the discussion in Chapter 7.
8. See Peter Beaumont, 'Hamas destroys al-Qaida group in violent Gaza battle,' *The Guardian*, 16 August 2009, http://www.theguardian.com/world/2009/aug/15/hamas-battle-gaza-islamists-al-qaida; and 'Gaza Islamist leader dies in raid,' *BBC News*, 15 August 2009, http://news.bbc.co.uk/2/hi/middle_east/8202746.stm. Qaradawi commented at the time that Hamas was justified, as the group occupying the mosque was violent, and was not open to non-violent negotiations. See: https://youtu.be/8VSECTsDlaU.
9. In Arabic, *nubāḥ* is necessarily the act of a canine, unlike the English word 'barking'.
10. Gomaa points at the army in front of him as he says this.
11. These sentences are stated in Egyptian dialect and are unclear.
12. In their detailed report on the massacre, HRW found little evidence of any violent intent on the part of the protests against the security forces. See: Omar Shakir, *All According to Plan: The Rab'a Massacre and Mass Killings of Protesters in Egypt* (New York, NY: Human Rights Watch, 2014), available at https://www.hrw.org/report/2014/08/12/all-according-plan/raba-massacre-and-mass-killings-protesters-egypt.

13. For a discussion of the soundness of this report, see Ch. 5, n. 42.
14. See Ch. 5, n. 43 above for a discussion of this report.
15. For the phrase *yiḍrab fi-l-malyān*, see El-Said Badawi and Martin Hinds, *A Dictionary of Egyptian Arabic* (Beirut: Librarie du Liban, 1986), 834.
16. There is in fact extensive documented evidence that the soldiers clearing Rabaa chased protestors into buildings in order to torture and or kill them. See: Shakir, *All According to Plan*.
17. This report is of dubious authenticity. See Ch. 5, n. 35 above.
18. Gomaa gesticulates here, making a cutting action with his hand.
19. A reference to the Qur'anic verse 54:45 in which the disbelievers of Quraysh are addressed, and threatened with these words, referring to them in the third person.

BIBLIOGRAPHY

Abaza, Mona. 'Two Intellectuals: The Malaysian S. N. Al-Attas and the Egyptian Mohammed 'Immara, and the Islamization of Knowledge Debate.' *Asian Journal of Social Science* 30:2 (2002), 354–83.

Abdelkader, Deina Ali. *Islamic Activists: The Anti-Enlightenment Democrats*. New York: Pluto Press, 2011.

Abdo, Geneive. *The New Sectarianism: The Arab Uprisings and the Rebirth of the Shi'a-Sunni Divide*. New York: Oxford University Press, 2017.

Abou El Fadl, Khaled. *Rebellion and Violence in Islamic Law*. Cambridge: Cambridge University Press, 2001.

———. 'The Centrality of Sharī'ah to Government and Constitutionalism in Islam.' In *Constitutionalism in Islamic Countries: Between Upheaval and Continuity*, eds Rainer Grote and Tilmann Röder. New York: Oxford University Press, 2012.

———. 'The Praetorian State in the Arab Spring.' *University of Pennsylvania Journal of International Law* 34 (2013): 305–14.

———. 'Failure of a Revolution. The Military, Secular Intelligentsia and Religion in Egypt's Pseudo-Secular State.' In *Routledge Handbook of the Arab Spring: Rethinking Democratization*, ed. Larbi Sadiki, 253–70. London & New York: Routledge, 2015.

———. 'Egypt's Secularized Intelligentsia and the Guardians of Truth.' In *Egypt and the Contradictions of Liberalism: Illiberal Intelligentsia and the Future of Egyptian Democracy*, eds Dalia F. Fahmy and Daanish Faruqi, 235–52. London: Oneworld, 2017.

———. 'Dominating Religion in Egypt's Pseudo-Secular State.' http://www.abc.net.au/religion/articles/2013/09/15/3848943.htm. Accessed 5 March 2018.

Abū Dāwūd. *Sunan Abū Dāwūd*, eds Shu'ayb al-Arna'ūṭ et al. Beirut: Dār al-Risāla al-'Ālamiyya, 2009.

Abū Zayd, Waṣfī 'Ashūr. *al-Qaraḍāwī: al-Imām al-Thā'ir: Dirāsa Taḥlīliyya Uṣūliyya fī Ma'ālim Ijtihādihi li-l-Thawra al-Miṣriyya*, 2nd edn. Cairo: Dār al-Maqāṣid, 2017.

Achcar, Gilbert. *The People Want: A Radical Exploration of the Arab Uprising*, trans. G. M. Goshgarian. Berkeley: University of California Press, 2013

———. *Morbid Symptoms: Relapse in the Arab Uprising*. Stanford University Press, 2016.

Adang, Camilla, Hassan Ansari, Maribel Fierro, and Sabine Schmidtke. *Accusations of Unbelief in Islam: A Diachronic Perspective on Takfīr*. Leiden: Brill, 2016.

Agrama, Hussein Ali. *Questioning Secularism: Islam, Sovereignty and the Rule of Law in Egypt*. Chicago: University of Chicago Press, 2012.

Alibašić, Ahmet. *Political Opposition in Contemporary Islamic Political Thought in the Arab World*. MA dissertation. Kuala Lumpur: International Institute of Islamic Thought and Civilization (ISTAC), 1999.

———. 'The Right of Political Opposition in Islamic History and Legal Theory: An Exploration of an Ambivalent Heritage.' *Al-Shajarah: Journal of the International Institute of Islamic Thought and Civilization (ISTAC)* 4:2 (1999), 231–96.

Allal, Amin and Thomas Pierret. 'Chapitre Introductif: Les Processus Révolutionnaires Arabes en Actes.' In *Au Coeur des Révoltes Arabes: Devenir Révolutionnaires*, eds Amin Allal and Thomas Pierret. Paris: Armand Colin, 2013.

al-Anani, Khalil. 'The 'Anguish' of the Muslim Brotherhood in Egypt.' In *Routledge Handbook of the Arab Spring: Rethinking Democratization*, ed. Larbi Sadiki, 227–39. London & New York: Routledge, 2015.

———. *Inside the Muslim Brotherhood: Religion, Identity, and Politics*. New York: Oxford University Press, 2016.

Anjum, Ovamir. *Politics, Law, and Community in Islamic Thought: The Taymiyyan Moment*. Cambridge: Cambridge University Press, 2012.

———. 'Mystical Authority and Governmentality in Medieval Islam.' In *Sufism and Society: Arrangements of the Mystical in the Muslim World, 1200–1800*, eds John Curry and Erik Ohlander. London: Routledge, 2012, 71–93.

———. 'Qaraḍāwī, Yusuf al-.' In *The [Oxford] Encyclopedia of Islam and Law*. Oxford Islamic Studies Online, n.d. http://www.oxfordislamicstudies.com/article/opr/t349/e0107.

———. 'Salafis and Democracy: Doctrine and Context.' *The Muslim World* 106:3 (2016), last accessed: 13 May 2020.

Apter, David E. "Political Religion in the New Nations." In *Old Societies and New States: The Quest for Modernity in Asia and Africa*, ed. Clifford Geertz. London: Collier-Macmillan, 1963.

Al-Arian, Abdullah. 'From the Ashes of Rabaa: History and the Future of Egypt's Muslim Brotherhood'. *Centre for Middle East Studies Occasional Paper Series*, November 2015, https://www.du.edu/korbel/middleeast/media/documents/occasionalpaper4.pdf, last accessed: 13 May 2020.

Arjomand, Saïd Amir. *Revolution: Structure and Meaning in World History*. Chicago: University of Chicago Press, 2019.

Armbrust, Walter. *Martyrs and Tricksters: An Ethnography of the Egyptian Revolution*. Princeton: Princeton University Press, 2019.

Asad, Talal. 'The Idea of an Anthropology of Islam'. *Qui Parle* 17:2 (2009), 1–30.

al-ʿAsqalānī, Ibn Ḥajar. *Taqrīb al-Tahdhīb*, ed. ʿĀdil Murshid. Beirut: Mu'assasat al-Risāla, 1999.

———. *Sharḥ Nukhbat al-Fikar fī Muṣṭalaḥ Ahl al-Athar*, ed. Ṭāriq Abū Muʿādh. Riyadh: Dār al-Mughnī, 2009.

Ayubi, Nazih. *Political Islam: Religion and Politics in the Arab World*. New York, NY: Routledge, 1991.

al-Azami, Usaama. 'Neo-traditionalist Sufis and Arab Politics: A Preliminary Mapping of the Transnational Networks of Counter-revolutionary Scholars after the Arab Revolutions.' In *Global Sufism: Boundaries, Structures, and Politics*, eds Mark Sedgwick and Francesco Piraino. London: Hurst, 2019, 225–36.

———. 'Abdullāh bin Bayyah and the Arab Revolutions: Counter-revolutionary Neo-traditionalism's Ideological Struggle against Islamism.' *The Muslim World*, 109:3 (2019), 343–61.

———. 'Legitimizing Political Dissent: Islamist Salafi Discourses on Obedience and Rebellion after the Arab Revolutions.' In *Salafi Social and Political Movements: National and Transnational Contexts*, ed. Masooda Bano. Edinburgh: Edinburgh University Press, 2021.

———. 'Locating *Ḥākimiyya* in Global History: Premodern Islamic Conceptions of Sovereignty and their Islamist Reception after Mawdūdī and Quṭb.' *Journal of the Royal Asiatic Society* (forthcoming).

al-ʿAẓīmābādī, Shams al-Ḥaqq. *ʿAwn al-Maʿbūd Sharḥ Sunan Abī Dāwūd*, ed. ʿAbd al-Raḥmān M. ʿUthmān. Medina: Muḥammad ʿAbd al-Muḥsin, 1969.

Badawi, El-Said and Martin Hinds. *A Dictionary of Egyptian Arabic*. Beirut: Librarie du Liban, 1986.

Bagley, F. R. C. (trans). *Ghazālī's Book of Counsel for Kings (Naṣīḥat al-Mulūk)*. Oxford University Press, 1964.

Bano, Masooda. 'Protector of 'al-Wasatiyya' Islam: Cairo's al-Azhar University.' In *Shaping Global Islamic Discourses: The Role of al-Azhar, al-Medina, and al-Mustafa*, eds Masooda Bano and Keiko Sakurai. Edinburgh: Edinburgh University Press, 2015.

——— (ed.). *Modern Islamic Authority and Social Change, Volume 1: Evolving Debates in Muslim Majority Countries*. Edinburgh: Edinburgh University Press, 2018.

——— (ed.). *Modern Islamic Authority and Social Change, Volume 2: Evolving Debates in the West*. Edinburgh: Edinburgh University Press, 2018.

———. 'At the Tipping Point? Al-Azhar's Growing Crisis of Moral Authority,' *International Journal of Middle East Studies* 50:4 (2018), 715–34.

———. *The Revival of Islamic Rationalism: Logic, Metaphysics and Mysticism in Modern Muslim Societies*. Cambridge: Cambridge University Press, 2020.

Bano, Masooda and Hanane Benadi. 'Official Al-Azhar versus al-Azhar Imagined: The Arab Spring and the Revival of Religious Imagination.' *Die Welt Des Islams* 59:1 (2019): 7–32.

Bano, Masooda, and Keiko Sakurai (eds). *Shaping Global Islamic Discourses: The Role of Al-Azhar, Al-Madinah and Al-Mustafa*. Edinburgh: Edinburgh University Press, 2015.

Bano, Masooda (ed.). *Salafi Social and Political Movements: National and Transnational Contexts*. Edinburgh: Edinburgh University Press, 2021.

Barraclough, Steven. 'Al-Azhar: Between the Government and the Islamists.' *Middle East Journal* 52:2 (1998), 236–49.

Barrons, Genevieve. "Suleiman: Mubarak Decided to Step down #egypt #jan25 OH MY GOD': Examining the Use of Social Media in the 2011 Egyptian Revolution.' *Contemporary Arab Affairs* 5:1 (2012), 54–67.

Bassiouni, M. Cherif. 'Egypt's Unfinished Revolution.' In *Civil Resistance in the Arab Spring: Triumphs and Disasters*, eds Adam Roberts, Michael J. Willis, Rory McCarthy, and Timothy Garton Ash. Oxford: Oxford University Press, 2016, 53–87.

Bayat, Asef. *Revolution without Revolutionaries: Making Sense of the Arab Spring*. Stanford University Press, 2017.

al-Bayhaqī, Abū Bakr. *al-Sunan al-Kubrā*. Ed. Muḥammad 'Aṭā. Beirut: Dār al-Kutub al-'Ilmiyya, 2003.

Bebawi, Saba, and Diana Bossio. *Social Media and the Politics of Reportage: The 'Arab Spring.'* New York: Palgrave Macmillan, 2014.

Belal, Youssef. 'The Life of *Shari'a*.' PhD Dissertation. University of California: Berkeley, 2017.

———. 'Islamic Law, Truth, Ethics.' *Comparative Studies of South Asia, Africa and the Middle East* 38:1 (2018), 107–21.

Bin Bayyah, Abdullah ('Abdullāh b. Bayya). *Tanbīh al-Marājiʿ 'alā Ta'ṣīl Fiqh al-Wāqiʿ*. Beirut: Markaz Namā', 2014.

Bin Bayyah, 'Abdullah. *Al-Irhāb: Tashkhīṣ wa-Ḥulūl*. Riyadh: al-'Ubaykān, 2007.

Bin Bayyah, Abdallah, et al. *In Pursuit of Peace: Framework Speech for the Forum for Promoting Peace in Muslim Societies*. Abu Dhabi: FPPMS, 2014.

Brockopp, Jonathan E. *Muhammad's Heirs: The Rise of Muslim Scholarly Communities, 622–950*. Cambridge: Cambridge University Press, 2017.

Brooke, Steven, and Elizabeth R. Nugent. 'Exclusion and Violence After the Egyptian Coup.' *Middle East Law and Governance* 12:1 (2020), 61–85.

Brown, Jonathan. 'Salafis and Sufis in Egypt.' *Carnegie Endowment for International Peace, Carnegie Papers (Middle East)*, 2011.

———. 'Even If It's Not True It's True: Using Unreliable Hadīths in Sunni Islam.' *Islamic Law and Society* 18:1 (2011), 1–52.

———. *Misquoting Muhammad: The Challenge and Choices of Interpreting the Prophet's Legacy*. Oxford: Oneworld, 2014.

———. *Hadith: Muhammad's Legacy in the Medieval and Modern World*, 2nd edn. Oxford: Oneworld, 2017.

Brown, Nathan J. 'Post-Revolutionary Al-Azhar.' *Carnegie Endowment for International Peace*, 3 October 2011, http://carnegieendowment.org/2011/10/03/post-revolutionary-al-azhar/, last accessed: 12 February 2021.

———. 'Contention in religion and state in postrevolutionary Egypt.' *Social Research* 79:2 (2012), 531–50.

———. 'Egypt's Constitutional Cul-de-sac,' *CMI Insight*, March 2014.

———. *Arguing Islam after the Revival of Arab Politics*. Oxford: Oxford University Press, 2016.

Bruns, Axel, Tim Highfield, and Jean Burgess. 'The Arab Spring and Social Media Audiences.' *American Behavioral Scientist* 57:7 (2013), 871–98.

al-Bukhārī. *Ṣaḥīḥ al-Bukhārī (al-Jāmiʿ al-Ṣaḥīḥ al-Mukhtaṣar)*, ed. Muṣṭafā Dīb al-Bughā. Beirut: Dār Ibn Kathīr, 1987.

———. *al-Tārīkh al-Kabīr*. Hyderabad: Dāʾirat al-Maʿārif al-ʿUthmāniyya, n.d.

Burhani, Ahmad Najib. 'Fatwās on Mohamed Bouazizi's Self-Immolation: Religious Authority, Media, and Secularization.' In *Sharia Dynamics: Islamic Law and Sociopolitical Processes*, ed. Timothy P. Daniels. New York: Palgrave Macmillan, 2017, 63–89.

al-Būṭī, Muḥammad Saʿīd Ramaḍān. *Fiqh al-Sīra al-Nabawiyya*, 10th edn. Damascus: Dār al-Fikr, 1991.

Cavatorta, Francesco, and Fabio Merone (eds). *Salafism After the Arab Awakening: Contending with People's Power*. Oxford: Oxford University Press, 2017.

Cook, David. *Martyrdom in Islam*. Cambridge: Cambridge University Press, 2007.

Cook, Michael. *Commanding Right and Forbidding Wrong in Islamic Thought*. Cambridge: Cambridge University Press, 2000.

———. *Ancient Religions, Modern Politics: The Islamic Case in Comparative Perspective*. Princeton: Princeton University Press, 2014.

Crone, Patricia. 'Did al-Ghazālī Write a Mirror for Princes?' *Jerusalem Studies in Arabic and Islam* 10 (1987), 167–91.

———. *Medieval Islamic Political Thought*. Edinburgh: Edinburgh University Press, 2004.

al-Darʿī, Muḥammad b. Nāṣir. *The Prayer of the Oppressed*, ed. Hamza Yusuf. Sandala Productions, 2010.

Daulatzai, Sohail, and Junaid Rana (eds). *With Stones in Our Hands: Writings on Muslims, Racism, and Empire*. Minneapolis: University of Minnesota Press, 2018.

Decosimo, David. 'An *Umma* of Accountability: Al-Ghazālī against Domination.' *Soundings: An Interdisciplinary Journal* 98:3 (2015), 260–88.

al-Dhahabī, Shams al-Dīn. *Mizān al-Iʿtidāl fī Naqd al-Rijāl*, eds ʿAlī Muḥammad Muʿawwaḍ, et al. Beirut: Dār al-Kutub al-ʿIlmiyya, 1995.

———. *Tārīkh al-Islām wa-Wafayāt al-Mashāhīr wa-l-A'lām*, ed. Bashshār 'Awwād Ma'rūf. Beirut: Dār al-Gharb al-Islāmī, 2003.

Dīb. 'Abd al-'Aẓīm (ed.). *Yūsuf al-Qaraḍāwī: Kalimāt fī Takrīmihī wa-Buḥūth fī Fikrihi wa-Fiqhihi Muhdāh ilayhi bi-Munāsabat Bulūghihi al-Sab'īn*. Cairo: Dār al-Salām, 2004.

Eickelman, Dale F., and James P. Piscatori. *Muslim Politics*. Princeton: Princeton University Press, 1996.

ElMasry, Sarah, and Neil Ketchley. 'After the Massacre: Women's Islamist Activism in Post-Coup Egypt.' *Middle East Law and Governance* 12:1 (2020), 86–108.

El Shamsy, Ahmed. *Rediscovering the Islamic Classics: How Editors and Print Culture Transformed an Intellectual Tradition*. Princeton: Princeton University Press, 2020.

Elston, Mary Beinecke. 'Reviving Turāth: Islamic Education in Modern Egypt.' PhD dissertation. Harvard University, 2020.

Esposito, John L. (ed.). *The Oxford Encyclopedia of the Islamic World*. New York: Oxford University Press, 2009.

Esposito, John L., Tamara Sonn, and John O. Voll. *Islam and Democracy after the Arab Spring*. New York: Oxford University Press, 2015.

Euben, Roxanne, and Muhammad Qasim Zaman (eds). *Princeton Readings in Islamist Thought: Texts and Contexts from al-Bannā to Bin Laden*. Princeton: Princeton University Press, 2009.

Fadel, Mohammad. 'Public Authority (Sulṭān) in Islamic Law.' In *The Oxford International Encyclopedia of Legal History,* ed. Stanley N Katz. Oxford: Oxford University Press, 2009, https://www.oxfordreference.com/view/10.1093/acref/9780195134056.001.0001/acref-9780195134056-e-663, last accessed: 12 February 2021.

———. 'Modernist Islamic Political Thought and the Egyptian and Tunisian Revolutions of 2011.' *Middle East Law and Governance* 3:1–2 (2011), 94–104.

———. 'Islamic Law and Constitution-Making: The Authoritarian Temptation and the Arab Spring.' *Osgoode Hall Law Journal* 53:2 (2016), 472–507.

———. 'Review of Law and Revolution: Legitimacy and Constitutionalism After the Arab Spring. By Nimer Sultany. Oxford: Oxford University Press, 2017.' *Law & Society Review* 52:3 (2018), 810–13.

———. 'Political Legitimacy, Democracy and Islamic Law: The Place of Self-Government in Islamic Political Thought.' *Journal of Islamic Ethics* 2:1–2 (2018), 59–75.

Fahmy, Dalia, and Daanish Faruqi (eds), *Egypt and the Contradictions of Liberalism: Illiberal Intelligentsia and the Future of Egyptian Democracy*. Oxford: Oneworld, 2017.

Falk, Richard. 'Reflections on Revolution, Politics and Law: The Unfolding Process in the Arab World.' *Transnational Legal Theory* 4:1 (2013), 83–107.

Faris, David. 'Dissent and Revolution in a Digital Age: Social Media, Blogging and Activism in Egypt.' *European Journal of Communication* 29:3 (2014), 392.

Feldman, Noah. *The Fall and Rise of the Islamic State*. Princeton, N.J.: Princeton University Press, 2008.

Filiu, Jean-Pierre. *The Arab Revolution: Ten Lessons from the Democratic Uprising*. New York: Oxford University Press, 2011.

———. *From Deep State to Islamic State: The Arab Counter-Revolution and Its Jihadi Legacy*. Oxford: Oxford University Press, 2015.

Freer, Courtney. *Rentier Islamism: The Influence of the Muslim Brotherhood in Gulf Monarchies*. Oxford: Oxford University Press, 2018.

Friedlander, Nuri. 'Gomaa, 'Ali.' In *The [Oxford] Encyclopedia of Islam and Law*. Oxford Islamic Studies Online, n.d. http://www.oxfordislamicstudies.com/article/opr/t349/e0122, last accessed: 23 April 2020.

Funatsu, Ryuichi. 'Al-Kawakibi's Thesis and Its Echoes in the Arab World Today.' *Harvard Middle Eastern and Islamic Review* 7 (2006), 1–40.

Gaborieau, Marc, and Malika Zeghal. 'Autorités religieuses en islam.' *Archives de Sciences Sociales des Religions* 49:125 (2004), 5–21.

Garden, Kenneth. *The First Islamic Reviver: Abū Ḥamid al-Ghazālī and his Revival of the Religious Sciences*. Oxford University Press, 2013.

Gauvain, Richard. 'Salafism in Modern Egypt: Panacea or Pest?' *Political Theology* 11:6 (2010), 802–25.

Gerges, Fawaz (ed.). *The New Middle East: Protest and Revolution in the Arab World*. Cambridge: Cambridge University Press, 2013.

Ghanem, Hafez (ed.). *The Arab Spring Five Years Later: Case Studies*. Washington, DC: Brookings Institution Press, 2016.

Ghanem, Hiba. 'The 2011 Egyptian Revolution Chants: A Romantic-Muʿtazilī Moral Order.' *British Journal of Middle Eastern Studies* 45:3 (2017), 430–42.

Gomaa, Ali (Jumʿa, ʿAlī). *Fatāwā al-Imām Muḥammad ʿAbduh*. Cairo: al-Jamʿiyya al-Khayriyya, 2005.

———. *al-Mutashaddidūn: Manhajuhum wa-Munāqashat Ahamm Qaḍāyāhum*. Abu Dhabi: Dār al-Faqīh li-l-Nashr wa-l-Tawzīʿ, 2015.

———. *Responding from the Tradition: One Hundred Contemporary Fatwas by the Grand Mufti of Egypt*. Louisville, KY: Fons Vitae, 2012.

Gräf, Bettina. 'Media Fatwas, Yusuf al-Qaradawi and Media-Mediated Authority in Islam.' *Orient – Deutsche Zeitschrift Fur Politik Und Wirtschaft Des Orients* 51 (2010), 6–15.

Gräf, Bettina, and Jakob Skovgaard-Petersen (eds). *The Global Mufti: The Phenomenon of Yusuf al-Qaradawi*. London: Hurst Publishers, 2009.

Grewal, Zareena. *Islam is a Foreign Country: American Muslims and the Global Crisis of Authority*. New York: New York University Press, 2013.

Hafez, Mohammed M. *Why Muslims Rebel: Repression and Resistance in the Islamic World*. Boulder: Lynne Rienner Publishers, 2003.

Hallaq, Wael B. *Sharī'a: Theory, Practice, Transformations*. Cambridge: Cambridge University Press, 2009.

———. *The Impossible State: Islam, Politics, and Modernity's Moral Predicament*. New York: Columbia University Press, 2013.

Hamid, Sadek. *Sufis, Salafis and Islamists: The Contested Ground of British Islamic Activism*. London: I B Tauris, 2016.

Hamid, Shadi. *Temptations of Power: Islamists and Illiberal Democracy in a New Middle East*. New York: Oxford University Press, USA, 2014.

———. *Islamic Exceptionalism: How the Struggle Over Islam Is Reshaping the World*. New York: St. Martin's Press, 2016.

Hamid, Shadi, and William McCants (eds). *Rethinking Political Islam*. Oxford: Oxford University Press, 2017.

Hamzawy, Amr. 'Egyptian Liberals and Their Anti-Democratic Deceptions: A Contemporary Sad Narrative.' In *Egypt and the Contradictions of Liberalism: Illiberal Intelligentsia and the Future of Egyptian Democracy*, eds Dalia F. Fahmy and Daanish Faruqi. London: Oneworld, 2017, 337–60.

Hashemi, Nader. 'The Arab Spring, U.S. Foreign Policy, and the Question of Democracy in the Middle East'. *Denver Journal of International Law and Policy*, 41:1 (2012), 31–46.

———. 'The ISIS Crisis and the Broken Politics of the Arab World: A Framework for Understanding Radical Islamism.' In *Routledge Handbook on Human Rights and the Middle East and North Africa*, ed. Anthony Chase. London: Routledge, 2017.

Hashemi, Nader, and Danny Postel (eds). *Sectarianization: Mapping the New Politics of the Middle East*. London: Hurst Publishers, 2017.

Hatina, Meir (ed.). *Guardians of Faith in Modern Times: 'Ulama' in the Middle East*. Boston: Brill, 2009.

———. *'Ulama', Politics, and the Public Sphere: An Egyptian Perspective*. Salt Lake City: University of Utah Press, 2010.

Hellyer, H. A. *A Revolution Undone: Egypt's Road Beyond Revolt*. New York: Oxford University Press, 2016.

Herman, Edward S., and Noam Chomsky. *Manufacturing Consent: The Political Economy of the Mass Media*. New York: Pantheon Books, 1988.

Hillenbrand, Carole. 'Islamic Orthodoxy or Realpolitik? Al-Ghazālī's Views on Government.' *Iran* 26:1 (1988), 81–94.

Hirschkind, Charles. *The Ethical Soundscape: Cassette Sermons and Islamic Counterpublics*. New York: Columbia University Press, 2006.

Høigilt, Jacob, and Frida Nome. 'Egyptian Salafism in Revolution.' *Journal of Islamic Studies* 25:1 (2014), 33–54.

Ibn Balbān al-Fārisī. *Al-Iḥsān fī Taqrīb Ṣaḥīḥ Ibn Ḥibbān*, ed. Shu'ayb al-Arna'ūṭ. Beirut: Mu'assasat al-Risāla, 1991.

Ibn al-Ḥajjāj, Muslim. *Ṣaḥīḥ Muslim bi-Sharḥ al-Nawawī*. Cairo: al-Maṭba'a al-Miṣriyya bi-l-Azhar, 1929.

Ibn Ḥanbal, Aḥmad. *Musnad al-Imām Aḥmad b. Ḥanbal*. Beirut: Mu'assasat al-Risāla, 1999.

Ibn Ḥazm, *al-Muḥallā bi-l-Āthār*. Beirut: Dār al-Kutub al-'Ilmiyya, 2003.

Ibn Mājah, *Sunan Ibn Mājah*, eds Shu'ayb al-Arna'ūṭ, et al. Beirut: Dār al-Risāla al-'Ālamiyya, 2009.

Ibn Nāṣir al-Dīn. *Tawḍīḥ al-Mushtabih*, ed. Muḥammad Na'īm al-'Araqsūsī. Beirut: Mu'assasat al-Risāla, 1993.

Ibn Rajab al-Ḥanbalī. *Jāmi' al-'Ulūm wa-l-Ḥikam*, ed. Māhir Yāsīn al-Faḥl. Damascus: Dār Ibn Kathīr, 2008.

Ibrahim, Ahmed Fekry. *Pragmatism in Islamic Law: A Social and Intellectual History*. Syracuse: Syracuse University Press, 2015.

'Imāra, Muḥammad. *Thawrat 25 Yanāyir wa-kasr ḥājiz al-khawf*. Cairo: Dār al-Salām, 2011.

Ismail, Salwa. *Rethinking Islamist Politics: Culture, the State and Islamism*. New York: I. B. Tauris, 2003.

Jackson, Sherman A. *Islamic Law and the State: The Constitutional Jurisprudence of Shihāb al-Dīn al-Qarāfī*. Leiden: Brill, 1996.

Jamali, Reza. *Online Arab Spring: Social Media and Fundamental Change*. Waltham, MA: Chandos Publishing, 2015.

al-Jawziyya, Ibn Qayyim. Ḥādī al-Arwāḥ ilā Bilād al-Afrāḥ, ed. Zā'id al-Nushayrī. Jeddah: Dār 'ālam al-Fawā'id, 1428 [2007].

Jum'a, 'Alī (cf. Gomaa, Ali) (ed.). *Fatāwā al-Imām Muḥammad 'Abduh*. Cairo: al-Jam'iyya al-Khayriyya, 2005.

———. *al-Mutashaddidūn: Manhajuhum wa-Munāqashat Ahamm Qaḍāyāhum*. Abu Dhabi: Dār al-Faqīh li-l-Nashr wa-l-Tawzī', 2015.

———. Responding from the Tradition: One Hundred Contemporary Fatwas by the Grand Mufti of Egypt. Louisville, KY: Fons Vitae, 2012.

Kamrava, Mehran (ed.). *Beyond the Arab Spring: The Evolving Ruling Bargain in the Middle East*. Oxford: Oxford University Press, 2014.

Kandil, Hazem. *Soldiers, Spies and Statesmen: Egypt's Road to Revolt*. London: Verso, 2012.

———. *Inside the Brotherhood*. Cambridge: Polity Press, 2015.

Keaney, Heather N. *Medieval Islamic Historiography: Remembering Rebellion*. New York: Routledge, 2013.

Kenney, Jeffrey T. *Muslim Rebels: Kharijites and the Politics of Extremism in Egypt*. Oxford University Press, 2006.

Ketchley, Neil. *Egypt in a Time of Revolution: Contentious Politics and the Arab Spring*. Cambridge, UK: Cambridge University Press, 2017.

al-Khansā', *Dīwān al-Khansā'*, ed. Ḥamdū Ṭammās. Beirut: Dār al-Ma'rifa, 2004.

al-Khaṭīb, Mu'tazz. *Yūsuf al-Qaraḍāwī: Faqīh al-Ṣahwa al-Islāmiyya: Sīra Fikriyya Taḥlīliyya*. Beirut: Markaz al-Ḥaḍāra li-Tanmiyat al-Fikr al-Islāmī, 2009.

al-Khinn, Muṣṭafā. *al-Manhal al-Rāwī min Taqrīb al-Nawāwī*. Damascus: Dār al-Mallāḥ, 1998.

Kirkpatrick, David D. *Into the Hands of the Soldiers: Freedom and Chaos in Egypt and the Middle East*. London: Bloomsbury, 2018.

Korb, Scott. *Light Without Fire: The Making of America's First Muslim College*. Boston, MA: Beacon Press, 2013.

Krämer, Gudrun. *Ḥasan al-Bannā*. Oxford: Oneworld Publications, 2010.

———. *Demokratie Im Islam: Der Kampf Für Toleranz Und Freiheit in Der Arabischen Welt*. München: Verlag C. H. Beck, 2011.

Krämer, Gudrun, and Sabine Schmidtke. *Speaking for Islam: Religious Authorities in Muslim Societies*. Boston: Brill, 2006.

Lacroix, Stèphane. *Awakening Islam: The Politics of Religious Dissent in Contemporary Saudi Arabia*, trans. G. Holoch. Cambridge, MA: Harvard University Press, 2011.

Lacroix, Stéphane, and Jean-Pierre Filiu (eds). *Revisiting the Arab Uprisings: The Politics of a Revolutionary Moment*. Oxford: Oxford University Press, 2018.

Lane, Edward William. *Arabic-English Lexicon*. London: Williams & Norgate, 1863.

Lauzière, Henri. *The Making of Salafism: Islamic Reform in the Twentieth Century*. New York: Columbia University Press, 2015.

Lav, Daniel. *Radical Islam and the Revival of Medieval Theology*. Cambridge: Cambridge University Press, 2012.

Lesch, Ann M. 'The Authoritarian States Power over Civil Society.' In *Egypt and the Contradictions of Liberalism: Illiberal Intelligentsia and the Future of Egyptian Democracy*, eds Dalia F. Fahmy and Daanish Faruqi. Oxford: Oneworld, 2017, 121–74.

Lipa, Michal. 'Internal Determinants of Authoritarianism in the Arab Middle East. Egypt before the Arab Spring.' *Hemispheres: Studies on Cultures and Societies* 31:3 (2016), 57–67.

Lombardo, Paul A. *Three Generations, No Imbeciles: Eugenics, the Supreme Court, and* Buck v. Bell. Baltimore: The Johns Hopkins University Press, 2008.

Lynch, Marc. *The Arab Uprising: The Unfinished Revolutions of the New Middle East*. New York: Public Affairs, 2012.

——— (ed.). *The Arab Uprisings Explained: New Contentious Politics in the Middle East*. New York: Columbia University Press, 2014.

Lynch, Marc, and Jillian Schwedler. 'Introduction to the Special Issue on 'Islamist Politics after the Arab Uprisings''. *Middle East Law and Governance* 12:1 (2020), 3–13.

Mahmood, Saba. *Politics of Piety: The Islamic Revival and the Feminist Subject*. Princeton: Princeton University Press, 2005.

Mandaville, Peter. *Islam and Politics*, 2nd edn. London: Routledge, 2014.

March, Andrew F. *The Caliphate of Man: Popular Sovereignty in Modern Islamic Thought*. Cambridge, Massachusetts; London, England: Harvard University Press, 2019.

Masoud, Tarek. *Counting Islam: Religion, Class, and Elections in Egypt*. Cambridge: Cambridge University Press, 2014.

Mathiesen, Kasper. 'Anglo-American 'Traditional Islam' and Its Discourse of Orthodoxy.' *Journal of Arabic and Islamic Studies* 13 (2013), 191–219.

Matthiesen, Toby. *Sectarian Gulf: Bahrain, Saudi Arabia, and the Arab Spring That Wasn't*. Stanford: Stanford University Press, 2013.

Mehta, Uday Singh. *Liberalism and Empire: A Study in Nineteenth-Century British Liberal Thought*. Chicago: University of Chicago Press, 1999.

Meijer, Roel (ed.). *Global Salafism: Islam's New Religious Movement*. London: Hurst Publishers, 2009.

Mitchell, Richard P. *The Society of the Muslim Brothers*. Oxford: Oxford University Press, 1969.

Mohamed, Eid, and Dalia Fahmy (eds). *Arab Spring: Modernity, Identity and Change*. New York: Palgrave Macmillan, 2020.

Moll, Yasmin. 'The Wretched Revolution.' *Middle East Report* 273 (2014): 34–9.

———. 'Subtitling Islam: Translation, Mediation, Critique.' *Public Culture* 29:2 82 (2017), 333–61.

———. 'Television Is Not Radio: Theologies of Mediation in the Egyptian Islamic Revival.' *Cultural Anthropology* 33:2 (2018), 233–65.

Momani, Bessma, and Eid Mohamed (eds). *Egypt beyond Tahrir Square*. Indiana University Press, 2016.

Moosa, Ebrahim. 'Aesthetics and Transcendence in the Arab Uprisings.' *Middle East Law and Governance* 3:1–2 (2011), 171–80.

———. 'Political Theology in the Aftermath of the Arab Spring: Returning to the Ethical.' In *The African Renaissance and the Afro-Arab Spring: A Season of Rebirth?*, eds Charles Villa-Vicencio, Erik Doxtader, and Ebrahim Moosa. Washington, DC: Georgetown University Press, 2015, 101–20.

———. 'Recovering the Ethical: Practices, Politics, Tradition.' In *The Sharīʿa: History, Ethics, and Law*, ed. Amyn B. Sajoo. London & New York: I. B. Tauris & The Institute of Ismaili Studies, 2018, 39–57.

Mouline, Nabil. *The Clerics of Islam: Religious Authority and Political Power in Saudi Arabia*, trans. Ethan Rundell. New Haven: Yale University Press, 2014.

Muedini, Fait. *Sponsoring Sufism: How Governments Promote 'Mystical Islam' in Their Domestic and Foreign Policies*. New York: Palgrave Macmillan, 2015.

Muzakkir, Muhamad Rofiq. 'Understanding the Discourse of 'Alī Jumʿah on the Military Coup During the Arab Spring in Egypt.' *Ilahiyat Studies* 10:2 (2019).

al-Nadwī, Muḥammad Akram. *Kifāyat al-Rāwī 'an al-ʿAllāma Yūsuf al-Qaraḍāwī*. Damascus: Dār al-Qalam, 2001.

———. *Madrasah Life: A Student's Day at Nadwat al-ʿUlamā'*. London: Turath Publishing, 2007.

Nakissa, Aria. 'The Fiqh of Revolution and the Arab Spring: Secondary Segmentation as a Trend in Islamic Legal Doctrine.' *The Muslim World* 105:3 (2015), 398–421.

Nasr, Seyyed Vali Reza. *Mawdudi and the Making of Islamic Revivalism*. New York: Oxford University Press, 1996.

Nugent, Elizabeth R. 'The Psychology of Repression and Polarization.' *World Politics* 72:2 (2020), 291–334.

Osman, Amr. 'Past Contradictions, Contemporary Dilemmas: Egypt's 2013 Coup and Early Islamic History.' *Digest of Middle East Studies* 24:2 (2015), 303–26.

Owen, John M. *Confronting Political Islam*. Princeton: Princeton University Press, 2014.

Pierret, Thomas. 'Syrie: l'islam dans la revolution.' *Politique étrangère* 76:4 (2011), 879–91.

———. *Religion and State in Syria: The Sunni Ulama from Coup to Revolution*. Cambridge: Cambridge University Press, 2013.

———. 'Les salafismes dans l'insurrection syrienne: des réseaux transnationaux à l'épreuve des réalités locales.' *Outre-Terre* 44:3 (2015), 196–215.

———. 'al-Būṭī, Muḥammad Saʿīd Ramaḍān.' In *Encyclopaedia of Islam, THREE*, eds Kate Fleet, et al. Leiden: Brill, 2015.

al-Qaraḍāwī, Yūsuf. *Ẓāhirat al-Ghuluww fī al-Takfīr*, 3rd edn. Cairo: Maktabat Wahba, 1990.

———. *Bayyināt al-Ḥall al-Islāmī wa-Shubuhāt al-ʿAlmaniyyīn wa-l-Mutagharribīn*, 2nd edn. Cairo: Maktabat Wahba, 1993.

———. *al-Ḥulūl al-Mustawrada wa-Kayfa Janat ʿalā Ummatinā*, 5th edn. Cairo: Maktabat Wahba, 1993.

———. *al-Ḥayāt al-Rabbāniyya wa-l-ʿIlm*. Cairo: Maktabat al-Wahba, 1995.

———. *al-Marjiʿiyya al-ʿUlyā fī al-Islām li-l-Qur'ān wa-l-Sunna*, 2nd edn. Cairo: Maktabat Wahba, 2001.

———. *Min Fiqh al-Dawla fī al-Islām*, 3rd edn. Cairo: Dār al-Shurūq, 2001.

———. *al-Dīn wa-l-Siyāsa: Ta'ṣīl wa-Radd Shubuhāt*. Dublin: al-Majlis al-Ūrubbī li-l-Iftā' wa-l-Buḥūth, 2007.

———. *Min Hady al-Islām: Fatāwā Muʿāṣira*, 4 vols. Kuwait: Dār al-Qalam, 2009.

———. *Fiqh al-Wasaṭiyya al-Islāmiyya wa-l-Tajdīd*. Cairo: Dār al-Shurūq, 2010.

———. *Fiqh al-Jihād: Dirāsa Muqārana li-Aḥkāmihi wa-Falsafatihi fī Ḍaw' al-Qur'ān wa-l-Sunna*, 3rd edn. Cairo: Maktabat Wahba, 2010.

———. *Kayfa Nataʿāmal maʿa al-Turāth wa-l-Tamadhhub wa-l-Ikhtilāf?* 3rd edn. Cairo: Maktabat al-Wahba, 2011.

———. *25 Yanāyir Sanat 2011: Thawrat al-Shaʿb*. Cairo: Maktabat Wahba, n.d. https://www.al-qaradawi.net/sites/default/files/pdf/801ba-alqaradawy-walswraa-elmasria.pdf, last accessed: 12 February 2021.

Quisay, Walaa. 'Neo-Traditionalism in the West: Navigating Modernity, Tradition and Politics.' DPhil dissertation. University of Oxford, 2019.

Qureshi, Jawad Anwar. 'The Discourses of the Damascene Sunni Ulama during the 2011 Revolution.' In *State and Islam in Baathist Syria: Confrontation or Co-optation?* Boulder, CO: Lynne Rienner, 2012.

———. '[Book review:] Thomas Pierret, *Religion and State in Syria: The Sunni Ulama from Coup to Revolution*.' *Milestones: Commentary on the Islamic World*, 2018. https://www.milestonesjournal.net/s/syrian-ulama.pdf, last accessed: 23 April 2020.

———. 'Būṭī, Muḥammad Saʿīd Ramaḍān al-.' In *The [Oxford] Encyclopedia of Islam and Law*. Oxford Islamic Studies Online, n.d. http://www.oxfordislamicstudies.com/article/opr/t349/e0027.

———. 'Nadwī, Abū al-Ḥasan. ' In *The [Oxford] Encyclopedia of Islam and Law*. Oxford Islamic Studies Online, n.d. http://www.oxfordislamicstudies.com/article/opr/t342 /e0350.

Rabb, Intisar. *Doubt in Islamic Law: A History of Legal Maxims, Interpretation, and Islamic Criminal Law*. Cambridge: Cambridge University Press, 2014.

Radsch, Courtney C. *Cyberactivism and Citizen Journalism in Egypt: Digital Dissidence and Political Change*. New York: Palgrave Macmillan, 2016.

Ramadan, Tariq. *Islam and the Arab Awakening*. Oxford: Oxford University Press, 2012.

Ranko, Annette, and Justyna Nedza. 'Crossing the Ideological Divide? Egypt's *Salafists* and the Muslim Brotherhood after the Arab Spring.' *Studies in Conflict and Terrorism* 39:6 (2016), 519–41.

Al-Rasheed, Madawi. *Muted Modernists: The Struggle over Divine Politics in Saudi Arabia*. Oxford: Oxford University Press, 2015.

Rock-Singer, Aaron. *Practicing Islam in Egypt: Print Media and Islamic Revival*. Cambridge: Cambridge University Press, 2019.

Rougier, Bernard, and Stéphane Lacroix (eds). *Egypt's Revolutions: Politics, Religion, and Social Movements*. New York: Palgrave Macmillan, 2016.

Rutherford, Bruce. *Egypt After Mubarak: Liberalism, Islam, and Democracy in the Arab World*. Princeton: Princeton University Press, 2008.

Sadiki, Larbi (ed.). *Routledge Handbook of the Arab Spring*. London: Routledge, 2014.

al-Sarhan, Saud (ed.). *Political Quietism in Islam: Sunni and Shi'i Practice and Thought*. London: I. B. Tauris, 2019.

Schielke, Samuli. *Egypt in the Future Tense: Hope, Frustration, and Ambivalence Before and After 2011*. Bloomington: Indiana University Press, 2015.

———. 'There will be Blood: Expectation and Ethics of Violence during Egypt's Stormy Season.' *Middle East Critique* 26 (2017), 205–20.

Schmitz, Charles, and Robert D. Burrowes. *Historical Dictionary of Yemen*, 3rd edn. Lanham, Maryland: Rowman & Littlefield, 2018.

Scott, Rachel M. 'What Might the Muslim Brotherhood Do with Al-Azhar? Religious Authority in Egypt.' *Die Welt Des Islams* 52:2 (2012), 131–65.

Sedgwick, Mark. 'The Modernity of Neo-Traditionalist Islam'. In *Muslim Subjectivities in Global Modernity*. Leiden: Brill, 2020, 121–46.

Sedgwick, Mark, and Francesco Piraino (eds). *Global Sufism: Boundaries, Structures, and Politics*. London: Hurst Publishers, 2019.

Shaham, Ron. 'The Rhetoric of Legal Disputation: Neo-*Ahl al-Ḥadīth* vs. Yūsuf al-Qaraḍāwī.' *Islamic Law and Society* 22:1–2 (2015), 114–41.

———. *Rethinking Islamic Legal Modernism: The Teaching of Yusuf al-Qaradawi*. Leiden: Brill, 2018.

Shakir, Omar. *All According to Plan: The Rab'a Massacre and Mass Killings of Protesters in Egypt*. New York, NY: Human Rights Watch, 2014.

al-Shāṭibī, Abū Isḥāq. *Al-Muwāfaqāt*, ed. Mashhūr Āl Salmān. Khobar: Dār Ibn 'Affān, 1997.

Shavit, Uriya. 'The Muslim Brothers' Conception of Armed Insurrection against an Unjust Regime,' *Middle Eastern Studies* 51:4 (2015), 600–17.

Sheline, Annelle R. 'Shifting Reputations for 'Moderation:' Evidence from Qatar, Jordan, and Morocco.' *Middle East Law and Governance* 12:1 (2020), 109–29.

Sivan, Emmanuel. 'Sunni radicalism in the Middle East and the Iranian revolution.' *International Journal of Middle East Studies* 21 (1989).

Skovgaard-Petersen, Jakob. *Defining Islam for the Egyptian State: Muftis and Fatwas of the Dār al-Iftā*. New York: Brill, 1997.

al-Ṭabarī. *Tafsīr al-Ṭabarī: Jāmiʿ al-Bayān ʿan Taʾwīl āy al-Qurʾān*. Cairo: Dār Hajar, 2001.

al-Takrūrī, Nawwāf. *al-ʿAmaliyyāt al-Istishhādiyya fī al-Mizān al-Fiqhī*. 2nd edn. Damascus: Dar al-Fikr, 1997.

Tammam, Husam. 'Yūsuf al-Qaraḍawi and the Muslim Brothers: The Nature of a Special Relationship.' In *The Global Mufti: The Phenomenon of Yusuf al-Qaradawi*, eds Bettina Gräf and Jakob Skovgaard-Petersen. London: Hurst Publishers, 2009.

Tareen, SherAli. *Defending Muhammad in Modernity*. Notre Dame: University of Notre Dame Press, 2020.

al-Tirmidhī. *al-Jāmiʿ al-Kabīr (Sunan al-Tirmidhī)*, eds Shuʿayb al-Arnaʾūṭ, et al. Beirut: Dār al-Risāla al-ʿĀlamiyya, 2009.

al-Tukla, Muḥammad Ziyād b. ʿUmar. *Fatḥ al-Jalīl*, 2nd edn. Beirut: Dār al-Bashāʾir al-Islāmiyya, 2008.

Ulrichsen, Kristian Coates. *Qatar and the Arab Spring*. New York: Oxford University Press, 2014.

———. *The United Arab Emirates: Power, Politics and Policy-Making*. London: Routledge, 2016.

———. *Qatar and the Gulf Crisis*. New York: Oxford University Press, 2020.

Wagemakers, Joas. *A Quietist Jihadi: The Ideology and Influence of Abu Muhammad al-Maqdisi*. Cambridge: Cambridge University Press, 2012.

Warren, David H. 'The *'Ulamā'* and the Arab Uprisings 2011-13: Considering Yusuf al-Qaradawi, the 'Global Mufti', between the Muslim Brotherhood, the Islamic Legal Tradition, and Qatari Foreign Policy.' *New Middle Eastern Studies* 4 (2014).

———. 'For the Good of the Nation: The New Horizon of Expectations in Rifa'a' al-Tahtawi's Reading of the Islamic Political Tradition.' *American Journal of Islamic Social Sciences* 34:4 (2017), 30–55.

———. 'Cleansing the Nation of the 'Dogs of Hell': 'Ali Jum'a's Nationalist Legal Reasoning in Support of the 2013 Egyptian Coup and its Bloody Aftermath.' *International Journal of Middle East Studies*, 49:3 (2017), 457–77.

———. *Rivals in the Gulf: Yusuf al-Qaradawi, Abdullah Bin Bayyah, and the Qatar-UAE Contest Over the Arab Spring and the Gulf Crisis*. London: Routledge, 2021.

Wehr, Hans. *Arabic–English Dictionary*, ed. J Milton Cowan. Ithaca, NY: Spoken Language Services, 1994.

Wender, Andrew M. 'Beyond Resurgent 'Islamists' and Enlightened 'Secularists.'' *Sociology of Islam* 2:3–4 (2014): 268–82.

al-Yaqoubi, Muhammad. *Refuting ISIS*, 2nd edn. London: Sacred Knowledge, 2017.

Zaman, Muhammad Qasim. *The Ulama in Contemporary Islam: Custodians of Change*. Princeton: Princeton University Press, 2002.

———. *Modern Islamic Thought in a Radical Age: Religious Authority and Internal Criticism*. Cambridge: Cambridge University Press, 2012.

Zeghal, Malika. *Gardiens de l'Islam: Les ulama d'al-Azhar dans l'Egypte contemporaine*. Paris: Presses de la fondation nationale des sciences politiques, 1995.

———. 'Religion and Politics in Egypt: The Ulema of al-Azhar, Radical Islam, and the State (1952-94).' *International Journal of Middle East Studies* 31:3 (1999), 371–99.

———. 'The 'Recentering' of Religious Knowledge and Discourse: The Case of al-Azhar in Twentieth-Century Egypt.' In *Schooling Islam: The Culture and Politics of Modern Muslim Education*, eds Robert W. Hefner and Muhammad Qasim Zaman. Princeton: Princeton University Press, 2007, 107–30.

Zollner, Barbara H. E. *The Muslim Brotherhood: Hasan al-Hudaybi and Ideology*. London: Routledge, 2009.

Zulfiqar, Adnan. 'Revolutionary Islamic Jurisprudence: A Restatement of the Arab Spring'. *New York University Journal of International Law and Politics* 49 (2017), 443–97.

INDEX

Note: Page numbers followed by "*n*" refer to notes